WITHOUT FAME

Without Fame

THE ROMANCE OF A PROFESSION

BY OTTO EISENSCHIML

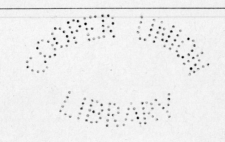
ALLIANCE BOOK CORPORATION

CHICAGO · NEW YORK

CONTENTS

FOREWORD

THE EVENTS related in this book are essentially true. At times I have used poetic license, and no attempt has been made to attain historical accuracy. Individuals, firms and localities are sometimes presented in disguise, so as to protect the privacy of people whose fates were interwoven with mine. Wherever only the given or family names of persons appear, they are not the real ones; wherever I have cited given and family names together, they are true, and have been used with the consent of the people mentioned, except when the latter were not within my reach. Any similarity between these fictitious names of persons or firms and actual persons or firms is purely coincidental.

If there are chemists called Martin, Manny or Skinner, they are not identical with the characters of this book. The true names of the demented broker Parker, of happy-go-lucky Dr. Oppen and the wily merchant Ainsworth were different; so were those of the lawyers Shaughnessy & Wettlesborough. All the firms I mention existed or still exist but, with the exception of the American Linseed Company and the United States Steel Corporation, not under the names I used; and if any firms, such as the Heavenly Health Company or Potthauser & Mettendorf, which bear these names or similar ones, do or did exist, they are not identical with those which play a part in this story.

—O. E.

WITHOUT FAME

ALONG THE BEAUTIFUL DANUBE

$\mathcal{V}$IENNA in the early December days of 1881. Along the broad *Ringstrasse,* once the site of the city walls, a one-horse carriage made its leisurely way past the Bourse. The Viennese, perhaps in a spirit of irony, used to call these vehicles *comfortables.* Inside, a little boy and his mother were returning from a visit, the boy enchanted by the unusual adventure of a ride and longing for a place on the driver's box. Suddenly a policeman stepped forward and ordered the driver to detour through a side street. A frenzied crowd filled the wider thoroughfare, milling and shouting; the blare of fire trumpets added to the excitement. On the right stood the Ringtheater, quiet and dark; but inside it was a hell-pit of roaring flames. During the first act of *The Tales of Hoffmann* a backdrop on the stage had caught fire. There were no asbestos curtains then, and the exits opened toward the inside. A panicky attendant had turned off the gas, in foolish fear of an explosion. Six hundred people died; but that night a new set of rules was born which provided safety for future theatergoers.

Of all this the boy knew nothing at that time. He experienced only the sensation of something unusual and took with him a vague recollection of a mad multitude struggling against rows of policemen and firemen, of contorted faces, imprecations, groans. It was the earliest lasting impression that engraved itself on the child's memory.

No one can grow up in Vienna without feeling the charm of its antiquity. It meets you in every street, in the quaint, ancient courts known only to the natives, through which they pass for short-cuts and on the walls of which posters from time immemorial have an-

1

nounced the owner's warning that free passage was subject to instant repeal. Not even the oldest inhabitants remembered such a repeal and, had one been issued, there would have been a riot. In these placid courts blind or crippled musicians played the songs of the ages, here and there intermingled with a modern tune. Then there were the old outer city gates, still functioning, not against armed enemies, but as toll stations for food brought in from the country. For many years it was the favorite sport of suburban schoolboys to smuggle things past green-clad officers to save the two-*Kreuzer* tax on a chicken and the four-*Kreuzer* tax on a goose. When the guards were too efficient, or the traffic too light for safe operations, we would climb over the walls. It was not quite so hazardous as it looked. We knew certain spots where bricks had been loosened and could be used as footholds on the climb up or down. Only one spot near the *Alserthor* was safe from these depredations. It was occupied by the old Insane Asylum. A few of us had once ventured into those eerie precincts and had been scared nearly to death.

When my older sister Helene was six, she brought home from school the tales taught to children at that age, and a wide-eyed youngster listened entranced as she retold them; how the Turks had come before the city in countless numbers, how the Emperor and half the army had fled, and the remainder had defended themselves against overwhelming odds. We would visit the narrow lane still known as the *Heidenschuss* (the heathen's shot), where one midnight a baker had heard suspicious sounds of digging under his cellar and where a whole regiment of besiegers had been drowned in water poured into their tunnel by Viennese housewives. At the *Schottenthor* the Mussulmen actually had once breached the walls, but had been repulsed by a brigade of women and children. And finally, when the fall of the city had been imminent, the watchful eye of the general, spying to the north from the spires of St. Stephen's Cathedral, had seen the rockets of a Polish relief army. In the early morning the Turks were routed; among their possessions were found brown beans which had a pungent fragrance and whose use had to be learned from prisoners of war. Thus it was that coffee came to the Western world.

The Viennese children of that time were taught history in their stride and hardly knew that they were learning it. When I was eight years old our teacher, a stocky little man named Korn, asked us one day to find out how the *Kandlgasse* (the Street of the Little Can), in which our school stood, had acquired its name. The next day saw many mothers with their offspring walking up and down the thoroughfare, but it was a long time before we discovered the old inn with its silver can swinging from the gable. When we triumphantly reported our achievement, we were met with a rebuff: had we noted the names of the cross-streets, and if so, had we speculated on their significance? In this way we learned that Bricklayers Lane had been the seat of the masons' guild in the medieval ages and Silk Street the headquarters of the weavers. From this nucleus our historical search spread fanwise through the city and finally throughout the whole country.

The old schoolmaster who thought that history, like charity, had best begin at home, has long been forgotten. Today pupils study the Battle of Marathon or the first World War, but they seldom know the history of their own home towns. To me this looks like building a thirteenth story without a foundation; but I am old-fashioned and most likely wrong.

Austrian school discipline in those days was severe, and physical punishment was meted out in liberal doses. Strokes on the palms with wooden sticks were applied to pupils of both sexes, and boys were often cruelly slapped and had their ears pulled on the slightest provocation. Another form of torture was solitary confinement after school hours, lasting up to six hours at one time. So far as I could observe, enforced discipline was not entirely successful and bred much resentment, especially among those who were chastised unjustly. I once received a resounding slap in the face, because the boy standing next to me had hit a wrong note in a community song, and I still carry with me an angry scar because of this miscarriage of justice. I have never afterward joined in community singing, no matter what the occasion. To me it is, next to turnips and boiled cabbage, the most detestable thing in the world. I have been beaten unmercifully, locked up and threatened with expulsion, but I have stood firm. No more community singing for me.

These strict educational methods were not altogether wasted, however; we did learn to master a variety of subjects by the sheer weight of external pressure. But our knowledge was acquired at a high price; we never had any relaxation, sport or play. During intermission we walked the corridors, and gymnastic exercises usually meant going through mechanical forms of knee-bending and other tiresome contortions in which we saw neither sense nor diversion.

The result of this restraint was an exuberance of spirit outside the school which manifested itself in regular warfare between individual schools or between entire city districts. For many years war raged between all the schools of Währing, the suburb in which my school was located, and the neighboring district of Hernals. As you walked along a street, a gang might accost you with the dangerous question: "Währinger or Hernalser?" Woe to you if you belonged to the wrong faction; the chances were that, unless you could signal for help in time, you were in for a lusty beating. Cruel? Perhaps. But somehow no one minded much, or was ever known to report his grievance to the police or to the school authorities. We had no playgrounds, no sport teams, no games. A safety valve had to be found, and was found. Everybody comprehended that vaguely, even those who were beaten up.

Although born in Vienna, I was an American, for my father was a citizen of the United States at the time of my birth. I scarcely knew my father, as he was a sickly man and usually away at health resorts. He died when I was not quite eight years old, and most of what I found out about him came to me in later years. He had been born near Pilsen in what was then the Austrian crown land of Bohemia, and when fourteen years old had been given by his parents a tray of merchandise and told to make his own living. So he trotted from farm to farm, selling and bartering his way through life. One rainy night he found himself without food or shelter, and seeing a farm near by, asked for a night's refuge. He was told to go to the pigsty which, so it was hinted, was a good enough place for him. My father slept with the pigs that night, but his soul revolted. It was the year 1848, and revolutionary thoughts were in the air. Within a few days he exchanged his trinkets for a bag of potatoes and a sack of beans and joined one of the squads of emigrants who were making their way out of Europe into the Promised Land. The tickets were expensive enough, yet everyone had to carry his own provisions on board ship. Three times the sailing vessel on which my

4

father was a passenger came almost within sight of New York, and three times adverse winds drove it back. The drinking water became fetid and provisions grew low. The ship's crew sold eatables at exorbitant prices, and complaints to the officers brought no relief. At last a landing was made and my father was ready to disembark, when news reached the boat that gold had been found in California. No one left the ship at New York; crew and passengers alike proceeded to San Francisco, arriving there after a perilous trip around the Horn.

My father made a lucky strike within a few weeks of setting foot on the coast. As a matter of fact, so he wrote his parents, he had become so rich that he could buy the whole village where they were living. Then ensued a long silence. The next letter was composed in a minor key. A few hours after the first news had been dispatched, an armed band invaded the tavern where my father was sleeping, and he was fortunate to escape through a window in his nightshirt. After that there were no more lucky strikes for him. He continued to prospect, mostly in Nevada, but all he gathered was experience, sore feet, and an incipient rheumatism which eventually cost him his life.

In 1861 he gave up prospecting and turned soldier. Joining an Illinois regiment, he fought in the battle of Shiloh, but the slaughter so disgusted him that he resigned his commission and became an Indian scout for the remainder of the war. Everything went well for a while, until one day he and four of his comrades were captured by a bloodthirsty Indian tribe. They were tied to trees, hooks were put into their bodies, and by means of merciless whippings they were driven to disembowel themselves. My father witnessed two such horrible deaths before rescuers arrived. After this close call, his decision to quit the Indian service is understandable. Taking out his citizenship papers in Nevada, he left the West, never to see it again. From the adventures of a scout he turned to the peaceful occupation of running a meat market in Chicago.

In 1872 the young butcher received word that his father had died and, seized with a sudden fear that he might never see his other parent again, he took the next boat to Europe. He need not have been in any such hurry, for as it turned out, his mother did not die until seventeen years later.

In Vienna he was introduced to a cousin whom he had never seen, and promptly fell in love with her. The affair led to an engagement and the engagement to marriage. As my mother was then nursing her old father and was unwilling to leave him, the butcher business in Chicago and an entire block of real estate in a choice neighborhood were sold for next to nothing, and my father started a new career abroad. His first venture was to act as manager for the Siamese twins, heralded as the great and only ones, the pathfinders for all imitators who were to follow in their wake. The venture might have turned out profitably, in spite of my father's lack of experience in the theatrical field, had it not been for the frightful ugliness of the two Oriental females. Wherever they were scheduled to appear, big crowds gathered at the depots, but after one look at the twins promptly decided to stay at home.

The panic of 1873 did the rest. When that year closed, my father was penniless and had to begin all over again. He started manufacturing photographic apparatus, a business about which he knew nothing. Nevertheless, by sheer ability and helped by the advent of amateur photography, he soon owned a big enterprise. I can testify to that, for on my way home from school I used to step in and empty the wastebaskets of foreign stamps, of which there were vast numbers every day. In this way I started the nucleus of a collection which, in the days of inflation following the World War, became one of the most valuable items in the family's inventory and secured for my brother-in-law a leading position on the Vienna Stamp Bourse, an institution which in the heyday of its existence took itself as seriously as the New York Stock Exchange.

What ruined the firm after my father's death in 1888 I never did find out. His partners were relatives, and I heard stories of ballet dancers and expensive presents made to them. I only know that this firm of my father's, whose name still appears on the backs of many old pictures in photograph albums from Egypt to Spain and from Patagonia to Newfoundland, went bankrupt, and that suddenly we found ourselves as poor as the proverbial church mice.

Father remained an American citizen and was extraordinarily proud of it. The American bar in the *Kärntnerstrasse* knew him as a frequent visitor, and he set up drinks for anyone who spoke English. He was easily imposed on by strangers, especially by inventors of all kinds; that much I gathered from table conversations and the frequent protests of my conservative mother. Otherwise I recall only that he talked to me about a man named Lincoln and another named Grant, both of whom he seemed to admire a great deal. He also admonished me never to give up my American citizenship.

"Finish your studies in Europe," he used to say, "but when you have your diploma, go to the United States before the ink on it is dry." It was good advice, and I resolved to follow it.

The family today still owns a stock certificate of a non-existent Nevada gold mine. It was taken in exchange for a block of valuable ground on the West Side of Chicago and is the only thing left of the parental estate.

We lived in a quiet residential district, but a streetcar that passed our house furnished us children no end of excitement. It ran up a hill so steep that two horses could not pull it; hence, a man riding a third horse joined the team at the bottom of the incline; on reaching the top, where the street took a sharp turn, he would disengage his horse by a deft movement which disconnected a coupling. If he succeeded, the movement of the streetcar continued without interruption; if he did not, there was a delightful confusion of horses, reins and hooks, and a still more delightful exchange of compliments between driver and rider, all in the choicest *patois*, such as only grownups were supposed to hear. There came a day, though, when the streetcars did not run, when the lights in the house were turned low and the conversation was carried on in whispers. No one seemed to know just what was wrong. I sneaked out to the corner to get information from a policeman.

"They're striking," was his reply to my anxious question. He pronounced it "stricking," which to me meant "knitting," and my eyes opened wide in wonder and awe.

"You mean the conductors and drivers are at home knitting socks?" I ventured.

"That's what they say," he responded, as much puzzled as I.

The word "strike" had not yet found its way into the German vocabulary. Troops were marching through the streets all night, and no one thought of sleep. Nothing much happened, after all, and we did not guess that what we were witnessing was a reverberation

7

of the Haymarket riots in far-away Chicago and the demand of labor for an eight-hour day.

Discipline at home was as strict as that at school. We children had to be in bed at half-past eight sharp every night; all food set before us had to be eaten to the last crumb, a rule which led to violent upheavals, especially on my part, as I have always suffered from a strong aversion to all green and red vegetables. Newspapers, magazines and books in our limited library constituted things that were "not for children." Any infringement of the household regulations was punished by having to eat in the kitchen, by elimination of favorite dishes, or by whipping. Our meals were simple; after the death of my father we usually ate a supper of potatoes with butter, or dry bread with tea. Monday was washday and a festival for us, as the meal was fetched from a nearby restaurant. The one dish we always bought was a cheap sweet-sour hash, a Viennese specialty called *Peuschl,* which was neither good-smelling nor good-tasting: but it provided excitement, especially for me who did the fetching. I could linger in the smoke-filled basement of the restaurant, listening, watching, with my money clutched tightly in my fist, and studying what was for me a new world.

In the house where our modest apartment was located lived an uncle of mine, my mother's only brother and the only rich man I knew for the first twenty years of my life. He would hardly be called rich by modern standards, but in the minds of our family he loomed as somebody of stature. At the age of sixteen he had come to Vienna from a little Czech town and obtained employment as a messenger boy in a banking house. The wild inflation markets of 1872 occurred at that time, and there seemed to be no cloud on the horizon. Like everyone else Uncle Anton invested his savings in stocks and kept pyramiding his profits until they reached the astounding figure of fifty thousand dollars. Then he did the smartest thing of his life; he cashed in.

Uncle Anton's luxurious apartment was directly above ours. It boasted of gas light where we used kerosene, of a gas stove where we used coal, and it even had a bathtub. Yet his home life was not pleasant. He had been tricked into marrying a tall, ungainly woman by the name of Antonia who, by tacit agreement, was called Tante Toni, to differentiate her from my mother's sister who had the same name and whom we designated as Tante Tini. Tante Toni came as close to my conception of a witch as any human being could without actually riding a broomstick. She had a long, hooked nose, stooped shoulders, and could casually utter venomous insults in a grating nasal twang. We were hardly ever invited to her house, and the few times we went we did not get enough to eat.

After I had left Vienna, I did not see Uncle Anton and his wife for many years, not until the war was over. By that time they had lost their factory, their house and everything else they had possessed. My uncle had to sneak into coffee shops where once he had presided as an honored customer, with a bottle of homemade coffee under his vest, and shyly kibitz at a game of tarok or checkers.

There was an old grandmother in our family, a beautiful, white-haired woman full of quaint ideas and sayings. One of her favorite bits of philosophy was that reading was a waste of time. She maintained that in novels, "they" either got each other in the end, in which event the story was like a thousand others; or "they" did not get each other, in which event you got mad and wished you had not started the book. History was a bunch of lies, science something that would be obsolete before you had finished reading the volume. Hence, no reading. What the old lady's age was no one knew. When the census taker came around every ten years she always told him she was "somewhere in the seventies." She had been telling him that for thirty years.

One of the great ambitions we youngsters nursed in our souls was to discover a fire, if only once in our lives. In those days, before the general use of the telephone, people reported fires by running to the nearest engine house, and whoever got there first was entitled to a reward of one florin, about forty cents. When I was eight years old my great moment came. A bakery stood not far from our house, and one day I noticed thick waves of smoke belching from its doors and windows. The engine house was about half a mile away, but I am sure I made the distance in almost nothing flat. When I got there, I was so out of breath that I could only scribble the address on a piece of paper. Unfortunately, someone with longer legs had been there before me, and the engines were already thundering down the street, three horses abreast, with a bugler standing next to the driver and sounding his ♩♩♪ in imposing grandeur. The bugled notes, echoing from the walls of the houses, gave the scene a musical background which no siren or bell can rival. I think even today that a horse-drawn engine, with the beautiful animals straining against the yokes and the driver bent forward, is the most exciting spectacle in the world. "My" fire was quickly brought under control, but for a time I felt like a hero just the same.

Whether our financial condition at that time was really perilous or whether my mother practiced economy only out of habit, I do not know. The fact is that in our family money was being saved in queer ways. We rarely had butter on our bread; usually we had lard or grease, and we always teased our mother for spreading it on the smaller side of the slice, or threatened to drop it on the floor to find out which side was buttered. On the other hand, we always seemed able to afford hired girls, usually stout, hefty Bohemians. One of these kitchen maids was named Karoline; she could not speak a word of German and was kindness itself. She shared with us her portion of all dishes we liked, and when we wanted something between meals she put on the bread everything there was in the house. In this way we fared well and learned Czech besides, which was a profitable investment, for my mother and Tante Tini, her sister, often talked in their native tongue between themselves when they did not want us to understand what they were saying. This was a great incentive for us to pick up as much of a Czech vocabulary as we could.

My mother had been born in the German part of Bohemia, but when she was still a baby, her family had moved to the town of Rokycany in the Czech-speaking part of the country. There she learned Czech in the streets, for her father permitted only German to be spoken in the house. My mother's German was perfect, but there were several words which she pronounced with a slight foreign accent, and it was our great delight to lead the conversation at the table in such a direction that she would be forced to use these words. I remember two of them—*Kürschner,* meaning furrier, and *Dresden,* the Saxon capital. It was not easy to weave topics around a furrier and a foreign city, and our glee when we succeeded in entrapping Mother was that much more triumphant. Perhaps in recollection of her own linguistic home discipline, my mother did not allow us to speak the Viennese *patois* at home, not even among ourselves. This, I believe, was a mistake. We became accustomed in this way to speak a pure German which later set us apart in school from other children and caused us to be regarded as hothouse plants, which we really were not in any sense of the word.

The greatest economy was practiced in regard to our clothing. My older sister was the only one for whom new wearing apparel was ever purchased. Bertha, next in age, had to wear her castoffs, and when she outgrew them I, like Achilles in his youthful days, was dressed as a girl and remained in female disguise till I was six years old and ready for school. Laughed at by my playmates and with bitterness in my young heart, I went through those years a martyr to a balanced budget. Later, when coats and pants became an absolute necessity, my mother took me to a store and bought me clothes several sizes too big for me to grow into. There were no stores with fixed prices at that time, at least not where we did our shopping, and a purchase of this kind sometimes took a couple of hours before an agreement was reached between my mother and a worn-out salesman. In the course of the bargaining, I had to put on and take off pants and coats a dozen times, as my prospects of owning them dimmed or brightened. To take them off was only a stratagem, of course, because I knew my mother would come off victoriously. She always did.

When I was about four years old, tidings reached us that Tante Tini had broken up her household in Budapest and was moving to Vienna with her husband, a wild-mustached Hungarian, and her three boys, Zsigo, Fred and Hugo. Zsigo was my uncle's son by a former marriage and was then about fourteen years old. His arrival upset our best traditions. He wanted to be a circus rider, and we all became his willing slaves. We had to learn all kinds of acrobatic stunts, such as standing on each other's shoulders, turning somersaults and other elementary tricks of the trade. It was not long before I could jump on Zsigo's shoulders and stand there, trembling, but with a smile, while he raced around the room. He used to give little clucking sounds which were inaudible to the audience but which gave me warnings of sudden twists and turns, so that I could throw my weight to the opposite side in time to avoid a spill. Everything would have gone on splendidly had not our mothers once surprised us. Our acrobatic stunts came to a definite halt. Zsigo disappeared from his stepmother's house soon thereafter and joined a circus. We were never allowed to inquire about him, but by listening in on the Czech conversations of our elders we gleaned that he was traveling through Europe in tights and tinsel, probably living mostly on glory and the smell of horses. Many years later my uncle suddenly went on a trip; when he returned he wore a black band on one arm. Zsigo had fallen from a trapeze in some southern Slavic town and after a few days had died in a little white-washed room overlooking the Adriatic Sea, with a gypsy woman doctoring him into eternity.

Tante Tini had the exterior of a saint but the soul of a Spanish inquisitor. Compared to the discipline in her house, ours was a home of wild Indians. She directed her husband and her children by mere motions of the hands. No one was allowed to speak until addressed by her. She was possessed of great social ambitions and read nothing but court notices and gossip about the nobility. When we were invited to her house we had to obey the latest rules of etiquette, as she perceived them. We never knew whether to hold our knives in the right hand or in the left, whether to use a spoon or a toothpick, whether to wipe our mouths vertically or horizontally. Tante Tini did not criticize us directly, but she managed to get her disapproval across by directing her remarks to her own children.

"Hugo, don't fidget in your chair," would not mean that Hugo had fidgeted, but the guilty one understood the reprimand.

Tante Tini used to cultivate a French accent, even where it hurt. A wagon was a *wagong* to her, a baron a *barong*. She also had picked up a few stray bits of English, and in later years when I was back on European visits, she would introduce every second sentence with "last not least," which seemed her favorite expression. She brought it out with apparent nonchalance, but I always saw her watching me out of the corner of one eye.

"Why, Auntie," I exclaimed then, "you speak English like a . . . ," and trailed off into a mumble.

We would never have accepted an invitation to Tante Tini's had there not been some salvage in it for us in the form of special delicacies. In those days the Imperial Court used to sell the leftovers from the Emperor's table to the common herd at bargain prices, and my aunt stood in line for hours, glorying in the feeling of being so close to the throne. She came home with all sorts of squashed cookies and similar remainders of a royal repast. We never had anything like that at home, and every bite into these luxuries was heavenly bliss.

The town of Rokycany, where my mother had spent most of her youth, was a settlement of about six thousand people, not far from Pilsen. When the war of 1866 broke out and the Prussians began to pour through the country, stories of rape and plunder swept before them. The stories were probably untrue or much exaggerated, but my grandfather took no chances. He packed the family into a railroad coach and selected Vienna as his new home.

My mother had been trained as a governess, spoke English, German, French and Czech, and was well versed in literature and the fine arts. We had to speak French at the table and were supposed to do so among ourselves, too, but we never did. At the table we became adept at gestures in order to avoid speaking at all. Piano also was taught us by our mother and, according to the methods in vogue then, in the driest and most repugnant manner. As we were used to similar ordeals at school, we did not mind greatly.

Since we were not allowed to read books or newspapers, attend the theater, or play much in the streets, Mother provided entertainment by telling us stories, a task she performed extremely well and with a delicate sense of the dramatic. Her text-book usually was the *Gartenlaube*, a tepid weekly containing mildly interesting illustrations. The story we liked best and which my mother had to repeat until she was threatened with brain fever, was called "The Four-Fingered Man." It dealt with a great bank robbery in Paris. The theft amounted to millions of francs, and the only clue the police had was the hazy description of a man who had only four fingers on his left hand and was always seen wearing black gloves. The upshot of the story was that the thief really was a normal, five-fingered man, and his four-fingered left glove had been a clever ruse. The amateur sleuth who solved the case received a reward of a quarter of a million francs.

What would we do if we should ever have a quarter of a million francs! Let's see, that was about 100,000 florins. Would we be satisfied with that? Mother thought it was enough, but my sisters and I, after hearing the story a few times, only sneered at such a bagatelle. A full million for us, or nothing! So we had nothing and went to bed feeling like millionaires.

Our school life did not furnish much excitement. When I was ten years old and had passed through four years of grade school training, my mother decided to have me skip the last grade and enter high school. Such a procedure was possible, provided one were willing and able to pass a special examination. There were two different types of high schools to choose from in Vienna: *Realschulen*, where one went to prepare oneself for real life, and *Gymnasien*, where one became a devotee of grand learning. The *Realschulen* taught French and English, the *Gymnasien* Latin and Greek, and against geometry and stenography taught by the former, the latter countered with fine arts and literature. Poor people who expected to work for a living were sent to the *Realschule*, and so there I went. The familiar *Du* was changed by the teachers to the more formal *Sie*, and we were suddenly called by our family names. Each branch of learning was taught by a different teacher; unlike American students we did not change rooms, but stayed where we were, the teachers doing the traveling.

Before I was accepted as a high school student the hurdle of tuition had to be overcome. There were public high schools too, so-called *Bürgerschulen*, which were free, but they did not afford their graduates the right to enter college. As a rule, it was not difficult to obtain a remission of all or half of the tuition fees; but I was an alien and naturally not entitled to the privileges of a citizen. My mother, however, was an expert in taking hurdles. She gathered up reams of documents, certifying to our extreme poverty, to my excellent character, to my brilliant scholarly achievements. After a futile struggle, the school authorities gave up. I received the benefit of free tuition, provided I would maintain the highest rating in deportment and be an honor student. I found the latter requirement the easier of the two.

It is difficult for me to judge the system by which we were taught in the first high school grades. In some subjects, such as geography and history, we certainly received a most thorough training. When we studied a country, we had to stay with it until we could draw a map of it by heart, together with its rivers, cities and mountains. I think I could draw them now, almost fifty years later, with my eyes shut. In my opinion, this is the only way to learn geography. Our lessons in history were equally thorough. But the method that worked to advantage in these two studies did not work well in languages. The slogan, "Give them the fundamentals," got us only grammar and isolated words, but left us unable either to speak or understand French and English. We could read *Gulliver's Travels* or Rousseau's *Emile*, but when I came to America I did not know enough everyday English to get my shoes shined.

Our daily adventure consisted in climbing the old city walls to and from school. By that time the municipality had posted policemen at our most popular clandestine crossings; I don't know why— probably just because we enjoyed the sport. This sort of restriction embodied the entire philosophy of life which prevailed in those days. What people liked to do was bad for them, and vice versa. When children wanted to read, it was bad for their eyes. When we wanted to play, we were told to study instead. When we were sick and burning with fever, the last thing we got was a drink of water; and if a medicine was not bitter enough to warp one's tongue, it could not possibly do any good. Parents, teachers and doctors were all agreed on these points, and no doubt meant well. On Sunday afternoons we had to take long walks, mostly along the dreary *Gürtelstrasse*, a belt boulevard which paralleled the lines of the outer city walls and showed here and there some trees and grass plots, thereby giving the illusion of being part of the Great Outdoors. Of course, the grass plots were all fenced in, and even the trees had wire guards around them to keep children and dogs at a respectful distance, but as the remainder of the streets were simply narrow stone canyons, the *Gürtelstrasse* on a Sunday afternoon presented a veritable style show. One of my sisters always had to hold my hand, even after I wore long pants, and the promenading took place at a snail's pace. Ever so often, Mother told us to open our mouths and breathe deeply. I have never since walked for pleasure nor without a fixed goal if I could help it. When the weather made these openair riots of ours impossible, we were made to stay at home and read classics, all of which were selected for us with due care for our morals.

One evening Mother and I took a stroll along the *Kaiserstrasse,* where we then lived. Suddenly a newsboy darted across our path, a big stack of extras under his arm. Ordinarily, newspapers could not be sold on the streets in Austria at that time, and our curiosity was aroused. A tall man snatched one of the sheets from the boy and looked at it. As he read, I saw him turn pale. Then he stepped on a curbstone and with a simple gesture quieted the crowd which had quickly gathered around him.

"Crown Prince Rudolph Is Dead," said the big headline which he read aloud. A few short paragraphs followed, giving a bare outline of the Mayerling tragedy and ending with this cryptic editorial remark: "We know the truth, but we are not permitted to print it."

When the man finished reading, there was deep silence. Then some people started talking in hushed tones; soon thousands found their voices, until a curious low hum seemed to vibrate over the city. Thus began that whisper about the drama of Mayerling which has not stopped since, and which will probably go on until this mystery is solved, if ever it is.

Crown Prince Rudolph was, I believe, the only member of the Austrian court who was really popular with the common people. They liked to talk about him, his talents, his virtues, his escapades. His vices were condoned, because they were human. Who could be true to a woman like Princess Stephanie, and how could one blame a young man for seeking occasional release from an unbearable court etiquette? Even the royal carriage driver, a Mr. Bratfisch *(fried fish)*, was popular, perhaps because his name was so typically Viennese. It was said that the crown prince's ideas were modern, almost radical for his time. Old coffee-house habitués never ceased to assert that the first World War would have been avoided had Rudolph lived.

Emperor Francis Joseph, the crown prince's father, was respected for his uprightness and pitied for his misfortunes, but he was not loved. His picture hung in every schoolroom in Austria; underneath there was a long printed list of his titles which we hated, because we had to learn them by heart, and which we ridiculed, because we did not understand them.

"Francis Joseph I, By the Grace of God Emperor of Austria, King of Hungary, King of Bohemia and Moravia, Knighted Count of

Tyrol, Vorarlberg and Istria, Knight of the Golden Fleece . . . ," it was difficult to remember all. We never found out what a Knighted Count was, but we assumed that it was a sort of brevetted Count who had not passed his final exam. Francis Joseph was a fine specimen of physical manhood, six feet tall, handsome, chivalrous. He would have made an excellent subaltern officer, with his worship of etiquette, detail work and honorable traditions. As a ruler of a vast empire he was a failure. He lacked statesmanship and was handicapped both by his natural limitations and his upbringing. His linguistic talents were poor, and of the fourteen Austro-Hungarian languages he spoke only German well, although with a Viennese accent. The Hungarians and Czechs snickered when he addressed them haltingly in their respective tongues, and therefore he visited their capitals only on rare occasions. According to law, he had to be crowned in Budapest as Hungarian king but, free from legal compulsion in Bohemia, he refused like courtesy to the Czechs. This was a fatal error. Yet Francis Joseph was a nobleman at heart who lived according to his own code of honor.

Emperor Francis Joseph, we used to mock you because you uttered the same banalities at all public functions; but you always arrived on the minute, and you honored the beautiful phrase that punctuality is the courtesy of kings. You did not always understand your people, and they thought themselves suppressed; they have discovered since what real suppression means. You believed in the ancient prerogatives of the nobility, but there was peace and justice in the land, and the word *graft* had no equivalent in any of the languages spoken where you reigned.

Francis Joseph I, By the Grace of God Emperor of Austria, King of Hungary, and Knighted Count of Tyrol—one of those who criticized you and laughed at you in his youth, now salutes you!

When I was about ten years old, my mother announced that we were going to spend the summer in the country. What windfall made this possible I do not know, but we asked no questions. The choice, strange to relate, did not fall on a place boasting of some foul-smelling mineral water, supposedly good for our blood, but on a little village called Emmersdorf, where we went in a steamer up the Danube. The boat, an old side-wheeler, was called "Valerie"

17

after one of the archduchesses who was greatly beloved by the populace, according to the loyal press. The name, however, was of little importance to us. We roamed the boat from bow to stern, and sometimes dared to look down into the turbid stream which we had never seen before. Even my mother caught some of the excitement, and her "Don't go near the railing, children!" did not carry the usual tone of conviction. The dining room looked very inviting; Viennese can eat at all times, and the tables were already set for lunch early in the morning. Our own lunch, of course, came out of a paper bag, but we looked into the *Speisesaal* while we ate it and felt like first-class passengers.

In Emmersdorf we found lodgings with the local postmaster in a house on the river's edge. Grapevines twined along the façade of the house, and a little garden with pear trees looked out across the Danube toward the beautiful monastery of Melk. We did not know what to do first; there was so much that was new. The postmaster let us help him assort the daily mail which was brought into town by the "Valerie" one day and by her sister ship, the "Rudolph," the next. I was allowed to walk with the mailman on his delivery route, and when he was sick one day I did all the delivering myself. The mailman's black and yellow service cap hung down to my ears, but I felt as proud as Lucifer as I rang doorbells with the touch of authority.

The Danube between Emmersdorf and Melk is about half a mile wide, but all the current was on the opposite side. Though you could wade out from our shore to the middle of the stream, the channel was hundreds of feet deep on the farther side; and the current was so swift there that even the steamboats could not plow upstream without the aid of a chain which stretched below the surface and into which the vessels were hooked, much like old cable cars. There came a time in midsummer when the water was very low and the "Valerie" did not dare make her regular landing at Emmersdorf. The postmaster had to take a small rowboat to fetch the mail at Melk. I was aching to go along with him, and after repeated warnings on his part and coaxings on mine, I was told to hop in. All the way across he told me what was going to happen: the first part of the trip would be uneventful, but wait till we got to the deep channel. If a skilful boatman were not at the helm, an upset was inevitable. So we rowed slowly across over water that was almost as calm as a lake. Suddenly the boatman sang out, "Hold tight!" and a second later the little skiff spun around like a top and began shooting downstream with incredible speed. I held on as tightly as I could, and I am sure I was as white as a sheet. Slowly and skilfully the mailman steered toward shore, and we landed about a mile below our destination. The deep channel was not more than fifty feet wide, but we had been carried that far down the river in crossing this short stretch.

I would have given anything to avoid the return trip, but I had no choice. I found my fear greatly lessened, though, and later I lost it altogether and even learned to navigate the boat alone.

Not far from Emmersdorf, on a high embankment, stood the two neighboring towns of Krems and Stein. Both were old and picturesque, strangers to modern customs, and still surrounded by medieval walls and moats. No tourists ever came their way, for which I used to offer thanks to the powers that be. Krems and Stein were old Austria at her glorious best.

The two towns always had been bitter rivals, and their history was one of perpetual warfare. In the seventeenth century, when the Swedes pillaged the countryside, Krems and Stein were besieged, and it is said that after every shot fired at the invader they fired one at each other, as a reminder of their perennial feud. After a few weeks, they both had to surrender to the enemy.

Krems has an old church in which stands a headless statue of the Holy Virgin. Thereby hangs a story. After the Swedes had captured the place, a captain of their army entered this shrine and, to show his hatred for the Catholics he was fighting, drew his sword and decapitated the statue; but when he rode away, the head rolled after him. He rode faster and faster, the sweat of panicky fear drenching him. He raced through the barracks and circled the walls of the town at a furious gallop. It was no use—the head was always behind him. Finally he turned to face his ghostly pursuer. As he pulled his pistol, two cannon balls fastened together with a chain came hurtling across the Danube and beheaded him. The horse shied and galloped away; the horrified townspeople saw the officer's head rolling behind the fleeing animal, until head, horse and dead rider all vanished over the parapet and were not seen again.

The next morning the head of the Holy Virgin was found lying at the foot of the statue to which it belonged; but on the wall of the town, near the spot where the hapless officer was last seen, there had appeared over night the outline of a man on horseback, with his head missing. The crude sculpture can still be seen there today. The man in the street calls it The Headless Man, *Das Mandl Ohne Kopf.*

The summer that year was exceptionally dry, and the Danube shrank more and more. One day we were sitting in our little garden when we saw the "Valerie" painfully puffing her way upstream. The next moment we heard three shrill whistles. The signal was repeated over and over. As with one stroke all work in the village stopped; everyone rushed to the river's edge and jumped into whatever boats were handy. I was told to take an oar and row furiously.

"What's wrong?" I asked between breaths, and the answer was, "The 'Valerie' is stuck on a sandbar."

I rowed as never before in my life, feeling as if I were out to rescue my lady-love. It was a good mile down to the steamer, and when we got there passengers were already being transferred to small boats. We received our load in good time, two elegant ladies who screamed most of the time and jumped out of our skiff before we had beached it. As they splashed into the water their screams sounded more natural. Altogether, it was a never-to-be-forgotten adventure.

The Danube at Melk, even in midsummer, is an ice-cold body of water, and for bathers not only a torture but also a danger. Due to the irregularity of the currents, it is full of invisible whirlpools, and careful swimming is necessary to extricate oneself from these death traps. I was repeatedly told that if I should be caught in one to strike squarely through it and not follow the natural panicky impulse of trying to escape the outer edges. There the speed is at its maximum and the most powerful man will be sucked to his grave. I had occasion to prove to myself the wisdom of this life-saving rule; for on venturing out near the middle of the stream I was once caught in one of those treacherous vortexes. For a second, fear almost paralyzed me. I felt my feet being drawn from under me, while my body began to spin in a dizzy fashion. Then

reason reasserted itself and I became obsessed with a cold fury.
To me the whirlpool was a living monster, hungry for another victim.
It was a fight of brute force against brute force. No, not that. That
was just what the monster wanted; only cool judgment on my part
could overcome his superior strength. Remembering my lessons, I
threw myself on my back to get my feet up, then turned around
and struck out to the center of the whirlpool with all my power. A
moment's rest there, and then out of it, downstream where the current was with me. The fight was terrific, as first my feet and then
my body had to disentangle themselves; but I was moving faster
than the swirling waters and got away. I have ever since entertained
a wholesome respect for fast-moving rivers.

I shall never forget our trip back to Vienna. The Danube flows
through a beautiful valley called the Wachau, where both shores
are adorned with the ruins of old castles, each of which has helped
make history. There is the old fortress of Aggstein, where a robber
baron once stretched a chain across the river and made all merchants
his captives. Then he would hold them in his castle for ransom;
after they had paid, he was wont to show them his "rose garden."
This was a little balcony leading out from one of the towers over-
hanging the Danube. As soon as the unfortunate guest had been
shoved out, the door was locked behind him and he could either
starve to death or jump into the river. There was Dürenstein where
Richard the Lionhearted was once confined until his troubadour
Blondel found him by singing a song known only to himself and
the royal prisoner. Along this route the Nibelungs had traveled on
their way to Hungary, and not far from Melk the great Rüdiger
von Bechelaren had his home in a village whose name, Pöchlarn, is
still reminiscent of those legendary days.

As the Danube leaves the narrow valley of the Wachau, it makes
a sharp turn. In the middle of the river there was at that time a
little island, long since blasted away by government engineers. The
terrific currents created here were known to the skippers as the
Wirbel and the *Strudel*, whirlpools which had something in common
with Scylla and Charybdis. It took expert seamanship to navigate
these parts, and at the time we made the trip the danger was by no
means negligible. Everybody was called on deck and given a life
belt, the captain and a big seaman stood at the rudder, and with both

paddle wheels violently in reverse, the boat shot out into the pool, apparently headed straight toward a rocky promontory. On top of this rock a band was playing, perhaps to drown our cries of terror. We seemed to hurl ourselves directly at the rock, and held our breath. One more second and the boat must break to pieces. Then, at a shrill whistle, the captain and his helper threw themselves onto the wheel, the rudder flew about, and with a graceful movement the vessel swerved, the railing of the deck not farther than a few feet from the musicians. The band stopped playing instantly, hats were thrown into the air, women stopped crying, and the show was over. After that the remainder of the trip faded into insignificance.

CHAPTER 2

*

NEW VENTURES IN AN OLD CITY

*W*HEN I WAS THIRTEEN years old, the question of my future began to be discussed with increasing seriousness. I only guessed this, as the discussions were never held in my presence. Uncle Anton, our official guardian, as well as other bearded elderly relatives began gathering at our house, and one or the other asked me what I would like to be some day. Eventually my mother announced the verdict to me. I was to finish high school at the age of fourteen, then take a one-year commercial course and graduate as a merchant's apprentice. I was speechless with horror. All my dreams of great achievements, of adventures in foreign lands, of making a name for myself, were threatened by this hideous scheme. For the first time in my life I rebelled, rebelled openly and fearlessly. It was my life that was being shaped, and I would defy this whole pack of unromantic old fogies who cared no more about my future than they did about last week's weather forecast. I talked myself into a white-hot fury. Just let those old vultures come to the house again, I would show them. My mother argued with me, but I remained firm. When she asked me what I would want to be, if I had my own choice, I replied, "A chemist."

On my frequent stamp-collecting visits to my father's office, I had talked now and then with my uncle, who had charge of the manufacturing part of the business, and he used to remark how much more successful his operations would be if he had some knowledge of chemistry. He was constantly handling solutions of silver salts and other chemicals about which he knew very little, and sighed over his lack of chemical training. He also visualized many inventions and improvements that a chemist could bring to bear on photography. I had heard my father say once that without chemists there would have been no photography. It was a chemist who had developed the wet plate, a chemist who had changed the wet plate to the film that made snapshots possible. Our business could not afford to hire chemical help, but secretly I expected to supply the scientific link that would make us undisputed leaders in our field. As I gradually absorbed remarks which I only partly understood, my imagination was fired. I pictured myself as a mighty inventor and the pioneer of great things. Although all I had seen of chemistry up to that time was my uncle measuring a liquid before he poured it from one glass container into another, my decision was made. I would be a chemist and nothing else. After my first important discovery I would come home and buy my mother a house and a two-horse carriage and we would go shopping in the *Kärntnerstrasse*.

All these plans and hopes came streaming out of me in an incoherent torrent as my mother sat listening in silent amazement. Finally, and with great reluctance, because one did not usually talk about such matters to children, she told me something of our distressing financial situation. My father had left only a little insurance; this was now about eaten up, and my sister Helene was already at work as a stenographer, although she was only fifteen years old. Bertha would follow in her footsteps a few months later. If I meant to study chemistry I would have to support myself and contribute to the family's income as well. It was a question of take it or leave it.

I provided the answer by going to work at once. I could think of only one way by which I could make money, and that was to tutor other boys who had trouble making the grade. I knew some of them; so I picked out those whose parents were fairly well-to-do and offered them my services. Thus began my long and heartwrenching career as a mentor. It was to last many years.

My first pupil was a boy my own age who attended the same class I did. I had to spend three hours a week with him, going over our lessons until he mastered them. For this work I received the equivalent of two dollars a month. It took me a long while to adjust my own mentality to the level of my pupil. Teaching is perhaps never an easy occupation, but to teach backward children exclusively, as I had to do, drains one's nervous energy to the vanishing point.

24

In a way it was fortunate for me that my first charge was an unusually stupid boy. Sometimes it took me hours to get one simple idea across, but I had the satisfaction of seeing my classmate pass his examinations. Soon my reputation grew. Instead of my looking for pupils, pupils were looking for me. In the beginning I taught whatever subjects they wanted to learn; I rehearsed with them the catechism, French grammar, or German history with absolute impartiality, and sometimes I learned more through them than they learned from me. After a while I taught only the subjects I liked, and at much better prices. My professors began to recommend me to anxious parents, and by and by the idea spread that no pupil of mine had ever been known to flunk. This was not true, of course, but my average was fairly good. The teaching staff was genuinely grateful to me and to all other tutors, because our work made the progress of the classes smoother and more uniform. Before long my school-free afternoons were completely taken up, and I realized a substantial sum from my tutoring. The problem of my future was settled for the time being.

If there is any way of making money which entails greater effort than that of teaching backward pupils, I have yet to experience it. Some of them were downright feeble-minded, and when I had finished coaching them I felt almost feeble-minded myself. Other boys would be quite normal in certain studies, but woefully deficient in others. It was they who gave me the most worry, because they were so deserving of help. One of them was a shy, red-haired youngster with a fine family background, quite intelligent, but lacking all linguistic sense. He twisted his German in the most incredible manner. His blue eyes had the haunted expression one sees in people who have been kicked around or laughed at all their lives. I used to stay awake nights trying to invent rules that would be useful to him. His parents were wealthy importers, and his mother never neglected to serve me tea and cookies, a kindness for which I am still grateful. She would then give me a long look, hoping for a sign of encouragement, but for a time I felt as hopeless as she did. Suddenly, one day, I found the key to my pupil's brain. I had him read juvenile stories and retell them to me in simple language. His self-confidence and power of expression rose simultaneously, and he passed his examinations in a blaze of glory. Twenty years later the boy was torn to pieces by a Russian shell and his parents committed suicide. His only sister, a beautiful little girl who used to come into the room once in a while to listen, is a grandmother today, and still corresponds with me occasionally.

One of my pupils was quite normal; he had done well in his studies up to a certain time, but after that he had started to slump so badly that his parents became seriously alarmed. I was called into consultation and soon found the cause of the trouble. The boy had one day obtained a copy of Jules Verne's *Twenty Thousand Leagues Under the Sea,* and from that moment on had read one Verne book after another, to the exclusion of everything else. He had become Jules Verne crazy. Instead of reporting this to the family, I reached an agreement with him; he was to read Jules Verne stories to me for half an hour, provided he would listen to me the other half, and for every Verne page I let him read he was to study one page of the school curriculum. The scheme worked to perfection, but had one bad after-effect. I became so interested in Jules Verne myself that I neglected my own studies and had to use all my will power to extricate myself before it was too late.

In the midst of my merry-go-round of studying and tutoring, I went through an attack of scarlet fever. By the time I had recovered, vacation time was near, and Mother worried about where to send me for convalescence. She finally wrote to Uncle Joe, a brother of my father's, who had a farm in the little town of Schwihau in Bohemia, and I was most cordially invited to spend two months with him. Mother wangled a half-fare ticket out of the railroad and, trembling with excitement and loaded with motherly advice, I started on my trip.

After several hours of travel we crossed the borderline of Bohemia, and soon the conversation of the passengers turned from German to Czech. I found that I had forgotten my Czech almost completely and could catch only a word here and there without grasping the meaning of the sentences. In subsequent years I often found myself in countries whose language I did not understand; but this was my first experience of that kind and it made me feel like an outcast.

I knew nothing about my uncle or his family, and when we

slowed down toward sunset and the conductor announced, first in Czech and then in German, "All out for Švihov—Schwihau," I was almost frightened.

It seemed to me that the whole town was at the depot. A tall man who looked a great deal like my father jumped at me, lifted me in his arms and kissed me; next came a stately, matronly woman who introduced herself as my aunt and did the same; and then I met six children, ranging from a boy and girl about my age down to a newborn baby. When we walked off, the rest of the crowd followed us. The arrival of a visitor from Vienna was an event in this town of fourteen hundred inhabitants, and as I looked with amazement at the people trailing behind us, my aunt assured me that there were still some persons left who had not come out to see me, although they would be watching from curtained windows as I was marched past them.

My uncle owned a house, a few teams of horses which were for hire, a brick factory and several farms. I wanted to absorb so many things at once that it almost drove me frantic. I had to learn the difference between wheat, corn and barley; how to milk cows; why a team of oxen had to be muzzled before they were taken out to harvest a field of clover. I wanted to take up horse-hitching, bricklaying and the Czech language all at once. There are many things I never did learn, but on the whole I did not do badly, for every item added to a knowledge of zero mounts visibly.

I can still see before me that peaceful Bohemian village of Schwihau. Like all its neighboring towns it was built around a square where stood the city hall, the church and the leading shops. Geese were all over the place, got into everybody's way, and never accelerated their pace unless they were shoved; then they retaliated with a vicious hiss. The horse and oxen teams seemed to have a thorough understanding with these feathered pedestrians, for I never saw a dead goose on the streets. On Saturdays and Sundays the square was lined with booths where farmers sold apples and plums, while others offered cakes, soap and trinkets of all kinds at ridiculously low prices.

To my great pleasure I found my knowledge of Czech coming back to me rapidly, and this made it easier for me to cultivate the people of the community. The inhabitants of small towns have always intrigued me more than those who live in big cities. One will usually find many more interesting persons in smaller settlements, persons who have preserved their individualities and who have thoughts and philosophies of their own. In Schwihau lived an old man who had to be wheeled around in a chair and who was considered queer. I used to visit him, and he would tell me of days gone by when he had been a young soldier. During a battle in the war of 1866 he found himself in the front line while the Austrians were storming a Prussian battery. Noticing a four-leaf clover at his feet, he could not resist the impulse to pluck it, and as he stooped down, the battery let go with a double charge of canister, killing or wounding everyone in the company except him. Another time he had found himself in deadly hand-to-hand combat with a Prussian infantryman and had stabbed him with his bayonet. As the Prussian fell, he moaned, "My poor wife and children," and died.

"I have never forgotten that I murdered a husband and father," the invalid said, "and I can't ever get those words out of my mind. That's why they think I am queer; perhaps I am."

Years ago a play which was having a big run all over the United States contained a line to the effect that there are as many interesting people in Kokomo as there are in New York. I would add that they are also easier to find. Schwihau had its vegetarian, quite a novelty in those days, a woman suffragist, and a small merchant who knew ancient philosophy by heart and recited Shakespeare to his customers.

In a village not far from Schwihau stood a little rapeseed oil mill. One day I entered it and, introducing myself to the foreman as a future chemist, begged him to show me around. He laughed good-naturedly and showed me what was to be seen, which was not a great deal. When he told me that they sent samples of oil and oil-cake regularly to a laboratory in Prague for analysis, I pricked up my ears. Apparently there was a demand for chemists, even in villages.

Upon my return to Vienna I entered the higher grades of the *Realschule*, and there was no more turning back now from my college career. A new set of professors took charge and treated us like grownups. Among these instructors were many we made fun of, either because of their accents or for some little mannerisms; but one day someone by accident found a copy of the school payroll. When we discovered how little pay the teaching staff received, we had a change of heart. We were old enough by that time to know what money meant and to understand the difficulties our teachers must have faced in order to live decently at salaries ranging from twenty to eighty dollars a month, the latter sum being the top remuneration paid to any of them.

It was at that time that we received our first instruction in chemistry. We beheld with wide-open eyes the miracle of two parts of hydrogen gas and one part of oxygen combining to form a tiny globule of water; we saw the violent reaction that follows when ammonia and hydrochloric acid are brought in contact. Then and there, I think, all of us decided to become chemists and to contribute valuable discoveries to mankind. I was allowed to take home some metallic sodium, and terrified the whole family when I let it loose in a basin of water. Fortunately, our enthusiasm was kept within bounds by the chemistry professor himself, a dried-up little man named Seidl, with an exasperatingly slow and distinct enunciation, who insisted on the greatest exactitude in our speech. Woe to anyone who would use personal pronouns which were not closely connected with the preceding noun. Did we mention a mere "she," the response would be, "By 'she' you mean the battleship 'Hiawatha,' I presume." If you inadvertently used an "it" out of turn you received a fishy stare and a slow, "You are perhaps referring to one of the students in this room?" When we were given problems during class, some enthusiast might jump up and exclaim, "I've got it, Professor," but he was quickly subdued by, "You have *what?*" And when he answered, "The solution, Professor," he was told that he had not completed the sentence; then he would comply, only to be told that he did not have the solution, he only thought he had it. On one occasion a boy asked to be allowed to leave in order to see a doctor, because a cinder had blown into one of his eyes. He was obviously in distress, but Professor Seidl was not so quickly moved.

"You have no cinder in your eye," he announced deliberately; "the cinder is between your eyelid and the eyeball." And with that comforting assurance the sufferer was permitted to leave. Had we been keen enough to recognize it, we should have known that we

29

were receiving sound mental discipline together with our chemistry lessons; but it was not until many years later that the value of succinct and precise language was understood by us, if indeed all of us profited by the training.

There was another professor in our school, a well-dressed man named Leon Kellner, who still cherished ideals. He told us that he kept one composition of each student, in the hope that one of them would some day make the world's *Who's Who*. His basement and garret were full of old papers, but he was still hoping. I met him twenty years later when he was an old man and long retired.

"Did you ever get your wish?" I asked him. He shook his head. "Not yet," he said, "but give the boys time. One of them still may become famous some day."

In one thing Professor Kellner and I agreed perfectly. We both had a dislike for honor students. I was forced to be one for the sake of my tuition, but I detested those who were striving for distinction only because it gave them an imaginary blue ribbon around their necks. Professor Kellner was of the opinion that honor students never amounted to much in later life. Good marks, he would say, were largely the result of a retentive memory, but what use did the world have for retentive memories? One did not pay people to know the telephone directory by heart.

My sister Helene was now seventeen or eighteen years old and had become private secretary to an old friend of the family, a man by the name of Morgenstern, who had hired her originally straight out of school. He owned a box factory, and always treated my mother and, in fact, all of us, with the utmost consideration. My sister Bertha was working as a stenographer for a firm of downtown lawyers.

Wages were pitifully small for office help of all kinds. Helene was considered a topnotcher when she got seven dollars a week. Later, when she was paid about twice that much, as private secretary to a prominent man whose speeches she wrote, her salary was headline news.

It was not surprising that under these conditions a ground-swell of unrest began to manifest itself. Employees had the effrontery to ask that all shops be closed on Sunday, something unheard of, and they even paraded the streets to popularize their demand. Elaborate arguments were conducted in the papers to prove that such an innovation would spell ruin for everyone. Then a Socialist paper, the *Arbeiter Zeitung,* was born and espoused the cause of the working classes. The police promptly dispersed all demonstrators, but the unrest continued. We children were naturally in favor of better working conditions, but my mother could not understand what this world was coming to and kept wishing for the good old days when, so we youngsters supposed, people worked all the time.

One evening, as I was coming home from my last lesson of the day, I met Mr. Morgenstern.

"I have good news for you," he confided to me. "Your sister's salary will be doubled, beginning tomorrow. She will live in a hotel, and the company will pay all her expenses." I rushed home to tell Helene what I had heard. Instead of being elated, she appeared greatly worried. The box business had not gone at all well lately. Hungary, the great market for the output of Viennese factories, was building plants of its own, and prices had slumped badly. The next day Mr. Morgenstern was taken to the Psychopathic Clinic, and then to the insane asylum. I visited him there once. The poor man had faded to a mere shadow, mumbled incoherently, and when I handed him an orange as a present from my mother, he wolfed it down like an animal. In all my horror and pity I could not help wondering what Tante Tini would have thought had she seen his manners. A few weeks later Mr. Morgenstern was dead. My sister was out of a job, and the sinister spectre of poverty lifted its head in our peaceful home. Something had to be done, and had to be done at once, to bring relief, while a feverish hunt went on to find Helene another position.

A family council was held, and it was decided to try a financial experiment. Tante Tini's husband, Uncle Adolf, a thoroughly subdued man who had been in turn a watchmaker, a tailor and a poultry dealer, had acquired considerable experience as a buyer of eggs, chickens, ducks and geese. The export of goose livers to Strasbourg, where they were worked into *pâté de foie gras* for re-export, was becoming a regular industry, and good goose livers commanded a high price in Vienna. In order to qualify, the liver had to be extraordinarily large, soft and almost white in color, and

geese were being forcibly fed in cages until their organs degenerated. It was difficult, however, to tell from the outward appearance
of a goose whether or not she would yield a desirable liver, and this
is where Uncle Adolf was importuned to take a hand. He went
marketing for us with the absolute assurance that he could draw no
blanks; he explained to us so carefully how, by a few skilful finger-
ings of the breast, the interior condition of the fowl could be
determined, that we gained absolute faith in his judgment. So one
day he went out marketing for three geese. They were duly delivered to our kitchen, and we all stood breathlessly around Mother
as she carefully cut her way into their interiors. Great caution
was essential, so as not to open either the gall bladder or the
intestines, as such a slip would have been fatal. All three geese
turned out to be very healthy specimens, and their livers were not
worth saving. We ate goose in all possible variations for weeks,
goose with rice, goose with dumplings, goose with potatoes, and
yet the end was not in sight. The three geese seemed to last forever.

After this debacle, we children held a conference. Why employ
Uncle Adolf at all? His explanations had been so lucid and logical
that they could not be all wrong. Could we not try our own skill
at selecting degenerate geese? We borrowed what money we could,
and when we had enough for one goose we went shopping. I am
sure no one was as unpopular as ourselves that day in the open-air
market place where we did our buying. Individually and collec-
tively we squeezed each goose, left our fingermarks all over the
poultry stands, played one dealer against another, and finally bar-
gained the last one down to a point where he did not even say
"Thank you" when we paid him, an unusual breach of etiquette in
pre-war Vienna. When the goose was opened it produced a liver
that was so beautifully enlarged, so pathologically wrong in every
respect, that an exporter paid us three times the price of the entire
goose and exhibited the sickly organ in his show window for several
days. After that we retired our uncle, and there was always a near-
panic on the poultry market when the three "goose-brats" came
along looking for a purchase. We did remarkably well in the liver
business and gave it up with genuine regret when Helene found herself another position.

My sister's new employer, a Mr. Pompl, owned a racing stable and a wine business. He cared little about the wine business, but in a city where wine and horses enjoyed a high rating, he was a man of distinction. The newspapers often asked his opinion on questions of the hour and, although Mr. Pompl had few noteworthy opinions, he was always anxious to oblige. He handed the job over to my sister, who in turn submitted it to our family circle. Three children then knelt on their chairs, heads bent over the table under the kerosene lamp which hung from the ceiling and, amid much giggling, concocted words of wisdom which supposedly flowed from the pen of our illustrious principal. We had certain standard formulae from which we never deviated much. Christmas sales invariably broke all previous records. On the first of the year we always predicted prosperity. In spring, we forecast bountiful crops; if they materialized, we patted ourselves on the back; if they did not, we consoled the country by pointing out that lesser quantities meant higher prices for the farmer. We used long words that made Mr. Pompl scurry to the dictionary to find out what he had said. Sometimes my sister brought home reprints from provincial papers or letters of congratulation, whereupon we marched around the table Indian fashion and let out ungodly yells of triumph, much to Mother's consternation and silent disapproval.

For his intellectual achievements Pompl eventually received the title of Court Counsellor and was actually introduced to Francis Joseph I. Mr. Pompl bowed deeply to the Emperor, whereupon the latter nodded his head and said, "Very nice, very glad, very nice." That is what His Majesty always said on such occasions, but Pompl boasted that the Emperor really had seemed glad to meet him and that the imperial intonation of "very nice" had sounded in his ears like so much poetry.

I was now sixteen years old and entering the last year of my studies at the *Realschule*. Spring would bring with it the dreaded *Matura*, an all-embracing examination about which we had heard dark hints since our freshman days. In this exam you were likely to be asked questions touching on any study in the curriculum of the past seven years; besides, so the rules said, you were expected to be familiar with anything an educated person was supposed to know. This took in a lot of territory. The examination was not conducted by the regular teaching staff, but by a State Commission and, worst of all, the students had to appear in full dress regalia. A movement was on foot, even in those days prior to the turn of the century, to restrict the number of college students. The intellectual proletariat was assuming threatening proportions, it was said. In short, there were more college graduates than the country could absorb. It was rumored that the *Matura* was a sort of elimination exercise, and that the State examiners had orders to flunk everyone they could.

I started clearing my decks. I had worked extra hard at accumulating a little surplus cash by using my vacation to steer some stragglers toward a happier future, and it was understood that I need do no tutoring during the last semester. One thing worked in the students' favor; the professors were on our side, partly from personal sympathy, but mostly because their own standing depended largely on our success. The school which showed the largest percentage of honor graduates and the smallest number of failures was rated the highest. In order to become an honor graduate, one had to announce his ambition beforehand, and especially difficult questions were prepared for these prospective victims.

The *Matura* consisted of an oral and a written section. The written examination started in June, and those who failed were automatically out for that year. Special rules prevailed to erect obstacles as severe as human ingenuity could devise them. We were placed in a large room, far apart from each other, and guards were stationed in front of us and behind us to preclude all possible communication. The papers were on German, French, English, mathematics and solid geometry, each lasting from four to eight hours. In German composition we were, like Walther Stolzing in *Die Meister-singer*, allowed only nine errors, but there was no Beckmesser present to warn us as we scribbled along. In French we had to follow rapid dictation and transcribe it into German at once; we then took dictation in German and translated it into French at greater leisure. Our tormentors had not missed many tricks in making our task difficult. There would be sentences in English, for example, which bristled with interpolated phrasings that are foreign to the German language and were therefore the cause of much head-scratching and despair. Even as I took down the dictation, I could detect various traps which I knew would catch all but the most wary.

When the oral examinations were held, four weeks later, we found that only twelve of us were left out of seventeen; five had been eliminated as unfit. Three of us applied for honor questions, I by necessity, the others by choice. What they did to us beggars description. Eventually I passed, but I still have nightmares about some of the questions put to me.

What to do for a little recreation? My money was exhausted and I did not want to impose again on the hospitality of my uncle in Bohemia. Yet that country held a strong fascination for me, and I had conceived a great liking for its people. Out of my longings emerged a resolution to take a hiking trip through both the German and the Czech sections which were supposed to be in a constant turmoil of strife against each other. If I could get as far as Pilsen by train, I thought I had a scheme which would obviate further financial difficulties.

The trip to Pilsen was undertaken. I carried with me a knapsack and about a dollar's worth of change. After four weeks of travel, I came back with twice that much and had robbed no one.

Starting from Pilsen in a southwesterly direction, I traversed country with which I was already familiar. I would walk a few miles until I came to a fair-sized village. There I would introduce myself to the local priest—Bohemia is predominantly Catholic—and offer my services for cleaning and cataloguing his library. My offer was usually accepted with surprised pleasure. For a couple of days I stayed as a guest in the priest's house and had an opportunity to familiarize myself with the community and its inhabitants. Payment I neither needed nor demanded; nevertheless, some grateful *padres* often slipped me a couple of florins when my work was done. In this fashion I traveled along, coming upon isolated German villages nestled among Czech neighbors and finding nothing but mutual good will over the entire countryside. At a little town named Drosau I was told that I was now leaving Czech territory behind me; the next town, which was only half a mile away and whose church spire was plainly visible, would be German. I had always wondered what a linguistic boundary line was like. Was there a no man's land where both languages were spoken, or was there a sharp dividing line? I discovered that the line could not have been drawn more sharply with a razor. In Drosau the children playing in the streets could not speak a word of German. When I spoke Czech to the children in the next village, fifteen minutes later, they gaped at me as if I had been a visitor from Mars. The grownups were not much different, only more polite. One thing that struck me as particularly distinctive was the way in which the German Bohemians buried their dead. Over each grave were planted the boards which once had been parts of the deceased person's bedstead, and on each board one could read part of his life story. I thought it a pretty custom.

Try as I would, I could discover no animosity between the Czech and German population of the country. Whenever I asked what the shouting was all about, people merely shrugged their shoulders and said, "Ask the politicians." I did not have to ask the politicians, for I could see what they were doing. They had to have strife, or else some of the most popular names would be forgotten over night. Evidently it was easier to become famous by tearing down than by building up.

Between the supposedly warring factions, Germans vs. Czechs, the Austrian government trod with circumspection. Each railroad station had the name of the town in both languages displayed with entire impartiality. The city of Budweis, for example, would display the words Budweis-Budějovice on the side fronting the road to Vienna, but Budějovice-Budweis on the side turned toward Prague. In front, the signs Budweis-Budějovice and Budějovice-Budweis appeared side by side. Wherever the district was inhabited by both Czech and German people, conductors, policemen and other officials spoke both languages. But it was all to no avail. Trouble was brewing, and everyone felt that the politicians would use every opportunity to stir the unsavory pot.

In order to understand the background of all this agitation, it must be remembered that after the debacle of 1866, Austria and Hungary, independent in all but diplomatic representatives, postal service and army, had concluded a treaty which was to be renewed every ten years, at which times their respective assessments for the maintenance of these common services were to be readjusted. Originally, Hungary had paid only thirty per cent, while Austria contributed the larger share; but Hungary was becoming a prosperous industrial country, and the Austrian taxpayers refused to bow to what they described as Hungarian imposition. The head of the government at that time was Prime Minister Count Badeni, a Pole. He had witnessed session after session of delegates arrive at a deadlock, and the day on which these negotiations must be concluded, November 30, 1897, was fast approaching. Every Austrian deputy who would vote for a maintenance of the *status quo* was in for bodily punishment; every Hungarian who would vote for a change was equally doomed. In the meantime, if the impasse could not be ended, the essential functions of the monarchy would break down.

In this dilemma, Count Badeni shrewdly but unscrupulously undertook to split the Austrian delegation. He promised the Slavs that if they would vote with him he would favor them in their perennial tug of war with the German minority.

The Germans in Parliament were hopelessly outnumbered, but they put up a strenuous fight. First they introduced resolutions of all kinds, asking for a teller's vote which took hours; then they complicated matters by asking for a vote on their resolution to have a teller's vote taken. For a few days this scheme worked; then Badeni had his partisans change the parliamentary rules, so that it was no longer workable. The Germans now resorted to whistles, drums and trumpets to make further deliberations impossible. Badeni had the sergeant-at-arms confiscate the noisy instruments. The hard-pressed Germans tried every parliamentary trick known, to tie up all proceedings beyond November 30; but November 29 came, and only one minority speaker remained to them, Dr. Otto Lecher of Brünn (Brno), in the province of Moravia. When he finished speaking the vote would be taken. Everyone knew who was bound to win.

Lecher did something heroic. He spoke without interruption for twenty-eight hours. His colleagues kept him going with coffee and other stimulants. When he concluded, the time limit had passed. It looked as if he, singlehanded, had forced the course of history. But at the last moment, Badeni marched troops into the Parliament and had all the German deputies removed by force and thrown into jail. The vote proceeded without further interruption.

I was a student at the Vienna Polytechnical Institute when all this happened. News of Count Badeni's despotic procedure reached us as we were attending morning classes. The effect was electrical. Professors and students alike left the classrooms instantly. When we reached the streets, big crowds of people had already assembled, and everyone was in an ugly mood.

"To Parliament!" someone shouted, and toward the Parliament building we marched, although we never got within a mile of it. Tens of thousands of workingmen were streaming through all the radial thoroughfares that connect the *Ringstrasse* with the suburbs, and all these waves of humanity seemed to have the same goal. In vain, hundreds of policemen and whole companies of cavalry threw themselves against the crowd. The riders were swept off their horses and brushed aside, but none was hurt. Although a revolution was in the making, the natural humor of the Viennese asserted itself on every possible occasion. I remember a mounted police officer riding along our front shouting, "Disperse! Disperse!" Everyone ran, except one fat citizen who held his ground. "Disperse, sir," the officer yelled at him; whereupon the fat man pointed to his stomach and woefully said, "I wish I could, but I can't." Everyone laughed, including the policeman, and there was no bloodshed.

I was shoved around with the crowd and suddenly found myself inside the University building. According to an ancient custom, the police could not invade the school grounds, but they did shoot at us from the street, while we in turn hurled at them chairs and inkwells and anything else that was handy.

At three o'clock the government surrendered by releasing the imprisoned deputies, and the revolution was over. I hurried to the office of the *Neues Wiener Journal*, a large newspaper, and asked them if they wanted my story. They accepted eagerly. I suddenly had become a student-journalist.

A few days later the *Neues Wiener Journal* called me in for an important assignment. All colleges were still closed, and the editor gave me orders to find out when they would reopen. It was a vital question, and the papers tried eagerly to supply the answer. I knew some of the professors fairly well, but they were sworn to secrecy. Nevertheless, by casually conversing with them and drawing what I thought were justifiable conclusions, I arrived at a satisfactory answer. The next morning my article was at the top of the page.

The editor considered it a real scoop, for later events proved that I had guessed right. The colleges opened on the day I had predicted. After that I was the star student-reporter of the *Journal*. Ordinary reporters walked or took the streetcar, but I could travel nonchalantly in two-horse carriages, when the occasion warranted, and I had a very generous expense account. More valuable than that, I had a press card. I would not have changed places with the Emperor of China.

CHAPTER 3

*

PREPARING TO SERVE MANKIND

$\mathcal{B}$EFORE ENTERING the *Kaiserlich-Königliche Technische Hochschule,* I had to overcome once more the resistance of my mother. She was determined to make a civil engineer of me, because the government at that time was contemplating the erection of many public works, and civil engineers were assured of immediate employment. My choice was chemistry, of course, and I stuck to it with unshakable determination.

I had taken considerable chemistry in the *Realschule* and liked it. The magic of turning a colorless liquid pink or purple by the addition of a few drops of phenolphthalein or some other mysterious indicator had appealed mightily to my imagination. Long and tedious studies had taken the place of the first fascinating experiments, but my enthusiasm had not diminished.

I had also asked the advice of my professors, but none of them knew much of practical things. There were chemists in the world, to be sure, and as the papers never reported that any of them had died of starvation, it was reasonable to infer that they were making a living. More than that I could not get out of them, probably because it was not in them.

I still had pictures of Lavoisier and Liebig in my mind; within me surged the hope of making great inventions, as they had done. I felt that I had to become a chemist, although up to that time I had never met a chemist, except my teachers. Like hundreds of other students, then and now, I was entering the long, dark tunnel of a college course without a definite idea of what would be waiting for me at the other end.

The amount of chemistry we were allowed to imbibe in the first two years at college was not enough to give anyone mental indigestion. While officially we had no compulsory curriculum and could attend lectures or not as we saw fit, there were a few classes we had to take sooner or later, but most of them bore little, if any, relationship to chemistry. The ways of the German educators are not always easy to follow, but it seems to me that they stumble sometimes over their own thoroughness. An American child learns swimming by being thrown into the water. In Germany he is first taught correct breathing, for the sake of endurance; then anatomy, so he knows which muscles pain him; and then first aid, just in case. If he lives long enough, he may in the end get a swimming lesson. Our *Polytechnikum* worked along similar lines. In order to understand chemistry we had to study physics, and in order to understand physics we had to study higher mathematics. For two years we heard lectures on everything except chemistry. Had it not been for our laboratory work, we would not have known toward what goal we were headed.

One of the most interesting courses I took was economics, although it was less the subject than its exponent that made it so attractive. Professor Hermann was a man of many original ideas. Some thirty years before, he had invented the postal card. It seemed rather odd to me that the postal card had to be invented by someone, but the fact is that only sealed letters had been in use before Hermann hit on the idea of a single piece of paper which would carry stamp, address and message all in one. Aside from this creditable achievement, Professor Hermann had conceived many strange and brilliant theories. The one I remember best dealt with the thought that children, after their birth, still undergo the evolution of the far distant past, much as an embryo passes from the worm stage to that of a human being. To him a newly-born baby was still more monkey than man, as shown by the tremendously strong grip in its fingers and by its delight in being swung high in the air. The tendency of youngsters to jump out from hidden places to frighten others was reminiscent of the cave days, and children's frequent preference of green apples to ripe ones denoted to Professor Hermann the age when most of our temperate zones were covered with glaciers, and fruit never ripened. He also held forth a remarkable theory that by a proper tabulation of all gaps in our knowledge, new inventions could be greatly hastened, and he demonstrated the idea by practical tests which often produced astounding results.

It was not long before my finances began to bother me again. Laboratory work was expensive, especially for one as awkward as I, who broke beakers and thermometers wholesale. I still tutored and wrote for the *Neues Wiener Journal,* but I needed more income, and needed it badly. College students in Vienna had many privileges, such as reduced rates in restaurants, and we could buy standing-room tickets in the best theaters for a dime or two. But cheapness is, like so many other things, a relative matter, and to me who did not have a dime to spare, a dime ticket was beyond reach. Then an accidental remark of a fellow student gave me an idea which relieved my pecuniary distress, at least for the moment.

Among our more or less compulsory studies was one called Elementary Machinery. The professor who retailed this knowledge to us was a small, wheezy-voiced man called Nottinger who, in addition to his unintelligible mode of speech, scrawled his figures and drawings on a wet blackboard, claiming that the scratching of chalk on the dry board irritated him. The result was that by the time the writing became legible, his lecture was a few minutes further along, and the students quit in droves, because they could not follow it. I was a pretty good shorthand writer and managed to keep up with the lecturer. One of my classmates asked me to let him copy my notes, so he could stay away entirely. I consented, of course, but it gave me a bright idea. If I did this service for one, why not extend it to some two hundred others who were equally perplexed? No sooner did the thought strike me than it was executed. I bought myself a multigraph machine and let it be known that I would sell the entire year's lecture course for eight dollars. The scheme took like wildfire and the lecture room became alarmingly empty. In order to forestall possible trouble, I handed Professor Nottinger a sample copy of my, or rather his, work. He was delighted.

"Did I really put that so well," he asked, "or did you polish it up for me?" I disclaimed all credit, and he asked me to let him have a complete set at the end of the year. He confessed that he had always wanted to compile his course in written form, but had never found the time. Incidentally, I was exempted from examination in Elementary Machinery on the debatable assumption that I had become familiar with the subject while making my copies.

We were required to average twenty hours a week in the analytical laboratory, and it still breaks my heart when I contemplate that waste of time. Routine analytical chemistry has long become a mere mechanical art and should be separated from the curriculum of a real chemistry student. There may have been a time in the dim past when physicians had to mix their own prescriptions and chemists had to do their own analytical work, but these days are gone. Hundreds of years ago it may have required the brains of a savant to determine the temperature in a room; today anyone can look at a thermometer. The filling station attendant who puts his spindle into a battery fluid gets the specific gravity as accurately as the best chemist. Analysts constantly invent simple devices like spindles or thermometers, and each of them throws a few confrères out of employment. Most routine analytical work can be done today by high school youngsters. They may not know the underlying principles of what they are doing, but their results are acceptable, nevertheless.

In my opinion, the study of analytical chemistry should be left to those who wish to specialize in it. The majority of chemistry students could put to better use the short time allowed them for the preparation of their careers.

Viennese schools in the last years of the nineteenth century were the meeting places of many queer students from many queer places. They came from every country in the Balkans and the Far East, and when you walked through the courts or corridors you could hear more tongues wagging in outlandish languages than were heard by the builders of Babel. Our laboratory had its share of these oddities. I recall in particular a tall, rawboned Russian from Kazan, whom no one could rightly understand and whom we all regarded with a good deal of awe. We used to call him Klobunishky; his real name was too hard to pronounce. He came and went much as he pleased and seemed to be bursting with money. The class wit composed an obscene poem about him which—in expurgated form—ran something like this:

This Klobunishky has the dough;
His strength is physical, not mental.
He does not need to give a damn,
Nor gives a continental.

Klobunishky once engaged in a lengthy piece of laboratory work. The task allotted to him proceeded slowly; finally the day came when he had condensed his result in the form of a small amount of liquid; he was within one day of his goal. At this moment someone opened a window, and a sudden gust of wind upset his beaker. There was a profound silence. None of us knew what to expect. But the big fellow only started to whistle, picked up the broken glass, and started his work over again.

A few more weeks passed; this time he had his results in a crucible which needed only to be weighed to finish his thesis. Going to the balance room he stumbled and broke the crucible. The whole laboratory stood as petrified. The Russian got up, whistled, and went out to the cloakroom. A minute later he returned with his cane. He opened all his drawers and closets, took out the glassware, and proceeded to smash everything in sight: beakers, flasks, burettes, and all. Then he picked up his cane and went away whistling. When he did not show up for a few days, we ascertained his address and called on him. We found him in bed, fast asleep, with a half dozen empty vodka bottles lying on the floor and one of them, half emptied, clutched tightly in his hand. Soon afterward he disappeared and was not heard from again.

During the first year at the Polytechnic I was vouchsafed a strange demonstration of telepathy. I asked my neighbor in the laboratory to cut with a knife a steel wire which I was holding taut between my hands. He hacked away with gusto, but hit one of my fingers instead, with the result that the top joint was left dangling by a mere thread, while the blood spurted all over the place. I hurried to a first-aid station, then rode home, as I was feeling a bit faint. When I arrived I found my mother sitting on the stairway, deathly pale and in an agony of suspense. She was waiting for me; something had told her I was coming home. She had been working in the kitchen when she received a sudden subconscious flash that I had met with an accident. She could not guess what had happened, but had seen blood on the walls and on the floor. My mother always had premonitions, and they never failed her. Whenever she dreamed that she had lost a tooth, someone in her circle died within a day or two. It was not a desirable gift to possess, and I inherited the worst part of it. I sometimes have a presentiment of impending disaster, and it always comes true; but since I do not know its nature or the direction from which the blow is about to fall, I would willingly dispense with this strange power.

Vienna at that time was the home of many Englishmen, probably because British capital controlled the local gas works and other public utility plants, and as Englishmen remain what they are all over the world, they banded together, rented a little piece of land in the Prater, and started the First Vienna Cricket and Football Club. The invasion of the sacred Prater, that great island forest preserve which has been the playground of the Austrian capital since the time of the Romans, was frowned upon by the Viennese. The indignation was not directed against the Englishmen, but at Empress Elizabeth, whose wild expenditures in foreign countries taxed her husband's private purse to such an extent that he was forced to sell part of the Prater grounds. Nevertheless, many spectators turned out to see the Englishmen in their strange antics of cricket and football. Cricket never aroused much response, but football soon became very popular. The first purely native club found me among its charter members, in spite of the protests of my family, who looked with aversion on this violent exercise. I was then eighteen years old, had never indulged in any kind of sport, and became wildly enthusiastic about the game. When football practice was called I would cancel all other engagements, and when there was a game on, a straitjacket could not have kept me from attending. The football we played was the English brand, known as association football, where the use of hands is taboo. I chose the position of goalkeeper, but my zeal was greater than my ability, and I was gently demoted to the position of second, and later to third substitute guardian of the goal. We had no coach of any kind, and what we learned we had to pick up from our English opponents who had some former professionals among them. I still recall one of their forwards, a man named Windett, and one of their halfbacks, a powerful fellow called Nicholson. Both became the heroes of all Viennese boys, and their memories are still cherished among the old-timers.

In the meantime, other European countries had also taken up football, and clubs were founded in Hamburg, Berlin and Prague. One day we received a letter from an English professional club, the Thames II, offering to play us all if we would defray their expenses. How we did that I do not know, but we managed it, and the Thames II came to Vienna for a two-day match. On the first day they were to play a team composed only of locals, and on the second day a team combined of everything we had to offer.

When those English boys started to play we looked like dummies in a show window. We had never learned the art of teamwork, of flat passing, or of any other fine points, and our visitors ran all over us. What irritated us particularly was that the Thames goalkeeper sat between his posts writing picture postcards and never even looked up to see what was going on. They knocked out our first goalkeeper, and the second soon followed in his wake. This was my great chance. By this time the score was 9 to 0. I had hardly taken my place when the balls started whizzing at me and past me in a way I had never seen before. I threw my body against them when they were out of reach of my hands, and I must have stopped quite a few, for I was black and blue for a week afterward. Nevertheless, the game ended 15 to 0. The next day the battle order was issued to make that Thames goalkeeper get on his feet, no matter what happened. The English team had not been scored against on their whole Continental trip, but our aggressive tactics bore fruit. By neglecting our defense altogether and sending the entire team into the forward line, we managed to score one goal, at what price I would rather not say.

We had about thirty paying spectators those two days, and collected a total of four dollars in admission fees. Twenty years later I saw a combined Viennese team play the champions of Ireland before 60,000 spectators, and there was nothing cheap about the tickets, even when measured by American standards.

When I chose to tutor in those days, I moved in pretty high society. One of my pupils was a young artillery officer who was carrying on a private war against everything that looked like an equation or a calculus, and he lost every time. I had to call on him at eleven o'clock in the morning so as not to interfere with his other duties—I never did find out what they were—and this upset my own schedule; but he paid me a fancy price, fed me sumptuously, and always found an excuse to skip the lesson. He entertained me by the hour with recitals of his love adventures, mostly with ladies of the stage, and he knew everyone in town worth knowing. Eventually his father, a high staff officer, lost patience with him and had him transferred to a provincial garrison. With him Vienna lost one of her most charming seducers and I a choice slice of my income.

Another of my charges was the son of a secretary to Baron Rothschild, then reputed the richest man in Austria. The lessons took place in the Rothschild palace, known widely for its beautiful gardens which, I am ashamed to confess, did not interest me at all. I just about knew the difference between a rosebush and a pine tree, and much more than that I have not learned since. The secretary was a loyal official, and his admiration for the family he served expressed itself in heaps of anecdotes which he was fond of telling. One or two of them have remained in my memory. During the commune in Paris in 1871, an investor came breathlessly into Baron Rothschild's office in Paris with a big bundle of banknotes in his pocket, wanting to know what to do with the money. The Baron advised him to buy French government bonds, then selling at seventy or thereabouts.

"What," exclaimed the visitor, "buy French government bonds when the streets of Paris are running with blood?"

"You fool," was the reply, "do you think you could buy them for seventy cents on the dollar if the streets of Paris were not running with blood?"

Another time a caller was kept waiting in the anteroom for some time, and when he was finally admitted into Rothschild's presence, he commented on some of the financial literature he had read while waiting.

"You advocate the purchase of an eight per cent stock," he said, "and you say it is a good investment. You also advocate a three per cent bond and you say it is a good investment. Which of the two do you advise me to buy?"

The Baron smiled. "If you want to eat well," he said, "buy the eight per cent stock; if you want to sleep well, buy the three per cent bond."

I never met any member of the Rothschild family, but the stories I heard gave me a fairly accurate picture of their personalities and of the homely wisdom which was the cornerstone of their fortunes.

Among the many privileges accorded to college students was a membership in a medical aid society, where advice and treatment were ours for a fee not worth mentioning. One day a classmate asked me why I had not had myself sent out to the country somewhere during the summer; everyone was doing it.

"But I am not sick," I remonstrated.

"Yes, you are," he said, "you've got softening of the brain. The society is itching to show you a good time, and you can't even take the hints they throw at you."

Thus it was that I contracted rheumatism, and that is how I was sent to Baden to take the curative baths there. I did not know that I was forging the first link in a chain which would tie me more and more to that beautiful little town in the foothills of the Austrian Alps.

Baden lies about fifteen miles south of Vienna, and was then one of the most popular summer resorts for the middle class burghers of the metropolis. To me it was Paradise. There were the ancient Roman baths, the modern parks, an open-air band concert three times a day and—this is what took my breath away—an outdoor arena where light operas and comedies were presented afternoons and evenings. If I could only afford this luxury, my happiness would be complete.

The medical aid society had handed me a sum equivalent to eight dollars, plus free bathing tickets, and told me to stay as long as the money lasted. This was by no means intended as a joke. Students were supposed to know how to live on next to nothing. I immediately started to cast a budget. If I paid two dollars a month for a room and ate only two meals a day, the money could be made to hold out several weeks. There were not many other expenses. I needed no shaves because my mother insisted that I let my beard grow; it would be silky, she said, if I did not shave. In the meantime, she saved the outlay for a razor. The laundry could be taken care of by my landlady; she was an invalid, and in exchange for the washing I agreed to wheel her to the concerts every day. The problem of the theater still remained; no matter how I figured, I could not manage it. I even tried looking into the arena from the branches of nearby trees; but the walls were just high enough to preclude such artistic piracy.

Finally I decided on a bold move. I would go to the *Direktor's* office, beard the lion in his den, and ask him for free tickets. And so, with my heart hammering audibly, I was ushered into the presence of Herr Alfred Schreiber, who was the presiding genius of the *Stadttheater*. I came straight to the point. I was crazy to see his shows, but I had no money; would he let me in free? Mr. Schreiber, who had been sitting at his desk, now rose, and I could not help admiring the beautiful physique of the man which, together with a marvelous profile, gave him the appearance of a Roman god. At least that is the way he looked to me.

"Young man," he said, "I ought to throw you out. But what good would that do me? You may not believe it, but I am just as broke as you are." I surprised myself by not running away.

"A man who's broke," I suggested, "has one advantage; he has nothing to lose. Let me in, and perhaps I'll bring you luck." I have no idea what made me say that, for I did not know then what a superstitious lot theatrical people are; but I saw at once that I had hit a responsive chord.

"All right," Mr. Schreiber said, "maybe you will. Free standing room only for you, and on Saturdays and Sundays you stay away. Understand?" I did, and said so with tears in my eyes. Just as I was about to leave he called me back.

"I was a student once myself," he said in an undertone. "If no one is looking, I'd try to get in on Saturdays and Sundays too, especially if there were empty seats going to waste." I left hurriedly. Never before in all my life had the sun shone so brightly.

I did not see Baden again until almost twenty-five years later, and my first visit was to the theater. To my great sorrow, Schreiber had died in the meantime. A daughter of his still lived, however, a middle-aged married woman to whom I was introduced. The postwar inflation had then set in, and Schreiber's daughter found herself in straitened circumstances. Her rooms were still filled with beautiful furniture and the many gifts her father had received during his lifetime; but her husband's pension was a mere pittance in the depreciated currency. Knowing the pride of her class, I told her I had promised Mr. Schreiber that if the time ever came when I could reimburse him for his free tickets I would do so, with interest. The little scheme worked, and I was thereby enabled to repay part of my old debt. I also bought a number of tickets each day for impecunious students. Unfortunately, this brought the whole affair to the attention of the newspapers, and a loquacious ticket-seller who knew the value of publicity helped to make live news out of it. According to his version I, as a small boy of fourteen, had been crying at the entrance to the playhouse when Herr Schreiber saw me and asked me the reason for my tears. When he learned that I wanted to see the show, he lifted me in his arms and carried me into one of the loges, and after that I became his mascot, bringing him full houses and everlasting prosperity. And now, twenty-five years later, I had returned, a rich man. Finding Mr. Schreiber's daughter impoverished, I had bought her a new house and furnished it as for a fairy princess. It was a good story, even if untrue, and made the rounds of the European press, into Germany, Poland, Denmark and Russia. The farther it traveled the more bizarre it grew, until very little resemblance to the facts remained.

All this, of course, was then still far in the future, and even farther from my dreams. The brave little stock company which Schreiber directed had a big repertoire, and I got to know many of the beautiful old Strauss, Zeller, Suppé and Milloecker operettas which are now almost completely forgotten. Milloecker lived in Baden at that time, and I often watched him from a distance as he sat on a bench in the Kurpark, drawing lines in the sand with his cane. When he left his seat, I immediately occupied it, hoping for some inspiration, but none ever came; nor could I decipher his scrawls, which I tried to interpret as musical sketches.

Where are those melodious operettas which once had such a hold on the world's audiences? Strauss' *Ali Baba* or *A Night in Venice*, Millöcker's *Apajune*, Suppé's *Boccaccio*? Some day an enterprising radio manager will rediscover them and make himself popular. In the meantime, the American public is made to hear *The Blue Danube* over and over again, while the more adventurously inclined conductors give their hearers the overture to *Die Fledermaus* or some other Viennese composition which, although worked hard, has not yet been worn quite to tatters.

After my return to Vienna, my enthusiasm for music continued. Although I could not go to the opera often, I took a serious interest in it, as did everyone else in Vienna. The city had no such thing as a baseball team on which to vent its local patriotism, and therefore lavished its affection on the theaters, principally on the Imperial and Royal Opera. In a manner of speaking, we knew each member's past record, playing position and batting average. What had happened the night before on the stage of the opera was sure-fire news and more exciting than politics or crime.

One night the management did something unusual. It brought out a young, unknown singer named Roth, fresh from a musical academy, and put her into the role of Gretl in Humperdinck's *Hansl und Gretl,* then a comparatively new opera. The young lady did exceptionally well and earned the applause of her skeptical and somewhat blasé listeners. The father of the new star happened to be a printer on a local daily, and when he read the glowing review he was setting in type, he became so confused that he printed the column upside down. All Vienna laughed about his mistake, and some cried, too. Miss Roth had captured the metropolitan heart overnight.

A few weeks later the brilliant star disappeared from the sky. A wealthy man had come along and married her. She was not again heard in public.

I had not seen Miss Roth perform, but something rebellious stirred within me. Did a person who was endowed with a special gift that could make others happy have the moral right to withhold it from common use? Did Mozart have the right to burn his music or Edison his models? I worried a lot about this on long, lonely walks. If all gifted people had moral obligations toward their fellow creatures, how about those whose special talent was money-making? I wondered whether moneymakers would ever have enough decency or foresight to share the fruits of their ability with others less fortunate. If they did not, would the community some day take it away from them through taxes or by still more drastic means?

51

I discussed this thought both at home and at school, but the results were discouraging. Of course, a singer had the right to marry a rich man and abandon her public career if she chose. I was called an iconoclast, a communist. I discovered that once my opponents had found a label for me, intelligent discussion ceased; but my doubts kept haunting me.

I had passed my nineteenth birthday and was entering the last two years of my college courses. Our chemistry studies now began in earnest, but there was little cohesion between the various courses prescribed for us. The Austrian colleges did not only practice *Lernfreiheit,* which meant that every student could study what he wanted, but also *Lehrfreiheit,* which meant that every professor could, within wide limits, teach what he wanted and use his own way of doing so. As a result of being taught by several methods at once, our immature minds did not know which way to lean. We had a professor in inorganic technology, for example, who touched on only three chapters of the entire field during the year—blast furnaces, sulphuric acid and gold mining. He took us through each chapter with extreme thoroughness; I imagine his belief was that it is better to know a few things well than to spread oneself thinly over a wide surface. If that was his idea, he should have said so, and we would have understood. But he did not, and therefore encountered much resistance and unfavorable criticism. Another professor followed exactly the opposite procedure and gave us a little bite from every loaf. He was lecturing on organic technology, and we got a glimpse of breweries, aniline dyes, yeast factories, oil wells and a dozen other subjects, all of which left us completely bewildered. If that was chemistry, we would not master it in a hundred years. In between, we heard lectures on all kinds of subjects delivered by assistant professors or guest speakers. Arrhenius had just published his studies on ions and was promptly laughed out of court by the older faculty members, while the younger assistants, when they were alone, would speak of him in terms of highest praise. Roentgen had discovered X-rays and the Curies were studying a substance called radium. A revolution was brewing in chemistry, just as in politics.

The turmoil in politics was, of course, much more audible than that in science. People were now demanding universal suffrage, something that we knew existed in America, England and France, but which still had to be fought for in Austria. Why should people without a property stake in the community have the right to vote, the old folks wanted to know. And what good would it do if they did vote? The younger generation was of a different opinion, and rifts appeared even in well-regulated bourgeois families. Then there was the Slavic question which would not down. The Czechs were dreaming of Pan-Slavism to unite Russians, Poles, Czechs and Serbs into one great bloc. The Germans countered with Pan-Germanism, and the Socialists talked universal brotherhood of all working classes, irrespective of nationality. It was difficult for any individual to stay out of this strife, even had he so desired, which as a rule he did not. Anti-Semitism also began to raise its ugly head. A *Bürgermeister* named Karl Lueger had been elected in Vienna on a purely anti-Semitic platform, in spite of the united opposition of the press. When the Emperor confirmed him, the conservative classes stood aghast. During the campaign, Lueger had promised to tear the *Peuschl* out of every Jew living, *Peuschl* being made of the lungs and livers of sundry domestic animals. When he came into power, however, he made friends of the Jews and ousted the English capitalists from their possession of the utility plants, installing municipal power and streetcar lines instead. Those were lively times, and the older inhabitants shook their heads dubiously over their cups of coffee and games of tarok or chess.

It was about that time that I fought my only duel, and no one was more astonished than I that I had to do it. The students observed certain codes of behavior, one of which was that any offense committed by one student against another had to be settled by means of the sword, provided the offended party willed it so. One day, while walking in one of the college courts, I inadvertently bumped into a fellow student. I apologized, but he sent me his seconds who asked for "proper satisfaction." I could have refused, but by this time I was just as angry as he, and so I accepted. Never in my life had I held a sword in my hand, while my opponent was known to be one of the best fencers in Vienna. Friends wanted to rush me to their fraternity house to give me instructions, advising me that I could ask for a six weeks' extension because of my lack of training. I had other plans, though. I asked for a week's time and spent a few hours handling swords, so as to get my muscles accustomed to the heavy weapons then in use.

Student duels were not always the dangerous combats they were pictured to be. Each combatant had two seconds at his side, and although they were not supposed to do more than see that the rules were obeyed, each held a sword in his hand and parried any blow that looked dangerous, explaining matters afterward as well as he could.

I knew, of course, that no amount of training I could undergo in a short time would offset the skill and experience of my antagonist, and I therefore decided to break away from all established customs and fight along a new line. As soon as the signal for the start of hostilities was given, I lit into my opponent like a madman. I knew nothing about *primas* and *secondos,* nor the proper way to parry them, but my opponent never had a chance to attack me. I had to keep up my slashing tactics or be hacked to pieces. A cry of dismay arose from our seconds, and after a few minutes they stopped the fight. This was not a student's duel, they said, but butchery, and likely to lead to serious bloodshed. I replied that I did not care; the more blood the better, and to the devil with refined methods of adjusting such a fatal insult as bumping accidentally into another man. My own seconds were as dumfounded as the rest and did not quite know how to handle the situation. In the end we all shook hands and called it a day. For weeks afterward I could feel myself being pointed out on the college grounds, but just what was whispered I did not know and did not much care.

I really had more important things on my mind than duelling. My poverty began to irk me again. In the last two years, all students had to take excursions into chemical factories, and those trips cost money. Most of my colleagues had substantial amounts sent them from home, while I not only had to meet my own expenses, but in addition had to create a surplus. As a consequence, I had to forego much fun, and I would have had to forego much more, had it not been for the generosity of an assistant professor who guessed my troubles and often relieved them with finesse and tact. This assistant, a Doctor Reich, impressed me as a man of unusual talents.

54

He later became one of the leading patent specialists on the Continent, but at that time, his talents were overshadowed by his irrepressible sense of humor and his vast store of good stories, not all of which were fit for print.

One of our excursions carried us into the town of Kattowitz in southeastern Silesia, on German soil. The Prussian hand lay heavily on this region, which was largely inhabited by Poles and, although the use of the Polish language was forbidden, I heard it spoken on all sides. One night as we were walking to our hotel, some dimly outlined figures appeared as if from nowhere and threw heavy stones at us, presumably because we were conversing in German. Future events were casting their shadows ahead, long before anyone dreamed that there could ever be such a thing as a World War.

On these excursions we naturally inquired into the living conditions of the chemists employed by the plants we visited, and we were thoroughly disillusioned, if not actually frightened at our prospects. These predecessors of ours, many of whom had graduated from our school, were leading a disconsolate existence; they often lived hundreds of kilometers from the nearest cultural center, among strangers whose language they first had to learn before they could discharge their duties. Usually their homes were nothing more than a part of the factory in which they worked. Recreation consisted of card playing at the village inn, where a special room was reserved for the *Honoratioren*, meaning the local doctor, the priest, the postmaster and the elite of the plant employees.

I followed some of the chemists on their daily rounds. They looked bored and disgusted. One of them took me along without enthusiasm. It was his duty to supervise a sulphuric acid plant in a small Hungarian village. The official language was Magyar, and all reports had to be made in that tongue, but the workers spoke Slovak among themselves, while in the laboratory and in the private offices I heard mostly German. An air of restlessness hung over the entire institution. The laborers were visibly undernourished, the officials underpaid; the intercourse between them was sullen. Neither class understood the other well, literally or otherwise. Commands were given harshly and obeyed lackadaisically. The technical staffs hailed either from Vienna or from Budapest, and each treated the other as intruders. What kept them in forced solidarity was their common fear of the workers' passive resistance, that dreaded intangible weapon of the downtrodden. Orders would be executed within the exact meaning of the words, but not within their spirit. On one occasion I heard a chemist ask a girl to run back to the laboratory to see if he had left his spectacles there. The young woman came slouching back after a while.

"Yes, sir," she said.

"Yes, what?" the man thundered.

"Yes, you left your glasses there," she answered, looking stupid, but with a mischievous glint in her eyes.

The foreign-born technicians had trouble pronouncing certain words in the local language, and this often lent itself to misinterpretation and gave the workers many chances for open ridicule, of which they availed themselves gleefully. In fact, it seemed their favorite mode of amusement.

The chemical plants were in operation day and night, and all employees worked in shifts. Chemists worked twelve hours, like everyone else. I did not see how they could find time to keep abreast of new developments, let alone make inventions; but when I expressed this thought I met only stares or contemptuous smiles. I would find out in time, they said, and one of the younger men hinted that after a while I, like the rest, would learn to get my inspiration from a bottle.

It was all very exasperating.

On the way home, Doctor Reich twitted us unmercifully. Who had bidden us to become chemists anyway, he asked. We had it coming to us. "Serving mankind," as Professor So-and-so always said—well, these chemists we had seen were serving mankind, weren't they? He had us all so desperate before he finished that we considered ending our chemists' careers and becoming dry-goods clerks instead. The difficulty was that in order to become a dry-goods clerk you had to be apprenticed first, and no one over sixteen could be apprenticed. Damn it, stick to chemistry then, and trust to luck that you at least would land a job in some city and not out in the sticks.

If I had ever had any doubts in my mind about following my father's advice to start my career in America, these trips into the twilight zone of European civilization dispelled them effectively.

But when I broached the subject at home I met with opposition. My mother was set against my plan to emigrate. Her argument was that if a chemist had to starve, he could do it at home as well as in America. She told me gruesome stories of my father's sufferings out West, stories I now heard for the first time. She painted the picture as dark as she could, but I stood pat. As always, we ended by compromising. I could go whenever I pleased, provided I would pay my own expenses and continue my contributions to the Viennese household, month after month, without any omissions or alibis. I agreed.

Several things remained to be done before my emigration project could be made feasible. First, I had to make sure that my American citizenship was still intact. Fortunately, my mother had, a few years before, applied for the pension due a widow of a Civil War veteran. It amounted to some four hundred dollars a year and would have transformed our lives into a riot of luxuries. We came close to getting it, too, but unluckily my father's papers were in very poor order. His name was spelled differently on every document, and he had never taken the trouble to correct the errors. The upshot was that, although the State Department officially recognized all of us as American citizens, the pension was denied us on a technicality. For me the establishment of the citizenship was of primary importance. I verified its validity at the American consulate and, to make doubly sure, had a passport issued to myself so that I could enter the United States as an American citizen any time I chose.

Only the final exams now remained. They, like the *Matura,* were conducted by a State Commission. I hardly gave them any thought. Studying had become a routine business with me. By constantly coaching other minds, my own had become machine-like in its operation. I found it much easier to tutor myself than to tutor others. Many mnemotechnical tricks I had taught my pupils now stood me in good stead. I also practiced a rule I had laid down to those who studied under me. They were not allowed to touch a book for three days prior to an examination. I had found that this period of rest gives the brain time to revivify itself and puts all stored-up knowledge into its proper perspective. It was early summer, and for three days I loafed through the beautiful Vienna woods and parks, saying a silent adieu to many spots that held pleasant memories. Now that I was about to leave, Vienna looked more enchanting than ever, even to me who could call every cobblestone by its first name. I knew everything about the city that could be learned by wandering around and studying; I knew nothing at all about the things that cost money. Many were the embarrassing moments that would greet me on my arrival in America. How was Schöner in the *Siebensterngasse* and the *Rathauskeller* and the famous Raindl Quartette in Grinzing? I knew nothing about them. The Vienna of the tourist who had money to spend, the Vienna that laughed and waltzed, I would not know for many years to come.

The examinations came and went. When they were over, the president of the college delivered his customary speech about serving humanity, and we all decided right then and there to sacrifice our very lives for mankind. I was greatly surprised to hear him announce that my four years' average had been equalled only twice in eighty years. This proved nothing but that I had a well-trained memory. It was, with one exception, the last time the diploma was ever mentioned by me or seen by others. I suppose it is still somewhere around, and if anyone should dig it up, he will read that "because of brilliant performances in many fields," the faculty awarded me the highest honors without a full examination. On suspicion, as Elbert Hubbard might have said.

I did not waste much time looking at my diploma, but shook hands with my classmates and hunted up timetables for Hamburg. I was headed for America by the first outbound boat which fitted my pocketbook.

CHAPTER 4

LIVING DOWN A DIPLOMA

I HAD ARRANGED it so that I could spend two or three days in Berlin, a city I had never seen. I was overwhelmed by its metropolitan ways and, naturally enough, made comparisons between the German and the Austrian capitals. Measured by the speed of transportation, the cleanliness of its streets and its modern architecture, Berlin was undoubtedly top dog; but what Berlin lacked was the antiquity, the grace, the intimate charm of pre-war Vienna.

A former schoolmate of mine was then living in Berlin. I was astounded by what three years in Prussia had done to his Austrian dialect; no trace of it was left. In contrast, I remembered a Prussian who had lived in Vienna twenty years and who still spoke German with a Northern accent. I had a lot of other things to worry about then, but I was puzzled. Many years later I published my observations in a now defunct magazine. Evidently dialects of later origin revert easily into the roots from which they have sprung, while the mother tongue remains more or less inflexible. An American in England will lose his accent in a few months, but an Englishman, transplanted from home, will talk like an Englishman to the day of his death.

From Berlin it was only a few hours to Hamburg. The ship on which I had engaged passage was an old converted cattle boat, called the "Pretoria," scheduled to make the voyage to New York in seventeen days. Well, I was in no particular hurry. The "Pretoria" smelled of cattle, was full of rats, and could have had a great many other faults for all I cared. She took me to New York for fifty dollars, and she was good enough for me. When we lifted anchor and sailed out into the North Sea, my outstanding emotion was curiosity. I had learned by that time to take a detached view of many things, myself included; climb up a tree, so to speak, and look at myself crawling along, wondering where the next step would lead me. The next chapter of my life promised plenty of excitement for myself, both as an actor and as a spectator.

I suppose I ought to say here that I was greatly thrilled by the ocean, by the machinery of the boat, by the coasts of Holland and France as we saw them glimmering in the distance. But I was not. What thrilled me were the meals in the dining room. To be allowed to eat all you wanted, to have eggs or sausage even for breakfast, and to be waited on besides, those were things to write home about.

In my suitcase I carried many letters of introduction. They were addressed to all kinds of people, lawyers, merchants, even a detective, ranging in places of residence from Texas to Manitoba. I heaved them all overboard the second day out, and I have never regretted doing it. I shunned the German emigrants on the boat and tried to associate with returning Americans so as to get acclimated. Aboard the ship was a German Protestant minister who had lived in Philadelphia eighteen years; he told me that he had an equally perfect command of German and English. This filled me with awe and still would, if true, for I have never reached this pinnacle of perfection. After living in the United States for over forty years, I still have a German accent and certain linguistic shortcomings which I try to hide. I cannot, for example, figure rapidly in English. When I add a long string of figures, it is always six and three is nine, plus four is thirteen, *und sechs macht neunzehn, bleibt eins.* As I do this silently I hope no one will ever know it.

I envy that Protestant minister and wonder if he can really think of such words as "tadpole," "pencil mark," "voting power" and "lipstick" with equal speed in either language; I can't.

The dining-room stewards discovered that I could play the piano, and asked me to enliven the time for them while they were setting the tables. They did not want highbrow music, they said, such as most passengers always wanted to unload on them, but street tunes with a rhythm. I was glad to oblige, and in return was taken into their confidence. They were getting only thirty marks, or about eight dollars a month, from the steamship line, and were held responsible for all breakage and thefts at their tables. This meant that tips made up almost their entire net income, and it was interesting to hear them figure in advance what profits the voyage had in store for them. They certainly were fine judges of human character. My own steward told me that he could tell the occupation of any passenger I might point out to him.

"That fellow with the long beard is a fur dealer from Canada," he said. "That man with the florid complexion runs a saloon in Brooklyn. The chatterbox with the red sweater is a schoolteacher. She will kick at everything served to her, and then eat potato peelings all winter long to make up for this trip." So he would go on, and all his diagnoses proved nearly perfect. He had a special aversion to one woman who sat at our table and who seemed to me quite amiable.

"Amiable!" he sneered. "You just wait. On the day before we land, she'll pick a quarrel with me so she can save herself the tip. If she does, it'll cost her plenty." The quarrel came off on schedule; there was no tip. I still can see the unfortunate lady rushing desperately from one end of the pier to the other looking for her baggage, with a lot of unnaturally polite and grinning stewards disclaiming any knowledge of its whereabouts.

It took the "Pretoria" the full seventeen days to cross the ocean. The good old boat was nearing her last days. Three years later she was sold to the Russians, who used her as a troop transport in the Japanese war; before she reached Port Arthur she was sunk. If rats really leave a boat before it goes down to Davey Jones' locker, there must have been a mass exodus that set a world's record.

When the "Pretoria" steamed into New York Harbor, I had no feeling of elation; all I felt was fear, fear undisguised and uncontrollable. I was to pass the Statue of Liberty again many times, returning from European trips, and never have my emotions failed to register an echo of that first panic. Sailing up alongside the famous skyline has always filled me with the icy dread of the unknown.

Two cousins of mine were at the dock in New York to greet me. They could give me very little time, they said, because it was a Saturday; both were running saloons and expected to do a land-office business on that intensely hot August day. It was a great relief to be welcomed by relatives, even if my stay with them lasted only two hours. Their brother, they told me, was expecting me in Pittsburgh; one of his friends had connections with the steel industry and hoped to find me a place in some laboratory. Consequently, I was bundled into an early afternoon train and told to get out when the conductor shouted "Pittsburgh." That the train would arrive at half-past two in the morning was something my cousins had overlooked. They were typical New Yorkers, to whom even Pennsylvania was *terra incognita*.

I was too frightened on the trip to enjoy it. I listened to the conductor's calls with rapt attention, but it would have taken a more practiced ear than mine to understand his slurring announcements. If the word "Pittsburgh" was not mentioned, I trembled for fear that the train was not going there. If it was mentioned, I was afraid that we were at a transfer point. When we pulled out of Philadelphia the same way we had gone in, I felt sure that I was on the wrong train, and was almost ready to jump off, when a sympathetic passenger explained to me that the Pennsylvania Railroad uses a Y in switching its cars in and out of that city.

We reached Pittsburgh on time, and my cousin Jules was waiting for me. He was a dapper blond man with a wicked little mustache and laughing eyes. I took to him at once. He made me sip a cup of coffee at the station restaurant and then took me to a hotel where, of course, I did not sleep a wink.

Pittsburgh did not present its best side at the time of my arrival. The new Union Station was just being built, and passengers had to walk across planks and over temporary staircases. The temperature had been very high for days, and the streets were full of dead horses which could not be removed as fast as they fell. I was greatly surprised to find that water in some restaurants was served in blue glasses. The reason was that Pittsburgh had no filtering plant, and the water, taken from the Allegheny River, was often so muddy that a little camouflage was considered advisable.

Typhus and typhoid fever were raging continuously, and my cousin had just recovered from a severe attack of the latter. He was still taking his temperature and pulse now and then, and told me how happy he was that he now had a blood relation in town to look after him in case of sickness. As matters turned out, it was he who had to look after me first, but I really think my presence gave him some confidence. When I moved away from Pittsburgh he resumed the checking of his temperature, a habit which I had succeeded in laughing away, and his condition became steadily worse until he died. I was at his deathbed with the doctor who had treated him for twenty years. I asked what Jules had really died of, and the doctor replied, "From taking his pulse too often."

Jules was a traveling salesman who carried his sample case of laces up and down the countryside into all the towns and villages between Wheeling and Altoona. Traveling through small towns at that time was not done *de luxe*. There were no automobiles, so everyone was a slave to train schedules. There were no movies and no reading lights in the hotels. A salesman could hardly do anything but date up a waitress, play poker, or else drink himself into a stupor. I caught the tail end of this period on my first business trips.

My cousin had great news for me. A position in a laboratory at one of the outlying blast furnaces was being held open for me and I was to report immediately. It was a twenty-mile ride to the suburb of Rollins, mostly along the Chatonquin River. Factories of all kinds were stretched out in the valley, with just enough space for railroad tracks to squeeze their way in and out. Over all these homes of industry hung a dense pall of smoke. It all looked beautiful. Smoke has always been an inspiration to me; where there is smoke, there is life. To look down on smoke is, in my opinion, to look down upon sweat, and the industrial body can no more function without one than without the other. If anyone wants to live in a nice clean town he is welcome to it. For myself, I'll take the soot and the grime, if you please.

We finally reached the town of Rollins, and there before me on a triangular piece of river bottom lay the Barbara Furnaces, which were to be my future home. Fire and cinders were belching from the top of one of the blast furnaces, and a shower of small missiles greeted me as I stepped off the streetcar. To me it was glamorous. The car had stopped at what was called the main gate; but there was neither a real gate, nor a fence, nor a watchman. I simply walked in and asked my way to the laboratory. It proved to be a small, two-story brick building in the center of the yard, and I looked at it with trepidation. Would I get my position and, if I did, could I hold it? What little I had learned of steel and iron seemed to dissolve into nothing in the face of realities. But it was now too late to worry about that. I climbed the iron stairs with a weak stomach and asked for Mr. Kern, the chief chemist.

Mr. Kern was a small man from whom combativeness seemed fairly to radiate. He always held his head at a challenging angle, his eyes shone like those of an insulted prize fighter, and what he lacked in size he made up in lung power. When he opened up with his voice you could hear it booming a block away. I stammered a few well-rehearsed words and handed him my diploma, thinking it would serve as a good card of introduction; he tore it out of my hand, gave it one contemptuous glance and then threw it back at me unread.

"We don't want no university nonsense around here," he bellowed; "this is a factory laboratory, and the quicker you get that through your Dutch head the better we'll understand each other." He then told me I was hired at fifty dollars a month and to start work next morning.

The nearest large town to Rollins was Morningport. It had a department store and a small frame hotel, and I decided to make my headquarters there. Room and board could be had for five dollars a week, which was eminently satisfactory, for it would easily leave me my margin of fifteen dollars a month which I had agreed to send home. The world was a good place to live in, after all.

The work assigned to me was peculiar. It appeared that the Chatonquin River carried in its yellowish waters a large but variable amount of sulphuric acid, evidently from the discharge of pickling plants farther upstream. If this water had been allowed to feed our boilers without previous treatment, quick corrosion and great financial damage would have resulted. It had therefore become the practice to neutralize the acid with soda ash, and my job was to sample the river water, determine both its acidity and the amount of neutralizing salt required, and then check my results by sampling and analyzing the water from forty-eight boilers twice a day. If I did not prescribe enough soda ash, corrosion would still go on, although at a diminished rate; if I put too much in, the boilers would

LIVING DOWN A DIPLOMA

foam. The latter contingency was the one I dreaded most, for each boiler was equipped with an automatic whistle which blew whenever the water rose to a certain point. Many were the nights when I had miscalculated, or else the acid had suddenly changed, and my shame was proclaimed in New Year's fashion to the entire neighborhood.

The collection of the samples was the worst part of my job. Little valves, high up on the boilers, had to be turned to let the water flow into my containers, and usually the high pressure forced both steam and jets of hot water on my hands and face, until pieces of my skin were dangling from every part of my body. I protected my hands with gloves and used all the armor I could think of, but my sufferings continued with little or no abatement.

The burns on my face and body, bad as they were, really bothered me less than the way I had to travel on my sampling trips from one set of boilers to another. The sets were connected only by narrow planks, strung up some eighteen feet from the ground and without railings. On these swaying boards, hardly more than a foot wide, I had to balance myself, with two pails of scalding hot water on each arm, and I did not like it. I always have had a horror of great heights, and no one could ever make me enjoy mountain climbing. This work presented all the hazards of mountain climbing and none of its beauty. No, I did not like it a bit, and every day was a day of terrors for me.

The other employees of the laboratory were friendly boys who helped me as much as they could. The first assistant to Mr. Kern was a young man called Harry. He was a man who neither smoked, drank, nor swore, a combination which ordinarily would have made me suspicious. In Harry's case, all suspicions would have been unfounded. He was really a twenty-four-carat diamond. The first Christmas day I spent in the United States, Harry and his wife bought me a little box of candy out of their scant savings, on the general idea that I might be lonely. I have never forgotten that. Harry had no understudy, although everyone thought that a kind-hearted, elderly chemist named Louis should have had the place; he had been in the laboratory long enough to own it; but when I saw him twenty years later he was still one of the crew, analyzing slags.

Mr. Kern's bark was worse than his bite. He had been born in

Berlin and preserved his knowledge of German in that warped and anglicized form which I soon got to know as Pennsylvania Dutch. Outwardly he raised Cain with all of us from morning till night, but he often translated unintelligible orders for me or assisted me in various ways. Shortly after my arrival, he invited me to his home. He had married a woman of Irish parentage, and they had several boys, all of whom looked exactly like their father. Kern also introduced me to a Swiss doctor, and through him I became acquainted with more people and never felt lonely. My English, though, was still very bad. People understood me well enough, but I did not understand them. My greatest fault was my involved language; the constant teasing of my co-workers in the laboratory soon cured me of that, however.

"Having nothing else to do," they would ape me, "and wanting to please me, will you clean the immediate vicinity of my table?" That was the result of my having been fed on Shakespeare and Swift. I changed my reading matter, bought only dime novels, and soon learned to say ten-word sentences in five words rather than in twenty.

Only one little thing always stood between Kern and me: I would not use the common mouthpiece of the laboratory wash bottle through which everyone blew whenever his work demanded it. I would have preferred my own wash bottle, of course, but since such a luxury was beyond my reach, I always carried in my vest pocket a piece of rubber tubing which I attached before putting my mouth to it. Whenever Mr. Kern saw me doing that he grew furious, and one time he threw the bottle through a closed window, threatening to throw me after it if I persisted in my habit. But persist I did, regardless of consequences, and I finally tamed down my chief to the point where he would merely drop sarcastic remarks about Mamma's darling and collegiate snootiness.

Weekdays we worked from eight to five, Sundays only till noon. My free afternoons I spent with my cousin in the city. He lived in a boardinghouse with nice people, and those hours away from the blast furnaces were great holidays for me. Jules introduced me to a few young ladies, but with questionable results. My English was not good enough for lively conversation or quick repartee. What I needed still more than conversational gifts were American manners, the lack of which caused me some embarrassing moments;

there would have been many more, had it not been for the kindly help given me by some young ladies of the neighborhood. One dashing girl in particular, who had brown, curly tresses, spent a lot of time tutoring me, but I am afraid I proved as dumb as some of my former pupils. I see her now once in a while. Her hair has turned gray and she wears glasses; but when we are together she still corrects me with the same candor and energy as of yore.

It did not take me long to become accustomed to the atmosphere of the laboratory, and soon I began to nose into the work done by the remainder of the staff. Altogether we were ten men, with two more on night shift. I used to return in the evening and try to learn their tasks. No chemist in the furnaces, except myself, had ever received chemical training in any school, not even the chief, Mr. Kern. He was self-taught throughout, and had worked his way up from a water boy. For a while I looked down upon him with a secret sense of superiority, until I became better acquainted with him. He ran into me one time, during one of my nightly excursions, and told me that I knew nothing. He snapped his fingers to describe what he thought of my diploma and my degree. To prove his argument, he challenged me to analyze a sample of pig iron, using all the books I wanted. I took him up, and for a week I worked with what my books described as a "rapid analytical method." When I had finished, the figures ran up to about eighty-seven per cent, instead of totaling one hundred. Kern did not laugh; he just said that I had done better than other college graduates he had known. I then watched him do in a few hours what I had done in a week, and when he had finished, his results figured up to 99.81%, which was well-nigh perfect.

By this time I was beginning to understand the routine of the place. Whenever a blast furnace was tapped, a boy would dip out some of the molten pig iron at intervals and cast the samples into a bucket of cold water. The quickly formed pellets were then hurried to the laboratory, where the sample boy smashed them to powder with a sledge hammer. From here on the chemist took over. The powdered iron was dissolved and a test run for silicon and sulphur, before the train with the molten load was allowed to depart for the steel plant across the river. The maximum time allowed for this analytical work was eleven minutes, and in order to accomplish it, suction filtration was used, and a specified quantity was weighed out so as to eliminate figuring. In cold weather extra haste was necessary to prevent freezing up of the ladle cars, and often the four shrill whistles of an impatient train crew would spur a perspiring chemist to his topmost speed. If the iron was of good quality, the train was allowed to proceed; if not, the product was dumped into molds and stored up for other uses. As blast furnaces normally are never shut down, this work went on day and night, on Sunday, Christmas and the Fourth of July. One time, when an epidemic of typhoid fever struck the district, I was kept on my job for fifty-six hours, without so much as ten minutes' rest. The number of our furnaces had by that time increased to seven, and the samples followed each other as fast as one man could handle them. After my fifty-six-hour run, I was relieved by a chemist from some distant subsidiary company but, in line with the prevailing custom, I received neither a word of appreciation nor a penny for overtime.

Other men in the laboratory analyzed the iron for phosphorus, which took more time, and still others had to keep an eye on the slag to see that it did not carry away too much iron. The highest grade work was that of testing the iron ore, the coke and the limestone that went into the furnaces. This work was done by the first assistant, and in some important cases by the chief chemist himself.

The town of Morningport was beyond the inner Pittsburgh streetcar zone, and it cost ten cents to ride to the city. As my cousin lived in what was then known as Allegheny, it took another nickel to get there. I found that my expenses were growing, and as I knew of no immediate way of increasing my income, I decided to economize, something I never liked to do and am not good at. Not far from my boardinghouse I had discovered another place with a sign reading "Room and board for $3.50," and as soon as there was a vacancy, I moved in. To save a quarter I hired a Negro to help me carry my trunk. The distance was only half a mile, and everything would have worked out well had the European trunk not suddenly parted in the middle, strewing my belongings all over the sidewalk. My Negro quietly faded away, leaving me to my fate. A kindly policeman gave me a helping hand and, accompanied by half the youthful population of the town, I entered my new home.

I soon discovered why the rates were so cheap. Three of us were expected to occupy one bed, and no trio was allowed to sleep more than eight hours, as the next shift was already waiting for its rest. I stood this life as long as I could, which was not very long, I am afraid, and then moved again. I had spotted a room just outside the town limits, where I could get a bed for myself alone, plus board, for no more money. The joker was that the little building stood in a triangle, surrounded by switchtracks on all sides, so that the house literally shook day and night, while the noise of whistles, bells and rumbling trains made sleep appear like a half-forgotten saga. I fled after I had used up my week's prepaid lodging, and this time I moved from Morningport to a little village on the top of a hill. It bore the inviting name of Mountainglory. There, in a little frame house, I found a garret room for five dollars a month. Meals I decided to take elsewhere. I was fed up with boarding house diet anyway, and wanted to select my own menus.

Mountainglory is now a modern town of some twenty-five thousand inhabitants, but when I moved there it was just an irregular patch of straggling frame and brick houses, strung along the rim of a ridge which overlooked the Chatonquin Valley and our blast furnaces. No regular road led down to the plant, and vehicles would have had to detour several miles. As no one drove to the furnaces, the problem never arose. We climbed up and slid down as best we could, and in wintry weather our best was none too good. Those who were careless on the way down were in danger of being pitched onto the tracks of several railroads which passed through a cut between the factory grounds and the hillside. It was a calamity that happened now and then, without arousing any particular attention, for we workers were supposed to take chances with our lives all day long. The freight trains which continually moved in front of the gate rarely allowed free spaces for through passage, and even if the cars were standing still they were not always uncoupled for our convenience or safety. At first I found it difficult to board fast-moving trains on one side and jump off on the other, especially as the lunch basket which was slung over one arm impeded my movements. If you missed your foothold you fell under the wheels. Many did.

Inside the mill there was a like disregard for human life. Little

switch engines scurried through the yard, and if anyone was tres-
passing on the tracks he was likely to be run over. The train crews
seemed convinced that if they had given the unfortunate victim a
warning whistle they had done their duty. Our casualty list was
not small. I was one of the few who knew the figures, because for
a while it was part of my job to flag trains to take the injured to
the nearest hospital, fifteen miles away. I stopped them all, freight
trains or the New York Limited, and usually received a juicy round
of abuse, for neither engineers nor conductors enjoyed carrying
away a mangled piece of humanity in the express car and losing
two or three minutes of their precious schedule into the bargain.
The people who were calmest about the situation, I believe, were
the workers themselves. The men who fell were considered soldiers
on a battlefield, who accepted their risks as a matter of course.

My new home on top of the hill brought me many new contacts,
for Mountainglory was not without its social aspirations. We had
church bazaars, picnics and debating clubs. For any inhabitant
to exclude himself or be excluded was unthinkable. My landlord
was deacon of a little church, and his wife was a leading member
of its women's auxiliary. I suddenly found myself playing the
church organ or dissecting roast chickens at Methodist parties. I
was equally bad at both, but others were no better, and there was a
scarcity of young men. One day someone came forward with a
plan to start a volunteer fire department. Collections for an engine
went on for a year; then came the drills, which were good fun. We
had no horses and therefore had to drag the engine ourselves to all
kinds of places in response to imaginary fire alarms. Then, during
a stormy and ice-cold winter night, we had the only real fire which
occurred while I was a member of the department. I rushed out
in shirt, trousers and untied shoes; my task was to help douse the
side of a frame building so as to prevent a spread of the conflagration. I stood on a stepladder, about half way up to the roof, and
had to hand water buckets to the man next in line. I know that
half the water never reached its destination, for I could feel it running down my back. We all looked like icebergs when we finished.
While the fire was raging the excitement ran high, but the morning
after was uncommonly gray.

A railroad ran its right of way on top of the Mountainglory hill through the center of the little town. There were four tracks, all of them busy night and day, so busy in fact, that when one night a wreck somewhere down the line stopped traffic for an hour, the entire village was awakened by the unusual silence. Walking along the tracks was my favorite relaxation. I could walk there for hours, my eyes following the rails until they merged into the western horizon, my mind miles beyond that. "Canton, Fort Wayne and Chicago," the conductor at the Union Station used to cry. Fort Wayne, Indiana; what romance in the name! The whole history of the early settlers seemed to be embodied in it. And Chicago! Would I ever see it? The conductor sometimes added, "and all points west"; but that was beyond my dreams. If I should ever see Fort Wayne and Chicago I would be happy.

Mountainglory had a little library, and from there I borrowed schoolbooks on American geography and history, over which I pored during mealtimes and at odd moments. I found that Mountainglory had played quite a part during Braddock's march to Fort Duquesne, and I believed that young Washington might have camped somewhere around the level spot where our depot stood. Nobody else seemed interested, though, and after my sensation had fallen flat I continued my studies in strict privacy.

My evenings were almost entirely devoted to furthering my technical education. This meant that I would go down to the plant again immediately after supper to learn and practice every method of analysis used in the laboratory, and then extend my excursions into the rest of the mill. I took a hand in everything that presented itself. I learned to do much work around the blast furnaces, delved into the mechanics of the loading process, and even ran trains carrying molten pig iron across the bridge. Sometimes I worked as a fireman and sometimes as an engineer, and there was little enough romance in either job. The regular fireman would stand next to me, grinning, and watch me do everything wrong until he showed me how to shovel coal with the least exertion and the greatest efficiency. I discovered that a fireman feels the slightest incline in the roadbed or a headwind, which would escape a pedestrian altogether, just as a bicyclist feels it by the increased strain. Even today I cannot watch a train pull uphill without a sympathetic heartbeat for the fireman, although automatic stokers and whatnots have since eased his work. I also learned to respect the accomplishments of an engineer. The manner in which the train under my guidance would jerk and hit the curves erratically was painful, and when I looked over my shoulder I could see the liquid iron flying in streams from the ladle cars.

Incidentally, I met all sorts of people during these nightly wanderings, and by and by I learned a few expressions in almost every known language. I found later that these little quips were worth a college course. The foreman who can slap a man on the back and call him a dirty name in his native tongue will never have any trouble with his crew, no matter how hard he drives it.

Shortly after my arrival in the United States, President McKinley was shot. Although it may seem a far cry from the assassination of the Chief Executive to the job of an obscure cub chemist in a Pittsburgh blast furnace, I almost lost my job on account of it. Among the German papers to which I still subscribed was a Viennese magazine called *Die Fackel (The Torch)*, which appeared between flaming red covers and had the picture of a torch on the cover. It looked like a revolutionary propaganda sheet, but was in reality a witty one-man paper, without any political leanings, much in the style of Elbert Hubbard's *Philistine,* which was then at its best. I had a terrible time explaining *Die Fackel,* but luckily Mr. Kern, my superior, could read German, and he convinced those higher up that the magazine, and presumably I too, was quite harmless. Thereupon I gave orders to have the cover removed before the paper left Vienna, and the incident was soon forgotten—not, however, before it had produced an unexpected aftermath.

Living in Mountainglory at that time was an Alsatian by the name of Mende, a short, stocky man with an enormous head and small twinkling eyes that made you his friend the moment he looked at you. I had noticed him on the streets here and there but did not know that he was the manager of the large glass factory in town. Mr. Mende evinced some curiosity to meet the "little anarchist" of whom rumors had reached him, and one evening I was invited to his house for supper. It was one of the great events of my early American days. Mr. Mende occupied one of the showplaces of the village, so I put on my best suit and my choice behavior for the occasion. A hired girl asked me to wait in the parlor. I noticed a piano there and, having nothing better to do, I sat down and played "The Last Rose of Summer." I varied and modulated it as I went along, my mind at ease with the world, and every fiber of my body softened under the influence of this luxurious home. Finally I stopped and turned around. Behind me stood the whole Mende family, transfigured and still as statues. I jumped up in great embarrassment, but Mr. Mende begged me to play the song just once more. For thirty-five years, whenever I visited them, I played "The Last Rose of Summer" to the Mende family. It was our theme song, the great enduring link in our long friendship. Up to his last moment my friend Mende declared that no one could play the old song as well as I did; I really think that every time I played it afterward it brought back to him the days of his prime manhood and his happy years in Mountainglory. He became richer and much more famous in later life, but I do not think there ever was a moment when he would not rather have gone back to the house where we first met.

Mr. Mende spoke and wrote English, French and German, mixing them up into a blend that was all his own. His wife was a Belgian and preferred French to English. There were also two daughters, Vionne and Vinta, aged thirteen and eleven, both pictures of high-bred daintiness. Vionne looked like a silhouette from an artist's sketchbook, and Vinta, with her dreamy eyes and fine hair, reminded me of a fairy queen I had once seen on the stage. When I last visited her she had an eleven-year-old daughter who looked just as her mother had looked at that age, and the mother was still a fragile beauty who brought to mind a French miniature or rare porcelain. A third daughter, born much later, was called Vignette. She was a fluffy-haired blonde baby with the profile of a cameo. I did not see her again until she was a grown-up young lady.

After supper Mr. Mende broached the idea that I give him lessons in chemistry. He was a glassmaker of some renown, he told me, and came from a long line of glassmakers; but rule-of-thumb methods were being replaced by chemical principles, and he felt that it was necessary for him to fall into line. *In fine,* he offered me a dollar an hour to come over three times a week and teach him as much chemistry as I could, I to select those parts I considered most important for his particular needs. He knew nothing about chemistry and I knew nothing about glass. The two negatives, so

Mr. Mende chuckled, should make a positive. Mr. Mende had the nicest, most persuasive chuckle I have ever heard.

In order to get my bearings on this new problem I decided to pay the glass factory a visit. Mr. Mende offered to show me around, but I declined. I had learned enough about factory life by that time to know that it is not the wisest thing in the world to be introduced as teacher's pet. The first visit I would make alone; the personally conducted tour could wait.

The Mende Glass Company was in some ways a singular institution. It consisted of three distinct departments: the office, the furnace room and the decorating section. The office was an ordinary American office where English was spoken, the furnace room where the glass was melted and blown was in the hands of Belgians who talked only French, and the decorating department was run entirely by Germans. Each division had its little reception room, and the girls who presided over their respective desks looked as typically American, French and German, as if a Hollywood casting director had selected them.

I addressed the Belgian girl in my most elaborate French. *"Veuillez me donner . . . "*

She shook her head. "You may say *'Voulez-vous me donner'* to me," she said; "I am only a factory girl, not a princess."

A friendly smile robbed the remark of all possible offense. When I walked out into the furnace room, I noticed that her verdict had already preceded me by that invisible grapevine route which is common to all places where men work in overalls. The verdict must have been favorable, for I received pleasant nods from everyone, and no one accidentally spilled hot glass over my clothes, as they often did to other visitors.

The blowing room was dominated by a huge Belgian known to everyone as François. Glass blowing was an art which had been handed down from father to son for no one knew how many generations. Mechanical inventions had not yet replaced human craftsmanship, and glass blowers were a highly paid, highly respected lot who did pretty much as they pleased. It was fascinating to see men form glass into almost any shape imaginable. It looked easy enough, but actually required years of experience. Big buckets of beer stood around the room, and whenever one of the blowers finished a difficult piece of work he would imbibe incredible quantities of the inviting drink and proceed to sweat it out again in the next fifteen minutes. The beer was furnished by the management, purchased by the truckload, and was regarded as indispensable.

François probably did not look upon my coming without some misgivings, but an incident happened which earned me his respect and affection. Marianne, the little brunette reception girl, asked me one evening to play the piano in François' house in honor of some Belgian national holiday. A large crowd would be there, and in those days when radios were unknown and gramophones still screeching novelties, a piano player was a man of importance. When I arrived, many people had already assembled. It was a fearfully hot day and, noticing a glass of water standing on a table, I emptied it in one swallow. The next moment I thought my insides had caught fire. The glass had not contained water, but gin, and had been set aside to be used as an ingredient in a punch. For a minute there was a dead silence in the room; no one moved or spoke. Suspecting that a trick had been played on me, I gritted my teeth, walked over to the piano, and began to play; then the dam burst. François came over to me, slapped me on the back till my shoulder blade seemed to crack, and said, *"Eh bien, mon ami can drink, eh?"* One after another they came to express their admiration. A whole glass of gin in one swallow, and he did not wink an eyelash, did he? *Sacré Dieu,* they could not do it themselves! From that day I was cock of the walk in the Belgian colony; the only handicap was that wherever I called after that I was offered a water glass full of gin as a welcome greeting. Alcohol has never affected me much and, although I detest gin, I was willing to pay this price for my popularity.

François was married to a tiny Frenchwoman who bossed him around much as an animal trainer does an elephant. When they walked down the avenue they looked, so someone once said, like a dollar and a quarter. Nevertheless, they got along well together. Sometimes in the evening one could hear terrible screams from their cottage. The Belgians then commented with true French naïveté that big François was making love to his little Annette.

By the time I had grasped the fundamentals of glassmaking, I had come to a decision on what to do about my lessons for Mr.

Mende. I would select all the chemical elements which went into his manufacturing processes, and disregard all other chemistry for the time being. With this plan in mind, our lessons began.

Never was there such pleasure for me in tutoring as in the case of my old friend Mende. After all the simpletons that had passed through my hands, it was unspeakable joy to work with a mind like his. Thomas Lawson had not then written his *Frenzied Finance,* but a sentence he used there in regard to H. H. Rogers of Standard Oil fame often came back to me later when I thought of Mr. Mende. Rogers, so Lawson related, had a mind like a metallic wire netting; you said a word to begin a sentence and it traveled through his brain like an electric current; he would finish the thought for you before you had fully stated it. Mr. Mende was just like that. I had to ask him repeatedly if he was serious in taking lessons from me; he knew so much more than I did. But he assured me that I was earning my money several times over and that I was not to worry.

After a while a new idea came to me. I drew a big map of Mendeleyeff's periodic system of elements and presented it to my pupil. That theorem, I explained to him, was the key to untold new inventions, if one could only ferret out its many hidden secrets. Mr. Mende was speechless. For hours and hours he sat in front of the big canvas, his inventive mind digging deep under the surface of the periodic system and receiving from it messages that were denied to ordinary men. Mendeleyeff's table became a fetish with my pupil. He thought and spoke of it all the time and, I almost believe, prayed to it when he was alone. Our lessons degenerated into monologues on his part. I wasn't teaching him; he was teaching me. His untutored but brilliant mind spun curious visions around the chemical elements, and I interrupted him only when I knew positively that he was off on a wrong tangent.

The first tangible result of our sessions was not slow in developing. The Mende Glass Company manufactured a red glass which was bought chiefly by railroads for use in semaphores and on the rear of trains. I was told that Mende's had the reputation of making the best red glass in the country, but now my pupil made some improvements which eliminated so much blue and yellow that his product was beginning to be considered almost perfect in its redness. Orders began to pour in from all over the continent, and competitors

were driven to frantic efforts to catch up. Mr. Mende attributed all
these innovations to Mendeleyeff's table and, indirectly, to me. Our
lessons became informal chats, as between two friends. With a
bottle of French wine between us and the air thick with the fumes
of good cigars, he would often talk of Greek and Roman philoso-
phers, all of whom he understood thoroughly. By and by I also
learned his personal history. He had come to the United States as
a young boy and had received practically no schooling. As a little
boy he carried beer buckets to the factory where his father was
a glass blower, and he naturally followed in his footsteps. But
Mr. Mende was soon more than a glass blower; his special genius
was the designing of lamps and lampshades. Often I watched him
take a piece of paper to explain a point in the art of designing, and
then, as his pencil went over the paper in rapid strokes, some work
of art would be born out of nothing and be finished to its last detail.
Now, at the age of thirty-eight, he was vice-president and manager
of his company; at heart, however, he was not a businessman but
an artist. He was an artist in everything he did, in his reading, in
his recreations, even in his eating. When he took me to a French
restaurant downtown, I began to learn the difference between a feed
and a feast, and incidentally between an ordinary host and a prince.
Once I suspected that the waiter had cheated him by a considerable
sum, and told him so.

"He cheated me by exactly two dollars and fifty cents," Mr. Mende
affirmed. He had known it all the time, but had not said a word.
Would he spoil his own humor by quarreling with a *garçon?* Would
he embarrass his guest for the sake of two dollars and fifty cents?
Not he. Mr. Mende may not have had a formal education, but he
surely had something much rarer than that. Mr. Mende had breed-
ing.

About that time a little incident occurred which was of no great
importance in itself, but which brought unexpected consequences in
its wake. Each blast furnace in our plant was equipped with a
pyrometer, an instrument designed to measure the heat inside the
furnace, so as to insure its proper regulation. Should a furnace get
too cold and freeze up, the loss could be measured only in thousands
of dollars. These pyrometers were enclosed in little structures that

looked like telephone booths, and were carefully attended by the assistant superintendents, both day and night. An automatic recording device made it possible for the superintendent to see what the heat had been in each furnace during the past twenty-four hours. One night, while meandering around our plant, I noticed that one of the pyrometers had broken down and was not registering. I looked high and low for the assistant superintendent in charge, but could not find him. It developed later that he had been gassed and was then lying unconscious in an out-of-the-way spot. I knew enough about pyrometers to make temporary repairs, but one of the main connecting lines in this one was broken, and it would have been hopeless to look for the break in the dark. I therefore stood by all night, regulating the instrument by hand, until the day shift came on and I could turn the job over to someone else. Within two or three hours the matter had passed out of my mind.

A few days later a boy from the main office came over and asked for me. He was a loose-mouthed, homely piece of humanity, much disliked by everyone; he always had a cruel leer on his face and seemed to enjoy mischief more than anything else in life.

"The big boss wants to see you," he said to me.

"What for?" I asked, in natural amazement.

"How should I know?" he sneered at me. "Probably wants to fire you." And with that he shuffled out.

I had never been in the main office, nor had I ever talked to the "big boss," although I had seen him, of course, from a distance. He was a tall Swede by the name of Lund who wore a long, brown beard which made him look older than he was. To be invited into his presence meant something portentous; what it was I could not imagine.

I was ushered into the presence of the mighty Mr. Lund without much ceremony, and the eyes of the entire office staff burned on my back as I went through the door of his private office.

"Tell me something about yourself," he began the conversation, harmlessly enough.

There was not much to tell. When I started to talk about my studies, he quickly lifted his hand. "No nonsense, please," he said. "Your worst handicap is your college career." There went another chance to display my diploma.

Mr. Lund then began to ask me all kinds of questions about blast furnaces, open hearth furnaces, Bessemer converters, the reason why limestone was put into furnace charges, the meaning of phosphorus in pig iron, and such. Finally he came to the point. A great shake-up was in contemplation. Mr. Kern was slated to become assistant superintendent and had—do miracles happen?—recommended me as his successor; me, the bottle washer, the boiler sampler, the last man in line. In the end, the miracle was not allowed to happen. Mr. Lund concluded, quite sensibly I thought, that I was too young and inexperienced after less than one year of service, also that my English was still too stuttering. He would make me first assistant, though; for Harry, the present incumbent, was also leaving for greener pastures. All Mr. Lund wanted was my assurance that I could do the work and would introduce no college tricks. We shook hands on that, and when I left the office I felt like shouting it out to the world: I was first assistant chemist of the Barbara Furnaces with a salary of seventy-five dollars a month!

In due time Mr. Kern moved out of the laboratory, and a new chief chemist moved in, a Mr. Tompkins, up to now first assistant in the famous Montague Steel Works, where puddlers were reputed to earn between fifty and a hundred dollars a day and came to work wearing gloves and driving two-horse carriages.

Mr. Tompkins was the exact opposite of Mr. Kern. Where Kern was temperamental and irritable, Tompkins was calm, dignified, inscrutable. Where Kern was short and blond, Tompkins was lanky and dark. Their only common meeting ground was that both were excellent chemists. My new superior had had no more formal schooling than the other, but he was more scientifically inclined and always ready to add to his vast store of knowledge. As an analyst I have scarcely seen the like of him. When he grasped an Erlenmeyer flask in his long, artistic fingers and shook it with a circular motion, he was gracefulness itself. No one ever doubted his results. Mr. Kern haunted the laboratory for a while and frowned on all innovations the newcomer had quickly installed. Only once did he use his prerogative as the higher officer to criticize openly. Mr. Tompkins met the onslaught with a Mona Lisa smile against which there was no defense, and the innovations stood as ordered. After that we no longer saw Mr. Kern on his old stamping-grounds.

As first assistant I had to carry quite a few responsibilities. The more difficult analytical tasks were mine, and I had to supervise the work of all others. What was more onerous was that I had to jump in and pinch-hit everywhere, whenever the occasion demanded. When men got sick or quit in the middle of the night, which happened not infrequently, I had to answer the emergency call to duty, and many a time I slid more than I walked down the hill in complete darkness to take the absentee's place.

Since Mr. Tompkins also lived in Mountainglory, we often walked home together. As I got to know him better, I learned that he had only taken his present position to escape the job of first mate in the big steel laboratory which he had occupied too long, he thought. Better be captain of a flea circus than first mate of the United States battle fleet, as he expressed it. His ambition was to be director of a big scientific laboratory or superintendent of an important steel plant, and he looked on his stay at the Barbara Furnaces only as a steppingstone toward a brighter future.

Under Mr. Tompkins' management the laboratory took on new life. The record for determining silicon and sulphur was broken again and again until it stood at seven minutes. The percentage of iron content in an ore was approximated in four hours. Just then some chemist in a neighboring laboratory discovered a new method by which the old way of analyzing steel and iron for manganese was reduced to the mere reading of a color scale. Time was marching on, even then.

CHAPTER 5

SMOKESTACKS AND BLAST FURNACES

*U*NDERNEATH OUR LABORATORY
was a basement in which samples of ore, limestone and coke were
assembled and dried in large flat pans before being delivered to the
chemists for their work. Over this basement presided an elderly
man with a beard whom I had heard mentioned as George Markley,
and whom I had often seen as he balanced himself precariously on
the edge of a gondola car with buckets on each arm. Markley was
the official sampler of the plant. In order to expedite the assortment
of the materials furnished us, he met incoming freight trains several
miles out and, jumping from car to car, he took some lumps of coke
here and some lumps there, or handfuls of iron ore or limestone, as
the case may have been. When the train pulled into our yard the
sampling was finished. The cars were then held on the track until
the laboratory decided if, where and how to use their contents, and
as trackage was limited and demurrage expensive, speed was the
watchword all around.

I had never paid much attention to Mr. Markley until he met me
one day in the yard and asked me to step into his place and eat my
lunch with him. After a few commonplace remarks, he asked me if
it was true that I had studied in Vienna, and when I confirmed this,
he looked at me curiously.

"The place where Doctor Gall lived," he said with almost religious
awe.

"Doctor who?" I asked.

He stared at me incredulously. "Now you're fooling," he remarked. "Of course you know Doctor Gall, the father of phrenology."

This was Greek to me, and I said so. Phrenology? I had never heard of it; and was it a science? If so, I certainly would have heard about it at college. What was phrenology, anyway?

Mr. Markley was taken aback, but not discomfited. He asked me to sit still for a minute while he studied me, and then he laid his hands on my head, took a few rough measurements, and sat down again. "You love languages," he said, "but you hate mechanics. You think best when you are on your feet, and the faster you walk, the quicker your thoughts come to you. You appreciate a good meal, but you can live on dry bread if you have to, and even get a kick out of it, because you have a sense of romance; as you munch your crust you dream you are Robinson Crusoe eating his last provisions, and you wonder where the next meal is coming from."

"Stop!" I cried. "You didn't get that from measuring my head. Somebody told you."

Markley became very serious. "I never joke when I talk phrenology," he declared. I believed him.

Markley continued with his analysis, and when he finished I felt as if I had been completely undressed. The matter was disturbing, not because of my own experience, but because I was half convinced that phrenology must rest on a solid foundation if it could produce such astounding results. After mulling things over in my mind for a while I decided to put Markley to a test. I had some old German magazines, and from them I cut the pictures of two men. One of them had been convicted in a famous forgery case, and the other was a murderer. These photographs I submitted to my mentor for his expert opinion. Markley was not satisfied with the pictures and did not think it fair to have to base his judgment on them. One was a three-quarter view and gave him no clear idea of the distance between the eyes, and there were similar objections to the other. I took his hesitation as one takes the preliminaries of a singer who explains that he is hoarse, does not have the proper music with him and all that, and then proceeds to sing endlessly, nevertheless. Markley's reluctance was genuine, I know now, but I coaxed him along and he finally adjusted his glasses and scrutinized the pictures carefully.

"This man," he pronounced after some deliberation, "is a first-class pen-and-ink artist. His sense of color is less pronounced, but he could paint if he wanted to. Too bad that he is dishonest; I am afraid he will some day put his talents to improper use. If he does, he will be a counterfeiter or a check-forger." I did not comment, but an imaginary hat came off my head.

"The second man," Markley continued, "has cruelty and cunning written all over his head. Look at the width behind the ears, look at the curves on the side of his skull. I don't think I would want to meet him in the dark when he's angry. He would crush a human life as you or I would a fly."

I stood up and bowed. The college graduate humbly asked the sampler for permission to study under him. If this was phrenology, I wanted to know more about it. Thus began an interesting time. Every noon saw us bent over newspapers, scanning the illustrations, measuring, analyzing, debating. When we ran out of papers we dragged surprised and protesting men from the yard into our improvised human laboratory. I bought myself a plaster of Paris bust and a set of books, over which I pored at night. I got into everybody's hair, literally speaking, for no person within range was safe from my hands. In the beginning, I am afraid, I was not always tactful, for many times my victims would blush violently when I blurted out the results of my findings. Later I learned to use discretion.

I visited Markley in his home and watched him work. On the door he had an imposing brass plate, "George Markley, Phrenologist," and in his parlor he was not a factory hand in dirty overalls, but a gentleman in a long black coat with a turned-down collar and a flowing black necktie. His pink cheeks, healthy face and humorous wrinkles around the eyes made people like and trust him, and I am sure that in his modest way he did a lot of good. I brought many of my friends to see him, and they all went away satisfied, if thoughtful. When there were no customers, Markley would tell me of Doctor Gall; how he had collected skulls for his early studies, how the University of Vienna had compelled him to leave Austria, and how he had been persecuted in Germany until he found refuge in Paris, only to be banished from there, so that he was forced to spend the end of his life in England. What had happened to Gall's original collection of skulls Markley did not know, and he would have given his right arm to see it. Many years later, walking through an obscure museum in a small town near Vienna, I accidentally found it. It was housed in a little room which I believe had not been opened for years. When Gall fled Vienna in 1814, he had hidden his treasures there to preserve them. I thought of Markley, how he would have revered every head in the exhibit and how he would have longed to read the notes in Doctor Gall's own handwriting. But by then Markley had been dead a long time.

The second summer of my stay in Pittsburgh brought me a new experience. Mr. Tompkins had gone on a two-week vacation and left no address. I was in charge of the laboratory and no end proud of it. The first evening found me exhausted and unable to sleep. In the morning I went to work with a severe headache. Markley advised me to stop eating. He often went without meals for days at a time, and once had fasted for nineteen days without any harm to himself. On the contrary, he claimed to have felt better than ever, with all his organs rested and every bit of poison out of his system. I had no time to be sick, so I took Markley's advice. I have no doubt that it saved my life.

The days dragged on interminably and my headache increased steadily. I could feel my body burning up with fever, but did not take my temperature for fear of discovering an unpleasant truth. Toward the end of the second week I fainted on three successive days, and each time it was more difficult to bring me to. At last, on a Monday morning, Mr. Tompkins returned. I had all my reports written up, but he merely glanced at them.

"You look funny to me," he said; "better go and see a physician."

I went to see my old Swiss doctor in Morningport, who gave me one quick examination, took my temperature and told me that, scientifically speaking, I was dead. No one could live with a 106° fever. He wanted to call an ambulance, but I boarded a streetcar instead and went home. An hour later Cousin Jules was at my bedside. He was shocked when he saw my little garret room where one could hardly stand up, and insisted that I go to the Allegheny Hospital where he could be close by. So I was strapped to a board and put into a horse ambulance for a twenty-odd-mile drive. It was fearfully hot inside this little closed vehicle, and as the country through which we rode was a succession of hills and vales, I slid from one end of the ambulance to the other and received a shaking up which would have driven a less sick man to the brink of insanity. I arrived at the hospital exhausted and wringing wet; when the nurse asked me how I felt, I answered, "disgusted." She wrote the words "patient delirious" on my chart and called the doctor. He could do nothing. I had gone through an attack of typhoid fever on my feet and, thanks to Mr. Markley, had taken the proper measure to insure my survival. Continued fasting was about all the hospital could prescribe for me, and in a short time I was discharged.

My illness had raised havoc with my finances, and again I had to think of new sources of revenue. The first thing I did was take up newspaper writing again. I wrote a few sketches for the Pittsburgh *Courier* and sent some articles to the *Neuer Wiener Bote*. Both accepted my contributions readily enough, but the Viennese paper always kept urging me to make my pictures of American life and episodes more bizarre. Their readers expected it, and they were entitled to get what they expected. The Munich *Beobachter* had an American correspondent whose articles were constantly held up to me as examples. I remember one of his monstrous stories. Train service between New York and Chicago, he wrote, was too slow, but the railroads claimed that their trains were already running at the maximum speed the roadbeds allowed. So a clever way was found to expedite service. Every station was equipped with a moving platform which was set into motion when the trains approached, until its speed was the same as that of the train. The result was that the loading and unloading of passengers took place without the trains having to slow down. I countered by relating unusual events from the grist of the daily press, and proved to my editors that truth actually could be more fanciful than fiction. Thus the rivalry between the Vienna and Munich papers went on, to my great amusement and financial gain.

In retrospect, I am not very proud of my journalistic achievements, for in my small way I contributed to a lack of understanding between two peoples by overemphasizing the abnormal part of the news in order to make the contributions more readable. This was a sort of censorship or, at best, improper propaganda. If an editor should choose to print nothing but the crimes and scandals of his community, he would soon have his readers believing that the decent

85

part of the population was a negligible percentage of the whole. Part of the blame properly belonged to my editors, of course, and the pressure they exerted on me; but to a larger extent I plead guilty on my own account.

After I had quit my European correspondence, my successor drew his share of distorted pictures. He wrote one time that he was talking to a multimillionaire on the street in front of a railroad station. Suddenly the rich man disengaged himself with a mumbled excuse, hastened to the sidewalk, and helped a lady carry her suit-cases to a taxi. He then returned to the correspondent, exhibiting a twenty-five-cent piece. "I am never ashamed to make an honest penny when I have a chance," he remarked. Aside from the utter nonsense of the narrative, the fact that no redcap would give an outsider an opportunity for such easy money would, of course, not occur to a European reader. But the impression would remain that all Americans are uncultured money-grabbers; Messrs. Schmidt-hofer and Wittenheimer in their German homes would wisely nod their heads; you couldn't fool them; they had known it right along. I have often wondered whether wars could not be minimized, if each nation were to see its prospective enemies through the eyes of a truth-loving, sympathetic press.

Since my promotion I had doubled the amount I sent to my mother, and as neither the Pittsburgh nor the Viennese papers paid fancy prices for my contributions, I reluctantly went back to tutoring in order to fertilize my barren treasury. My first pupil was a young girl, the daughter of a German glass decorator, whom I taught piano. If I thought that I had tasted the cup of tutoring to its last dregs, I found myself mistaken; nothing in my past experience could compare in nerve-exhaustion with piano lessons. My blue-eyed pupil was pretty enough to be an artist's model, but I quickly saw that she would never be able to tell a funeral march from a waltz, and she simply grew fat on discords. My landlady then had me take her seven-year-old son in hand; compared to him my German girl was a genius. I told him once, in a moment of anger, to go out and climb a tree. He took me literally, ruined a pair of trousers and skinned his leg. This finished my career as a music teacher.

One day I received a letter from the superintendent of an ice plant; he asked me if I could initiate him into the mysteries of ammonia and its function in a refrigeration plant. I could and would, for a dollar an hour and carfare. His office was the hottest place I have ever worked in. Steampipes were strung all through the building, and their radiation, added to the natural heat of a Pittsburgh summer, made tutoring there almost impossible. My pupil noticed my suffering, and told me how to cool off; there, behind heavy wooden doors, was the refrigeration room where the temperature was four degrees above zero. I jumped up, put on my coat and was ready to start, when he interrupted me.

"No coat, please," he said. "My men go back and forth in their shirt sleeves all the time, and they never get sick. Of course, some of them die of pneumonia the first week, but those whose skin takes proper care of the change in temperature survive and never again catch a cold."

Here was a sporting proposition. I took off my coat and began the test. Five minutes outside, five minutes inside; then again five minutes sweating and five minutes of teeth chattering. When I emerged the last time the superintendent smiled sardonically.

"Now you go home," he told me, "and throw away all your heavy underwear and overcoats and the like. If you survive you'll never use them again, and if you die . . ." He shrugged his shoulders.

I did as I was told. My astonished landlady took over my raincoat, all my woolen socks and other winter garments, and was greatly elated to have so many gifts for the poor. I went about my work and waited for a pneumonia that did not come. I have not since worn an overcoat or woolen underwear. On cold days I am cold, but I don't ever know or care whether or not I have a handkerchief in my pocket, and when I cough it is usually only a warning sign to someone around me to change the subject of the conversation.

For many years I carried a light overcoat on my arm so as to impress upon people the fact that I could afford to wear one if I wanted to. Later I dropped even this pretense and immediately became known as an eccentric. This, as I see it now, is the ultimate goal of human freedom. If you are known as odd, peculiar —cracked, when you are out of earshot—you can do anything you like. You can defy conventions, make your own rules, and still remain reasonably popular. Verily, it is great to be known as an eccentric, and many a silent toast have I drunk to the ice plant superintendent at Pittsburgh and to his made-to-order brand of Spartanism.

My landlord at Mountainglory was having financial troubles too, and one day he asked me if I would board with his family rather than eat out. By that time I was so full of pork chops and fried eggs that I would have joined the zoo for a change of diet; hence, I readily accepted the invitation. Moreover, I induced some draftsmen from the Barbara Furnaces to do likewise. Before we knew it, the house was filled to capacity with roomers and boarders. The other boarders were all Swedes, Norwegians and Danes, and the conversation at the table was Scandinavian from soup to nuts. This suited me splendidly; I picked up a lot of whatever it was, for I never could tell the three languages apart. In the course of time I could talk Scandinavian fluently, if not correctly. In later years I once tried to put my knowledge to practical use. I happened to have dealings with several Swedish factory superintendents, and one evening took them all out to dinner. When the proper time arrived, I rose and addressed them in their own language. It was only a short welcome speech, but I thought it would go over best in their native tongue. When I finished there was an embarrassed silence. Finally one of the men got up.

"We are all second-generation Swedes," he explained, "and did not understand you. Won't you please repeat what you said in English?"

Among the roomers was an elderly couple whom I detested, probably because they always seemed to be occupying the bathroom when I wanted to get in. I discovered what others have discovered before me—how easy it is to detest people before you know them and how difficult it is afterward. One evening they were introduced to me, and I was invited into what they called their apartment. They were a Mr. and Mrs. Holcomb, and he was a night watchman in our furnaces. The conversation, which I had feared would alternate between the weather and neighborhood gossip, quickly took an unexpected turn. Mrs. Holcomb wanted to know all about the Austrian court; had I ever seen the Emperor, and did I think that the Archduchess Elizabeth was happily married? I had once, by merest acci-

dent, seen Crown Prince Rudolph just before he lost his life at Mayerling; beyond that, my contact with or interest in the Habsburg
family did not go. Mrs. Holcomb then startled me by telling me
that she had been presented at most European courts, including that
of Austria. Her husband was a younger brother to a lord, but had
forfeited his rights, I never knew why. Mrs. Holcomb was a Vir-
ginian by birth and came from one of the oldest colonial families,
which she proved in true womanly fashion by exhibiting a foot which
called for a size two-and-a-half shoe. Living in the shabby atmosphere of a down-at-the-heel boardinghouse, her mind loved to
dwell on the past, and as I proved a good listener, I was always
welcome at her rooms.

She often gathered young people around her, and we played
parlor games. Among the girls I met was one called Mabel, an outstanding beauty; we boys vied with each other for the privilege of
taking her home, but the lot usually fell to an impressive young man
by the name of Monty, the son of a local merchant, a boy gifted
with an irresistible charm. His voice was velvety and seemed full
of suppressed laughter; he knew the best stories, could tell them
well, and girls flocked to him as naturally as iron shavings to a
magnet. But he had eyes only for the village belle, Mabel, who
was unapproachable. She would not even let Monty kiss her good-
night when he escorted her home, which was really flouting an
unwritten code; no one but Mabel could have gotten away with it,
especially with Monty. Then one day, quite suddenly, the two
were married. I never saw Mabel again, but I did see Monty twice
in later life. The first time he called on me, five years after his
marriage, I heard that they had four children. The laughter was
gone from his voice and the charm out of Mabel, so he intimated.
I did not see Monty again for a long time. When he did visit me he
asked me to cash a check. The next day the police were looking for
him. He had misappropriated some funds in Pittsburgh and, on his
way west, had left a trail of bad checks behind him. Mine was among
them, but I hope the law never caught up with him. I like to picture
him sitting in the parlor, with all eyes on him, relating Munchausen
tales with inimitable humor and showing more courtesy to old Mrs.
Holcomb than to any of the young ladies present. To think of him in
a dreary prison cell would have been heartbreaking.

Life in the laboratory was beginning to grow monotonous. I had learned nearly everything it had to offer. My reputation as a chemist was slowly rising. Several times, when two laboratories could not agree on an analysis, I was chosen arbitrator, which was considered quite an honor. Mr. Mende then gave me a difficult problem for my spare hours. He wanted to match a certain purple colored glass used in lampshades. He could not produce it and asked me to take a hand in the experiments. It was an interesting problem and I spent much time and effort trying to solve it; but I never succeeded, and I do not know to this day how it is done. Only one European glass factory had the secret and guarded it well. The work I did along this line kept my head down to the grindstone, and my failure to get satisfactory results kept it out of the clouds.

An amusing controversy which broke out at that time helped to enliven our days. We had a yard foreman of Irish descent who was endowed with the typical combativeness of his race. Among other duties, he had to keep intact the platforms upon which the molten pig iron ran from the furnaces into the ladle cars, and as the heat of the metal constantly produced cracks in the brickwork, he was condemned to the Sisyphus labor of repairing something he knew would not last. Finally he had what he thought was a brilliant idea. He ordered some huge chains from the Montague Steel Works and tied them around the platforms so that they looked like the hulks of immense battleships. Now let the brickworks crack if they could; begorra, he would show them. Well, the brickworks did crack and so did the chains, as was to be expected. The foreman cursed and, in a letter to the steel works, claimed that their chains were not of the quality they had been when he was young. The chemists from Montague replied that the foreman had set himself against the laws of Boyle and Gay-Lussac, as well as the law of molecular expansion. Our foreman swore that he was as law-abiding as any citizen of the United States, and with a flood of profanity brought the correspondence to a close.

The winter was ushered in with a severe cold wave, which caused one of our furnaces to freeze up. Days of great anxiety followed. Lights were kept burning in the plant office all night long, and worried officials held conferences, while the electricians inserted carbons into the interior of the cold giant tower. With a great spluttering, hot white sparks slowly penetrated into the interior of the furnace. It was tedious work. Tension spread over the whole plant, until it became almost tangible; it was heightened by the necessity of dynamiting our ore piles which had become so hard that the steam shovels made no impression on them. As I watched the work of the electrician one day, a fantastic thought shot through my mind. If we could support the heat of the carbons by the use of oxygen, progress might be hastened by whole days. Instead of supplying heat to the iron until it melted, the burning of the iron itself would add heat to that furnished by the electricity. It would be a pretty trick if it worked. I quickly looked up the caloric values and found to my joy that when iron burned it produced almost as much heat as coal, the only difference being that its initial burning point was higher. Well, the electricians would have to see to it that the oxygen was carried to the point where the electric current was creating a small, but white-hot surface; after that the process of melting the iron would be self-supporting.

Trembling inwardly, I entered the office and laid my plan before an astonished and incredulous board of experts. I was cross-questioned in a not too friendly or intelligent manner. The main counter-argument appeared to be that the scheme had never been tried before. I had collided with that sacred rock called Precedent upon which innummerable new ideas have been shipwrecked since the days of Adam and Eve. The electrician was called in, and he sneered at my plan. He had handled frozen furnaces before and did not feel the need of advice from a greenhorn still wet behind the ears. It was Mr. Lund, our superintendent, who threw his weight into the scales in my favor. After all, the main responsibility was his, and he was probably the only one in the crowd with enough scientific training to understand my train of thought. I suggested that water-cooled pipes be made to carry the oxygen to the point of contact, but I was voted down. Porcelain tubes were procured instead, a tank of oxygen was shipped in by express, and with much anxiety the experiment was launched. When the first blast of oxygen hit the small white point at the end of the carbon rod, the glow spread at once to a larger area. A few seconds later, however, the porcelain tubes melted in the terrific heat, the fireworks went out, and it was all over. Before the water-cooled tubes could be provided, the electrician, by dint of extraordinary efforts, had broken through the frozen crust and the furnace functioned again. Whether or not the oxygen scheme could be made to work was debated for a long while, but I stood aloof. It has since become the standard method of re-opening frozen blast furnaces.

It may have been a coincidence, but when Christmas came a few days later, I was asked to spend the evening and following day at Mr. Lund's home. No one but his personal friends were invited, and I was the only person present who was not of Scandinavian birth. The superintendent's house, an imposing-looking mansion, stood on a hill across the Chatonquin River and commanded a beautiful view of the valley below. We ate and drank incessantly, and all business talk was barred. The Lunds were charming hosts, and their Christmas festival still stands out in my memory as one of the most pleasant events of my Pittsburgh days.

I had now been in Pittsburgh a year and a half, and my circle of friends and acquaintances had grown considerably. Besides most of the inhabitants of Mountainglory, I knew many people in Morningport and other nearby towns; my social relations in Allegheny also had proceeded along pleasant lines. I did not impose much upon my cousin for introductions; he had told me once that all one man could do for another was to kick him in the pants; after that, the kicked one had to do his own running. This was sound philosophy. Jules' boardinghouse, where I went for my Sunday dinners, was a lively place, and the table talk furnished spice to meals which were excellent in themselves. Radios had not yet been invented, and people found much sport in supplying their own entertainment. To understand all the teasing remarks which flew back and forth, one had to be fairly intimate with the background of the boarders, of course; one had to know that one lady came from Erie, where the grass was said to grow on the sidewalks, an accusation which never failed to draw fire from the infuriated native of that city. To understand the refrain of a homemade song which said something about someone being "always in the hallways," one had to know that an affair was in progress between the landlady's older daughter and one of the roomers.

A young merchant named Baker was the life of the party. He knew all the latest songs, saw every show in town, and could repeat all the vaudeville jokes he had heard. They lost nothing in his telling. Also in the group was a very old man with a long German name which I have forgotten, whom everyone addressed as Colonel. He had been a soldier in the Civil War, I believe, although he was significantly silent on this point. He was of dignified appearance, but in reality was a great intriguer who loved to push people into embarrassing situations. At one time I was the butt of one of his little jokes. Among the boarders was a very prim maiden schoolteacher who blushed easily and earnestly. I happened to be reading a copy of the *Philistine,* which always had on its front cover some immortal saying of Ali Baba, who was supposed to be Elbert Hubbard's major domo. "If you must belli-ake," it read, "do it in private." I asked the Colonel what that meant, and he seemed to ponder the question very seriously. At last he shook his head and suggested that I ask the schoolma'am. The result of his advice was that the young woman ignored me ever after.

Across the street from Jules' boardinghouse lived a prominent oculist, who was a frequent visitor in the White House and was said to have made eyeglasses for all the Presidents since Grant. One of his daughters, Lucy by name, was about my own age, and we became good friends. Pittsburgh and Allegheny, like the rest of Pennsylvania, were closed tight on Sundays, and we two liked to spend the afternoons roaming through the countryside. I think we were about the only people who ever thought that the environs of the steel city were worth seeing. There was no streetcar in town that we did not take to the end of the line; from there we tramped through the woods and ravines and climbed the hills with which the landscape was dotted. Bellevue, McKeesport, Aspinwall or Swissvale—all the suburbs looked good to us. Only those who do not know Pittsburgh the way we did will deny that it is picturesque, interesting, beautiful.

My association with the people in my cousin's boardinghouse caused me to reflect on the relative financial status of the different groups in which I was moving. My cousin's income, entirely derived from peddling laces for a New York importing house, amounted to about five thousand dollars a year, he told me, and he did not work very hard at his job. A fur salesman at the table made twice as much, and Mr. Baker, who ran a small liquor concern, also seemed to be very well off. On the other hand, I had found out that when Mr. Kern was chief chemist at the Barbara Furnaces, his salary had been ninety dollars a month; Mr. Tompkins was now receiving one hundred and twenty-five, and Mr. Kern's income as assistant superintendent had gone up to one hundred and fifty. Mr. Lund as superintendent was reputed to command a salary of six thousand dollars a year. He had to carry the responsibility of an investment amounting to many millions, had to run an army of a thousand men and a miniature railroad besides, and devote day and night to his job, including holidays. There was something wrong with this picture, but I could not put my finger on it. I only felt that the manufacture of iron and steel, which we did for small wages and under considerable personal danger, was infinitely more valuable to the human race than the selling of laces, fur or liquor. Yet, compared to the money these other people were making, we got almost nothing.

In viewing this problem I was entirely free from personal bitterness or envy. My monthly income was more than I needed, and what I earned in addition I was able to put aside. But if I was satisfied, my mother and sisters were not. They could not see why, after two years in America, I still carried a lunch basket to work, went around in overalls, and was not making at least a million dollars a year.

Mr. Tompkins was frequently away on trips, and during his absence, while I had charge of the laboratory, I met Charles M. Schwab, then president of the United States Steel Company, of which the Barbara Furnaces were but a small unit. My meeting with this man, whose name later became a household word in America, was brought about by an unusual incident.

I was sitting at home one evening, studying and writing, when my landlady announced some strange-looking visitors who were downstairs waiting to see me. When I stepped into the parlor, I saw a Catholic priest, a young woman in black, and two elderly couples who were seated uncomfortably on the edges of chairs, awaiting my arrival. What they wanted to see me about was this. The husband of the young woman, a Croatian, had suddenly disappeared, and there seemed to be no doubt that he had been killed. He had been employed in the Barbara Furnaces as a bin worker, and his job had been to walk along the edges of the large, cone-shaped limestone hoppers called bins and see that the passage of the stones into small cars through the narrow openings at the bottom continued without interruption. It happened once in a while that these openings clogged up, in which case the bin worker, by means of a long iron rod, had to break up the jam. One morning Jan had not come home and, on the rim of the bin, they found his coat containing a bank book which showed a balance of some seven hundred dollars. The inference was plain. Jan had bent over too far in an endeavor to keep the stones moving, had fallen into the bin and been carried to the top of a furnace, either unconscious or held a screaming prisoner by the weight of the load. All this was told me in bad English, interspersed with many sobs and Slavic words, the priest carrying on the thread of the tale, while the others put in a word here and there, telling me what a good husband Jan had been, how he had always given his earnings to his wife, had never got drunk, and how the two had saved up their money to return to the Old Country some day and buy themselves a farm.

The nub of their story was that the company had refused to pay the widow any compensation for the death of her husband. When she presented her claim at the office of the Furnaces, some clerk had thrown her out. She then conferred with her priest, and the two went to a local lawyer of their own nationality. Months passed, but no action was taken. My visitors told me that I was known as a friend of the workmen; would I not take the matter to headquarters and see that justice was done?

I was slightly acquainted with one of the minor claim agents of the company and the next day went downtown to present the widow's case. The agent was a repulsive, sinister-looking little man with arbitrary manners, a despot in his own domain.

"No *corpus delicti*," he snapped at me. "How do we know the man did not run away from his wife and plant his coat as fake evidence?"

I pointed out that the bank book in the inside pocket allowed the fair conclusion that the man had died. I also mentioned that the case was already in the hands of a lawyer. At this he laughed noisily. Sure it was in the hands of a lawyer; the claim agent had already paid the lawyer; now did I expect him to pay the widow, too? So that had been the game, and that was the reason the lawyer had taken no action. I was furious and told the little snake across the table that I would get the legal compensation for the widow, if I had to go to the president of the company. Thereupon the claim agent bent over toward me and intimated that perhaps something could be done after all. Was the young widow good-looking? Yes, she was. And—this with a wink—how good was she in bed? Being her champion, I should know.

I got up without another word. Mr. Schwab's office was on the next floor, and I walked straight into it. I told my story without any comments or recommendations, just stating the facts as I had heard them. He did not interrupt me once, but jotted down the names I gave him, thanked me, and waved me out. A few weeks later the widow received her compensation; and when I came downtown next time, there was a different name on the door of the claim agent's office. I never again heard from the claim adjustor, the priest, or the widow.

I saw Mr. Schwab once more, a few months later. He was on an inspection trip through our plant, and I can still see him before me as he walked along in his shirt sleeves, a broad grin on his good-natured, intelligent face, with a word of encouragement or advice here and there. He had worked his way up from the bottom and was Charlie to all men.

Many years afterward, when Mr. Schwab was seventy-two years old, he was sued for a large amount of money. It was the kind of case that most men of his prominence would have settled out of court, to avoid publicity; but Charlie went through with it and won. Before he left the witness stand, he asked for and received permission to make a statement while he was still under oath.

"I am an old man today," Mr. Schwab said, "and I look back on a long and checkered career. I want to say that ninety per cent of my troubles have been due to my being good to other people. If you younger folk want to avoid trouble, be hard-boiled and say *no* to everybody. You will then walk through life unmolested, but—" here the old-time smile lit up his face—"you will have to do without friends and you won't have much fun."

Charlie Schwab was a great man, great in his strength and great in his weaknesses.

I came near having a claim of my own against the company about that time. A new fad had invaded blast furnace chemistry. It spelled gas analysis. According to this latest scientific craze, all mysteries of steel and iron manufacture could be solved by means of gas analysis. I was ordered to buy an expensive outfit, and we started to analyze everything gaseous within reach. No one knew at that time how to interpret blast furnace gas analyses, not even we chemists, but the work went on with undiminished zeal. The Montague people were doing it, and so were the laboratories of our competitors, the Eleanor, Jane and Irene Furnaces. They were probably not quite sure either of the why and wherefore, but they worked as hard on gas analyses as we did.

Blast furnaces have an ugly habit of getting congested at times. The men say the furnace is "hanging." No iron comes out at the bottom, and now and then burning gases belch out from the top, sometimes accompanied by a shower of hot cinders. Those were anxious times for the attendants, but there was little they could do to relieve the congestion. In the end, things always adjusted themselves; amid a rumble like that inside a volcano, some crust that had formed broke, a tremendous flame shot out from the top, and the furnace would begin to function normally again.

One day the superintendent called me to his office and told me to go up to Number Five furnace, which had been hanging for a day or so, and take a sample of gas from the top. We both knew that this was no ordinary job, and I suspect that he called me into his sanctum to give me an opportunity to protest. However, I was a soldier on duty, and neither I nor any other chemist would have refused an assignment because it was dangerous. I told a boy in the laboratory to come with me and help carry the apparatus. There were no stairs leading up to Number Five furnace, so we had to climb a one-hundred-and-six-foot ladder which led straight up alongside the furnace and which, as I found when we reached the top, was not even fastened to anything; it just leaned against the furnace. From the top rung of the ladder we had to swing ourselves through an opening in the platform with our legs dangling in space. I saw the ladle cars with molten iron moving along the tracks under me, and thought of a man who had fallen into one of them some time before and who, although almost burned to a crisp, was said to have lived for twenty-four hours.

Atop the furnaces everything was quiet. My intention was to open a cock, attach a rubber hose, fill the gas receptacles and depart, trusting to fate that the furnace would not belch while we were within reach of the flames. I told the boy to stay always twenty-five feet away from me, and if he should see me being gassed, not to come near me, but to run for help. I opened the cock, but I never attached the hose. The pressure inside the furnace must have been terrific, for gas rushed out at me so fast that I had no chance to move out of its way. I could feel myself going; first my legs became paralyzed, then my body. I still could shout, and I yelled to the boy to run for his life. Whether or not I really uttered an intelligible sound I do not know. All I saw was that the boy, with terror written all over his face, jumped to my rescue. The gas got him in mid-air, so to speak, and he was lying unconscious at my feet before I, too, succumbed.

When I came to it was hours later. Someone, I thought, was pounding at my head with a sledge hammer. By and by, I realized that a big Slav laborer was knocking my head against an iron railing, shouting at me to come to, as the platform on a hanging furnace was not a pleasure resort. The words were different, but that was their meaning. As soon as I sat up, my rescuer took the boy in hand. I have seen many people knocked unconscious in my time, but this is the only instance where I witnessed one person knocking another into consciousness. Our lifesaver was a watchman who made the rounds over the tops of the furnaces once in twenty-four hours; it was sheer luck that he had found us so soon. When I could talk again, I tried to thank him, but he would not listen, and his English being poor, his "never mind" took the form of "go to hell." He did not have to urge us to descend hurriedly. We broke every instrument on the way down, but we didn't care. My head ached atrociously, and I suffered from nausea.

On the way home I found myself climbing the hill on hands and knees, and when I reached my bed I threw myself upon it without undressing. One of our boarders, a draftsman named Thefeldt, came to see me. He was a great believer in whisky as a remedy. When he could not sleep he took whisky to make himself sleepy; when he was too sleepy in the morning he took whisky to wake himself up. Now he pulled a bottle out of his pocket and handed it to me. I had never tasted straight whisky before, but I was desperate enough to try anything and took a good-sized drink. Five minutes later my headache and nausea disappeared as if by magic. I got up, ate my supper, and next day was as good as new. By tacit agreement, no further samples of gas from the tops of hanging furnaces were ever asked for while I worked in the laboratory.

Among the improvements talked about in the iron industry at that time was a novel idea which promised great economies. The idea was to dry the air which is constantly pumped into blast furnaces to keep the combustion going. This drying process, it was thought, would save the heat necessary for the evaporation of the atmospheric moisture and therefore increase the output. It was understood that one competitive blast furnace plant was being equipped with a big refrigerator plant for this purpose. It occurred to me that there was another way of accomplishing the same results, and at much less cost. If the air could be led over unslaked lime, the lime would absorb the water; when the lime had become saturated, it could be heated and converted again into unslaked lime, and this process could be repeated indefinitely. I was so taken with my embryonic invention that I went to a patent attorney whose advertisement I had seen in the papers, and had him prepare the necessary application. In the meantime, I worked hard every evening to overcome some practical obstacles which presented themselves. I found that it was not so easy to make the lime perform in accordance with my wishes; mechanically and chemically my plan was weak. I was saved the humiliation of having to acknowledge my defeat in public, for one day my patent attorney absconded with the money of all his clients, and it was discovered that he had never made the patent applications for which he had collected. I wished him Godspeed on his flight.

The Barbara Furnaces did not pay the men in checks, but in cash; every week a heavily guarded car pulled into one of our sidings, and we received our wages through a barred window. One day each man was handed an envelope together with his money. It contained an announcement that the parent company had installed a profit-sharing system. I believe it was the first of its kind, and it created great excitement. The employees were given the right to buy a share of the preferred stock at a price quite a bit below the quoted market value, and in addition, we were to receive five dollars a share extra at the end of each year we stayed on the job. It was a very fair proposition, but its reception was anything but friendly. Little groups of men were soon standing around the yard, throwing suspicious glances toward the office building from which no great amount of kindness had ever been known to flow. In the saloons of the neighborhood the discussion was carried a step further.

"There's a catch in it," said one self-appointed spokesman, "you can take it from me; we men never yet have gotten something for nothing."

"You can bet on that," said another man, spitting at a far-off cuspidor; "I have worked for this gang for nearly ten years; we do the work out here, and the white-collared sissies downtown and in New York get the big dough."

The consensus was that a plan which required a deduction from the weekly pay envelope was bound to be crooked. If the fellows on top were so damned big-hearted, why didn't they hand over some more wage-money and be done with it? Nevertheless, some of us bought the stock, but before we had paid for it, the bear market of 1903-04 broke the quoted price below ours, and we all withdrew our down-payments and called it quits. The "I told you so's" had it. Instead of promoting good will, the scheme had stirred up bad blood in the men, and it was not long before it bore sour fruit.

The resentment against this profit-sharing system which the men felt was not easy to explain. Perhaps the plan contained too much brain and not enough heart. Workers are human; a half-day off, with a baseball ticket to boot, might have created more good will than the well-meant bonus scheme, worked out by auditors who had never worn overalls, whom the men had not met and whose motives were therefore suspected as inimical.

About this time, an episode intervened which was destined to have quite an influence on my future. Louis, our crack slag analyst, had been acting mysteriously for some weeks past. He smiled to himself all day long, and gave out hints that he had something up his sleeve that would shortly make him a rich man. One afternoon, just before quitting time, he took me into a corner and confided in me. It appeared that he had met an inventor by the name of Martin who had been able to extract nitrogen from the air and who was now privately selling stock in a company which would revolutionize a large section of the chemical industry. Louis had already invested four hundred dollars, practically all his savings, in the new enterprise, and what he wanted me to do was to investigate the invention hoping that I would confirm his good judgment. In this he was not much different from other investors I have met since, who do their investing first and their investigating later. A meeting was arranged, and shortly afterward I confronted Mr. Martin in the basement of a house where a pilot plant was supposed to be in operation. Martin was a tall, well-built man, with wonderful oratorical powers and a magnetism that held you spellbound. He expressed his delight in meeting a graduate of the famous Vienna Polytechnical School, and invited the entire neighborhood to witness the critical examination of his process by me, who had no connection with his venture, had never been seen by him before, and who would be allowed to ask any questions I liked. Mr. Martin, so he vowed to the crowd of some fifty or sixty burghers, would stand or fall by my judgment.

The project, as Mr. Martin outlined it, was without doubt theoretically correct. He proposed to send a high-voltage spark through a closed chamber containing air and thereby produce nitric acid, just as it is produced by nature during an electrical storm. The question was, of course, whether or not the process was economically feasible. To demonstrate this, the pilot plant had been built, but it was not yet in operation. The opinion I gave to Louis and his friends was in line with these considerations. In spite of my many well-emphasized *ifs*, everyone was quite happy, no one more so than Mr. Martin himself. I was to see more of him before many months had elapsed.

Right then, more important events crowded everything else out of my mind. Mr. Tompkins took me to his private office one morning and told me that he was going to accept a position as superintendent of a steel plant a hundred miles away. His appointment was only temporary, to last three months. I was to take his place during his absence and keep it permanently if he chose to remain away. Should he, on the other hand, return after that period I was to relinquish my post and resume my former position as first assistant. I agreed at once. My salary was fixed at one hundred and ten dollars a month and was to go up to one hundred and twenty-five after the interim. Once more I felt that I had struck gold.

Before Mr. Tompkins left, he gave me some serious advice. The men who had been my colleagues so far, he said, would now be my employees, and between a boss and his employees there was only one relationship. Either you treated them like dogs—he used a stronger expression—or else they treated you like one. He urged me to raise a row with each man at least once a week, whether he had it coming or not. I did not accept Mr. Tompkin's method then, and never accepted it afterward, but I have often thought of it, and more than once I have been tempted to admit that he was right.

Although I was only twenty-three years old, I was now in full charge of an important department, with fourteen men working under me. This was not according to Hoyle and was bound to have repercussions. My position was not made easier by the fact that, with the exception of the sample boys, all my employees were older than I and had been my superiors not so long ago. I knew that I had to watch my step and that it would be myself against the whole plant. The other foremen, too, were considerably older and could look back on much longer service. They could hardly be expected to treat me as their equal.

The first shot in the incipient warfare was fired a day or two after Mr. Tompkins' departure. At a quarter to ten the reports of the morning's work were always laid before the chief chemist, and he reported in person to the superintendent a quarter of an hour later. When I looked at the analysis of the slag from furnace Number Four, I almost fell off my chair; it showed at least three times the maximum amount of iron permissible. I immediately called for a duplicate test and then went out to see what the night's run at that furnace had yielded in the way of slag. There, sure enough, in their proper places, were slag samples which convinced me at a glance that the analysis was correct. Armed with a supporting sample, I communicated my findings to Mr. Lund. The superintendent agreed that the laboratory figures looked correct, but at my request he at once instigated an investigation which revealed that someone had perpetrated a hoax on me by switching samples. The lightning of Mr. Lund's rage did not descend on me, but upon the jokesmith. The first attack had been successfully met.

A few days later the yard foreman came to see me. A brother of his, he told me, owned a mine out near Denver and had sent him an ore sample to have it analyzed for gold and silver content. Would I oblige a friend and undertake the analysis? I recognized the piece of stone immediately as some gravel from the bed of a nearby railroad, but I only remarked that one piece of ore was hardly representative of a whole mine. If the foreman would come out with me I would show him how to get a good average sample. He followed me without misgivings, and I led him to the main line of the Pittsburgh and Western and started to pick up one stone after another. He laughed heartily, slapped me on the back, and promised to call off the dogs. The hazing period was over, and I was glad of it. Too many other things were waiting to engage my attention.

I had been informed by Mr. Lund that a company had been formed to dredge the bed of the Chatonquin River for iron ore. It was not so crazy a plan as one would think. For years the furnaces of the district had blown fine ore dust into the river bed, and a deposit worth salvaging should have accumulated there. Iron ore from the Mesaba Range was getting worse in quality anyway, and we had to reduce our specifications constantly to meet the offerings. The dredging was started, and a barge anchored in midstream, containing a heavy load of ore dust, was pointed out to me. I was ordered to bring in an average sample and report on it. The Chatonquin River was swollen by recent rains, and I hesitated to send anyone out, especially as I was given no means to get to the barge. There was nothing else to do but to go there myself. I had the carpentershop rig up a float for me and, with buckets strung along both arms, I worked my way out, hand over hand, using as my guide line one of the ropes by which the ore-bearing vessel was tied to the shore. It was a hair-raising operation. The raft was too light for my weight and was swamped, and as the return load was bound to be heavier by many pounds, I navigated back to make the little float more buoyant.

In the meantime, George Markley had heard of the matter and was furious that I had infringed on his, the chief sampler's territory. What he really meant, I believe, is that it was his business and not mine to take such chances. Soon I had volunteers from all sides who wanted to be in on the adventure. It was just like Tom Sawyer's experience in whitewashing his fence. We finally built a seaworthy raft to hold three men and used loops of rope to work our way out. Even then it was not a pleasant trip, and we were all glad to feel firm earth under our feet again. I have only to close my eyes to see the rushing floodwaters of the Chatonquin around and under me; it is anything but a sweet memory.

After three months I had the laboratory running on its own momentum and was beginning to enjoy myself, when one morning Mr. Tompkins showed up again. He had not liked his new job and was back again to his old one. I relinquished my position with outward grace, but inside of me something snapped. After three months as chief chemist, I was once more one of the crew. A raise in salary or any other promotion is a one-way street; I had stopped being boss, but I could not mingle with the rest of the laboratory employees on the old footing. I was neither fish nor fowl. Mr. Tompkins took good care to let me know that he was again my superior, and that did not make my life more pleasant. Then came the last straw. One pay day we each found a slip in our envelopes notifying us that our wages were reduced ten per cent. After tossing through a sleepless night, I reported to Mr. Lund next day and handed in my resignation. To my astonishment, Mr. Lund objected strenuously. He asked me to defer my decision for one day, a request which I could not very well refuse. The following morning he informed me that I would not only be exempt from the reduction, but that a special raise in my salary had been agreed upon. A proper place would be found for me later. I was surprised that this announcement left me cold. Had it come two days earlier, I would have been elated; but now, after thinking a whole night over the hopelessness of my position, money did not seem so important. The steel industry no longer held what I desired. I wanted to get away from Pittsburgh and from analytical chemistry; I wanted to taste life out West and learn something new.

104

"Where are you going?" asked Mr. Lund, after I had convinced him that I was in earnest.

"To Chicago," I said, offhand.

"If you go to Chicago you will starve," he replied soberly. I was to remember these words many times in the months to follow.

At Mr. Lund's solicitation, I stayed on for a few days before taking leave. They were not agreeable days for me. I saw things I did not like. The men were all in a sullen mood. Sabotage went on even under the eyes of the foremen. Somebody shut off the cooling water from the tuyères (air inlets into blast furnaces) and a few thousand dollars' worth of machinery was headed for the junk pile. In further consequence, some furnaces had to be shut down, which resulted in more damage. Half of the switch engines suddenly developed boiler trouble, and in the laboratory glassware was being broken at an unprecedented rate. Those fellows around the green table who had figured out the profit-sharing system and had followed it with a ten per cent wage cut would not gain much by it, not if the men could help it. They were still paying dividends on the preferred stock, weren't they, the dirty so and so's? A story ran from one group of men to another that a big speculator in New York had bought one hundred thousand shares of the common stock. "Bet he doesn't even know the difference between crucible steel and cast iron," was the sour comment. I was glad when my successor was selected so that I was free to leave.

In my first free hour I took inventory of myself. I now had been a chemist for almost three years. I had gone up the ladder from the bottom. During the first days they had made me clean out toilets and unpack boxes, wash glassware and chase rats from the basement, but eventually I had landed fairly close to the top. What was the top like? A dreary enough place, I was forced to admit. Of all the departments the laboratory was the least respected. I had sat in on the factory council and had felt humiliated. The reason, as I saw it, was that while all other departments did constructive things, analytical chemists did mere check-up work; they were bookkeepers who kept watch over other people's work, but they did not contribute tangible profits of their own. Creative chemists were still scarce in the field of iron and steel, and laymen hardly knew that they existed. Analytical chemists, like bookkeepers, might cause damage by making mistakes, but it was beyond their power to distinguish themselves by doing something positive. When I had left the hospital and tried to collect thirty dollars a week on a health-insurance policy, the insurance company had refused to pay me more than twenty-five because, so they said, no chemist in the world was worth more than that.

Chemists from other industries whom I had met at meetings of the Society of Western Engineers were no better off than their colleagues in the iron and steel works. Some were college graduates, others were not; it did not appear to make much difference. They were a thoroughly disillusioned lot, the younger men rebellious, the older ones resigned.

There was old Dr. Mumford, as good a chemist as ever lived, who had just finished his thirtieth year with the T & T Chemical Company. It was generally known that for the past twenty years his salary had been the same, and when he hinted at a raise he had been threatened with discharge. A French chemist who lived close to me was getting ninety dollars a month; he had married a governess and she made him a good wife. Only the lack of money marred their existence and led to endless worries and disputes. She had nothing to wear, she said, and the children nothing to play with. Everybody else in town was making money, the real estate men, the clerks, the pawnbrokers; even streetcar conductors and night-watchmen were paid better than chemists.

The depressing thing about her argument was that she was right. What was it Doctor Reich had said? Better get out of this cursed profession while you have a chance; become a dry-goods clerk, grocer, anything, but get out. In Chicago I would start on a different career.

I had one hundred and eighty dollars in my bank account, which meant that I was fortified to send my mother her regular allowance for six months. The last pay check would take care of my train fare and incidentals. There were no tears in my eyes when I made my rounds saying goodbye. My cousin, the Mendes and a few other friends said their last farewells at the depot. "Canton, Fort Wayne and Chicago!" the announcer bellowed. This time the call meant me. What would there be for me at the end of the rails?

I did not see Pittsburgh again for twenty years. When I did, the

Barbara Furnaces had grown up. A high fence had been strung around the property; those who wished to pass through the gate had to have stamped permits, and one's arrival was telephoned ahead to the office. Big "Safety First" signs were posted all over the yard. A bridge spanned the railroad tracks. Human lives had become precious. But the old crew was no more. Mr. Kern had been killed in an accident, Mr. Lund had gone back to Sweden and taken his Scandinavians with him. Mr. Tompkins had realized his ambitions and become chief chemist and metallurgist for a large steel company. My old friend Markley had died. Louis, the slag analyst, was the only old-timer left. It did my heart good to see him. In this changing world he was the one permanent fixture that would represent the past as long as he lived.

CHAPTER 6

ODD JOBS AND ODD PLACES

CHICAGO! What would it be like? I could not sleep all night. I sat up in an ill-smelling smoker and rehearsed a poor actor who had to appear the next night in a part for which he was totally unprepared. Lucky fellow! He, at least, knew where he was bound and had a place he could call a temporary home. I did not have a thing in sight, and the only person I knew was a German engineer named Schloss whom I had once piloted around Pittsburgh while he was wearing out his swaddling clothes. I had landed him at the Westinghouse Electric Company at fifteen dollars a week, and when his people heard about it, they thought he had conquered America. In Chicago I found him working as a draftsman for the Northwestern Elevated Railroad, and I am certain they never had a more devoted employee. He was so enthusiastic that every day at the dinner table he would recite the names of all the stations, and from the look on his face the list sounded like the Song of Songs to him.

Schloss was living in a boardinghouse near Lincoln Park and naturally I, too, took a room there. The landlady was a large German woman who tried to hide her soft heart beneath a hard-boiled exterior. She never fooled her boarders for long, of course; they owed her right and left and constantly took advantage of her good nature.

My engineer friend proved a mascot right from the start. He dashed into my room the first evening and startled me with the news that he had a job for me. The Northwestern Elevated, he explained, was contemplating the building of an extension to the neighboring town of Evanston and was employing check-up men to find out if

108

the traffic warranted the new venture. Schloss drew elaborate maps for me and talked traffic density and other high-sounding terms with great eloquence. I was not a bit interested in details; all I gathered from his conversation was one word—*job*. What was it and when could I begin?

I started work the next day. We check-up men had to count the passengers on the streetcars which handled the influx and exodus of the Evanston population to and from the Wilson Avenue terminal of the Elevated Road, and we were posted at various intersections. I drew the corner of Glenlake Avenue, an unimportant street without a cross-line. Most cars just whizzed by without stopping, but I was paid to count the passengers they carried, whether or not any were discharged at my corner. The task seemed impossible to me, until an older hand showed me how to manage it. All you had to do was count the passengers who were standing, and then you added thirty-six to that number, on the axiom that no one would hang on a strap unless all the seats were taken. After a short while, the speed of the cars inconvenienced me no longer. What bothered me was the weather. Coming from the hot-house atmosphere of western Pennsylvania, with its stagnant and moisture-laden atmosphere, I found it difficult to get accustomed to the freshness of the air in the Windy City. I developed an ungodly appetite, by far too healthy for a newly arrived boarder, and my sleep was so sound that it was an effort to get up in time for the morning's labor. I must have done well at my post, for after a few weeks I was transferred to a more important corner, and my pay was raised from three to three and a half dollars a day. I enjoyed the work while it lasted which, to my regret, was not very long. It was still early spring when I was again a man without a job. It is not the most pleasant of feelings.

As I sat around after breakfast one day, a boarder who had recently moved in approached me and asked me to come to his room. I knew that he was married, and I had heard that his wife was sick; I therefore hesitated. He laughed, grabbed my arm, and told me not to be childish. What he wanted was to talk business with me. I went to his room with him, excused my presence to his bedridden spouse, and after a few preliminaries we got down to brass tacks. Could I keep my mouth shut and did I want to make some money? I could and I wanted. Well, here was the scheme, then. He and his partner—he never called her his wife—had been working a short-change game, and this is the way it was being done. The wife would go into a restaurant and order a light meal, paying for it with a dollar bill. When the change was brought back to her, she started a rumpus, claiming that she had tendered a ten-dollar bill in payment. The proprietor or cashier eventually took a hand in the altercation, and usually suggested that, if she could submit proof of her assertion, the proper change would be given her. The woman would act greatly embarrassed, and then suddenly pretended to have an idea. She said that while waiting for her check, she had glanced at the bill and now she could remember its number. Slowly, and with great concentration of thought, she put down the figures, and lo and behold, the top ten-dollar note in the cashier's drawer corresponded with her description. With many apologies she was handed her change. The cashier may or may not have remembered too late that just before he took part in the discussion, a stranger had walked in, bought a cigar, and handed him a ten-dollar bill.

The couple had worked this scheme for a long time, but now the woman was ill, funds were low, and would I act as the innocent restaurant guest or else as the cigar buyer? The split would be fifty-fifty either way. It was nice, easy money and a meal went with it. I thought it wise to tell the man I would think it over. When I came downstairs I found that the few dollars I had carried in my pocket were missing.

A few days later the couple was gone from the house. When the boarders compared notes in the morning, they found that the woman, dressed only in a robe, had knocked at each door during the night, and had coaxed as much as twenty dollars from the roomers by means of a harrowing tale that proved irresistible. They had not only spared me, but had stuck an envelope under my door with the money they had taken from me. Whether their conscience bothered them, whether it was just a whim, or whether the gift was intended as hush money, has remained an open question in my mind.

I was again eating up my savings and began to worry about finding something to do. In looking through the names of chemical firms in the classified telephone directory, my eye suddenly spied the familiar name of the Martin Development Company. Could that be the enterprise which was going to convert air into nitric acid? The picture of Mr. Martin flashed back to me, as he had stood in the Pittsburgh basement, haranguing the crowd, plausible, oratorical, convincing. The Red Book gave the address as Monmouth Street, a narrow thoroughfare near the downtown district where many manufacturing concerns were located. I went there in a hurry. The house I was looking for turned out to be a dingy old building with an incredibly large number of firms posted at the entrance; but the Martin Development Company was not among them. I hunted up the janitor, a taciturn man who either would not or could not talk, but who, upon hearing my earnest desire, took me by the arm and gently shoved me down the stairs into a dank basement. Before I had found my bearings, I heard the boom of a familiar voice.

"Well, of all things, if it isn't the Dutch chemist from Pittsburgh! Come on in; we're waiting for you." This sounded good to me, and I shook hands with Mr. Martin in true Western style. I was then introduced to a Mr. Manny, a miner from Arizona who had all his money tied up in the undertaking, and a Mr. Williams who was draftsman, electrical engineer and mechanical expert all in one. A stove stood in the center of the room, and a few chairs and spittoons were neatly grouped around it. In a corner I saw an apparatus of considerable dimensions, and the whole scene was dimly illuminated by a single electric light bulb. I sat down with the three men, and the conversation continued from where I had obviously interrupted it. Martin and Manny never could utter a sentence without spicing it with juicy swear words. There was no malice in the imprecations which rolled off their tongues like music. Manny was a tough-looking hombre—I was already falling into their jargon—and Martin did not look as prepossessing in overalls as he had looked in the black frock coat in which I had seen him last; but Williams was a most distinguished gentleman with a Roman profile that reminded me of Director Schreiber of the Baden Theater. He smoked incessantly and said little, but when he did speak, there was always sense and humor in his words. When I finally rose to go home, Martin called me to one side and asked me if I wanted to work for him at a salary of twenty-five dollars a week. I agreed readily, and the deal was sealed in a nearby restaurant over a cup of coffee.

I lost no time starting on my new work. A quick survey convinced me that the whole idea on which the company was expected to prosper had not yet passed the laboratory stage. In spite of the experimental apparatus built, the scheme still existed largely on paper. Mr. Williams and I decided to put our shoulders to the wheel and get some results. It was slow and uphill work for the two of us. During the day people kept coming and going. Most of them were prospective buyers of our stock who were being shown around; others had already sunk their money into the venture and were now hanging around to see their dividends sprout. Almost every one of them was hoping for a lucrative position as soon as we were started on a large scale. Martin's magnetic personality had worked miracles with people's pocketbooks. There was a real estate man who had mortgaged his home in order to invest in the Martin Development Company; there was a young farmer from Michigan who had sold his farm, there were bankers, grocers, carpenters, a minister or two and several lawyers. One of the last named was a very impressive-looking man who had learned all the semi-scientific talk which usually goes with the selling of stock in such concerns as ours and who often acted as volunteer guide to strangers or interested parties. Williams and I used to meet in the evenings to lay our plans, and when people began disturbing us even then, we got together elsewhere. Somebody had to do some work soon, or the whole outfit would burst like a soap bubble.

Martin was boiling over with enthusiasm and held long discourses on nitric acid and the benefits he expected to bestow on mankind. When we had our first unit going, wouldn't the world sit up and take notice? Here Martin the chemist changed subtly into Martin the prophet. He rose to his full height and his eyes took on a far-away look. He saw in the Western country hundreds of Martin units producing nitric acid for hundreds of worthless mines or claims now suddenly transformed into bonanzas; for, with cheap nitric acid as a solvent, silver and other metals could be extracted at ridiculously low cost. The name Martin would be famous all over the globe, and those who were associated in his work were riding with him to wealth and glory. To argue with him would have been like arguing with a dancing dervish. Williams and I knew that we had best get down to business and make our contraption work.

In order to stimulate the chemical reaction, Williams worked on the electrical side of the problem. Our sparks grew stronger and longer and more numerous and thereby more effective. I took on the chemical end and enriched the air by the introduction of oxygen. We also tried out the reaction under different pressures and with varying speeds of air circulation. Our program was fairly well laid out, and we thought that within a few months we should be able to report substantial progress.

These dreams were rudely interrupted before many weeks had rolled around, for we were calmly informed one Saturday that it would be a payless pay day. The treasury was as bare as Mother Hubbard's famous cupboard. A meeting at the corner restaurant brought out new and picturesque oaths but no easing of the exigency.

The real estate man who had mortgaged his home to become rich via the nitric acid route was acting as treasurer for the Martin Development Company. He was about forty years old, a very pious man who quoted the Bible continuously, but he was the only one in the company who had a good business head. He called us together and told us that only three dollars and twenty-three cents remained in the checkbook, and then followed it up with the reasonable suggestion that we go out and sell stock if we wanted to continue what he called our operations. He would try to raise funds that way, he said, and it was only fair that we should support him. I knew where I could sell fifty dollars worth of stock and therefore seconded his motion.

In our boardinghouse lived a German engineer named Lichter, a young giant with the strength of a bull and with a fine mind which harbored many unexpected and unusual quirks. One of them was a hobby the like of which I have never known again. He had a perfect mania for buying stock in dubious enterprises, just for the fun of seeing how his money was going to be filched from him. His room was decorated with trophies in the form of framed certificates, all of them utterly worthless. He was on the sucker list of every get-rich-quick scheme, listened eagerly to slick salesmen and then

113

attended every meeting that was called. His extraordinary size often scared the chairmen out of their habitual smiles, but he went there only for amusement. If the slickers worked carefully and skilfully, he praised them; if their object was too transparent, he delivered good-natured lectures to them. He did not want a knock-out in the first round, he said; he had paid his admission and wanted his money's worth. The poor fellows whom he thus confronted found themselves quite out of their depth, and he enjoyed their squirming discomfort. At the table he would sometimes give us lucid descriptions of these meetings, imitating the promoters with a marvelous talent and keeping up a never-ending series of enter-tainments. Even the stolid German boardinghouse lady, whose constant desire was to clear the table as soon as possible, or sooner, often stood by, enchanted with his stories, and someone said he had actually seen her laugh once or twice. Lichter was, among other things, a stockholder in a coffee plantation in Brazil, a gold mine in California, a flying device, a new shoe polish and a Central American rubber plantation. Now I proposed to make him stock-holder in a nitric acid concern. He had a check for fifty dollars made out before I got beyond my opening sentences. After that I sold blocks of fifty dollars each to two commercial chemists with whom I was slightly acquainted, and I am afraid they have never forgiven me for it. Then my stock-selling campaign came to an abrupt end.

At the next meeting of our crew it developed that all in all about a thousand dollars had come in. This sounded like good news to me, until I heard that half that amount had been contributed by a widow who had scraped together her all to become one of us. To this I objected strenuously. It was quite evident that whoever be-came a partner in our company was playing a long shot, and a widow's mite had no place on our collection plate. In a moment I had everyone up in arms against me. Would I take away from the poor the chance for a splendid investment? Were the good things in life for the rich only? I was a fine example of a loyal employee, I was; and so forth. I waited until they had talked themselves out, and then I let them have it. Investment, indeed. What we were selling were nicely framed dream pictures. Did I believe that nitric acid could be made from air? Yes, it could, and some day it would, but it might take years of hard work to do it and a whole staff of chemists to boot. It was all wrong to get a few dollars here and there from small people. What we needed was a hundred thousand dollars and behind it a group of men with vision, men who would know what chances they were taking, not little boobs who thought we would double their money overnight.

The meeting broke up in a row; immediately afterward the real estate man took me to his private office. He was pale and visibly upset. Did I mean what I had said? I did. Well, then he was the greatest boob of them all, and ruined besides. Was there no way out of it? He had been responsible for distributing more stock than anyone else; he had even given some people his personal note as security. Now he started to blubber and talk of suicide. I told him to brace up and try to interest some big organization in taking over the whole outfit. He wrote a letter that same day, and in a short time, back came a reply. The Eastern Products Company, Inc., a tremendously big concern, was interested and would send their Great Expert to Chicago on Wednesday next. I had resigned after the explosive meeting a few days before, but I agreed to be on hand for his reception.

Wednesday came, and the Great Expert with it. I often wonder what he thought when he was led down the stairs into our chilly basement. The important-looking attorney-stockholder who was always around appointed himself master of ceremonies. He gave the Great Expert our old sales babble, but when the visitor shot a couple of pertinent questions at him he graciously turned the meeting over to me.

All right, said the Expert, how much nitric acid can you turn out per unit and what is your cost? How strong is the acid when you draw it off and what arrangements have you made for its concentration? I told him that we had made no large quantities of acid, but had only plans, supported by laboratory experiments, which we expected his company to take over and carry through. At that he blew up, and I cannot blame him. Heaven knows under what impression he had started on his thousand-mile trip. As his cynical remarks were directed at me, I returned them with interest. If we had already accomplished all the things he had evidently expected to find, why did he think we needed him or his whole company?

If we were on a manufacturing basis, we could go to banks—yes, we had banks out here—and borrow on our merchandise. We also had sure-shot gamblers in Chicago who would take a chance on a flier with a one hundred per cent guarantee against loss by the First National Bank. With that I turned the meeting back to the attorney-stockholder and walked out. I was fed up with nitric acid, basements and Great Experts.

Not long afterward, I heard from the Martin Development Company for the last time. They had moved to a city in central Illinois, where Martin held the whole populace in the hollow of his hand. They had given him a factory, rent free, and every single inhabitant was, to use a modern term, nitric-acid conscious. The treasury seemed to be overflowing again, and I was invited to come back and occupy my old position at a much higher salary. I did not accept.

Looking back at this episode now, I believe Mr. Martin was absolutely sincere and honest. He always lived modestly and, if his scheme had yielded large profits, I think he would have given most of it to poor miners. It was not many years later that German chemists perfected a process for manufacturing nitric acid from air, and I was half proud and half sad to see that many points in their earlier patents bore a close resemblance to some of the ideas the Martin Development Company had embodied in its grand layout that was never allowed to blossom.

Here I was again foot-free, and once more I turned to the telephone book, that everlasting friend of the unemployed. Leafing idly through the pages, I found to my surprise that a man of my name was conducting a glazing shop in the loop district. I was far from anxious to meet him, but walked by there, just to get an idea of what his shop looked like. The place was a little basement affair, and out of it just then came a young boy of about fourteen who looked so much like most men of our family that I stopped, more in disappointment than in wonder, for I had secretly hoped that in coming to Chicago I would strike a town where I had no relations. My moment of hesitation caused the young man to ask me if I were looking for his father. I was not, and the father was not in, but I met his oldest daughter, to whom I introduced myself. It did not take long to establish our relationship. I thanked the young lady for her invitation to come to their house for supper, and as I said goodbye I was careful not to leave my address. I had more pressing problems on my hands than the cultivation of my social career, relatives or no relatives.

Among the chemists listed in the telephone book was one whose name sounded familiar to me, and I called him up. He turned out to be an old acquaintance from my earliest Pittsburgh days. Now he was superintendent of the Heavenly Health Company and, following his cordial invitation, I visited him in his office. The Heavenly Health Company was selling a liquid which was advertised to cure everything from astigmatism to tuberculosis and was apparently a very prosperous firm, for wagons piled high with cases of the precious fluid were streaming out from each of their many loading platforms, with others returning empty, hungry to be loaded up again.

I liked the office of the Heavenly Health Company; any man would have liked it for that matter, because it contained more pretty girls to the square yard than any place of business I have ever seen. My friend explained to me that they were part of a psychological sales scheme. The pretty girls were never pointed out to visiting customers or should-be customers; it was their silent mass appeal that was counted on to convince buyers that the mere inhalation of Heavenly Health fumes made people beautiful. The medicine itself was a mixture of water and a few other harmless ingredients, with just enough of a bitter taste to make sick people feel that, after an outlay of fifty cents and the suffering involved in consuming the bottle's contents, they had earned the right to a quick recovery.

Shortly after my visit, one of the popular magazines ran a series of articles on patent medicines and, among others, struck at the Heavenly Health people, publishing analyses of their medicine and other pertinent information. The next time I happened to pass there again, the stream of delivery trucks had dwindled to a mere trickle. I suspect that a good many pretty girls were looking for positions at the same time I was.

The monotony of my job-hunting days was somewhat enlivened for a time by the arrival of Emanuel Lasker, the chess champion, who had come to Chicago on a professional tour. Lasker had a fair command of English, but had trouble with what he called the American language, and I was engaged to act as his guide and interpreter. In my student days, I had once taken part in a simultaneous chess tournament against the famous Polish player Janowsky, and had been so fascinated by the way he kept chewing cigarettes instead of smoking them, that I forgot to make a move in time and forfeited my game. Lasker's style of playing was quite different. Where Janowsky was fond of daring attacks and long chances, Lasker's style, while just as brilliant, was more methodical and thorough. The kind of brain the man must have possessed was past my understanding. I sat next to him in a consultation game in which he and two players of the Chicago Chess and Checkers Club were pitted against the best local talent. Lasker had been sitting quietly for a while, pondering the next move, when he allowed himself a sudden outburst.

"Ask these dumbbells," he shouted, "if they can talk. Am I the only one who is playing this game?"

One of his partners suggested moving one of the knights a certain way.

"Move that knight?" Lasker barked. "If we do, we are checkmate in seventeen moves."

He rapidly reconstructed the chessmen on another board, moved the knight as suggested and continued the game from there on, while we watched, spellbound. Checkmate came in exactly seventeen moves. No matter how insulting Lasker got thereafter, no one dared open his mouth again.

I took one of the boards in a simultaneous exhibition against this master, and struck out ingloriously, as I had expected I would.

The German chess champion could be very entertaining when he wished to exert himself. He told me that he usually worked out his chess campaigns in bed. Now and then he would lie awake until morning, while he perfected new openings for his next tournament. Sometimes his nightly inspirations turned out well, at other times the light of day made them look foolish. In this respect a chess champion's mind evidently did not differ much from that of ordinary mortals. Lasker was ready with special traps for all opponents and studied their modes of thought as carefully as a baseball player studies the strong and weak points of an opposing team. He had great confidence in himself, but I think he was slightly afraid of Janowsky, whose erratic genius was quite unpredictable. He told me that he was also disconcerted by Showalker, because that imperturbable Kentuckian acted so deceivingly indifferent between moves. He had disliked the Bohemian Master Steinitz, from whom he had wrested the crown of the chess world in 1894, and whom he called the Shylock of chess. Steinitz had died in 1900, but his disciples were perpetuating his methods and were the objects of Lasker's wrath.

"All these fellows try to do is to capture one of your pawns," he declared, "and as soon as they have that, they hang on to their advantage like the devil to a sinful soul. Then they start crushing their opponent like a steam roller."

Lasker knew the history of chess backward and forward and was a great admirer of Paul Morphy, who had beaten the mighty Lowenthal at the age of thirteen, and then had stormed like a tornado over Europe in the fifties of the last century, uprooting established reputations like so many old trees by winning tournament after tournament; he had beaten Anderssen, that quiet German professor of mathematics, who had heretofore been regarded as invincible; at the age of thirty he had given up chess because there were no more worlds for him to conquer. But Lasker's favorite chess hero was André Philidor, a mysterious French composer and chess player who had appeared in London in the eighteenth century, and against whom the finest players had been helpless. Lasker yearned to know if he could have matched his genius successfully against that redoubtable Frenchman of long ago.

Lasker admonished me repeatedly to give up chess, even as a hobby. "If this game ever gets you," he used to say, "you are lost; and to be merely a good chess player will get you nowhere." In his opinion many a promising career had been ruined because men had loved this royal pastime unwisely and too well.

Lasker paid Chicago another visit during the World War. He had just won another world championship in St. Petersburg, and no longer needed me as a guide. He invited me to supper, during which he did all the talking, much to my delight. The life of a chess champion, so it seemed, had its drawbacks. There was room for only one champion, and no one had stayed on the pinnacle long.

119

The day would come, he sighed, when the crowd which now idolized him would have nothing for him but pity. If I remember correctly, Lasker held on to the top rung until 1921, when he was beaten by the young Cuban star, Capablanca. He regained the crown, and then retired from the game in 1924, still champion of the chess world.

Although I was sorely pressed for money, I was reluctant to go back to chemistry. Almost every chemist I met was hard up. If only there had not been that infernal lure of the laboratory! The finest resolutions in the world melted away when I saw an Erlenmeyer flask, or when the nauseating but beloved odor of hydrogen sulphide struck my nostrils.

The best plan I could think of was to try my luck at journalism. I had been considered a good reporter and feature-story writer before, and there was no reason why I could not earn my living that way. My calls at the offices of the *Tribune*, the *Record*, and the *News* ended in instantaneous failure. I did not even get beyond the reception clerk. I then tried the *Inter Ocean*, the *American*, the *Journal* and the *Post*, but they were all laying off men, not hiring them. The depression of 1904 was descending upon the country.

I had exhausted the list of the English papers, and now started my rounds of the German press. The *Abendpost* had nothing, neither had the *Illinois Staatszeitung*. One of the men at the *Abendpost* suggested with a smile I did not like that I might try the *Arbeiter Zeitung*, a paper of whose existence I was as yet ignorant. I looked up the address. The *Arbeiter Zeitung* was located in an unappetizing section of the Near North Side. In a few minutes I was standing in the editorial office. Five or six men were scribbling or typing, and none paid the slightest attention to me. At the last table sat an elderly man with a big dome of a head and a bitter face. He was, I found out, the editor-in-chief, and his name was Martin Drescher. When I finally picked up enough courage to interrupt him in his writing, he snarled at me more than he spoke.

"A job? A job is it you are looking for? Here?" Then he pushed up his glasses and looked at me as if I had been an exhibit from a museum. Before I could answer, he asked me if I had the price of a drink, and when I admitted that I had, he suggested that we continue our conversation in the saloon downstairs. We sat down and were soon joined by one after another of the remaining editorial staff. My interview, I figured, would cost me some money.

For a while the conversation turned on matters which I did not quite follow. Then, all of a sudden, Drescher flew at me with the question: "Why on earth do you want to write for a newspaper? You are a chemist, you say. Stick to it, then. We fellows know nothing, can do nothing, and therefore we have to do this plugging. If you try to work our side of the street you are no better than a dirty scab."

Bang! went the last of the liquor down his throat, to be followed by an angry call for more of the same. The others kept pace with their boss. Then Drescher started to talk in earnest. Did I know what he, the editor-in-chief, was getting? No? He'd tell me. Eighteen dollars a week. He would spell it out for me if I liked. For that money he had to write out all the editorials and handle the foreign news besides. The local news Fred was handling, but he was drunk half the time—what else could a man do with twelve dollars a week—so Drescher was doing his job, too. That was all child's play, though. The real daily worry were the editorialettes. Little two or three-line aphorisms, smart stuff, so people would snicker. Editorials were easy; you could use a lot of language and say nothing; these darned editorialettes, however, were just the opposite; you could use only a few words, but they had to be clever. To hell with the editorialettes, and Heinrich! another glass of the same.

Drescher had only one ray of hope for me. Could I translate a poem of his from German into English? There would be money in it. I thought I could. Next Sunday the Bakers' Union of Cook County was celebrating its twenty-fifth anniversary, and Drescher's memorial poem was to be printed and sung both in German and in English; it seemed that plenty of people could take English poetry and make it read well in German, but not many could do it the other way around. If I would wait a moment, Drescher would go upstairs and get his verses.

While he was gone, his editors told me that the man with whom I had been talking was the greatest living German-American poet. I took that statement with due allowance for their condition, but I was wrong. Drescher really was a poet. I do not pose as an expert on rhymed literature, but I think I know the work of a real genius when I see it. I got myself one of Drescher's books of verses, and read one of the poems at random. It was called *"Eine Wölfin hat mich gesäugt"* (A she-wolf has nursed me). It was a wild outcry of such fantastic beauty that I carry its memory with me even now, a generation later.

The verses which I was handed for translation were blood-curdling; they referred to the Haymarket riot in which the anarchistic *Arbeiter Zeitung* had played an important part, something I had not known. What interested me professionally was how cleverly Drescher had gotten around using the word *Union* in his anniversary rhymes. The German for Union is *Genossenschaft*, and I could not see how even the best of poets could get away with a word like that and still have his output called a poem. I had by far the easier task, and it took me very little time to finish my translation.

Next week I called again at the office of the paper to collect my pay. One of the co-editors caught me in the hall and told me that Drescher was as sore as an old bull elephant. I was dismayed; had my work been so terrible that it had disgraced him? The editor could not tell, nor could Drescher, he said, for neither knew enough English to judge. What had happened was this. After the poem had been sung in both versions, a friend of Drescher's had asked him since when was he translating poetry instead of writing it himself. When the astonished chief had denied the imputation, the friend had shrugged his shoulders and remarked that the English version was the better of the two.

Thus ended my job as translator for Mr. Drescher. I was told to collect my pay from the Bakers' Union, which then had its offices in the old Busch Temple. I wanted fifteen dollars for my work, but I did not collect so easily. The cashier asked me how many hours I had worked over it and when, for good measure, I told him eight, he offered me three dollars and eighty cents, figuring it at the union rate for bakers in Chicago, forty-seven and a half cents an hour. There was no higher calling than baking bread, the cashier declaimed, and I was to consider it an honor to be paid as much as one of their union men. I began to argue. My work had all been done at night; did not that call for overtime? The treasurer of the Bakers' Union pondered the issue, then agreed. "Time and a half, then," he decided, and I walked home feeling that I had not labored in vain.

I still had no job, and now I was beginning to be seriously worried. Technical men used to meet then at the old Quincy No. 9 or at the Red Star Inn on North Clark Street, where the owner, Mr. Carl Gallauer, not only served excellent food, but always had a kind word and a free hand for those of us who were in need of both. In neither place did I hear anything but tales of woe and apprehension from those of the guests who shared my predicament.

"Hold onto your combs," one of the old engineers used to preach daily, "lousy times are coming." He was wrong; lousy times were already upon us. It was back to chemistry for me again, only there were no jobs. I met the same applicants either going in or coming out of chemical plants all over the city, and we saved ourselves a lot of time by just shaking our heads at each other. My landlady began to look at me wistfully, but I anticipated no trouble in that quarter. For many weeks I had been teasing her by telling her that each week's rent would be the last. Nevertheless, something would have to break soon, or I was lost. I had written applications to almost every firm that could possibly have any use for a chemist, but had received no replies at all. I had called on dozens of houses, and all I ever got was a cigar from a kind-hearted employer. No one else gave me as much as a kind word. It would have cost them nothing, yet would have meant so much to me. My name and address must have been on file with every concern of any consequence in Chicago at that time, if I was to believe the promises made me by smiling switchboard girls.

Then one evening I had an adventure. I was alone at home; even the landlady had been tempted by the beautiful early summer day to take a walk in Lincoln Park. The doorbell rang and I went to answer it. If it was a beggar, I promised myself, I would take a dime away from him. To my disappointment, it was not a beggar, but a book canvasser.

"Young man," he addressed me as I opened the door, "do you sleep too much? I have a book here that'll keep you awake. What, you can't sleep? Here is one that I guarantee will make you doze off after you have read one chapter of it." He was an elderly man with refined features, and his eyes were like old wine.

"You interest me strangely, my friend," I told him. "I won't buy a book from you, but I would like you to come in and talk to me.

Perhaps I can even get you a drink if I can find where the landlady keeps the bottle." The old gentleman came in, wondering what was in my mind. I found the bottle, made him sit down, and then began asking him questions. Why had he picked on our house at this time of the day to sell his books? How did he select his books, and which ones sold best and to whom? Under the mellowing influence of the landlady's brandy the old man started to talk. He had picked our neighborhood because farther south, on the Gold Coast, all the people had charge accounts with downtown stores and therefore did not buy from itinerant book agents; he never went farther west, because the people there were too ignorant to read books. In the moderate-priced boardinghouses—I admired his tact—was where his field lay. There the people had intellect and a little money, but no time to go downtown to shop. The books he carried were selected to fit different tastes; if an old spinster had opened the door he would have offered her a love story; jokes went well with traveling salesmen and poetry with young girls. There was an opening phrase for every prospect, and each one was well thought out.

"I can't tell you what you have done for me," I said as we parted, "but you will hear from me some day. When I land a position I shall send you a whole month's salary." What on earth for, he wanted to know; but I was not in the mood to enter into a discussion just then.

So this was the key to successful selling. No wonder I had received no replies to my letters of application. I had always started with, "I am a chemist, twenty-four years old, with three years' experience," and so forth. This book salesman had done nothing of the kind. What would I have thought had he come in with, "I am a book salesman, seventy years old, with ten years' experience, a wife and six children"? I probably would have said, "Oh, yeah?" and slammed the door shut. That, at least, was how my prospective employers had reacted toward me. No, this man had come in and offered me something he thought I wanted, a book to keep me awake, a book to put me to sleep. That was the way to make an impression, not my antiquated method of talking about myself.

I tried out the new idea at once. My letters of application took

124

on new life. "Would you like to hire a chemist who can make his salary twice over by increasing your profits?" I asked. I said nothing about myself at all; I did not promise to become a faithful, loyal employee. On the contrary, I acted as if it were up to the employer to hold out inducements to me. The responses were immediate and highly satisfactory. Could I conveniently come at eleven o'clock or, if not, change the time for the appointment by telephone? From a mere job-hunter I had lifted myself suddenly into the rank of a businessman who was offering a deal and was being met on terms of equality.

One of the letters I received came from a firm named Sears, Roebuck & Company. They called themselves a mail-order house. I did not know what a mail-order house was, nor did anyone else at our boardinghouse table. They were located near Fulton and Desplaines Streets, close to the downtown district, and when I went there the following morning I found an unprepossessing old structure which looked anything but inviting to me. I had just left a concern which could not meet its payroll, and I had scant appetite for another experience of that kind. As it happened, I was not destined to see what the interior of a mail-order house looked like at that time, for while I was hesitating on the doorstep, a young chemist whom I knew slightly came down the stairs and gave me the high-sign meaning "nothing doing." He and I had met before on our chase for positions, and I invited him into a nearby drugstore to get the details of this situation. I always think of Mark Twain's *Life on the Mississippi* when I remember the system in vogue among the jobless chemists and engineers at that time. The pilots on the Big River, so Mark Twain related, used to advise each other, as their boats passed, of the latest changes in the sand banks, and although no records were kept of the daily variations, each man at the wheel had to have them clearly in his head if he wanted to avoid delays, if not disaster. We unemployed did likewise, only our river was the city of Chicago, the channels were possible openings and the sandbars places to be avoided.

As we sipped our ice-cream sodas, this young colleague, whose name was Hildebrandt, told me that Sears, Roebuck & Company were not looking for a chemist but for a soapmaker, as they had decided to make their own soaps. He would have been qualified

125

to take the position, but conditions were not to his liking. In the course of our conversation, I broached a plan to him which had just flashed through my mind. Why could we two not make soap on our own account and sell it ourselves? Why couldn't we do it as well as Sears, Roebuck & Company? Hildebrandt was an eager listener. He could make a shampoo in his basement, if that was what we would agree on; could I go out and sell it? I thought of the book canvasser. If he could climb stairs and ring bells, so could I. A few days later our firm started to do business, and Sears, Roebuck & Company had a new competitor.

Now that I was putting the lessons of the old master to practical use, I found it a little difficult to make them work. Most women refused to open their doors to me, and the men I met displayed a deplorable lack of interest in a hair-wash. Nevertheless, we both kept plodding along, and soon added a face cream to our line. Women who shut doors when I said shampoo often opened them again when they heard the words face cream. We discovered that certain territories were more fertile ground than others, and that our sales depended on the right combination of correct approach plus a favorable time of day; even the days of the week made a difference. Our sales were invariably best on Wednesdays and Saturdays, possibly because these were the usual dating nights. We also decided to carry two different grades of shampoo, one for coarse or greasy hair, and one for the dry, soft type. Hildebrandt and I met every night to compare notes and improve our methods. I had seen in a show window the photograph of an actress whose fluffy hair surrounded her beautiful face like a halo, and I suggested that we each equip ourselves with a copy with which to dazzle our prospective customers. The picture proved a regular sesame for us. Every woman in town wanted to look like that picture and, with inward longing, usually bought both the shampoo and the face cream. Curiously enough, we had no trouble selling our weak shampoo to people with fine hair; our difficulties began when we had to handle females whose crowning glory did not rate so favorably. Only the most careful diplomacy could effect a sale in such cases, and I discovered that the easiest way was to let them all first have a try at what we called our gentle shampoo, and then give them the stronger one only if they asked for it. In the course of a few weeks I became an expert at judging feminine hair and complexions, and I cannot look at a woman today without a suppressed impulse to advise her. The problem is far less complex at present, of course, what with short haircuts and simpler coiffures. In 1904 the fashion decreed long hair and enormous pompadours, and the rats which were worn underneath presented cleansing problems of their own.

Soon we began to get repeat orders by mail, and my pride rose when once I received a call from a druggist in one of the neighborhoods I had worked. He wanted to stock our merchandise, because he was experiencing a demand for it. Then one day our promising young business collapsed. Hildebrandt had a flattering offer from out of town and departed with our precious formulae and with his manufacturing knowledge. I felt that I could not carry on alone, so I quit.

I had accumulated a little money and now felt it my duty to visit my old friend, the book canvasser. I offered him a check for the service he had rendered me, but he would not take it. Instead, he treated me in his whimsical way to another lecture on the art of salesmanship. It was his opinion that the selling of merchandise was easy; what was difficult was the selling of knowledge. He had once been a bookkeeper and had been kicked around from one job to another until he had become an old man whom no one wanted any longer. As an employee he had been a flop, he said, because he had not known then that the selling of professional services was an art like the selling of goods, only more so. If a canvasser approached his customers like a beggar, he was treated as a beggar; but all people looking for jobs acted like beggars, and that was why they did not get anywhere. Even after they had jobs, they let everybody in the office haze them, instead of asserting themselves, with the result that they lost everyone's respect and all chances for promotion. But that was the way with employees, he concluded; if they had either sense or courage they would not be employees. Now that he knew all this, the old gentleman remarked, the knowledge was of no further use to him. It was funny, wasn't it? I did not think it very funny, but it certainly gave me something to think about.

About this time I decided that I would call on my newly found relations, but I promised myself I would remain pretty well buttoned up during the proceedings. Becoming intimate with people was easy, I had discovered, but it was not so easy to become distant again.

My relatives lived on the northwest side of the city, in a section I had never visited, and after telephoning my cousin in her office and receiving a very cordial and pressing invitation for supper, I went there to make my call. The family lived on the first floor of a small, two-story frame building, and I was most graciously received. My uncle—he really was a first cousin of my father—looked so much like other members of our family in Europe that I felt I had known him for years. His wife, a small woman with a plump figure, was possessed of more tact and common sense than the sum total of many other representatives of the gentler sex. Then the children were introduced to me, one at a time. Stephanie, the oldest, I had already met; Minnie, the second, was a stenographer who, strange to say, was working in the same building in which the Martin Development Company had been located, so that I had probably passed her a dozen times. Then there was Bertha, a girl of about sixteen, with black eyes, long lashes and attractive ways. I thought she was the most charming of them all. By and by two boys came in, one of whom I had run into in front of the store; and finally there was pretty little Elsie, aged eight, who was called upon to break the embarrassment which generally develops at a meeting of new relations after the first questions have been asked and answered. Elsie obligingly stepped on a wooden box and recited "The One-Legged Goose" and, when the supper still was not ready to serve, gave an encore which dealt with an English soldier named Atkins.

I suspected that my aunt in her younger years had nursed a romantic streak, for her first daughter was evidently named for the wife of Crown Prince Rudolph of Austria, and the second after Wilhelmina, Queen of Holland. You could always tell the age of European girls by their names, and my aunt abandoned this practice after her first two children.

The supper was grand. Where is there a Viennese who would not unbend at the sight of *Knödelsuppe* and *Wiener Schnitzel?* My uncle had a fund of good stories which he told well, thus giving the meal its proper background. It was a perfect evening. Had I been able to look into the future, I would have known that I had just met my future wife.

CHAPTER 7

OIL FROM LINUM USITATISSIMUM

Y FINANCES had now reached an all-time low. When Schloss asked me one evening to go to the Red Star Inn with him, I refused. A nickel for a glass of beer was too much of a luxury for me. But Schloss was insistent. A young chemist named Avers was angling for a job at the Illinois Steel Company, but knew nothing about steel or iron analysis and hoped to profit by a talk with me. That settled it, of course. With a sigh I put on my hat and went.

I told Avers all I knew, and in exchange he told me of a possible chance for employment. His last job had been with a concern called the American Linseed Company; they operated a linseed oil extraction plant at South Chicago. The trouble with that job was that it lasted only a few months each year, was uninteresting, and did not pay much. The time for re-opening the plant was at hand, though, and if I wanted to make a try for it there was no time to lose. I scooted home and wrote one of my newly styled letters.

A few days later I received a reply. Would I call the next day at the office of the American Linseed Company in the Manhattan Building? The letter was signed by John W. Hirst, western manager. I knew nothing about linseed oil, but that need not deter me. In my heart I was wondering how the book salesman would go about clinching this position, but I did not want to ask him. I felt that I ought to know how to apply his lessons without being coached.

Early next morning found me in the John Crerar Library, reading everything on linseed oil that was on the shelves. The encyclopedias were about all there was, as no specific books on the subject seemed to have been written. I studied the chapters on linseed oil with great care. Linseed oil, I discovered, came from a plant called *linum usitatissimum*, indigenous (whatever that was,) to Asia Minor, Russia, the United States and Argentina, yielding an oil which had an iodine value of about 185, a saponification number of 190-193, and some other properties which were interesting, although entirely meaningless to me. I found that it could be refined by means of sulphuric acid or sodium hydrate and that it was used in the manufacture of paints, varnishes, enamel and linoleum. I kept repeating all this to myself as if I had been preparing for a quiz, and when the noon hour approached, I walked over to the Manhattan Building, shot up to the fifteenth floor, and was shown into Mr. Hirst's private office. An elderly secretary received me and engaged me in a desultory conversation. Before long we found that we had many tastes in common. I never called on Mr. Hirst later without spending half an hour with her, and we remained fast friends until she died, many years later, in retirement at Pasadena.

At last I was shown into Mr. Hirst's inner office. After the preliminaries were over, he asked me what I knew about linseed oil. Linseed oil? *Linum usitatissimum*, indigenous to Asia Minor and other countries, yielding an oil with an iodine value of 185 and subject to refinement by means of sulphuric acid or caustic soda.

"How on earth do you know all this?" Mr. Hirst asked me.

"Oh, one picks up things here and there," I replied smilingly.

"You are the first chemist I have ever met who knows something about linseed oil," he admitted. "You can have the job if you want it. It pays fifty dollars a month and you can start tomorrow."

When I thought of my emaciated bank account, the mention of fifty dollars a month made me feel faint. I remembered my mentor just in time, however.

"Fifty dollars a month?" I said in simulated disgust. "Did you say fifty dollars a *month?*"

Mr. Hirst began to fidget uncomfortably. That's all they had ever paid their chemists, he said. Yes, I countered, but none of them had known anything about linseed oil. I could not work for less than one hundred and twenty-five dollars a month.

"I concede you every point," Mr. Hirst finally said, "but the president of this company is in a hospital, and my authority does not cover a change in salaries. I will go as far as sixty dollars on my own responsibility, but that's as much as I can do. I'd hate to lose you, but this is my last offer."

Here was a fine kettle of fish. I could not possibly come down from one hundred twenty-five dollars to sixty, nor could I afford to lose the position. I decided to play *va banque*.

"Goodbye then, Mr. Hirst," I said, holding out my hand, "it was a pleasure to meet a man of your kind." With that I got up, turned and strode toward the door. If he let me go, I was beaten. I turned the handle of the door and had gone half through it when he called me back.

"Just a minute," he said, "isn't there some way in which we can get together?"

I had been doing some fast thinking. Yes, there was, I replied. I would work half a day for the American Linseed Company for sixty dollars a month, and guarantee to do all the work that had to be done. The rest of the time I would hire out my services to other firms. This would make me a hundred-and-twenty-five-dollar-a-month man, and neither I nor the company would be the worse off. Mr. Hirst agreed that it was a good plan. Could I start the next morning?

I could not, I said, certainly not. There was that World's Fair in St. Louis, and I owed it to myself to see it. After I had started in my new position, I would probably not be able to absent myself. Yes, a week or two would suffice to post me on the latest chemical developments at the Exposition. When I left Mr. Hirst, the expression on his face was such a mixture of incredulity, respect and resentment that I felt greatly elated. The proper selling of knowledge was apparently not only profitable, but could be amusing, too.

I was two weeks behind in my rent by this time, but I was ready to crowd my luck. Calling on my landlady, I put all my cards on the table and asked her to finance my trip to St. Louis. She had probably already rehearsed a collection speech for me, and my attack took her completely unawares. She succumbed. In a few hours I was southward bound to see the Exposition.

It was frightfully hot in St. Louis, and of all the things I saw I remember only the lemonade stands and a concert at the end of which the audience remained stuck to the newly painted seats.

My mind was not on vacationing, anyway, and I was glad when I received a telegram from my landlady advising me that the American Linseed Company wanted me to report at once. I rushed back to Chicago, wondering what it was all about. Mr. Hirst had intimated to me at our interview that they employed chemists principally because they had an expensive laboratory and would not otherwise have known what to do with it. What could have happened that required my presence so urgently?

I found out soon enough. Our company had a plant in South Chicago which produced a special refined linseed oil commanding a premium on the market. A tank car of this oil had been shipped to a varnish house in Detroit and been rejected because it discolored when heated in varnish kettles. A second and third car had followed the first and been rejected on the same grounds, so that all three cars were now standing on a siding accumulating service charges. Our customer was forced to use a competitor's oil, which appealed to him no more than it did to us. This constituted my problem, and I was told to go ahead and solve it.

My first impulse was to run away and hide where nobody would find me. I, who had never seen a linseed oil plant and did not even know what linseed oil looked like, was being asked to perform something that had the experts puzzled. Outwardly I preserved my calm.

"Get me all the correspondence on the complaint, please," I said, with the authoritativeness of a doctor in the sickroom, "and then wire for samples of the oil before and after the heat treatment." The whole office sprang to attention.

"Miss Shields, you will please send the wires as you are told," said Mr. Hirst, "and let our new chemist have the run of the place." I thought I would improve my position while things were coming my way, and asked Mr. Hirst to advise South Chicago that I would be out at the factory the first thing in the morning and to have everything in readiness for me. This sounded good and was bound to give me the right kind of start. Then I excused myself and hastened back to the library. Somewhere, someone must have had a similar experience, and if the gods were good to me, he had recorded it for my benefit. If he had not, I was as good as fired.

I sat in the library until it closed. When I left I was not much wiser than I had been before. I knew now that linseed oil had been in use since the fourteenth century, that it contained some unsaturated fatty acids and that it was used in Russia for edible purposes, all of which left me cold.

The plant which housed my laboratory was located several miles south of Chicago, not far from the Indiana state line. It consisted of nineteen buildings, covering several acres of ground, and had its own pier, jutting out into the Calumet River. The manager of the plant, a Mr. Moulton, and the superintendent, a fat German named Stock, were expecting me. I was shown the laboratory, a roomy, well-equipped place, consisting of an office, a balance room and the laboratory proper. I delved into my problem without wasting a minute after the introductions had been concluded.

First, what refining agent was being used in the plant: sulphuric acid or caustic soda? My question brought only astounded stares in response. No one here had ever heard of either method. I began to suspect that perhaps there were matters between heaven and earth that even the encyclopedias knew nothing about. At any rate, it might be better to let the others do the talking. By and by a picture of the operations emerged from the descriptions I listened to. The linseed oil in this plant was extracted by means of naphtha as a solvent, and therefore the oil was purer than that obtained by the more common mechanical crushing processes. Hence, it was not necessary to use chemical refining agents at all. Instead, the oil was agitated with a small amount of Fuller's earth, a clay of special color-absorbing properties, and was then filtered through cloth and paper. That was all. No one could understand why the oil should suddenly discolor under heat, something it had never been known to do before.

I rushed from one library to another, only to find that the books now knew less than I did. Then I remembered what my superiors in Pittsburgh—Kern, Tompkins and Lund—had always held against me. "What we don't like about you college graduates," they used to say, "is that you try to save yourselves all thinking by looking things up in books. Books! People never put really worthwhile information into books, because that's their bread and butter. When a book is written, either the material has become obsolete or the author is a has-been." I was more than half inclined to agree.

All the correspondence pertaining to the matter was now before me; it did not help much. Our Detroit representative had kept saying that, as such a discoloration had never occurred before, it could not have happened now. The customer kept reiterating that it had happened. It was a fairly intelligent correspondence, considering that it had been carried on between two sales managers who knew nothing about technical matters. I would have preferred a direct story from the Detroit chemists or from the men at the varnish kettle. They might have stated the problem more scientifically, which would have meant a lot. But I surmised that they were not considered smart enough to write out complaints.

I got out my overalls and went to work. I followed the process of our refinery from beginning to end. Perhaps there was something in the Fuller's earth that caused all this commotion. A thorough analysis of the clay, however, disclosed no possible source of trouble. It was just ordinary, chemically inactive clay.

I then put some of our refined oil into a miniature copper kettle, heated it to 600° F. for a few hours, just as our friends in Detroit were doing, and watched the process. When the heating was finished, the oil sometimes became discolored and sometimes it did not. This was absurd and contrary to all reason. I was tempted to believe that I was not dealing with chemistry, but with witchcraft.

Gradually I worked myself into a state of frenzy. I could not sleep, and while outwardly I bore myself, I hope, with becoming poise, I was in reality utterly discouraged. Day and night my mind raced around in the same worn-out channels, as I went over every item again and again. This was worse than one of the Anna Katherine Green detective stories then in fashion, for I did not even have a clue. No one had left a collar with a laundry mark or a half-burnt match lying around.

A half-burnt match! This was not a bad idea. The discoloration could be due to a burning process. Linseed oil was an organic substance like wood and would possibly char under heat. I decided to watch that process in detail. Up to then I had conducted my tests in a copper kettle and seen nothing but the final result. Suppose I were to do my cooking in a glass vessel, where I could observe what was going on? I jumped out of bed and caught one of the hourly horse cars which took the place of the cable-cars on Clark Street after midnight; then I had to take the South Side Elevated to the end of the line; then the little electric cars that went almost to the Indiana state line; a three-quarters of a mile walk across the prairies brought me from there to the plant. Heatproof chemical glass was not yet in use at that time, or at least we had none in our laboratory; but this did not deter me. Let the beakers crack, one after another; I was bound somewhere and I was on my way.

The first two beakers broke, but the third held. With an electric light bulb fastened on the opposite side, I sat on a high stool watching the oil rise in heat and then slowly get heavier and heavier as the hours passed. There was no marked discoloration. Another sample, another cook, and the same negative result. Dawn and morning passed and found me still watching, still hoping. Then, on the third attempt, the miracle happened. A tiny brown spot developed in the lower portion of my yellow liquid, turned darker and darker, and from this nucleus a greenish black spiral line began spreading through the beaker. It soon blended with the remainder of the oil, discoloring all of it. One drop of ink in a glass of water, as it were. Something in the oil decomposed faster than the oil itself. I had my clue. Now for the criminal.

Again I turned to the Fuller's earth as the most likely culprit. Suppose it contained little specks of alkaline dust; then suppose these tiny particles saponified the surrounding parts of the oil; under heat, the soap would char faster than the oil, and the decomposed soap would dissolve in black streaks. That was it, without doubt. I knew that linseed oil soap was green, and the spiral had been green before it turned black. Eureka, I had found it!

Every bag of Fuller's earth we had in stock was opened at once and analyzed for alkalinity; but as one test after the other showed up negative, my enthusiasm waned. There just was no caustic in our clay. "Follow the evidence as you find it, if it takes you through a window," one of our teachers had admonished us. There was no use trying to fool myself. I had to admit that my clue had petered out. I went to a hotel in South Chicago and sank into a sleep of utter physical and mental exhaustion.

Next morning things looked brighter again. In those detective stories the criminal never was discovered before suspicion had pointed at least to one innocent person. My experience was therefore running true to form. If I could only think of another suspect!

I went back to the plant for a consultation with the superintendent. Was anything used around the place which could possibly contain an alkaline substance? There was not, he thought. We were using only flaxseed, naphtha and Fuller's earth, and certainly there was no caustic in the flax or in the naphtha. I then went to Mr. Moulton, manager of the plant, and put the same question to him. He was doing all the purchasing and should know. Mr. Moulton, a thin, ascetic-looking man of taciturn habits, was none too friendly toward me, and I thought I knew the reason. All other chemists had considered him their superior and taken orders from him, while I held that I was chemist for the entire company; the laboratory was located on his premises, but that did not alter my complete independence. The problem I was investigating happened to be also his problem, but other plants would have theirs, too, and my allegiance was to all of them. This was my understanding and that of Mr. Hirst, but Mr. Moulton did not like it.

When I asked for his cooperation, he pointed to his purchase book and told me to help myself. Every item bought for his factory was entered in this volume, and I could study it to my heart's content. So far as he was aware, I would find nothing.

I studied the entries for the past six months. Mr. Moulton had bought brooms, sieves, valves, pipes, filter cloth and an innumerable array of incidentals. None could possibly have any bearing on our trouble. As a last hope I turned back to the more distant past, and suddenly I struck an item that made me whistle. Mr. Moulton had once bought a drum of caustic soda! I was over at his desk in one jump. What was this caustic soda used for? He shrugged his shoulders. To wash the floors, he guessed. Guessing wasn't good enough for me, and I rushed out to see the superintendent. What was the caustic soda used for? Oh, they used it for washing floors and filter cloths, whenever they had to be changed. Filter cloths! Holy—! Could it be? I flew to the filtering room. Old Ted, the man in charge there, always acted as if he owned the press-house with everything in it, and was not communicative, but I hammered at him insistently. Just how did he wash his filter cloth? Well, he said, there was nothing to tell. The dirty cloth was hung in a vat filled with a caustic solution and taken out again next day. I began to tremble all over; his next answer would either solve my mystery or else drive me out of the window, along with my evidence.

"Ted," I said, as unconcernedly as I could, "do you rinse the cloth in water before you use it again?"

"No, sir," he replied, "and what would that be for, sir?" Ted had once been a seaman in the British service, and used a "sir" after every comma.

"Ted," I said, "I could kiss you." With that I stormed out to get the superintendent. "Orders from headquarters," I snapped. "All filter cloth to be washed in naphtha from now on. Let's make a fresh batch of refined oil and filter it through naphtha-washed cloth."

We made batch after batch, until we had enough to fill a tank car. During all this time I did not leave the plant and had my eye on everything. I even tested the inner walls of the tank car for alkalinity and then had it wiped out with a rag soaked in linseed oil. When the car was filled, I tested samples from every corner of it before I gave the word to let it go to Detroit. Then I went home. The next few days would make or break me.

In a week or so, a telegram arrived from Detroit. The car had been accepted, and would we send two more in quick succession. Would we!

Mr. Hirst asked me to come in for a conference. He did not think they had ever before had a real chemist. What would I take to work all day long and give up whatever other connections I had made (there were none) to earn money during my free time? I thought I was worth a hundred and twenty-five dollars a month, if I was worth anything; but that was too much. They had never paid their chemists more than fifty dollars, and the jump was too sudden. We compromised on one hundred dollars, but I was to be given special privileges not heretofore granted to other chemists, such as the right to take in consulting work, provided it did not conflict with my duties.

In the following days I reorganized my private life, adapting it to the changed conditions. It was manifestly inexpedient to spend five hours on the way to and from work, and regretfully I said goodbye to my boardinghouse, to Mr. Schloss, Mr. Lichter and to beautiful Lincoln Park. Twenty years later I was to move back to within a few houses of my old abode, into much more elegant quarters; but the old boardinghouse, long since departed, had some charms which later surroundings could not replace.

The German landlady cried on my shoulder before she checked up on the items in my room. I would miss her, as I would miss Schloss' intimate tales of life on the Northwestern Elevated. His position was not to last much longer, by the way. After all the ambitious expansions of the road had been completed, he was dismissed and went back to Germany. When the first World War broke out he led a patrol across the French border and was one of the first to fall in the Great Slaughter. Lichter became an internationally recognized authority on automatic telephones. He has risen to the position of professor in a leading university, and sends me autographed copies of all the highly specialized books he writes. As a consequence, I know everything about automatic telephones, except how they work without a switchboard operator.

On the South Side, not far from the entrance to Jackson Park, I found a room with an elderly widow whose son was an engineer on the Illinois Central Railroad. She was a New Yorker and, although she had lived in Chicago for thirty years, still looked down upon the natives as slightly beneath her. I was destined to live in her apartment for eight years, but I never felt that I knew her. Life had not handled her with silk gloves, and she was bitter toward the whole world. The other roomers remained complete strangers to me at all times. Yet I grew to like this sort of life. There was no companionship, but neither was there any intrusion on one's privacy.

Within a few doors of my new residence was the terminus of an electric line which took me to my place of work. On the way to its other end, somewhere near the Indiana dunes, it had to negotiate twenty-three grade crossings. Some of these were switchtracks of steel and coke companies, and some were the main rights of way of eastern trunk lines, so that one never knew whether the trip would consume forty-five minutes or two hours. A law in force at that time limited the use of a crossing by a train to five minutes, but the engineers were rather liberal in interpreting the ruling, and more than once the enraged streetcar passengers had the engineers pulled out of their cabs by policemen to make them realize that, in theory at least, the law applied to big fellows and little ones alike. Quite aside from these delays, riding these street-cars was no pleasure jaunt. They were small and antiquated, and some of them were still equipped with oil lamps and coke stoves. Bad lights and violent motion on uneven rails combined to make reading impossible for passengers who valued their eyesight. I often took wide detours and paid double fares to ride on lines with better equipment.

The superintendent's daughter Gertie was supposed to help me in my work, but I had not yet seen her. When I did meet her, it was only because I arrived at the laboratory one morning at seven o'clock. Gertie blushed when she was introduced to me, for she was a very shy creature who had done her daily tasks before daybreak in order to avoid me. She was a pretty youngster of seventeen, with an enormous pompadour of which she was very proud, and which she was constantly readjusting. From that day on, Gertie stayed at my side uninterruptedly for thirty-four years, until death parted us. Up to the last she was as modest and shy as she had been that first day.

As daughter of the superintendent, Gertie Stock knew a great deal about the plant, and to me she was, in the beginning at least, a never-ending source of useful information. Her duties were light and had previously been performed by her older sister, who had just married. Every day Gertie opened the oil cake samples which the mail brought and tested them for their oil content. It was her duty to determine whether or not the out-of-town mills which used the time-honored hydraulic system to remove the linseed oil from flaxseed had obtained all the yield possible during the day's run. The samples from our own plant also had to be examined, of course. The analytical method which had been worked out for this purpose was easy to follow. A given quantity of the powdered flax residue was put into a glass tube with a tapering end which was closed with a wad of cotton. Quantities of carbon bisulphide were percolated through the tube until the solvent came through color-less. The carbon bisulphide was then evaporated and the remaining oil weighed. A child could have done the work.

Gertie did not know a thing about chemistry, but her father had run oil plants all his life, in America, Germany and Russia, and she had absorbed a lot of practical knowledge which made her invaluable. It did not take her long to become accustomed to me, and when I found that she was a graduate of the South Chicago Business College, I asked her to take my letters and act as my general assistant. She consented after some hesitation. and I succeeded in having her salary raised to suit her work. Instead of her former fifteen dollars a month, she was to receive four dollars a week.

After I had solved the mystery of the Detroit complaint I found I had practically nothing to do. Mr. Hirst seemed to have forgotten that I existed, and the rest of the company had never known differently. I asked Gertie how my predecessors had killed time, but she really could not tell. In her opinion, they had just sat around all day looking wise and pretending to be busy. I could see that if I did not want to stagnate, I would have to do something about it. While I was considering the matter, help came from an unexpected quarter.

One morning I received a letter from the Chicago sales manager, advising me that a sample of oil was being sent to me for analysis. I replied at once, asking what the analysis was expected to disclose. The sales manager, an old gentleman who had sold linseed oil since the days of the Civil War, interpreted my letter as a piece of impertinence and complained to Mr. Hirst. As a result I was asked to come downtown for a consultation.

Mr. Hirst opened the conference in his usual smooth manner and with a suavity that had earned him the nickname of "Oily John." He was sure that there had been a misunderstanding and that we both had only the best interests of the company at heart. No, said Mr. Sales Manager, there had been no misunderstanding. I was just a fresh college kid and had asked too many questions. On my part, I denied any intention of rudeness or unjustified curiosity. When a man goes to a doctor, I explained, he could, if he chose to, just say that he wanted an examination, and he would get it. If the doctor should ask what hurt his patient, would that be an impertinent question? And if the patient refused to answer because a good doctor should find that out himself, was he doing himself any good? The sales manager conceded that there was something in what I had said. Anyway, there was no secret about the whole matter, and he might as well tell me. A competitor of ours had undersold us on a big contract, and the price quoted had raised a question regarding the purity of his oil, of which the sample sent me was a specimen.

This explanation greatly simplified my task. At the price our competitors had sold these goods, they could have used only one of two adulterants—gasoline or kerosene. All higher-grade admixtures, such as cottonseed or corn oil, were out. Knowing this, I would be able to have my results in a few hours, whereas it might have taken me days had I been forced to test the oil for the other ingredients. In fact, had I not known that a possible adulteration was suspected, I might have gone off on a different tangent altogether and examined the sample for viscosity, drying and other qualities that had no bearing on this particular case.

I found the oil heavily adulterated with petroleum, and so reported. At that time, no purity laws on linseed oil had as yet been enacted, but there was a law against fraud, and our sales department used it as a club, with telling results. As our competitor's oil was moved out, ours moved in. The victory ended in a little celebration during which the sales manager and I toasted each other. We remained the best of friends ever after.

Linseed oil adulterators, or dopers, as they were commonly called, were a constant thorn in our side. They were selling goods all over the country at prices no legitimate manufacturer could meet. Their activities were centered in the city of Margarite, a western community of considerable size and importance. There they had put everyone else out of business. Every manufacturing plant using linseed oil, every wholesaler, even every little paint store, was covered by their sales campaign. In outlying places they used curious dodges to take away our trade. They would ship two or three barrels of oil into a town, consigned to a fictitious address. Then they would inform a local paint dealer that this merchandise had been shipped in by mistake and that, rather than pay double freight on it, they would let him have it at a discount. The scheme proved so successful that our sales department became frantic, for our business was dropping off in alarming fashion.

At this juncture Mr. Hirst asked me to step in to see if I could remedy the situation. I went out to Margarite and found things worse than I had expected. The dopers evidently were planning a cleanup, for what they were selling was really gasoline adulterated with linseed oil, rather than linseed oil adulterated with gasoline. I made small purchases all over the city and used the laboratory of a local college for my tests. The average composition of what I had collected was one-third linseed oil and two-thirds gasoline, which latter, in the days preceding the automobile, was more or less a waste product. Gasoline was even cheaper than kerosene and sold for less than one-tenth the price of linseed oil.

I tabulated my analytical results and took them to the city attorney; but he refused to take action and referred me to the attorney general in the state capital. This worthy gentleman evidently had been warned of my mission and gave me an unfriendly reception, intimating that I would be lucky to get out of the state without being arrested for defamation of character. I later found that his name was the same as that of the attorney for the dopers. As a last resort, I hunted up the food commissioner, but he was a manufacturer of macaroni and uninterested in anything that did not look like worms.

My mission had been a failure; but on the train back to Chicago, sleepless and smarting under my defeat, I began to form an idea which might turn defeat into victory. I hastened to acquaint Mr. Hirst with my plan. He laughed and told me to go ahead. We had nothing to lose.

A few hours later saw me closeted with the experts of the Underwriters Laboratories. If they would investigate, they might find that highly inflammable and explosive material was being stored in Margarite and the surrounding territory at ordinary insurance rates. This was important to them, if true. Two of their inspectors were immediately dispatched to the scene and purchased samples in many places. Tests showed that most of them caught fire when a match was held to them, while pure linseed oil does not ignite at ordinary temperatures. The fire insurance companies became properly excited when they were apprised of this situation, and cancellations of policies must have clogged the Margarite mail. Mr. Hirst could be depended upon to take care of the publicity. One morning all Margarite papers blazoned forth with headlines such as "Margarite on the Edge of a Volcano," "Greed Threatens to Destroy Lives," and similar scareheads. The dopers packed up their belongings and disappeared. We started doing business again.

Unfortunately, our victory was barren of results. When the worst of the storm was over, our fraudulent competitors crept out into the open again. They changed their letterheads and office addresses and also, with admirable cleverness, their methods of adulteration. Instead of using inflammable naphtha, they turned to less combustible paraffin oil. This made the mixture worse for painting purposes, but took the trump card out of our hands. Without the fire hazard the underwriters were no longer our allies. The operations of the dopers deteriorated into mere fraud, and fraud was not news, especially in the days before the National Pure Food and Drug Law. We had stopped up one rat hole, but we had left the rats unhurt, and plenty of other holes were available for them to hide in, should hiding again become necessary.

As I settled back to my regular duties, I began to get a better understanding of the firm I worked for. The American Linseed Company had been formed, shortly before I entered its employ, by a combination of many flax-crushing mills. Those were the days of big mergers, resulting in such corporations as the United States Steel Corporation, Standard Oil, Amalgamated Copper and others. Our company consisted of seventy-nine linseed oil plants located all the way from San Francisco to New York and from North Dakota to New Orleans. Only nineteen of them were in operation; the rest had been dismantled. Very little cohesion existed among these units and, but for the powerful personality of Mr. Hirst, who was the executive head of the manufacturing end, there would have been still less.

Mr. Hirst had spent his youth as a cowboy in Nebraska and once, when Indian troubles had broken out, was chosen leader of the white settlers. There was no fighting. No one ever fought when Mr. Hirst was around. He knew how to persuade almost anybody to do anything he wanted them to do. He could lower his voice and tell you confidentially something you had read two days before in the papers, and make you believe you had just been made the sole recipient of a state secret. While still a young man, he had been elected state senator, and by and by had drifted into the linseed

143

oil business. He was a clever and prudent mill operator, and the board of directors had made no mistake in giving him his present responsible position.

Mr. Hirst was the shrewdest grain speculator I have ever known. In a quarter of a century during which I watched his operations, he was rarely wrong on the market by more than a small fraction, and he never missed out on an important movement. When he read the daily flax reports aloud to me, which he often did, they meant nothing until he began to interpret them. He could read a whole story between the lines, and his deductions were so clever that listening to him was pure intellectual joy. One day in 1920, when commodity speculation ran rampant, we decided together that flax at six dollars a bushel was too high and formed a little pool to short the market. Prices broke almost immediately, and within two weeks or so had gone down to five dollars and forty cents. I took my profit in a hurry, but not Mr. Hirst. He stuck to the short side until the market fell to a dollar and a half, and thereby made a profit of four dollars and fifty cents a bushel, perhaps an all-time record in grain speculation.

Of all the men at our plant the one I liked best was Charlie, the meal house foreman. Charlie was a man I would cheerfully have backed as Mr. America, if such a contest had been thought of. He was tall, straight, good-looking, intelligent, loyal and dependable. You had a feeling when he was around that nothing could go wrong. Charlie was much in demand as a semi-professional baseball player, but he could tackle any sport and excel in it. I once saw him pick up a tennis racket for the first time and in the next few minutes give a good, experienced player a battle royal. His favorite sport was handball, and he soon had me playing it with fervor. The meal house, where Charlie reigned supreme, was a big, three-story structure built for the storage of meal, the by-product of flax after the oil has been extracted. We turned a section of this structure into a court, and invariably used the noon hour and Sunday forenoons to play a few games. Charlie was a past master at handball and had once beaten the champion fireman of South Chicago. The best score I ever made against him was thirteen against his twenty-one. It was a score that was talked about as something outstanding.

A few years later, when I had taken over the management of the plant, Charlie came to my office one day and asked me to employ a man named Fitz whom he had brought along and who was waiting outside. A request for a favor from Charlie was something unusual.

"What can the fellow do?" I asked.

"Nothing," Charlie replied, and when I looked my question, he added, "but he is the ex-handball champion of Australia." That, of course, altered matters.

"Show him in," I said. Fitz was a medium-sized man with a poker face and arms that hung down his sides like those of an ape. No one ever saw him smile or get excited. He did his work well, but he never talked. No one could find out where he lived. I do not know what Fitz's real name was, and I do not believe anyone else ever knew. As Fitz he went on the payroll, as Fitz he was accepted by the other men, and he was still Fitz when he left us. Whether or not I would employ him depended, of course, on his ability to beat Charlie and me. Fitz only shrugged his shoulders. He would take on Charlie and me as a team, spot us ten points and give us two serves for his one.

Fitz might just as well have given us twenty points as ten, for when he played us we were simply squashed. His balls had a speed that no eye could follow, and he would curve them in mid-air so you could not guess within six feet which way they would carom off. The final score in our first game stood at twenty-one to three, but I have a suspicion that even these three points were due to Fitz's generosity. After that we used every free hour to improve our game, and although not even Charlie could touch Fitz when he got going, we all became better players in the course of time.

Our plant was considered quite a show place, and once a squad of students from a western state university visited us. I showed them around, and when we passed through the meal house one of the boys remarked that one corner looked like a handball court.

"It is a handball court," I assured him.

"Too bad I can't have a little game," he ventured. I told him there was no reason why he could not be accommodated.

"But I am handball champion of our university," he warned me. I remarked that it would be so much less disgrace for us to be beaten. So the coats came off, and the champion with his runner-up

145

battled Charlie and me. They gave us a good fight, but we nosed them out by a small margin. Our opponents did not take their defeat in good grace, and one of them, with a sidelong glance at Charlie, let slip a word about ringers.

"Would you like to play a game of singles with another of our men?" I asked him. Of course he would. Whereupon I sent for Fitz.

The ex-champion slouched in, dirty, unkempt, his long arms swinging stupidly at his sides.

"Do I have to play against *that?*" the student inquired in disgust. Yes, I told him, just *that*. Fitz hung his cap on a nail, pulled up his sleeves, and the game was on. For a few minutes the Australian toyed with the visitor, then I flashed him the sign and he let loose in earnest. This time he fairly outdid himself. These were not balls that were whizzing around, but bullets, crazy bullets that swerved in ungodly curves and sounded like hammer blows when they struck the wall. The college champion missed them not by inches but by yards. Before the game was finished, he put on his coat and quit. He was still shaking his head when I saw the last of him, and I have often wondered what the students said to each other when they were again among themselves.

One of the linseed oil plants operated by our company was run by two of the dourest old Scotsmen known to history, a Mr. McLeod, who was the superintendent, and a Mr. Lawton who had charge of the refinery. There had been no occasion for me to come in contact with either of them, but eventually the necessity arose; it was to cause me much irritation.

Mr. McLeod had been shipping a special grade of refined oil to a varnish plant in a midwestern city. Suddenly a letter arrived from there stating that the steel storage tank holding our oil had rotted through, with the result that several thousand gallons had gone down the sewer. Mr. Hirst instructed me to investigate the matter and rectify it.

At Mr. McLeod's plant I was received disdainfully. He and Lawton had made and refined linseed oil for forty years, and had done it without a young whippersnapper of a chemist sticking his nose into their affairs. He would show me nothing, tell me nothing. All the time while this harangue was being delivered, I wondered.

not at what Mr. McLeod said, but why he always called me "Sammy." My wonder grew when he addressed as "Sammy" a young man I knew as John Reque (now a leader in the linseed oil and white lead industry), and I was utterly flabbergasted when he applied the name to a girl stenographer. I honestly thought the man was crazy, and so reported to Mr. Hirst. From him I learned that "Sammy" was not a name but an abbreviation of "You understand me?" This may have been so, but to me he was Sammy McLeod after that, and that nickname stayed with him until he retired.

Mr. Hirst could have forced the issue, of course, but that was not his way. Instead, he asked me to see the complaining firm and start my investigations from that end. The next morning I was at their place and looked with dismay at the corroded storage tank. It had big, ragged holes in it where the shell had given way, and there was no doubt that the fault was ours. We were in for severe damages.

My mind was full of trouble, but I was temporarily diverted by a meeting with an odd specimen of a varnish maker. He was of a type now unknown and even then practically extinct. This old man would not use a thermometer; he looked upon it with contempt. What kind of a kettle man did I think he was that he could not tell the temperature without a thermometer? I asked naïvely how he did it, and he gave me a demonstration. He used a goose quill, and he knew by the speed with which it curled up how hot the oil was. And what, I asked, did he do when he ran out of goose quills? That did not bother him at all, he said; he would then spit into the oil and estimate its heat by the sound of the sizzle. I went downtown, bought a thermometer and checked him. He never missed the correct temperature, even up to 600°F, by more than ten degrees, and usually came even closer.

When I returned to Chicago I went straight to Sammy McLeod and told him of my findings. The fault was his; blustering would do no good. If he had washed out the excess sulphuric acid from his refined oil, corrosion would not have taken place. I also intimated that I would not particularly care to be in his shoes just then. Sammy surrendered. Perhaps a few peppery letters which had accumulated in his files while I was gone had helped bring about his change of heart. Yes, they were using sulphuric acid, but they had never before found it necessary to wash it out. Would I show them how to do it, and get them out of their troubles?

Get them out of their troubles. How often I was to hear these words in years to come. The world seemed to think that all a man had to do to become omniscient was to walk through doors bearing the inscription, "College," and that a chemical diploma was a key to all the mysteries of the universe. I was glad that few of the people who put their trust in me during my stripling years were aware how little I knew and what utter helplessness often was hidden behind my confident smile.

As far as Sammy's problem was concerned, I felt sure that the excess acid had been the source of his downfall. The question was how to remove it. I tried to wash it out with water, but that was difficult. The water and the oil formed a stubborn emulsion which I could separate only by letting it stand for a long time, thereby tying up the plant. I then figured that the emulsion was due to the small difference between the specific gravities of linseed oil and water, only about six and a half per cent. If I could make the oil lighter or the water heavier, a quicker separation was, theoretically at least, inevitable. The gravity of oil diminishes under heat, while that of water remains about constant. I therefore put steam into the big vat in which I was conducting my experiments; the water did settle more rapidly, but still too slowly. Another discovery that disturbed me was that it required too many washings to remove the acid. The idea then presented itself to remove the acid, not by dilution but by neutralization. Remembering my experience with the Chatonquin River water and the treatment we had used, I threw soda ash into the wash-water. The result was disappointing; enough soap formed through chemical action between the alkali and the oil to form a worse emulsion than before; it resisted all my efforts to break it up.

Sammy McLeod and Lawton hung around me all day long. Very likely they were torn between the hope that I would preserve their jobs for them and the desire to see me make a fool of myself. I am afraid my heart was not without malice either, and I strung out my tests so as to give them time to repent and reform. A doctor had once told me, in a moment of confidence, that if he wanted to charge some patient a high fee he let him wait for his diagnosis. Waiting in trepidation, so the doctor expounded, softened a man's heart and loosened his purse strings. For me it was easy to withhold my prescription because I had none to prescribe, but I found that my mentor had been a clever psychologist. Both my dour Scotsmen became more gentle from day to day.

At last an approach to my problem from a new angle occurred to me. If I increased the weight of the water by loading it up with salt, I might force a separation. I sent to the nearest grocery stores, bought all the salt they had and dumped it into my recalcitrant mixture; it broke up as if by a magic wand. The problem was solved.

To chemists of today my problems of a generation ago must appear ridiculously simple. But in those days I was, so far as I knew, the only trained chemist in America working in this line. There were no books on the subject and I could consult with no other expert. I had read once of a man born on an island who by himself had figured out the multiplication table. Somehow this story came back to me then, and it comes back to me now when I think of my early primitive voyages over uncharted chemical seas.

On one of my first free nights I stole away to call on my friend, the book agent. He lived in a tiny apartment—he called it a hole— on the North Side, and was genuinely glad to see me. It was easy to talk to this man with the weather-beaten face and wise eyes. I believe his name was Bernard, but that is not important. To me he always appeared less an individual than a symbolic figure like Father Time or the Egyptian Sphinx. He was a listener of infinite patience and a speaker who used few words. I told him of all the fun I was having, and that the days which had seemed so long in the beginning were now far too short for me. He did not interrupt me, but failed to respond to my ebullient spirits. His verdict was that I was giving away too much good mental merchandise for too little money. He believed in fair bargains, he said, and I was being taken in by people who took advantage of my inexperience. I remonstrated. One hundred dollars a month was good money, even if I retained only part for myself; it was all I needed, and a surplus meant nothing to me. The old man shook his head.

"At your age," he said, "money means very little; but you will get older, become a married man and have children. You may remain an enthusiastic fool, but I doubt if your wife will be one. You may be satisfied to be a servant of mankind all your life, but your family won't be. What they will want is cash." A servant to mankind; here I had that expression thrown into my teeth again. Had not Doctor Reich said the same thing to us students long ago? Starve to death and hope that they will set up a monument to you with the inscription, "To a Servant of Mankind."

Bernard had been a servant. Yet, when he lost his last job because of old age, it had been the beginning of his real life. Some day I might want to break away and start a business of my own, with my savings as my stake. How much would I have? Nothing. He was willing to bet that there was not a salesman in my company's employ who did not draw more than I did, even if he was only an order taker.

I went home depressed and in deep thought. Money was such a sordid thing to talk about, and I dreaded the prospect of having to ask for a raise.

I had joined the American Chemical Society and attended a meeting of the Chicago section, then held in the Chicago Drug Club. Twenty-five members were considered a fine attendance, but most of the time fewer were present, and sometimes the supper table was set only for eight or ten. But what a fine body of men these early chemists were. The first to greet me, the stranger, was Gus Thurnauer. He always considered it his duty to make newcomers feel at home, and I bestowed upon him my silent blessings. Thurnauer told me that he had started out as a chemist with a smelting company. The firm manufactured, among other products, refined lead for use in paint, and great care had to be taken to select only metal that contained less than five-hundredths of one per cent of bismuth, as otherwise the white lead would have shown a gray tint. When Thurnauer had taken his position, no method for the determination of such minute quantities of bismuth existed, and he had to blaze his own trail. After a few years the smelting works closed up. Instead of looking for another position, Thurnauer went into business for himself, and with a former co-worker as partner, pioneered the manufacture of lead alloys and the die-casting of bronzes. Gustav was the only businessman in our midst, and I looked upon him with mingled respect and curiosity.

The man at the head of the table, whom all revered as the dean of the chemical profession in Chicago, was William Hoskins. He had been active in chemistry as far back as 1881, when only three men in Chicago were following the chemical profession. Bill Hoskins was a man whom no one ever forgot. He was of medium height and slight build; his intelligent face was enlivened by laughing blue eyes. Still in the prime of life, he could look back on an extraordinary career. His formal education had come to a stop after two years of high school training; yet he had been a member of the Illinois State Microscopical Society at the age of fourteen and its secretary three years later. Before Hoskins was twenty, he had invented a furnace which has remained standard equipment in assay laboratories to this day. His scientific curiosity knew no bounds. Chemistry, physics, botany—he was at home with all of them. Over one hundred patents were granted to him during his lifetime; how many ideas he gave away to others no one but he knew. He conducted what he used to call a rainbow factory, where he could allow his imagination free rein. If his dreams could be turned to practical use, he left the commercial development to others; if they could not, it was just as well. His activities covered an incredibly wide range. When he set his mind to work on a problem, it was as if someone had lit a lamp in a dark room. Once he met a billiard champion who claimed that good billiard chalk came only from France. Within a short time Hoskins produced it in better quality from native earth. He helped race-track owners to speed up races, and with equal success advised streetcar companies how to prevent fraud in the use of transfers. Perhaps the outstanding invention worked out in his laboratory was that of heat-resisting wires. Every electric heater, toaster or curling-iron bears the invisible mark of Hoskins' genius.

Most chemists in Chicago considered Hoskins their godfather and came to him for advice on their problems, technical or personal. His reception room was a free dispensary of good cheer, and people who had come in with bowed heads usually walked out with firm and buoyant steps.

151

William Hoskins is dead, but his inventions and the memory of his kindly deeds live on.

After Thurnauer had introduced me to the remainder of the group he gave me a sketchy outline of their backgrounds. The impressive man with the highly intellectual features and graying beard was Professor Julius Stieglitz of the University of Chicago, then engaged in his memorable work on catalysis. The man next to him was Professor Warren Smith of the Lewis Institute. He looked like a teacher in whom students would instinctively place implicit confidence, and from whose lips even the driest subject would become interesting. Dudley French, a young man my own age, with a cheerful face and a hearty laugh, was secretary of the Society; in days to come he would be known as one of the leading experts on the treatment of boiler water. William Brady and Leslie Touzalin were the outstanding iron and steel chemists of the section. I kept away from them. Iron and steel were things I was trying to forget. When I did get better acquainted with them, my vanity received a rude shock. Whereas in Pittsburgh we had been proud of our seven-minute record for analyzing pig iron for silicon and sulphur, they were doing the same work here in five and one-half minutes, merely by superior management. They had grouped all necessary apparatus within easy reach of the analyst, so that from the weighing of the sample to the final drop from his burette he did not have to move around more than three or four feet. Why had this idea never occurred to me?

Brady had studied to be an agricultural chemist and drifted into iron and steel work more or less by accident. He was a tall man with genial ways and a happy disposition which he not only manifested toward strangers but toward his own employees as well. He did not look at all like the popular conception of what a chemist should look like. His assistant Touzalin later invented a gas filter which, with due modesty, he named the Brady Filter, and which not only served the purpose of determining the amount of dust in blast furnace gas, but was also used by industrial cities to ascertain the quality and quantity of dust in municipal atmospheres. Touzalin was destined to become a prominent staff member of the Carnegie-Illinois Steel Corporation, and his inventive genius is still at work, mostly in the field of utilizing slag and other by-products.

'Another of Brady's chemists was Charles Kawin. Ambitious, energetic and resourceful, he was soon established in business for himself, and by and by his laboratories extended over a wide territory. He became one of the best known consulting chemists on foundry practice, and although today he proclaims himself a gentleman-farmer, he still keeps in touch with chemical affairs and nurses in his heart a feeling of gratitude and love for his erstwhile chief and teacher.

Ivan Bregowsky and LaVerne Spring also were introducing metallurgy into foundry work. Bregowsky was a Russian by birth; he had suffered the hardships of Siberian exile near the Arctic Circle, but his experiences had not embittered him. He and his wife were engaged in so many charitable enterprises that people often wondered if they had anything left for themselves. Spring was known to love three things: chemistry, music and children. The future would bring him honorary medals from scientific societies, but I doubt if he got as much pleasure out of them as he did from his non-professional activities.

One of those present was Victor Kadish, a young visitor from Milwaukee. Mr. Kadish had a vision. He wanted to help turn sewage into fertilizer and thereby dispose of the sewage problem from both a sanitary and an economic standpoint. Mr. Kadish lived to see his vision come true, and the sewage disposal system of Milwaukee is today one of the great achievements of chemical engineering.

The packing house industry was represented by a chemist named Richardson. I was a little afraid of Richardson. He did not speak much, had a stern exterior, and was self-contained. I did not know then that the man possessed a sensitive love of art and that his nature photographs would some day be admired at exhibits in America, London, Paris and Tokio. He and Mrs. Richardson were authorities on bird lore, and their collection of pictures, mostly taken in the wild stretches of the Indiana dunes, contained exquisite bits of rare beauty.

It was W. D. Richardson and chemists like him, such as Arthur Lowenstein and Albert Schmidt, who had been prime factors in utilizing everything in a pig but its squeal. The guides at the Yards and Chicago historians always quoted the epigram, but never mentioned the names of these experts who had given it birth. They were making their footprints in the sands of time, although nobody outside the profession took the trouble to notice. Apparently the world was not anxious to either notice or remember chemists. It preferred to name streets, parks and towns for dead real estate speculators rather than for men who had served mankind.

My company was still fighting the dopers. One of them swore to shoot me on sight because, acting on my suggestion, our company had hired a private detective to pick up samples of the doper's deliveries as they were made. These samples had been properly sealed in the presence of the customer and carefully analyzed. Adulteration was plainly established, and the state's attorney's office was prevailed upon to start criminal proceedings. In addition, we had recommended that the customers refuse to pay their bills, guaranteeing that we would defend their cases. The latter precaution was a wise one, for the criminal case was dismissed on a technicality. One of the civil suits then came up for a hearing, and our lawyers summoned me as their expert witness.

I confess that I was scared. I had never been in a courtroom or faced a judge, but I had heard a great deal about gruelling cross-examinations and the uncanny cleverness of the lawyers who conducted them. Hoskins, I knew, had a reputation as an expert in court cases, and from what I had heard, he would rather aid a young man in distress than do anything else. Hoskins was a successful consulting chemist in more ways than one.

I called on my colleague, and he put me at ease at once. In his characteristically genial manner he told me that he, too, once had been afraid of cross-examiners, until someone told him a story about General Grant's first campaign. When Grant saw the bayonets of the opposing force glint in the distance, his heart almost failed him. Then he started to reason with himself. If he were frightened, would not the enemy be equally so? Now, on the witness stand, Mr. Hoskins commented, the expert really had all the advantages. He knew the field better than the opposing lawyer and he was in the trenches awaiting the attack. This was good advice, and it often had a steadying effect on me afterward, when fear threatened to unnerve me.

Mr. Hoskins told me some of his own court experiences. At one time when he was a young man he had been opposed by an elderly, gray-bearded expert whose appearance oozed dignity and wisdom. Hoskins was asked by his lawyer to note on paper any mistakes the bewhiskered one might make during his direct examination; but at its conclusion the sheet was empty.

"Has he made no mistakes at all?" Hoskins was asked by his attorney.

"None," was the reluctant reply. The case seemed hopeless.

"Doctor," the lawyer addressed the witness, "have you made no mistake in the statements you have given to the jury?"

"I have made no mistake," the witness asserted.

"Are you sure?"

"I am positive."

"Doctor," the cross-examiner said suavely, "have you ever in your life made a mistake?"

"Never," was the reply. The lawyer turned to the jury.

"Behold here," he said, "the only man I have met who has never in his life made a mistake." There was general laughter. Everyone knew that the case was over.

"Suppose the old chemist had answered, 'Yes, I have made mistakes,'" Hoskins questioned, "what would have been the result?"

"I had him either way," the lawyer laughed. "In that case I would have asked him how he could be sure of being right this time if he had been mistaken before."

Many were the times this anecdote was discussed in chemical circles, and many were the suggestions offered as to the best answer to that tricky question. I never heard one, however, that seemed quite adequate.

In another case Hoskins was on the witness stand when the opposing attorney brought in a dozen formidable-looking books.

"This book," he announced, selecting one, "was written by Professor Smith of Columbia University. Do you consider Professor Smith an expert on this subject?"

"I do not," Hoskins answered. He had never even heard of either the man or the book.

"I have here a book by Professor Jones of Harvard," the lawyer continued. "You consider him an expert, don't you?"

"Indeed not," was the reply.

In this fashion the whole set of books was brought forth and disposed of.

"If you don't consider these authors experts," the lawyer finally exploded, "whom on earth do you consider one?"

"Myself," Hoskins replied, smiling.

When the doper's case came up for trial, I was not nearly so panicky as I had expected and acquitted myself tolerably well. We gained a complete victory, but it was not due to my brilliance, nor even to the merit of our case. The other side had sent samples of the oil to an out-of-town laboratory and submitted the analyses as evidence. The mistake they made was that they constantly referred to the laboratory and not to their chemists. Our lawyer refused to cross-examine, much to my surprise. When his turn came, he contended that a laboratory was a room with four walls and not an intellectual entity. How could a room analyze a sample or give an opinion? The Court had not been shown any connection between the room and any chemist, and the presentation of such evidence was utterly worthless. The judge agreed, and we won hands down, but I could find little joy in my heart. I felt that my first case had been won on a foul.

The campaign against the dopers kept me fairly busy. Gertie now did all the analytical work, for which she was eminently fitted. She was clean, accurate, conscientious and had little imagination, qualities which are essential for the establishment of facts. Soon I had to add another young lady to the staff, and a high school boy joined us shortly afterward. For me, trouble-shooting of all sorts became the order of the day. Our refinery in North Dakota showed too large a percentage of losses, our plant in eastern Ohio wanted to erect a laboratory, a dealer in Missouri complained that our oil would not dry properly. The trip to North Dakota has remained in my memory, for I was arrested for walking on the street without an overcoat when the temperature was twenty-five below zero and a fifty-mile gale was howling across the prairies. The police were about to turn me over to the psychopathic clinic, especially when they discovered that I was wearing only summer underwear, but I talked them out of it. I did almost freeze to death, though. Our mill was located a mile beyond the end of the streetcar line, and I just made it, walking against that subzero windstorm. Another twenty-five yards would have been the end of me. When I got into the plant I was so frozen that I lay down on a radiator to thaw out. As a child I had once, to my mother's horror, brought home a white mouse, stiff with cold and apparently dead. In my despair I had lit a fire in the stove and put the mouse on it. Suddenly the little thing let out a squeak, jumped off and raced around the kitchen, whether with pain or the joy of living I never decided. I thought of that experience as I lay there, unable to move a limb or even to explain my presence to the men who assembled around me. Some of them had the good sense to rub my body, and gradually I returned to normal again.

Our fight against the dopers was like Hercules' fight against the Hydra. We slew one firm and two others would spring into existence. Selling gasoline or kerosene at linseed oil prices was so profitable that it presented a continual temptation. I was getting pretty much discouraged, but Mr. Hirst took a calmer view of the matter. He thought the dopers would eventually hang themselves, if they were given enough rope. He was right, as usual, and the time of the hanging was not far off.

One day I received a letter from the state's attorney of Ohio asking me to call on him. The state was willing to pay my expenses and a reasonable fee. The next day saw me in the state capital closeted with some high officials. It appeared that a particularly daring firm of dopers had sold a quantity of adulterated linseed oil to the State of Ohio. They might have got away with it but for an unforeseen development. Part of the oil had been used to paint the buildings of the state university, and the paint had peeled off within three months. The professors of chemistry had observed this phenomenon with amazement, had analyzed the oil and discovered the swindle. The state's attorney not only wanted me to help in the prosecution, but I was also to help draw up a law to make further depredations of this sort impossible. He knew pretty much about my past experiences and, I suppose, had no one else with whom to consult. I was naturally delighted with the assignment. The state's attorney was young and filled with great zeal; so were the food commissioner and the few state senators who sat in on our deliberations. It would have been better had some older and wiser heads counseled us. As it was, I practically dictated the chemical section of the bill, while some professors of chemistry nodded their approval. I stuck in all the specifications I could, restricting the oil as to iodine, saponification and other values, and closing, so I thought, every loophole through which a doper might crawl back into the business.

On my way home I stopped at Cleveland. Our representative there, Mr. William Harshaw, was a man who had always impressed me as somebody worth knowing. Sometime before, when I had been with the company only a few months, a meeting of all sales representatives had been called in Chicago. Mr. Hirst had invited me too, so I could answer any technical questions that might arise. As I listened to the talk at this meeting I was astonished at the inane remarks and the general lack of coherence in the conversation. It seemed to me that everyone present talked about something different, and no subject was ever threshed out to a conclusion. In between I listened to plenty of poker stories and other irrelevant drivel. Mr. Harshaw had been almost the only one there who hewed to the line and contributed something substantial. He was not to stay with our company long. Although I never met him again, I read about him frequently in later years as the head of one of the largest chemical enterprises in the Middle West.

It was this Mr. Harshaw on whom I now called. I wanted his praise more than that of anyone else. To my disappointment, he was disinclined to give it. He thought the bill was entirely too complicated; in his opinion, laws should demand only that materials be pure; let each dealer defend his goods on this simple ground, and let the administrative part of the state governments take care of the chemical specifications.

I was completely crushed. It was too late now to make any changes, and the bill became a law as we had drawn it up. Before long Mr. Harshaw's views were vindicated. The dopers had little trouble confusing both lawyers and juries with the chemical terms we had used and, what was worse, they made up combinations which were not pure linseed oil but met all its analytical specifications. Aside from that, the linseed oil used by the trade changed rapidly from that time on. Whereas up to 1906, when this law was enacted, the United States had been exporting flaxseed, this condition reversed itself and we had to import flax from Argentina. The oil from South America differed from our domestic product and did not conform to our standards. The Ohio statute was copied by many other states, and I am sure that much linseed oil was sold which, although pure, violated the letter of the various state laws. It was a matter of man-made laws vs. Mother Nature. To put a law on the books is not difficult, but it is almost impossible to remove it. Not until 1927 did the State of Illinois, for instance, bring its statute up to date with the altered conditions. I do not know how many other states, if any, have since followed suit.

The Ohio Pure Linseed Oil Law would scarcely have been passed so easily but for the great pioneer work on food and drug adulteration done by Dr. Harvey Wiley and his associates prior to that time. Inspection of foods had been practically unknown until 1886, when the Bureau of Internal Revenue assumed authority over oleomargarine and butter, due to a tax law enacted in that year. The only interest the government had in the matter was the collection of taxes, and in this particular legislation, strange to say, the purpose was not so much to collect revenue as to tax out of existence certain products, such as colored oleomargarine. By and by other edibles were added to the list over which the Internal Revenue Department took jurisdiction, such as tea, cheese, flour and vinegar. Unfortunately, there were then few accepted standards of purity, and still fewer reliable methods of analysis. Hence adulterators were still able to flood the market with inferior or fraudulent foods and drugs, thereby reaping unholy profits.

The end of this deplorable state of affairs was in the offing, however. In 1883, a middle-aged chemist named Harvey W. Wiley had come from Indiana to Washington to head the Department of Chemistry. Surrounding himself with a few enthusiastic young helpers, he was to become the Nemesis of the food and drug brigands.

It took Dr. Wiley twenty years to organize the forces of law and decency. As chairman of the Committee on Food Standards of the Association of Official Agricultural Chemists, he first set up clear-cut definitions and analytical methods and thereby hit obliquely at the despoilers. By 1906 the country was ripe for a change, and Dr. Wiley undertook to convert Congress to his views. His appearance before the Interstate Commerce Committee was a milestone in human progress; in chemical circles it was talked about for many years. His assistants had worked for weeks preparing exhibits and selecting books of references; in fact, they were forced to hire a horse and truck to carry this material to Capitol Hill for the hearing. But when Dr. Wiley presented his arguments, he did not use a single exhibit or book. He had all his data in the back of his mind, and his two-day speech before a hesitant committee was one of the greatest orations ever delivered in a Congressional chamber. Had it been on a political subject, it would be classed with the speeches of Clay, Webster or Calhoun. But Wiley was only an underpaid chemist fighting for the health of his country. What a three-thousand-dollar-a-year public servant had to say could not be worthy of immortality.

After the Federal statutes had put food manufacturers under restraint, Dr. Wiley became the relentless scourge of all offenders, big and little alike. A guilty member of the fraternity once rushed to Washington to seek protection under the wing of a highly placed political friend. As his automobile passed the Bureau of Chemistry, a tire blew out. At this moment Dr. Wiley happened to emerge from the laboratory. Recognizing his discomfited victim, he stepped up to him and said, "You see, a fellow can get by everything in this city except the Bureau of Chemistry." It proved to be so in this case, and in all subsequent cases as well.

Among Wiley's disciples was a young chemist named Lucius Tolman, whom I came to know well. He had won his spurs in the study of aging whiskies and was the first to demonstrate that preservatives in food products could be dispensed with through plant sanitation. I met Mr. Tolman in Chicago when he was chief of the U. S. Central Inspection District, and found in him a colleague who lent a willing hand in the testing of a new analytical method I was sponsoring. He would have aided anyone suggesting an improvement or advancement anywhere, any time. Some day the packing house industry would find in him one of its most prominent leaders in scientific research. I was also able to enlist Tolman's support in our campaign against the linseed oil dopers, who were still far from beaten.

A CHEMICAL POTPOURRI

THE NEXT YEAR saw me in Vienna on a short visit. With the exception of my mother, who kept telling me what she-devils women were, the whole town seemed to be anxious to see me married off. My sister Helene's former chief, Mr. Pompl, the rich wine merchant and stable owner, was in the vanguard of the conspirators. He invited me to his office, "just for old times' sake," and then asked me the most intimate questions about myself. After I had answered him, he announced his decision.

"You can command a dowry of at least fifty thousand dollars," he declared. "Maybe we can stretch that a little. You are entitled to a good-looker, too. When do you expect to settle down?"

I could not help thinking of a bath-house keeper in Poland from whom I had once tried to rent a bathroom and who had wanted to know whether I liked it blonde or brunette. But Mr. Pompl spoke in so businesslike a manner and was so convinced that he was acting in my interest, that I could not get angry. I asked him jokingly if he had pictures of any such girls around. No, he had no pictures handy, but he would make one date after another for me, and with such finesse that the young lady would never know she was being looked over. I fled.

Curiosity prompted me to find out what had become of my former schoolmates. What I discovered confirmed my worst fears. They were scattered all over eastern Europe, mostly in little villages few people had ever heard of, and the names of which still fewer could pronounce. I visited only one of my friends, a husky chap with whom I had been quite chummy during our college days. He was employed in an out-of-the-way place where they spoke a gut-

161

tural tongue in which I did not even know the difference between yes and no. As our train neared its destination, the conductor handed each passenger a red card printed in several languages and containing the announcement that the district had been officially pronounced syphilitic. Proper precautions, described in detail, were recommended. My old college mate assured me that life in that neck of the woods was not worth living. His first position had been in a country where at least the female population had been attainable. According to him, the girls working in the factory had considered it an honor to sleep with chemists or other higher ranking officials, and when a girl had been so chosen, she wore a rose in her hair the next morning for all the world to see. Now, what fun was there in a lousy spot on the map like the one we were in if you took sex away? You could not play cards or get drunk all the time during your spare hours, even if the local plum brandy was cheap as mud.

One of my classmates had never moved away from Vienna. I was particularly interested in him because we had known each other since boyhood. His name was Bortschutsch, and he was quite as queer as his name. After he had graduated as a chemist he decided he did not know enough to face the world. Hence he made up his mind to take a course in civil engineering. When he got through with that he found that he should know more about plant architecture. When I met him he was planning to go to South America, where the chances for chemists were said to be particularly good. So he took up Spanish and Portuguese. I did not see him again until he was a man of forty. He had at last found his niche in life as a clerk in the patent office. His business was to open the mail and assort it. The letters were in many languages and touched on all kinds of subjects, and Bortschutsch was just the man to handle the job. It paid him twenty dollars a month. His prospects for advancement were nil, he told me, but—and here he smiled happily—there was not one chance in a thousand that anyone could or would want to displace him. Unless Bortschutsch was killed in the World Wars, he is probably still assorting letters for the Austrian patent office, if there is one left.

Upon my return to the United States, Mr. Moulton, the manager of the plant in which our laboratory was located, handed in his resignation. Thenceforth I took charge of both the mill and the laboratory. My salary was increased to one hundred and seventy-five dollars a month.

The new responsibility which had thus been suddenly put on my shoulders was not one which I could take lightly. Each of our nineteen buildings had a foreman, and the roster of employees contained about a hundred names. Up to this time I had been considered merely one of the foremen, but now I had become manager of the entire plant, and I suspected that obstacles would be thrown in my way. Gertie also was fully aware of the threatening danger. Even her father, the superintendent, would not be easy to handle, she warned me. As between her father and me Gertie's loyalty never wavered. I had championed her and made her what she was, my all-round assistant with a nice salary, and now she was going to stand with me at whatever cost.

Signs of the impending storm confronted me everywhere. The chief engineer, who always played endless games of solitaire, did not look up from his cards when I came in on my rounds. I took his deck, threw it out of the door, and told him it was a disgrace for a man of his standing to use such dirty cards. One of my foremen I found asleep on a bench; perhaps he was entitled to a little rest, but I took a pitcher of water and poured it over him. Before he had a chance to say anything, I offered him an alarm clock. He was still scratching his head when I left him.

The real battle was yet to come. Ted, the British ex-seaman who had charge of the filtering plant, was the only man who knew the location of the many pipelines which led to and from his domain. This prerogative had never been questioned, but it gave him an undue advantage. Therefore I requested Mr. Stock to get a map of these lines so that the office might have a permanent record of them. Gertie's father did not think Ted would give up his secret. What was more, he thought Ted was right.

"Mr. Stock," I said, "here are my orders. You will tear up all lines to and from the filter house and re-lay them. You will furnish a drawing of these lines to me, and to me only. After we get through with this job, I alone will know the layout, and anyone who wants to get information will come to me." I dictated these instructions to Gertie and told her to hand a copy to her father. Then I went out and fired the first foreman who crossed my path. He happened to be Billy, the foreman of the cooperage shop. I rehired him a few months later, and afterwards he was in my employ for thirty-odd years, until I pensioned him. I was sorry to make him the scapegoat, but war is war, and I was out to win this one.

From that day on everyone in the plant knew who was boss, and soon all of us were again on the friendliest terms. What began to worry me now was the safety of the men and girls entrusted to my guardianship. We had a quarter of a million gallons of highly inflammable naphtha circulating through the plant, and I shuddered to think what a single spark might do. The recommendations of the insurance companies were obeyed to the letter, but they were not strict enough for me. What good, for instance, were fire extinguishers in our case? Except under rare circumstances, we would be blown into eternity before we could use them. Why should we be sure of proper ventilation? If a leak in a naphtha pipe occurred, ventilation might make matters worse, for dense naphtha fumes are only inflammable, while diluted ones are explosive. I decided to adopt my own measures of protection. First, I ordered the men to shed their footwear at the gate and put on rubber shoes. This eliminated the danger of hobnailed soles coming into contact with metallic parts. I also had each workman examined for cigarettes and matches before he was admitted. Next, motors were removed from the buildings and put into outside sheds, and all electric light bulbs were encased in double wire nettings. Individual switches which might throw sparks were taken out, and all power and light was controlled from a distant place where naphtha fumes were not likely to penetrate.

In spite of all these precautions I did not sleep well. One night I went back to the mill, and as I walked through the percolator building, where the extraction process was carried on, I heard a workingman excitedly yell to someone to turn off a valve. This incident gave me something new to worry about. Suppose one of our Polish workmen was caught in an emergency; he might lapse into his native tongue, as people under sudden stress are likely to do, and his call would not be understood. No, this would not do. In this building, at least, only English- or American-born men could work. A notice to that effect was posted immediately.

The next morning I had a strike of the Polish crew on my hands. Mr. Stock came in and told me that a deputation was waiting to see me. I was quite willing to receive them, and soon they trooped in, strong, stalwart, dark-complexioned figures, with scowling faces, twirling their caps in their hands in a mixture of embarrassment and defiance. Then they all started to talk at once. They were good men, they said, had worked hard, had families, too. I tried to tell them they were not fired, only transferred, but they remained sullen. The work they were doing was the work they wanted, nothing else.

"Me strike," said the leader, and the rest of them echoed, "Me, too." No matter how I argued, they kept harping on the same refrain. I sparred desperately for time to give them an opportunity to cool off. Think as I might, however, no workable plan occurred to me. Then an idea flashed through my mind; if I could talk in Polish to these men, I felt I could handle them. Unfortunately, I could think of no Polish except swear words. But I had heard my mother say once that Polish and Czech were so similar that they were mutually understandable if spoken slowly. I would try it, anyway. I waved the men back as if I were going to make an important announcement.

"*Přijdte zítra,*" (return tomorrow) I said. For a moment they all stood like statues; then pandemonium broke loose.

"*Pan boss mówi po polsku,*" (the boss speaks Polish) they yelled, slapping their thighs and jumping up and down like children. Then they crowded around me, telling me it was *jutro,* boss, and not *zítra,* and wouldn't I say it again? Gone were their scowls and their threatening attitudes. They were as happy as boys and swore they would back me against all comers. I later had occasion to find out that they meant it. A plan which satisfied everybody was quickly evolved, and they all went enthusiastically about their new jobs.

The year 1907 was ushered in with great promises of prosperity. Everybody who could make the headlines predicted good times. Yet, wise ears could already hear the rumblings of an approaching crash. In the early spring the stock market plunged down violently. The papers called it a rich man's panic and tried to minimize its importance. A Chicago daily printed a cartoon showing a man in overalls going to work in a factory where every chimney was belching smoke. On his arm he carried one of those full dinner pails which was then the favorite slogan of politicians. In a far-off corner stood two speculators, bent over a stock ticker, tearing their hair. The workingman pointed at them with a smile. Their troubles meant nothing to him.

A few months later the storm broke. Factories shut down right and left, banks of importance closed their doors and, although the cartoonist did not portray it, the smile had presumably left the workingman's face. The stock market registered new lows every day, no one seemed to know why. An enterprising reporter crashed the office of a Wall Street king, to get his private opinion; the great financier declared laconically that evidently there were more sellers than buyers, which did not exactly clarify the situation.

I did not own any stocks, but at our plant we had plenty of trouble. The banks had stopped paying out currency, and we were driven to use checks. None of us relished this departure from the established routine. The men complained that they had to pay usurious discounts to get their checks cashed in saloons; the wives protested that their husbands spent more than they brought home, and I was unhappy because I could not balance the company's cash book. Our checks were considered the prize circulating medium in South Chicago and were being used as money. When we did get them back we often could not make out the original names or amounts, and the endorsements were so numerous that they overflowed to the face of the check.

I had to take a trip to Cleveland during those turbulent days, but our bank would give me only twenty dollars in money; the rest I had to take in Clearing House Certificates. In Cleveland no one wanted this Chicago currency, so I lived for days on peanuts and apples.

The panic of 1907 did much damage among my friends in Chicago. People were laid off everywhere, wages were cut, hours reduced. There were bankruptcies, soup kitchens and all the other backwash that follows a financial upheaval of magnitude. It seemed to me that, on the whole, people took their misfortunes in good humor. They ate cheap cuts of meat instead of steak, wore out their old clothes and took any job that offered itself at any price.

My book-canvassing friend apparently enjoyed the lean year. He now sold dime novels instead of dollar books and had in his stock pamphlets on how to live on nothing and be happy. The Americans of 1907 were a hardy race and asked no favors.

My newly found uncle suffered severely from the depression. Building operations were at a standstill, and his glazing business was sorely beset. Yet he and his family viewed the setback philosophically. In place of *Wiener Schnitzel* we now had goulash for supper when I visited there, but it was as tasty as any dish at the Auditorium Hotel. At least I supposed so, for I had never eaten at that elegant hostelry, which was then my idea of the last word in Chicago luxury. With the exception of Elsie, all the children were working. Even Hans, a child of eleven, kept a lemonade stand in front of the house and dished out drinks at a penny a cup.

It was on one of the visits to my relatives that I witnessed a peculiar accident. I was standing at a street corner, waiting to transfer, when I heard the siren of a fire engine; a few seconds later, a fire truck drawn by three horses rushed out from its quarters half a block away, heading toward the crossing. A streetcar had been standing at the nearby corner and had just started across the street when the engine thundered into it. There was a crash, followed by an ominous silence. A moment later a second engine was driven by. In the middle of the crossing, an overturned fire truck, three mangled horses, and a badly damaged streetcar formed a tragic heap. The tongue of the truck had gone completely through the streetcar and injured several people. Police soon appeared on the scene and cleared up the wreckage. The wounded were taken to a nearby hospital; the poor horses had to be shot where they lay. A police inspector took the names and addresses of bystanders and then ordered the crowd to disperse.

I tried to dismiss the ghastly scene from my mind and had almost succeeded when, several weeks later, I was requested to appear in the law office of the traction company. A shrewd-looking attorney questioned me about my recollection of the crash. Had I seen it from the very beginning? Had the fire engine given the proper signal to clear the street? Could the driver of the truck have stopped in time to avoid the collision? I could see the drift of his thoughts. Either the streetcar company or the city was guilty of negligence, and whoever stood convicted would be liable for considerable damages. I answered his questions to the best of my ability, but when he thanked me and bade me goodbye I suggested that he let me ask a question or two. My vis-à-vis gave me a queer look, but told me to suit myself. Did he know, I inquired, that the fault lay entirely with the driver of the fire truck and that I could prove it by indisputable evidence? My host jumped from his chair and came over to me.

"If you can do that, young man," he said, "you can have anything within reason from our company. But you'll have to show me."

I drew a sketch of the scene on a piece of paper. The first question on which the case hinged, I believed, was this: had the streetcar been standing or moving when the collision occurred? It had been standing; it had come to a complete stop at the time the fire truck had approached the crossing. Not only had I seen this, but it could be demonstrated. The tongue of the truck had left a hole on each side of the car; if the car had been standing still, both holes would be equidistant from the front platform; if they were not, the car had been in motion. I had measured the distance and therefore knew that the motorman had stopped instantly and that the car had been motionless when the crash occurred.

The attorney became quite excited. He called up the car barns and, on finding that the car had not yet been repaired, caused the measurements to be retaken. They were in conformity with my statement. He was about to express his gratitude when I waved him aside. Was the traction company's lawyer aware that a second fire truck had dashed by less than a minute afterward? He was not, had not inquired about it. Well, there had been one, and it had cleared the wreckage at full speed, proving that with proper skill the first driver likewise could have gone around the streetcar.

The attorney arose from his chair.

"I withdraw my former offer," he said slowly. "Will you give up whatever it is that you are doing and work for me as an investigator?"

I declined laughingly. I might not be equally lucky next time, and besides, I was fairly well off where I was.

"Very good," were the lawyer's parting words. "If you ever need me, call on me. I shall not forget you."

product, and our own experts had testified that it was linseed oil, pure linseed oil by inference, for they had said nothing about its being adulterated. It would be a joke long to be remembered.

Before I went on the stand I had the state's attorney impound the samples as court exhibits, and when I was asked the same questions as my predecessors, I refused to give any opinion at all. I was an analytical chemist, I protested, not a crystal-gazer, and I worked with chemical tools, not with my eyes and nose. The more the cross-examiner pounded me, the more I ridiculed the idea of handing out snap judgment as an expert opinion. He finally gave up. Now came our counterstroke. We put the doper on the stand and asked him to identify the three samples. He squirmed and twisted, but under relentless grilling he admitted that the linseed oil sample represented his own merchandise, as I had suspected. This admission finished his case. We had a sample of his oil sworn to by himself and obtained an adjournment until it could be tested. By the time the analysis came through, our opponents had fled the state. Whether or not the fraud charge against them was pressed I do not know.

This amusing experience created quite a stir in the state. I was invited to meet the governor, who asked me to help draw up a new law to protect the public against similar impositions in the future. We stopped up another loophole by limiting the amount of drier; but my inadequate Ohio law still clung to me like a millstone, and the new statute was still far from perfect.

I had hardly returned to Chicago when I was asked by another governor to appear before his state legislature and argue for a linseed oil law. One state after another then followed in quick succession. I visited about fifteen state capitals within a few months and became a fairly proficient lobbyist. My usual course was to first enlist the support of the state university. The chemical faculty always went along with me to a man, and with this local phalanx on my side, we easily overrode all opposition. The only real fights I had on my hands were in Kansas and Pennsylvania. I must have traveled back and forth a dozen times between Lawrence, the seat of the Kansas State University, and Topeka, the capital, and I thought nothing of getting professors out of bed in the middle of the night to jump into the fray. I commuted between Philadelphia and Harrisburg for two weeks before I overcame all obstacles. Twice daily I ate banana fritters, which the railroad diner always served with its meals. I shall remember them long after I have forgotten the remainder of this episode.

The uniform success which had attended me so far made me over-confident. I requested and received permission to invade the enemy's own state, where the doper was a well-known personage of great political power. I soon discovered that I was as welcome as the plague; even the university professors were distant or downright antagonistic. Only the state chemist, a young daredevil who had no political aspirations, was on my side; he was of great help to me by tipping me off to many of the opponent's machinations. I got my bill introduced both in the House and in the Senate, but then an invisible wall arose through which I could not break. One time at supper a stranger joined me and asked if I was an oil chemist. When I gave an affirmative answer (with reservations which I kept to myself), he inquired if I knew that it took grease to make the wheels go 'round. After which solemn statement he left my table. On another occasion I was discreetly warned to get out of town or take the consequences. One night I found a ticket to Chicago tacked on the bureau in my room and attached to it a hundred-dollar bill. I turned ticket and money over to the hotel detective, who probably kept **both**.

Day followed day, but no committee hearing was held. I was dying with ennui, but I could wait if others could. Then, one evening after I had gone to bed, an anonymous phone call aroused me to action. The committee was holding a hearing in the middle of the night and, in spite of its promise to notify me, had failed to do so. At the capitol the state chemist was waiting for me and conducted me to the committee room. I cannot truthfully say that the members present were glad to see me. At the head of the table sat a ruddy-faced, fat saloon-keeper from the capital's vice district, and at his side my old enemy, the doper, and his attorney, with whom I had battled in previous cases. I was curious to see what would happen.

The chairman asked me politely enough to state my case. He then held a whispered conversation with his two neighbors and rose.

"The law you propose," he announced ponderously, "would allow four per cent drier in boiled oil. Drier is not boiled oil, therefore

172

it is an adulterant. The people of this glorious state"—here his voice rose and he pounded the table—"are entitled to one hundred per cent pure oil, and by God, they are going to get it!"

Thunderous applause. I felt like joining in it. I could understand, suddenly, the satisfaction there is in losing when you are being laid low by a master stroke. I left, because any further effort on my part would have been a waste of time. In the hall the doper caught up with me.

"Why don't you let up and call it quits, son?" he said to me. "You have licked me all over the country. Can't you leave me alone in my home state? A fellow's got to make a living, doesn't he?"

I saw my old enemy once again, many years later, in a mountain hotel somewhere out West. He had suffered a paralytic stroke and had to be wheeled around in a chair. When he saw me he held out his hand. I had fought clean, he said, and it had been fun while it lasted. The whimsical smile of a dying man played on his lips, and when he wished me all the luck in the world, I believe he meant it.

Life at the plant had settled down to a routine existence. During the depression I had been told to lay off most men, but I had gone to the mat for them and blocked this injudicious move. As a result, all the men were now for me, heart and soul. I often sat down with one or another of them and by and by got to know them intimately. There were some curious characters among them. Ted, the foreman of the filter room, had been in the Boer War and was full of adventurous stories which he related in quaint British accents. Then we had Tim in the refining room, a tall, red-faced man who was universally addressed as the Chief, because he looked like an Indian. Tim could talk by the hour, not on what he had done, but on what he could do, if he had the chance. His fellow workers laughed at him behind his back, but later I got him a salesman's job, and his ready tongue proved to be a good money-maker for him and his employer.

Albert Stock, the superintendent, was also quite an interesting person. Quiet and unobtrusive, he was a wonderful mechanic and shrewd in his way. He had a knack of mixing his men so that neither too much animosity nor too much intimacy grew up among them.

Over a squad of Irishmen he would put a Swedish foreman, over a Polish crew an Irishman, and he knew just what reaction was likely to result from the commingling of different nationalities in given proportions. A small, short-legged man, he was always accompanied by a dachshund which looked and walked exactly like his master, with serious mien and slow, deliberate steps. This dachshund, named Jack, commanded general respect. No one could become familiar with him; he ignored men and beasts alike. But one day a miserable-looking white cur strolled into the yard, hungry for food and love, and Jack's heart softened. The newcomer, called Nellie, became Jack's inseparable companion. She adored him and even tried to imitate his walk, which would have been comical had not an almost human touch invested her behavior.

One of our young engineers, a handsome boy named Harry, was much tangled up in matters of the heart. One morning when I came out to work, there was no Harry. A police squad had pulled into the yard and hauled him off. No one knew what the charge was, but Harry had left an ardent call for help. I went to the station house and found the boy behind the bars, sad and sober. Harry was accused of an affair with a young lass who, finding herself pregnant, had taken this drastic step to remind her lover that she expected to be married.

I got Harry out on bail and took him to a lawyer. According to law, I found that a substantial bond for the benefit of the expected child would keep my man out of jail. I arranged for the bond and let the matter drop. That was not the end of the story, though. When the baby was born, it looked so much like its father that Harry, a trifle shamefaced, expressed his willingness to become a husband and settle down. Just when all arrangements had been made, the baby died. That was the end of Harry's one serious romance. He remained a bachelor for the rest of his life.

In the boiler room we had a man who was considered queer. He was about fifty-five years old, never spoke unless spoken to, never laughed, and talked more like a college man than a coal heaver. For years I just nodded to him, for he did not invite companionship. One day when the boilers were down and he had nothing to do, I found him sitting on a bench looking out over the Calumet River with such an expression of sadness as I have seldom seen on a man's face. He moved over and asked me to sit down. For a few moments we remained silent. Then, as if driven by an inward force he could not resist, he told me his story.

Once upon a time, many years before, he had been an engineer and had worked himself up to a fine position. Life had been good to him. He had married, was the father of two children, and as happy as anyone in the world. One day he took a customer to a restaurant, and as he handed his hat to the check girl his heart skipped a beat. He did not know what had happened to him, but he felt that this young woman would be the turning-point in his life. He would conquer her if it took all he had. From that moment he devoted his time and resources to his love-making. The check girl, bewildered by a passion the like of which she probably had never encountered outside of moving pictures, insisted on marriage. She was a divorcee with a twelve-year-old daughter, and a good woman, she said.

The engineer fought a furious battle with himself, but lost. He divorced his wife, left his children, sacrificed his position, gave up everything. Within a few months of their first meeting the two were married. The day after his wedding the bridegroom, torn by a longing to see his wife, left work early and came home in the afternoon. Taking three steps at a time, he rushed to the bedroom. Before it stood his stepdaughter, who told him that her mother was resting and could not be disturbed. He brushed the youngster aside, stormed into the room and found his bride in bed with another man.

That was the end of his story. He only added that he prayed for two things every night: that his first wife and children were happy, and that he might die. His second wish was fulfilled soon afterward. When our plant blew up he was one of those who went with it; not a shred of him was ever found.

The mating of Jack and Nellie was crowned by the birth of a single beautiful little dog which Gertie and I adopted. We called her Annie. A dog fancier would have hesitated to place her, for she had many strains in her. Annie became the apple of our eyes. She soon knew every corner in the office, the laboratory and the plant. From her parents she learned the art of stalking and catching rats, and when this trio went a-hunting it was a bold rodent who dared leave his hole.

175

Annie lived to a ripe old age, then wandered away and was not returned to us, despite the fantastically large rewards we offered. We had kept one of her pups, a black, velvety female called Bessie, on whom we now poured all our affection; but Bessie was poisoned by someone, and although I called our family physician to save her, she died. After that, neither Gertie nor I ever owned dogs again. It was too heartbreaking to lose them.

Our plant swarmed with rats and mice who waxed fat on the oil and oil cake on the ground. Rat-catching became the natural sport of all workers, and strict rules were set up for this continuous warfare. When the dogs were hunting, for instance, no human interference was allowed. I once saw a rat escape from a pile of bags which the dogs were besieging at the wrong end. One of the men called to the dogs, and the rat was caught. For this unfair act the man's lunch-box was thrown to the rodents as a peace offering. When rats were caught in traps they were not drowned; instead, they were given a chance for their lives. They were let loose in the yard, with the dogs so far behind them that escape was just possible. Once in a while some forty or fifty rats were thrown into a big empty vat and set against one of the dogs. If the rats had ganged up on their enemy, they could have made short work of him, but they never did. In a few minutes the dog killed them all, while the two dogs outside set up such a howl that one would have thought they, not the rats, were being slaughtered.

Whenever we caught mice or rats, it was interesting to watch their behavior. A mouse, caught in a cheese-baited trap, would invariably cower, broken-hearted, and never touch the bait. A rat acted quite differently. He would calmly eat the cheese, and then glare at us with hatred and defiance. I usually released the animals that had been so caught. The mice could hardly be induced to leave; the rats, on the other hand, would rush out at once, hunt a hole, and sometimes even glare back before they disappeared. Rats surely were worthy opponents.

We soon observed what others had already commented on, that no rat enters a trap in which one of its kind was recently caught, unless the trap has been thoroughly scrubbed or burned out. This phenomenon caused me a lot of speculation. What could it be that gave the second rat this timely warning? I did not believe in instinct and figured that the captive rodent had emitted an odor which was recognized by other rats as a sign of mortal fear. This explanation, if explanation it was, did not suffice. All the poor rat could do was to perspire, and perspiration should smell alike under all circumstances. I was to worry about this problem for years.

As I could not experiment on rats, I decided to experiment on human beings, and began studying human odors. It was a slow and difficult study; if anyone doubts this let him try it. People are not anxious to let you smell them, and the ordinary habits of bathing and perfuming throw additional obstacles into the path of the curious. Gradually, I began to notice differences in human exhalations. As odors cannot be described in ordinary language, I had to invent names of my own. One of the things I found was that the odor of each individual remains constant throughout life and is fairly independent of diets and other extraneous influences. I observed many other principles on which I was able to check up again and again. Never did I find, however, that the natural odor of a human being is influenced by his emotions.

Then, one day as I was lying in bed awaiting a late telephone call that would bring an important message, I noticed that my own odor, under the stress of my excitement, was different from the ordinary. I was satisfied that the difference was there. The explanation, though, remained as elusive as ever. Perspiration was perspiration, and there seemed to be no reason why its composition should change. Human sweat consists of organic acids and other products of decomposition, and I could not see how an emotion could effect a sudden chemical change in these waste products.

For a long time I engaged in this profitless speculation and hated myself for doing so. There certainly were more profitable problems to engage one's mind; yet I could not banish the riddle from my thoughts.

One morning, while I was driving on a boulevard, a possible solution flashed through my mind. I stopped the car so abruptly that the car behind crashed into it. A big man approached my front window, with a scowl on his not too handsome face.

"What on earth were you thinking of?" he demanded to know.

"I was thinking that I know now why a rat does not go into a trap in which another rat was caught," I told him. The man's scowl vanished, and a look of terror took its place. He backed away from me, jumped into his car, and drove off at top speed.

This is what had occurred to me. If the odor of perspiration was caused by the oxidation of waste products, this oxidation would be completed in the tubes leading from the sweat glands to the pores of the skin. But what would happen in case of a sudden shock, such as fear? Was it not at least possible that an involuntary contraction of the muscles might force the perspiration from the tubes before it was more than partially oxidized? Could this be the "cold sweat" which was supposed to cover people who were in fear of death? What was true of human beings would be true of rats. It was an interesting possibility, but I never found the time or the facilities to carry my studies further.

The big rodents which infested our plant had to be fought, but I thought they should be fought fairly and without undue cruelty. It seemed to me that traps and dogs might be eliminated, if rats could be caught like flies on flypaper. The sticky medium would only have to possess greater strength. Together with an old colleague and former competitor named Glenn Pickard I experimented until we had produced a suitable preparation; then we sent a sample to a company which specialized in rat extermination. The success of the new compound was instantaneous, and considerable business resulted. One day I heard that the basement of the apartment building in which we were living was housing a particularly wise old rat which refused to be tempted into ordinary traps. I decided to try our new invention. After covering a board with the viscous oil, I put cheese into the center of it and awaited developments. Next morning I found the cheese gone and the skin of two tiny legs embedded in the sticky compound. The brave rat had worked his way free from his prison. When I thought of the plucky little animal limping away in agony on two bleeding stumps, I was seized with such a feeling of remorse that I quit the manufacture of the rat-catching oil, although it had been both interesting and lucrative. To this day rats to me are foes I respect, and when I read of occasional campaigns against them, my sympathy is divided between the hunted and the hunter, treasonable as this attitude may be toward the human race.

My studies in human perspiration stood me in good stead later in my consulting work. Once a physician called on me to get my advice on a peculiar case he was treating. His patient was a woman of considerable means whose body odor was so strong that she had become morbid about it. She would not leave her apartment, shunned visitors, and was threatened with melancholy unless a remedy could be found for her affliction. At that time odor-removing preparations were not so well known as they are today, and the doctor was at his wit's end. Baths and diets had been of no avail and, as the woman was perfectly healthy, he could think of no new point of attack.

After experimenting for some time on myself, I succeeded in deodorizing myself completely for twenty-four hours at a time by the simple method of daubing my skin with a cloth dipped in chlorinated water. To avoid possible injury to the skin, I then removed the excess chlorine with a reducing agent. To be entirely without odor is a queer sensation. I suppose no one knows he is odorous, but let him remove all traces of his scent, and he will at once become painfully aware of something missing. It brought to my mind the story of the man who sold his shadow. The shadow was of no use to him, yet he was unhappy without it.

I handed the doctor a bottle of Eau de Javelle, a more elegant version of my chlorinated water, gave him a sulphur compound as an afterwash, and bade him adieu. A few weeks later I received a check for two hundred and fifty dollars and an anonymous letter from a lady in which she told me that I had saved her from suicide.

CHAPTER 9

OF GARBAGE AND DETECTIVES

*O*UR PLANT WAS now so well organized that it required little effort on my part to keep it running smoothly; yet, here and there a problem still arose which required my personal attention.

One of our best workers was an Irishman whose name was Danny. There was just one thing wrong with him—he drank at times. I caught him once under the influence of liquor and told him that there would be no second warning. I had a hundred lives in my care and could not take any unnecessary chances. The next time he would be through. A few days later Danny was drunk again and I fired him on the spot. He swore by everything holy that he would shoot me on pay day. A number of people heard his threat, and I received much well-meant advice. Gertie wanted to notify the police; her father suggested that we send Danny his money and then bar him from the plant. Charlie wanted me to take a revolver and shoot first. I declined all these offers. This was my fight and I was going to see it through in my own way.

Pay day came and Danny with it. He entered the office in line with the other men and I saw he was sober enough.

"Am I fired?" he asked as I handed him the money.

"You are," I said. "Next man, please." I suppose my Irish friend was all set for melodrama, but this prosaic procedure to which he had been accustomed for years threw him out of his stride. Involuntarily he stepped aside for the next man and, as he did so, lost his opportunity for either speech-making or shooting. He slunk out, and soon afterward I heard sounds of a scuffle. The Poles whom I had won over with my few words of Czech had been waiting for

Danny and gave him a healthy thrashing, telling him in their broken English that if he ever came back to threaten "Pan Boss" they would kill him. That was the last of Danny.

The one building in the plant which I rated as the greatest hazard was the still house. There the naphtha which was used for the extraction of the oil from flaxseed was re-distilled for further use. I used to think that if the plant should ever go up in a terrific holocaust, the still house would be the seat of the catastrophe. As events proved, I was wrong. Nevertheless, I had two of the most reliable men at work there, a Welshman named Hughes and a clean young American boy whom we called Stogie, because of his lean and lanky figure. No one else except the superintendent and I was allowed inside this building, and we inspected it carefully every day. Any slight leak there harbored great potentialities for evil.

One morning about eleven o'clock Stogie came rushing into the office with the startling news that Hughes had suddenly and mysteriously disappeared. I rushed into the still house and was immediately aware of an overpowering smell of naphtha. Without a second's hesitation I blew the alarm signal. In a few moments every wheel in the big plant stood still, water was thrown on the boiler fires, and all motors and lights were shut off. From Stogie's disconnected sentences, Mr. Stock and I reconstructed what had happened. Hughes had been pumping naphtha into a storage tank which was located beneath the floor, when the pump started to slow up. Thinking that the steam pressure was low, he had put on more steam, and when the pump came to a standstill, he opened the valve wide. What really had happened was that the storage tank was full, but this thought had not entered Hughes' mind. He had kept pumping until the storage tank burst under the pressure. Then he must have crawled below to see how he could stop the leak.

The space in which Hughes now lay, overcome by fumes and in imminent danger of death, was about three feet high and not easily accessible. I formed a rescue squad for which everyone volunteered. We took off our shoes, removed from our pockets everything that could possibly cause a spark, and formed a chain. I was the first to go in, but the inhalation of the concentrated naphtha fumes was too much for me; I lost consciousness before I had located our missing fellow-worker. Each man got a little farther, but we were all stretched out on the ground, deathly sick and gasping for air by the time we had found Hughes and pulled him out. He was frantic when he was revived and offered no excuse for his colossal blunder. I knew that the best of men have their off days and was quite willing to overlook his lapse.

Then one day real tragedy stalked through our plant. In Charlie's meal house we had large, hopper-shaped storage bins which held hundreds of tons of fine meal. The meal had to be continually transferred from one place to another so as to air it and prevent fermentation. This job was entrusted to an old man named Burke, a steady employee, well liked by all. His two daughters were also working in the meal house, sewing bags, a job they did with a skill and speed that always aroused my admiration. The bins were surrounded by a solid railing, and there was no danger whatever in the transfer of the meal, a mechanical and entirely automatic process. One evening old man Burke did not check out, and his daughters, guided perhaps by some premonition, suspected that he might have fallen into one of the bins. Their foreboding, unfortunately, was only too well founded. With great difficulty his inert body was lifted out of the dust and brought to our laboratory. There I worked on him for two hours, but I knew all the time that it was too late.

How Burke had fallen into the bin was never cleared up, although an inquest followed, and a noisy investigation by detectives from the coroner's office continued for weeks. The verdict was one of accidental death, but the mystery remained unexplained.

We had a space in the laboratory screened off as a first-aid station, where Gertie and I did what we could for the many small injury cases which are part of life in a factory. Ordinarily we dealt only with bruises and cuts, but soon people began trooping in with toothaches and other ailments, all of which we treated to the best of our ability and apparently to the entire satisfaction of our patients. Only once did we have a serious case, and one that should never have been entrusted to amateur hands. Flaxseed was usually brought to us in big cargo boats into which a conveyer was sunk from our elevator to lift the seed into our storage tanks. Whenever a boat was to be unloaded, the steamship company hired its own men to work in the hold of the vessel. One of these poor devils came too close to the conveyor and had his leg sucked in and crushed to pulp. They brought him to the laboratory, and when I looked at his injury and at the inadequate little first-aid box we had, I despaired. Gertie helped me like the thoroughbred she was, pale and trembling, but game. When the hastily summoned ambulance from South Chicago arrived after about two hours, the doctor assured us that we had saved a human life. Before me lay the unconscious form of our patient, minus a leg, and I wondered if the achievement was really worthy of commendation.

The first-aid department also had its lighter moments, especially after our office and laboratory force had grown to more substantial proportions. The plant employees would fake all kinds of injuries, the men to get a little free whisky and gentle treatment at the hands of a young lady, the girls to flirt with my chemists and hold hands with them. I let these matters go on until they were being overdone, and then I took a simple way of bringing them back to normal. The men were suddenly treated by men chemists who put alum into bleeding wounds, and the girls who came in with headaches were handed aspirin tablets instead of having their cheeks patted. All this was done in the spirit of good sportsmanship by both sides, and it was considered fun to play a game in which everyone tried to outguess the opponent's move.

One of the big cargo boats which carried our flaxseed from Duluth to South Chicago was in charge of an old captain who had grown gray in the service. His trips under load were a severe strain on him, while on his way back he went under ballast and made a holiday of it. He had half a dozen cabins in which he could accommodate friends at his discretion, or his lack of it, to judge from some stories which were being told in whispers. But there was warm blood in his heart and he claimed to have matched many a happy couple and stopped many more before they took the plunge into marriage. He often invited engaged couples to go to Duluth with him as his guests. After five days in close companionship, he used to say laughingly, they either could not wait to rush off to the marriage bureau or else they took different trains back to Chicago.

I had many good meals on board the old captain's boat, and I still like to think of his healthy and carefree ways and his homemade method of doing good in this world.

One morning as I glanced at the daily paper while riding to work, I saw an exciting headline. The Chicago Garbage Company, an extraction plant somewhat like ours, had been destroyed by an explosion, and several people had been killed or injured. I jumped off the car and hurried to the scene of the accident. I had to find out what had happened, what carelessness or act of providence had wrought this havoc. I broke through the police cordon on the strength of an old press card I still carried from my Pittsburgh days and soon confronted a disconsolate and almost hysterical manager. He did not know how the explosion had occurred, nor could he offer any suggestion; but he was also worried by another pressing problem. His firm was under contract to work up hundreds of tons of city garbage every day, and as the plant could not be rebuilt for some time, he saw before him a city deprived of an essential function and his company the victim of staggering damages. I thought that our mill, which was then shut down between seasons, could be quickly adapted to the extraction of his product and offered the distracted official my help. It was immediately accepted. We drew up a temporary agreement which gave our concern an opportunity to utilize equipment which otherwise would have remained idle, and offered the garbage company a way to live up to its obligations. Before the day was over our main office had approved the plan, and we set to work remodeling our factory.

The garbage-reduction process then in vogue was a comparatively simple one. The raw or green garbage, as it was called, was dumped from numerous wagons into a big pit, from which it was shoveled into drying ovens where most of the moisture was removed. Heavy stone mills pounded to pieces whatever solid material had been thrown into the pails by careless householders. The garbage was a mixture of fruit, peelings, meat, fat, porcelain ware, glass, cigar stumps, beer bottles, caps and rags, all of which was then extracted with naphtha. The fat thus obtained, called garbage grease, was sold to soap manufacturers, and the residue was used as fertilizer. Luckily, the drier plant had not been destroyed and as for the dried product, I saw no reason why we could not process it as well as the plant which had been wrecked.

When I broached the story of the new contract to Mr. Stock, he showed little enthusiasm. He foresaw many mechanical difficulties;

had I known what was ahead of us, I would never have closed the deal. Garbage is a material which waits for no one; it is produced hour after hour and must be disposed of as fast as it is delivered. Before we were anywhere near ready with our alterations, cars began rolling in, two, four, ten, twenty, an avalanche of cars, until our sidings were blocked completely, with additional trains being held on the main line. We toiled day and night, and finally started to operate. Then an unforeseen obstacle arose. The rags in the garbage wound themselves around our shafts and gears in such a compact pile that the machinery either stopped dead or else snapped in two. Our screw conveyors were hopelessly entangled and ceased functioning. After each desperately needed clean-up it was only a matter of hours before we were forced to shut down again. Instead of extracting a day's run of Chicago's garbage we could barely handle a small portion of it, and every time the switch engine shunted another train into our plant, I felt like the Danish king who had tried to keep out the tide with a couple of brooms.

In this perplexity we decided to do something radical. If we could not manage the rags after they had gotten into our extraction plant, we would see that the rags were kept out of it one way or another. We built a barbed-wire fence through which all the garbage would have to pass before it reached the intake. All night long, like the armies in the subsequent World War, we threw up barbed wires and held the strings close together so that rags could not pass between them. The scheme worked only too well, for within half an hour the wires were so clogged that neither rags nor garbage could penetrate. We put a whole crew to work keeping the fences clear, but it was a hopeless task. We then had kerosene poured over the rags and fire set to them with a blow torch. This expedient looked good until it started to rain; then it faded. In my despair I asked the city authorities to post notices everywhere, reminding the populace that rags were not to be thrown into garbage pails; but these notices made matters worse than ever, for they seemed to implant in otherwise law-abiding citizens a new idea of how to solve their rag problem. I finally put four men into each car before it was unloaded, to pick out the rags by hand, and by working all our schemes together, eventually we managed to hold our own against this insidious garbage flood.

185

In the meantime, all the rats and mice of South Chicago must have heard of our new enterprise and celebrated a grand rendezvous at our plant. The diet agreed with them, so far as I could judge, for their number and size increased beyond anything reasonable. Even our dogs became so tired killing them that they lay down panting and let the rodents run right past them. We got rid of this pest, however, by a simple device. As we always had some kerosene handy to saturate the rags, we now used it to soak all the garbage as it came in. The result was that the rats departed almost as fast as they had appeared.

I recall a curious incident in connection with this garbage work. We had a very reliable old man on our payroll, and I assigned him to the duty of keeping the intake conveyor free of obstructions. All at once he began to show signs of unusual hilarity; it was obvious that he was drinking. Stories reached me that he was celebrating every night and spending money like a sailor on shore leave. I became interested and took up an observation post from which I could watch the man at work. The conveyor he was tending made a sharp bend at one place and I saw that this spot received an undue amount of his attention. Close examination showed that our *nouveau riche* had made a hole in the casing there and from it rained pennies, nickels, dimes and sometimes even coins of larger denomination. I then had the conveyor tapped at different places, and we were amazed to see the amount of valuables people threw away. Besides money, we picked up watches, rings, brooches and other pieces of jewelry; we found pencils, fountain pens and cigarette cases; one time we even found a pearl necklace. Our pirate treasure usually ran to over thirty dollars a day in cash alone. I foresaw trouble and therefore ruled that everything of value was to be turned into a common fund, to be equally divided, day by day, among all the employees. It was an exciting game. How much valuable material was withheld from the pot I can only guess, but I know that one man took an expensive fur neckpiece from one of the cars, and I almost had a riot on my hands when I insisted that this piece of wearing apparel together with the more valuable jewelry be turned over to the police.

The whole episode had only one fault; it did not last long enough. Just as we had straightened out all technical kinks and were running neck and neck with the daily arrivals, the wrecked garbage plant went back into commission. Never before had our plant looked so quiet and deserted as it did after the noise and bustle of our garbage-reduction days had died away. The company paid a substantial bonus to all of us, but money could not compensate for what we had lost. We had lived in Klondike for a few months, and the gold fever had crept into our veins.

Things had just about settled down again to normal when suddenly, without warning, I found myself a police suspect.

After the unpleasant experience with our payroll checks during the panic days of 1907, I had decided to go back to our former method of paying the men in cash. As we carried practically no money at our mill, Charlie and I drew the necessary funds from South Chicago and brought them back in a little satchel. Charlie, a loaded revolver in hand, always kept some forty feet behind me while we walked and sat opposite me in the streetcar. This procedure was not much to my liking. We had to walk five blocks over prairie land in a suburb which was only a short distance from the Indiana dunes where, since the days of the car-barn murders, criminals had always found shelter. So far as I knew, our little village was without police protection. Moreover, I would have hated to see even a holdup man's blood shed for the sake of mere money.

Out of these considerations came the resolve to let the Inland Express Company deliver the cash to us every Tuesday morning. A train on the Monon Railway had a flag stop about three blocks from the entrance to our plant and ran a convenient train, carrying an express car. An express wagon could meet the train and get the cash to the office shortly after nine o'clock. The proper arrangements were soon made and proved very satisfactory. At least I thought so for a time.

One Tuesday morning Gertie and I were sitting in the office waiting for the payroll messenger. The night shift was lined up near the pay window, the envelopes were ready, and we were all anxious to proceed. The men needed their sleep, and we always did our best to expedite matters. Ten o'clock came, and still there was no money. At last I sent Gertie into a telephone booth in an adjoining room to find out what was wrong. Just as she was telephoning, the wagon rolled in, and the express driver handed me the canvas bag with the cash. The train had been late, he said, and the delay unavoidable. As I took over the money, Gertie came out of the booth and told the driver that his office wanted to speak to him; she then joined me at the desk. The moment my practical-minded assistant laid eyes on the money bag, she noticed that the seal was hanging loose, and naturally we did not unfasten the string with which the bag was tied. When the driver came out of the next room, which was in about a minute's time, we showed him what we had observed, whereupon we all got excited and opened the little sack. When we found that there was a shortage of exactly one thousand dollars, three pale faces stared helplessly at each other. We notified the South Chicago police, and in due course two detectives arrived and took statements from everyone concerned. What had happened was this:

The afternoon before, the money had been packed up by a down-town bank and properly receipted by an agent of the express company. This apparently left the bank with a clean bill of health. In the morning, the agent on the train had taken over the bag and accepted it after examining the seal. This cleared the main office of the express company. From then on matters became confused. The train was late; the agent in the express car had seemed in a great hurry to push on. Therefore, the express-wagon driver had accepted the bag without giving it more than a glance. The money had then been put into a safe at the rear end of the wagon, but in his haste the driver had not locked it. To make the issue still more involved, several children had been seen stealing rides on the vehicle, unbeknown to the driver. Nor was this all of it. I had held the ill-omened bag in my hand while neither Gertie nor the driver was watching me, and then Gertie and I might have manipulated the seal and abstracted the thousand dollars while the express agent was telephoning in the next room. Altogether it was a bad muddle, and anything but pleasant.

The police, forced to do something, arrested the driver. The express company discharged him, not because they thought him guilty, but because of his carelessness. Neither Gertie nor I was questioned further after our first meeting with the detectives, and we soon dismissed the matter from our minds.

I always took my morning and evening meals in the same restaurant and knew nearly everyone there. The cozy little place was run on a sort of family basis. The owner, a kind, elderly lady, would form the guests into what she considered congenial groups and make us all feel at home. It was therefore only natural that I took notice of a tall newcomer who sat all by himself and read a paper, something that was frowned upon by our hostess as a discourtesy to her other guests. To make matters more obvious, he hid behind his newspaper every time I looked at him. I was unashamedly thrilled. Could it be possible that I was being watched?

I resolved to make a test and next evening transferred my allegiance to another restaurant. Sure enough, my tall friend came in immediately after I did, this time wearing dark glasses, reading his paper, and otherwise behaving like a detective in a musical comedy. Well, if he was getting paid for this work, I was willing to let him earn his money. I had read once that wild animals enjoy the chase as much as the hunter, and I learned to believe it. In playing with my shadow I had all the advantages, of course. I would go into my old restaurant and tell the waitress not to serve me, as I was expecting a friend. A minute later the detective would come in. As soon as he had given his order and started to eat his soup, I was out of the door, watching him through the window. It was comical to see him stop eating, wipe his mouth, throw a bill on the table and rush after me. When he found me standing calmly on the sidewalk, he did not know what to do, and probably felt as ridiculous as he looked. Then I would board an elevated train, he following. At the next station I got out and waited for the next train. He had to do likewise, but had no place on the platform to hide, which was embarrassing. I began to sympathize with detectives in general and for my own in particular, and finally walked up to him to make a bargain. Each night I gave him my itinerary for the next day and told him to make himself less conspicuous, as otherwise I would give him the slip for good. He took the tip and never bothered me much after that.

Gertie told me that she, too, was under surveillance. In her case the sleuth had nothing to do but guard her house all night long. Gertie's life was such a simple one that watching her must have been a tyro's job. Only on the one day a month that Gertie took off to go downtown shopping did the detective have to do any gumshoe work. Then Gertie, too, caught the excitement of the chase and once eluded her pursuer at Marshall Field's store. It probably brought her as close to adventure as she ever came in all her life.

One evening I suddenly missed my detective. I became so disturbed that I immediately called up Gertie. Would she please look outside and see if her shadow was there? I was seriously concerned about mine. Yes, her guardian was also gone, and she felt as aggrieved as I did. Next morning I called the Inland Express Company and asked them if they had solved the mystery of the missing thousand dollars. They had, and they gave me an outline of the solution.

The express agent on the train had carried with him a deadhead passenger, a former employee of the company, who had begged for a ride. He was familiar with the delivery of payrolls, and when he saw the bag containing our money, the temptation was too strong for him. He broke the seal, took out a thousand dollars, and retied the string so it would pass a cursory inspection. The lateness of the train and the impatience of the conductor to shorten the stay at our flagstop were unexpected strokes of luck for the thief. They had caught him by putting a detective on his trail, after the fact of his stolen ride had been sweated out of the baggage man. He had lived normally for a few weeks, but then started to spend money recklessly, and that had given him away. He was arrested, and confessed. The head investigator of the Inland Express Company then invited Gertie and me to lunch. We accepted the invitation, together with his profuse apologies, and he entertained us for a couple of hours by relating some of his choicest experiences. To judge from them, the last thing on earth I would advise a would-be thief to do is to rob the Inland Express Company.

By 1908 several states had adopted purity laws on linseed oil, almost all of them copies of our original Ohio statute. Curiously, the execution of these laws met with one obstacle nobody had envisioned. The state chemists did not know how to analyze linseed oil. This was not altogether their fault. There was only one book available at that time which contained the requisite data, and even that volume, translated from the German, was obsolete in many respects and not always adaptable to American conditions. The methods described therein also bore the German tradition of heavy thoroughness, and were better fitted for university laboratories than for practical use. I was sorry to notice this, for the two authors of the textbook, Professors Benedict and Ulzer, had both been teachers at Vienna colleges. Benedict had died about two years before I entered the Polytechnical School, but his strong personality still lingered in many anecdotes which circulated among the students. One of his characteristics had been a caustic wit, tempered with much good nature. When he entered a laboratory and found a piece of filter paper or a broken beaker lying on the floor, he would immediately lay another piece of paper or glass alongside its mate, even if he had to break something to do it. If he found a leaking burette he would calmly pull out his handkerchief and wipe off the drippings. These practical, silent reprimands worked wonders, even if they caused great individual embarrassment. He also had a habit of engaging his students in friendly conversation, asking their views on different chemical subjects. Sometimes he would interrupt with short ejaculations, such as "Nonsense!" "How silly!" and so forth, but the student had to keep talking. Then, as likely as not, he would depart with a "You'll make your way." At other times his interjections would express admiration, "Grand, go ahead," or "Well, well, you *do* think," but he would leave a baffled student behind when he ended the discourse with a harsh, "In all my life I have never listened to such asininity." His examinations were mere formalities, for he gave out his grades on the strength of his personal impressions. No one had ever seen him without the stump of a cigar in his mouth, and eventually he died from cancer of the tongue.

I had now acquired four years of experience in oil analysis and, in order to dispel the confusion which benefited the dopers, I published a series of articles on linseed oil. The publication created some interest, and I was invited to read a paper on the subject before the American Chemical Society. All the addresses I had heard there had been carefully prepared papers which were read from manuscript, but I felt I could not follow this practice. In my opinion, to read a paper from notes is a discourtesy to the audience. If a man does not command his subject well enough to talk freely about it I do not think he is worth listening to. Moreover, to hear someone read is extremely tiresome, and professional men, even in their professional capacity, are human and deserve consideration. I thought then, and I think now, that I would just as soon appear before an audience without a necktie as with a sheaf of typewritten pages in my hand. I needed all my courage to take the revolutionary step I contemplated, but when the evening of my lecture came, I talked without written notes.

As my address proceeded, I could see the assembled members separate into two groups—the old, conservative section, antagonistic to my novel method, and the young progessives who seemed friendly and encouraging. The schism widened as I went on. A professor in one of the leading eastern colleges had put a chapter on linseed oil into one of his books, and I tore into it as an example of the way misinformation was being perpetuated through thoughtless repetition of half-truths or actual errors.

I had never before witnessed a discussion of a paper at our meetings, but we surely had one that night. Nobody got up for the expected formal motion to extend the thanks of the members to the speaker, and the old man in the front row, who invariably got his name into the record by solemnly seconding every motion made, was left high and dry. The conservatives were in a violent state of indignation because I had attacked Professor So-and-So, and threatened to write to him for a scathing denunciation of my criticism. I told them to go and do their damnedest. The younger element was delighted at the incipient conflict. It was quite an evening. Had I known it, I would have marked down that day as the turning-point in my career, for two people in the audience were much impressed with my remarks and later reacted to them in a way that helped change my entire professional life.

My articles on linseed oil were compiled into a brochure which bore the imprint of The American Linseed Company and was sent out free of charge to those who wanted it. I dispatched a copy to one of the country's leading libraries, but regretted it at once. I had given away a lot of inside information in my articles, and to spread it promiscuously was foolish. I need not have worried, however, for the booklet never appeared in the card-index catalogue. It had only paper covers, was sponsored by a business house, and therefore perhaps considered worthless. A year or so later a writer on technical matters came to our plant to gather material for a book. We could not possibly give him our processes or formulae and, as he was very persistent, the men in the mill fed him the most fanciful stories. All of them found their way into his book. The volume had quite an impressive cover and was immediately placed on the shelves of the library which had thrown my booklet into the ashcan.

My articles brought me into close contact with the officials of the states where linseed oil laws were being enforced, and in response to a special request I worked out a portable laboratory designed to test linseed oil samples on the spot. Any field inspector could be taught to do this after a few minutes of instruction. The introduction of this new instrument of war enabled us to make better headway against the dopers, and in most states they disappeared forever within a short time.

There was one flaw in our knowledge of linseed oil analysis. No way was then known by which the presence or absence of fish oils in vegetable oils could be determined. This problem vexed me greatly, especially as its solution would meet a practical need. Fish oils were selling at much lower prices than linseed oil, and not only did I suspect that they were being used for purposes of adulteration, but we ourselves were sometimes accused of doing so. Ever so often some customer claimed that he could detect the odor of fish oil in our goods, and I had no definite way of disproving his imputation. I therefore decided to make an attempt to bridge this gap in our knowledge.

Working for me at that time was a young chemist of great ability named Norman Copthorne; of the few natural-born chemists I have met in my life he was one. I had discovered his qualifications through an error of his, which was quite ingenious. Linseed oil, when kept in storage, throws down settlings, known in the trade as "foots." These foots have but little commercial value, and were usually ignored by the plant managers until the annual clean-up of all storage tanks was undertaken. Then these unwelcome settlings appeared at the bottom and had to be reckoned with. To sell them was next to impossible, and they could not be thrown away; they were not good enough for one and too good for the other. Some shrewd mill superintendent had at one time, previous to my employment, suggested that all foots be sent to the South Chicago plant where the oil should be extracted from them by means of our solvent process. This suggestion was greeted with general acclaim. The plants got rid of their waste, were credited in full with the equivalent of good oil, and we had a hundred and fifty thousand gallons of foots on hand. The extraction process had not worked out at all. We kept sending samples of these foots to possible users, but nary a bite did we get. Then, one year when there had been a failure of the flaxseed crop and prices of linseed oil went soaring, one of our old prospects remembered these foots, and soon they were moving out at a great rate. Before long we had cleaned up our entire accumulation. It was then that my young assistant sprang his surprise. He had seen our stock of foots dwindling, and now presented me with a sample of synthetic settlings. It was a perfect match. Only one thing was wrong with it, and that was the price. The synthetic product cost us twice as much as we could get for it, and though it was therefore of no practical value, I was happy to have on my force a man with such initiative and chemical talent.

Neither of us had the slightest idea of how to attack our problem of determining the presence of fish oil in linseed oil, and the more we studied it, the more puzzling we found it. Linseed oil and sardine oil are almost identical in their chemical composition; when heated, linseed oil smells quite a bit like fish oil, and when it is converted into soap, most users will complain of the fishy odor. That two oils derived from such divergent sources as flaxseed and fish should be similar in so many respects is extraordinary. If fish oils would dry as well as linseed oil, the parallelism would be complete, but there the similarity ends.

It took six months of hard work on our own time before we struck a promising lead, and six months more were required to finish our thesis before it could be published. If we had thought that the paper would enhance our reputation, we were headed for a fall. Very few people commented on it. My friend Tolman and the then state chemist of Illinois, T. J. Bryan, undertook to send samples of mixtures to many testing laboratories and established the efficacy of the new method. After that it was kicked around until, in 1925, it was adopted as official by the United States Department of Agriculture. By then the names of the two authors had dropped by the wayside, although the method still stands as the last milepost along this path. Two more servants of mankind had received their customary reward.*

About that time one of my trouble-shooting expeditions brought me to a large city in Tennessee. A leading white lead factory was located there, run by two elderly gentlemen who treated me with true southern hospitality. I appreciated their attitude the more as they had suffered some real damage in their lead-in-oil grinding department because of a mistake on our part. I still recall with pleasure the little cottage adjoining the plant where an old Negro served lunches of delicious fried chicken. In the course of our meals one of my hosts mentioned that they thought their white lead was more resistant to hydrogen sulphide fumes than competitive products, but that their salesmen seemed unable to make the most of this point. Hydrogen sulphide being a constituent of sewer gas, a house painted white would easily turn brown when subjected to the effervescences of an imperfect sewage system, and as the sanitary arrangements in many districts of the South were then far from perfect, the advantage of a gas-resisting white surface coating was obvious.

Back in Chicago, I gave this matter some thought and finally rigged up a little demonstrator for my southern friends. It consisted of a Kipp apparatus which released hydrogen sulphide gas at the operator's discretion and of a few panels on which different grades of ground white lead could be displayed. A five minutes' exposure, I found, was sufficient to prove the difference between various products. If the Tennessee white lead really was superior, here was a way to demonstrate it. The test spoke for itself, so much so that when I sent the contraption down to my hosts, I only told them to turn on the gas. All I added was that I felt impelled to show my appreciation for their graciousness.

A few days later I received a letter from them. Was I ready to take a position with their company as chief salesman at a salary of five thousand dollars a year? I had never sold anything bigger than a bottle of shampoo, and although I was flattered by the offer, I declined it, convinced that I was not fit for the position.

---

* The method was published in the *Journal of Industrial and Engineering Chemistry* in February, 1910.

Shortly afterward I unexpectedly had to go out selling for our own company, and so was given the opportunity to see whether or not I could do it. About ten years had elapsed since the formation of the American Linseed Company, and the high tide of the big business combines was beginning to recede. None of them had been able to achieve a monopoly in their particular domains, if that was their goal, and those connected with agricultural products had failed by the widest margins. People could buy mine after mine of copper or iron ores or control patents, but no one could constantly, year after year, monopolize an industry based on crops. Competitors had always been in the field, and new ones sprang up constantly whittling away our sales volume. I had nothing to do with the selling of linseed oil, but I suggested to our sales department that we were not playing our cards well. Our rivals were emphasizing their refined products to get an entry into the trade. This was a clever move, especially as we were not leaders in that part of our business, although we had in our naphtha-extracted oil an excellent basic material and were therefore in an advantageous position. With a few changes in our refinery, I thought, we could produce an oil of outstanding quality. I was told to produce it, and I did, with welcome help from Mr. Stock and others. The new product had some features which—so we flattered ourselves—no pressed oil made at that time could match. These I wrote out carefully; then I prepared a set of samples for visual proof and sent the lot to our sales department for action.

To my great disappointment not much happened. I did not know, of course, what our sales force was doing, but I did know that we shipped only about six thousand gallons of the new oil in a period of six months, which indicated rather clearly that the world was not being set afire. Then one day Mr. Moore, our specialty salesman, asked me to meet him. Breakfast time was the only hour he could spare me, he said, so would I meet him at, say, eight o'clock? I did not know Mr. Moore at all, but he had been described to me so often as a living dynamo that I expected to find my host another Teddy Roosevelt. Instead, I saw a tall, lean man with a pale complexion and the most voracious appetite I have ever witnessed. He ordered a whole fried spring chicken with French fried potatoes, and washed it down, as he expressed it, with two soft-boiled eggs and half a dozen cups of coffee. His invariable companion was a male secretary, half his size, who contradicted him continually and made intelligent conversation almost impossible. Whenever I tried to steer the talk into business channels, the two would start quarreling about some ridiculously unimportant matter, such as whether a certain incident had happened on the Pennsylvania Railroad or on the New York Central. It was only when I rose to go that Moore got down to business. My new oil was a flop, he told me, and could not be sold. I replied with some heat that it could be sold, but was not being pushed intelligently. Well, was his taunting comeback, if I knew more about selling than the sales department, why didn't I start a campaign myself? I assured him that I would.

When our western manager heard about this challenge he chuckled with glee. There was no love lost between him and the New York office. So far as he was concerned, I had *carte blanche*.

Mr. Curry, our youngest salesman, was selected to accompany me. He was an elegant young gentleman who made a fine appearance and could talk well, but better on polo, theaters and races than on oils. That did not matter greatly, for we were a good combination. Together we made a tour of almost the entire United States, lasting about three months, and took orders everywhere. In the beginning my partner, whose appearance was much more impressive than mine, led the conversation, until it was time to spring the technical talk, when I took up where he had left off. By and by, Mr. Curry tired of this performance and stayed in the hotel, leaving it to me to fill both speaking parts. I began to wonder what there was to this much-ballyhooed art of salesmanship. As I saw it, if you stated your case properly you were usually treated with courtesy. Sometimes your product fitted into the prospective buyer's setup and sometimes it did not. In one case you got an order, in another you went away without one, unless there was a chance for an argument. The upshot of our campaign was that we sold half a million gallons of oil in a year's time which, compared with the six thousand gallons shipped the previous half year, made the percentage of increase difficult to calculate without the use of logarithms.

The immediate result of this success, so far as it touched me personally, was that I was considered good enough to speak at conventions in place of salesmen, who heretofore had been given these assignments. I went to master painter conventions, conventions of dealers, conventions of manufacturers. I detested them all. I did not like the enforced hilarity brought about by immoderate drinking any more than I liked to answer offhand the trick questions which were shot at me. I was a poor public speaker anyway, lacked confidence and was so nervous that for the first few moments on my feet I could hardly hear my own voice. The only thing I could hear was the pounding of my heart.

Here and there other chemists were breaking out of their laboratories and entering the technical sales field. We often met on the same occasions and eventually formed a phalanx against all outsiders. I recall a master painters convention in a Pennsylvania town, where a little chemist who represented a paint manufacturing concern was being ragged on the platform by a half-drunk audience. The poor victim dared not strike back at his tormentors, as they were all prospective customers of his firm, so we other chemists jumped on the speaker's stand and blasted the hecklers out of their seats.

One of these chemists, a man named Pat, interested me in particular. He was a brilliant man, but very quick-tempered. He abhorred these conventions as much as I did, but while I fretted in silence, he drank away his sorrow until sometimes he was unable to stand on his feet when his turn came to address the audience. Once he was completely out at the critical moment, and I delivered his scheduled speech for him. Having heard it so often, I almost knew it by heart. After that we chemists often interchanged our talks just for the fun of it, and we all profited by the arrangement. There was a day when we all had finished our addresses and were on our way to a western city. In view of a heavy snowstorm which was blowing in from the north, the majority thought that a detour was the safest way, but Pat and I differed and took a direct train across the country. The result was that we were snowed in for twenty-four hours and did not arrive in time for our appearances. Thanks to our friends, we were not missed much, for they presented our addresses, and none of the audience was the wiser for it.

Incidentally, I found that being snowbound in a train was not so romantic as I had always pictured it. There was nothing to eat, there was no heat, there was no light. According to local law, the train equipment included canned pickles and biscuits, but when the conductor began to distribute these emergency supplies, we found the biscuits full of worms and the pickles so rotten with age that they crumbled to pieces when removed from their embalming fluid. We tried an expedition to get to the nearest settlement, but could flounder no farther than a few hundred feet, after which sortie we were glad to reach the shelter of our cars again before succumbing to the severe cold.

Traveling through the back country in the first decade of our century was hard work and entailed little pleasure. Many trains were slow and ill-equipped. Sleepers and diners were a rarity on all but the main lines of traffic, and many a night I had to sit up uncomfortably in an atmosphere that would have thrown a horse back on his haunches. We ate sandwich meals at way-stations, sometimes without bread, sometimes without salt, sometimes without meat. The hotels were mostly old and murky. Reading lamps were unknown; usually a single bulb hanging from the ceiling provided all the illumination. You were supposed to spend the evenings in the lobby, sitting around the stove, swapping stories, but these stories lacked wit and originality. The talks in the lobbies no more varied from one place to another than did the skimpy meals in the dreary dining rooms. One had to look at the newspaper, also skimpy, to see what town one was in, they were so alike. Only the largest cities had theaters, and these were usually given over to cheap vaudeville. Movies, then commonly known as nickelodeons, were coming in, but provided only banal entertainment not worth ruining one's eyes for. The nicest part of any traveling man's life in those days was the homecoming.

CHAPTER 10

"YOU ARE FIRED"

*D*URING THE WEEK, I usually spent the evenings at home. One night a visitor for me was announced, an unusual event which caused my landlady to prick up her ears. A bearded man was ushered into my room; the card he handed me indicated that he was in the real estate business. His story became more and more interesting as he unfolded it.

'Way back in 1869, he said, an Englishman whose name he had forgotten had conceived a clever idea. He had noticed that grease spots on paper made it transparent; others had undoubtedly made the same observation before him, but only he thought of putting it to practical use. Why not make an envelope, he speculated, with a grease spot on its face, so that the address could be read as through a window? It would save writing the address twice; besides, who had not experienced the agonizing doubt about certain letters having been put into the right envelopes? Plays had been written on the mixups brought about in this manner.

So far, so good. But then troubles arose. It was easy enough to grease up a piece of paper, but one could not make window envelopes that way. Ordinary grease did not form a regular outline, ran all over the paper in hot weather, and would have soiled the contents of the entire mailbag. So the idea had lain dormant until the Englishman's patent expired. People had played around with it here and there, but all trials had ended in failure. Then a Chicago merchant by the name of Julius Regenstein had taken up the orphaned invention and started a plant for window envelopes. He put a great deal of money into special machinery and added some ingenious mechanical inventions which made mass production possible. Everything went well for a while; then came disaster. The windows on the envelopes soon began to lose their transparency, and shipments came back almost as fast as they went out. When I saw the plant for the first time, the man in the boiler room stood knee deep in returned envelopes and was shoveling them onto his grates as fast as he could work. The heat in the plant was unbearable, but the pleas reaching the furnace man went unheeded. He had to keep the radiators hot just to preserve breathing space for himself.

"Else I'd have to keep the whistles blowing all day long to get rid of my steam," he remarked plaintively to me.

My caller was a real estate agent who had rented a North Side building to Mr. Regenstein and was seriously concerned about his lease. Would I help? I would, but not without a direct request from the Window Envelope Company. On that understanding we parted.

The expected telephone call came. I found Mr. Regenstein to be a large man with a fine brain and a wonderful sense of detachment from earthly troubles. He could get as excited as anyone and swear better than most, but I never saw the glint of humor leave his eyes, no matter what the provocation. Things that worried other men into insanity glided off his mind at will. When I first met him, and many times thereafter, his entire fortune was at stake; yet he was constantly joking, and his hearty laugh sounded as carefree as that of a child. His superintendent and loyal co-worker, Ernest Sauermann, was the exact opposite of his chief. He always looked worried, and his conscientiousness amounted almost to religious fervor. Mr. Regenstein usually referred to him as his funeral director. Times were to come when the plant had to be shut down because we could not produce one satisfactory envelope. Mr. Sauermann would then put up a cot for himself in the factory, to do or die there, while Mr. Regenstein took the next train for Excelsior Springs, leaving instructions that he was not to be bothered until things were on the mend.

Mr. Regenstein's heart was as big as his body. He made out a retainer check for me before he had fairly stated my task. Then he turned me over to his funeral director. When I heard the details of my problem, I felt very much like returning the check.

201

Mr. Sauermann told me quite frankly that he scarcely knew what he was doing or why he was doing it. Samples of oils and varnishes had been collected from both domestic and foreign sources, none had ever worked well, and almost every week a new mixture was tried. Test envelopes were sent constantly to distant lands, addressed to fictitious persons, and when the post office returned them after weeks or months of travel, they were studied for the effect time and climate had wrought on them. They usually came back with the window a mass of criss cross lines—"crystals" was the term used—and with their transparency gone beyond recall. The only envelopes not returned were those which were used immediately. No wonder the boiler room was the busiest spot in the factory.

The first thing I did after pocketing my retainer fee, I am ashamed to confess, was to go to Yellowstone Park. I felt like a diver who takes a deep breath before going down into the unknown, not sure when or whether he will come up again. I am glad I saw Yellowstone Park before automobiles were permitted to enter it, and when the entire season's visitors totalled less than those of one day in recent years.

Upon my return I felt that in order to start out intelligently I had to know why the windows lost their transparency. The lines which spread over the oiled area until the paper became opaque were usually formed like stars and bore in their outline a similarity to fungus growths. At this, a hazy recollection stirred in my brain.

In 1871, I remembered, some rare and valuable paintings in a Munich museum had been found covered with what looked like mould. The authorities, thoroughly frightened, called on Professor Pettenkofer, a leading scientist of the day, for advice. Pasteur had just published his epochal discoveries, and it was thought that bacteria might be at the bottom of this trouble. When Pettenkofer examined small pieces of the affected paintings under the microscope, however, he found that the cause of the opaqueness was something quite different. The thin varnish used by the old masters to protect their paintings had succumbed to time and atmospheric influences, and the numerous small cracks, through the reflection of light, gave the impression of gray mould, much as chipped glass looks white, although the glass itself is colorless. Pettenkofer proved his case by suggesting a simple method of correction. Exposing the cracked surface to the fumes of alcohol, he caused the gum of the varnish to soften and the cracks to close. The result was a quick and complete restoration of the old masterpieces, probably to the great chagrin of contemporary artists who had hoped to paint them over.

I had always liked this story, and at times, when lecturing on practical application of chemistry, had used it for a demonstration. In order to achieve the right dramatic effect, I carried with me a real oil painting which I had bought in a pawn shop. The picture may have been below par as a work of art, but it served its purpose. I would hold my masterpiece over a basin of boiling water, with the result that in a few minutes the entire painting was obscured by a white film. Then came the exposure to alcohol fumes, and presto! the original picture was restored. It was a nice stunt and always held the attention of the audience.

In the case of envelopes, alcohol would not work, of course, because the varnish used was not made of alcohol-soluble gum. Nor would it have been feasible to restore ruined envelopes. My problem was to prevent the surface from cracking in the first place. But how? The cracks were undoubtedly caused by a difference in the rate of expansion between dried varnish and paper. Paper expands and contracts rapidly with heat, cold and variations in moisture, while a varnish film is comparatively inflexible. As envelopes pass from hot offices to cold mailboxes, back to overheated mail cars and once more to the street, they undergo many changes in size. The varnish, being unable to follow, cracks off. We were dealing here with an inexorable law of physics. If our yard foreman at Pittsburgh had been unsuccessful in beating it with a set of heavy chains, how was I going to do it? I began to feel that the problem had no solution.

I had accepted a good-sized retainer though, and was honor-bound to match my wits against this apparent impossibility. I was quite ready to spend time on developing a varnish, but I was not willing to wait three or four months before seeing the results of each test. My next task therefore was to find a method by which I could determine in a few hours what nature would do to our windows in the course of months.

I shall not describe the labyrinth of ideas and errors through

203

which we worked our way before we began to see a ray of hope. Suffice it to say that without the mechanical genius of Mr. Sauermann and the patience of Mr. Regenstein, we would have continued to send an endless stream of letters to fictitious addresses in Singapore or Teheran. Together we untied one knot after another, until only one problem remained—how to overcome the law of expansion and contraction. And here I was as far away from my goal as ever.

One night a man who was contemplating a pleasure trip to Vienna called on me. He wanted me to suggest what he should see there. I began by telling him at random of a nail-studded tree which stands in the center of the city; how a witch who once lived in that tree had affixed to it a lock which no one could open. Every blacksmith tried it and left a nail in the bark to show that he had failed; for when he inserted his key, the witch gave it a half turn and blocked the attempt. Finally a bright young apprentice came along; he inserted the key upside down, and when the witch twisted it around, it fell into the right position and the lock sprang open—

I stopped abruptly. Before me I suddenly saw the answer to my puzzle. I would not have to suspend a natural law; all I had to do was meet it halfway. I could hardly wait to try out my inspiration. When I did, it worked to perfection, and it has continued to work that way for over thirty years. A good many chemists used to tell me how hard they had tried to match our varnish. Even Mr. Hoskins confided to me that he had spent two years on the problem before he gave up. I could not, of course, divulge a professional secret, and I was loath to discuss it, for the puzzle almost solved itself, once it had been reduced to its elements. At Sammy McLeod's plant our emulsion of water and linseed oil had defied separation until I hit on the ridiculously simple plan of decreasing the specific gravity of one constituent while increasing that of the other. In the case of window envelopes the process had to be reversed: we had to equalize the widely varying coefficients of expansion of paper and varnish. I did not put this into so many words, but I told Hoskins to read the story of the studded tree in Vienna or Poe's "The Purloined Letter." I am afraid he did not take me seriously. Few competitors do when you tell them the truth.

With the discovery of the magic formula our troubles did not cease; rather they began afresh. In his impetuosity, Mr. Regenstein ordered that no more envelopes be made with the old varnishes, in spite of my hectic protest that I was not yet ready to jump into quantity production. The result, as anyone might have foreseen, was misery. I could not duplicate my own results, the spoilage was enormous, and at one time we shut down the plant altogether and did not reopen it for seventeen days. During that period Mr. Sauermann and I stayed in the factory all night until we fell asleep on our feet. We were half-crazed with worry and lack of rest, while a frantic sales department wanted to know every hour when the plant would start up again. One Saturday noon I threw up the sponge and suggested that we all get drunk and not come back till Monday morning. The invitation was avidly snapped up. We all went to the nearest saloon and soon forgot about envelopes.

Monday morning I was on the job bright and early. Going over our experimental outfit, I discovered to my dismay that Frank, a usually reliable workman, had forgotten to turn off the fire under one of our kettles. This was the finishing blow. Now the varnish, exposed to extreme heat for two days, would be irretrievably ruined. We all felt like quitting for good. Nevertheless, we took what remained and finished our compound with it. It produced the best envelopes we had made yet. Frank's hurry to get to the saloon had solved our main difficulty.

Many minor kinks still remained, but they were ironed out one after another, and although others cropped up now and then, we mastered them. The making of window envelopes graduated into an industry governed by chemical control.

Billions of these envelopes have since rolled off the presses, and there are few people who have not either sent or received some of them. I would give a great deal to know if a single person, instead of taking these envelopes for granted, has ever wondered how windows are put into them, and how much worry, sweat and heart-blood it has taken to bring them to their present state of perfection.

Compared with the excitement and the turmoil at the Window Envelope Company, life in the linseed oil plant seemed dull and uninteresting. Not much more than routine executive work was left to me. I had disposed of nearly all pressing tasks and could not envision any new ones. At more and more frequent intervals I had to confess to myself that I was tired of my position. Moreover, I was becoming dissatisfied with the amount of money I was making. What my old book agent had predicted had come to pass. I was now thirty years old, and my rolling-stone age was over.

People still had curious ideas about chemists. In my Pittsburgh days no one had ever had a clear notion what a chemist was and what he did. Those who thought about it at all imagined he was a soda-water clerk with a diploma. Now chemistry was becoming better understood, but rarely to the advantage of the profession. My friends began submitting to me their home problems. I once had the good luck to restore a four-hundred-dollar wedding gown to a hapless bride who had spilled iodine on it. All I had done was to walk to the nearest drugstore, buy a nickel's worth of sodium thiosulphate, dissolve it in lukewarm water, and dip the gown into it. This piece of magic gave me a certain local reputation. Hostesses began pestering me with questions about fruit, food and ink stains, until I became wary about accepting dinner engagements. One time I found myself in the midst of several women, each of whom had a different stain on her mind.

"Ladies," I said, "let me tell you a story. There once was a hostess who complained to a visiting chemist about her inability to remove gravy spots from a tablecloth. He advised her to spread it on her lawn and let the ozone of the air bleach it out."

"And did the spots disappear?" one of my torturers asked me.

"Yes," I said, "and so did the tablecloth."

My audience did not like the anecdote, but it ended my scientific laundry work in exchange for meals.

One of my colleagues, a chemist for a large railroad, was so incensed at being questioned constantly on his profession that he carried a card in his vest pocket on which he had written, "I am a chemist for the K. & M. Railroad." This card he pulled out when someone asked him what he was. When the inevitable sequence came in the form of, "What does the K. & M. Railroad need a chemist for?" he parried it by pulling out a card from his other vest pocket. "The K. & M. Railroad," it read, "needs a chemist because it buys coal, oil and boiler compounds which must be tested."

As a matter of fact, a railroad chemist had to do more than analyze coal and oil. When George Davidson, for many years chief chemist of the Chicago & North Western Railroad, used to talk about his activities, we others wondered not at what a railroad chemist had to do, but if there was anything he did not have to do. Besides watching over the purchase of such widely different materials as boiler compounds, metal polishes, paints, car disinfectants, plush dyes and dozens of other items, he had to advise people who lived along the right of way of his railroad on the natural resources of the country or settle some of their personal troubles. At one time hog cholera broke out in one of the localities served by the Northwestern Railroad, and the animals were dying in large numbers. A quack veterinary appeared on the scene and took orders for a cholera cure in such astounding quantities that the railroad agents became interested and asked Davidson to analyze the nostrum. When Davidson showed it to be a mixture of clay and coloring matter, the quack disappeared in a cloud of dust, and some western farming communities were left with a new sense of obligation toward their railroad.

Davidson could tell by heart that the Overland Limited consumed fifteen thousand gallons of water in the two hundred and two miles between Clinton and Boone, and was able to cite the composition of boiler waters from Lake Michigan to the Black Hills of South Dakota. The laboratory of the railroad must have had a merry time varying the proper liquid diet for its locomotives as they traveled along. I still carried scars from the Barbara Furnace boilers on my body and did not envy these chemists their jobs.

If people did not bother chemists with foolish questions, they usually asked for free technical advice; never did I hear anyone offering me compensation. A fellow boarder who held a position in a lithographing firm once asked me to work out a problem for him; I did so, to his great satisfaction and pecuniary gain. When I suggested a fee, he was quite upset; one paid lawyers, sometimes doctors, but no one had ever paid a chemist. Mr. Hoskins, the leading consulting chemist in Chicago, had nursed this idea along by his free and easy hospitality. He dispensed advice like a public clinic, much to the despair of his competitors. There was Mr. Skinner, for instance—Doc Skinner to all who knew him—who ran a little laboratory on Adams Street and spent most of his time convincing his clients that he was paying rent and wages like other mortals and that occasionally he had to eat. They took his word for the rent and wages, but looking at his lean body they probably doubted that he ever ate, which was unfortunate for him. Skinner used to curse Hoskins in seven languages, but in his heart he loved that grand old man of chemistry just as we all did. Nevertheless, the fact remained that bills for chemical services were hard to collect.

Again I compared the income of many people I knew with those of chemists and pondered the iniquity of fate. I knew many men who had fine incomes or who owned lucrative concerns, but not one of them was a chemist. On the other hand, none of the chemists I knew was making as much as five thousand dollars a year, which was perhaps not surprising in view of the fact that the chief chemist of the United States Government received a salary of only three thousand. Low wages for analysts I could understand; but other chemists were either administering laws, creating wealth, or else effecting enough savings to justify a much higher compensation. I alone had instituted two measures in our company that showed a profit of fifty-five thousand dollars annually, and both of them I had dug up without outside help. What was the answer?

An accidental meeting with a large manufacturer of cosmetics gave me a glimpse of the truth. When I stepped into his office, I found him in an ugly mood. His chemist had developed and demonstrated a new vanishing cream which would be a great improvement; yet the president was disgusted.

"Here I come to the office at nine o'clock," he grumbled, "and the treasurer is waiting for me with a demand from the bank to pay up a loan. Then the sales manager comes in and shows me weather reports from Texas. The cotton crop down there is ruined and he wants to pull our salesmen out and throw them into Oklahoma, where the oil boom is growing. Then the superintendent comes in with a tale of woe; a competitor has just put his cream into a jar that opens more easily than ours. Our printer is next; a new state law in North Dakota requires us to put a special label on our merchandise. Then, just when I want to look at the mail, in comes that damned chemist. My God, do I have to put something into my jars, too, when I have my hands full with all these other things?"

So that was it. No wonder the treasurer, the sales manager, the superintendent and the printer were getting the butter and the chemist the skimmed milk. I suggested that the technical man had at least a nuisance value; if the improvement was important, he could take it to another house, couldn't he?

The president laughed.

"Let him go," he remarked. "For fifty dollars a week I can hire another who'll duplicate that great improvement or beat it. Now, if a good salesman threatens to leave me, he may take a lot of business with him. But a chemist? Pshaw! The woods are full of them. If one of them quits, the chances are that the next one will be better."

This executive was considered a humane and progressive man. In many other plants chemists were not even allowed to see the president. I wished other chemists could have been with me that morning, especially those who still could have quit the profession.

Something else about this conversation kept plaguing me. Was it because the chemist was getting only fifty dollars a week that the president had paid such scant attention to him? The sales manager and the others were probably drawing twice that much. A man with a small salary was not worth listening to; if he were, he would be getting more money. The chemist, on his side, probably felt that he would be getting more money if his superiors would only listen to him. It was the old story of which came first, the hen or the egg. I thought it might be worth trying to find out if bigger eggs would not produce bigger hens; if they did, and bigger hens would in turn lay bigger eggs, no one would care which of the two had come first.

The Window Envelope Company was having difficulties. The manufacture of the compound had been turned over to a local varnish maker who claimed to be following my instructions. Nevertheless, trouble arose frequently, and thousands of envelopes had to be thrown away. I blamed the varnish maker, while he, with equal conviction and superior profanity, blamed me and my formula. Quarreling was getting us nowhere; obviously our system was wrong. If the varnish were made under my supervision, one man would carry the entire responsibility. Mr. Regenstein was anxious to have me shoulder it, and so was I. The profit on the varnish, now flowing into other pockets, would cover my fee as a consultant. All I needed was a little plant of my own. As luck would have it, another concern was also anxious to have me open up shop. When I had made my address before the American Chemical Society three years previously, two railroad chemists had been in the audience; they had urged me several times in the interim to furnish their road with a special oil for painting freight cars. They were letting contracts to different firms, but the material was neither satisfactory nor uniform. Now they were looking for someone who was both honest in following an approved formula and capable of improving it. They thought I was that man.

All I had to do now was to get the consent of my firm to carry out this plan. To my surprise, I encountered no opposition. The only condition imposed on me was that I was not to devote my regular hours to the new business, but engage someone else to take charge. This was eminently fair and quite satisfactory to me. I selected a promising young man of my acquaintance for the job, and in a short time the Scientific Oil Company was born. My investment consisted of seventy-five dollars in cash and a huge surplus of extravagant hopes.

When I was ready to do business, the railroad gave me an initial order for no less than one thousand barrels of paint oil. This was almost too good to be true. I bought a little kettle, set it on loose bricks in a nearby prairie, equipped myself with a hand pump and compounded my first batch. It was approved and paid for. I shall never forget the thrill of making out that first bill on our new stationery, nor the pride I felt in depositing our first check in a brand-new bank account. I was launched as a full-fledged manufacturer in my own right.

With the Window Envelope contract and a thousand-barrel order of paint oil in hand I had no hesitation in renting quarters for my young venture. Across from the White Sox ball park I found a small lot with a stub switch track. There was no office, no toilet, only a little brick building which was half above, half under ground. It had originally been built to store naphtha for a rug-cleaning establishment. Price, however, was more important to me than conveniences. My young manager went in with me on a profit-sharing basis, and Billy, the foreman I had once fired in self-defense, became my working force. With our own hands we built a shanty out of two-by-four boards and corrugated iron and called it our office. The furniture consisted of two chairs, a stove and a slab of wood

life before me as on a screen, and wondered what the next reels would bring forth. I was now thirty-one years old. If I was to stop being an employee, this was the proper time. I knew of many people who had put off the day of their independence until they were too old to take chances. I was still unmarried and free to move where others were tied down with families.

For the first time, as I lay there day-dreaming, the thought struck me that now was also the time to make up my mind whether I wanted to get married or remain a bachelor. The idea of matrimony horrified me. Why shed the restraints of an employee only to go into a relationship from which one could not even resign? Yet the thought came back to me again and again. The question had to be faced some time. If men did not marry at my age, they usually dropped out of the race. It looked to me as if I were at more than one crossroad.

At a railroad station in Germany I bought at random a book called *The Joys of Married Life.* As I read it, my interest increased. The author was looking back on twenty-five years of connubial bliss and had observed much and well. If two healthy people who had sprung from the same soil were married, he had seen happiness follow with almost mathematical certainty. At first he had abhorred the idea of marriage, but the problems he had dreaded had solved themselves without difficulty. He cited two observations which impressed me. A girl who hummed or sang while she worked, he had noticed, always made a good wife, and the right kind of woman unknotted the strings of a package rather than cut them.

I could think of only one girl who met these specifications, and that was my young cousin Bertha in Chicago. Besides, she was lovely to look at and even more lovely in character. More impressive to me than anything else was that women seemed to admire her as much as men. One night I had taken her to a party where some old ladies with bitter tongues, believing themselves unheard, put every girl except Bertha through the acid bath of their gossip. For Bertha they had nothing but praise. But Bertha was a mere child. I had met her when she was sixteen or so, and in my mind she had never grown up. I did not recall ever having had a serious conversation with her. But when I thought that someone else might marry her, I felt unhappy.

Austria in 1911 was at her best. Gay crowds were everywhere. The soldiers one saw thought more of drinking and loving than fighting; passports were unknown. A new operetta by Lehar, called *The Merry Widow,* was setting people agog. The Vienna bourse was in the throes of a bull market. Clerks, policemen and nurse girls stood in front of brokerage offices. No one wanted to miss the easy profits. It was the last flicker of the great old empire before the World War extinguished it.

In the midst of these lazy summer days my loyal Gertie sent me a disturbing cable. The Scientific Oil Company was in trouble. A new competitive product was making serious inroads into our volume of business. I decided to return at once to set things straight, if possible. Evidently it would be wise to retain my position with the American Linseed Company for the time being. The day of my complete independence would have to wait.

The work I had done in Europe had not been without its attractions. The Germans had discovered a new process for the manufacture of fatty acids, and I had investigated its possibilities. It was the only time I went through pre-war German factories. The discipline which prevailed was impressive. I saw the deference of the workmen and heard the click of their heels as they stood at attention when addressed. All officials were called by military titles, such as Major Schmidt and Captain Mueller, for they were reserve officers and very proud of it. Once I was invited into the home of a Colonel, an occasion I would gladly have missed. I had completely outgrown the ceremonious formalities of European society, although I had never known them in such extremes in easy-going Vienna. A few bottles of wine were opened in my honor, but I committed a *faux pas* when I did not admire the cobwebs which denoted their age, and I probably made matters worse by overdoing my praise of the wine, about which I knew nothing except that I did not like it. We had some music later, everyone joining in the "Watch on the Rhine" and "The Lorelei," which reawakened my hatred for community singing. During the meal I was seated next to the hostess, who told me that she had three sons, all of whom held the rank of officers in the army. She was hoping that they would some day have the honor to fight and, if necessary, die for their Kaiser and Vaterland. I am afraid her wish was granted.

In Antwerp I visited one of our important oil-cake customers, with whom I was to arrange new terms for future shipments. Half a dozen men sat with me around an antique table in a room that must have been hundreds of years old. It had a low ceiling and small windows which were in wide contrast to the modern decorations. The meeting was carried on mostly in French, with Flemish, English and German words thrown in now and then for good measure. I lacked many French technical terms and was wringing wet with perspiration while negotiating our deal. At twelve o'clock sharp everyone left, and no one took the slightest notice of me. I was back at one, but the porter, who looked like a rear admiral, would not let me enter until three. The others evidently knew the customs, for they did not show up until then. One of them had the temerity to ask me where I had taken my lunch. I thought, "What do you care; you did not invite me," and told him of the little restaurant I had patronized. Whereupon they all turned their hypocritical eyes heavenward and told me of the many good places I could have chosen instead. It was a typical case of that much vaunted European politeness which is nothing but a veneer to hide the lack of true courtesy underneath.

I also had some business in London, Birmingham and Liverpool, and I felt less at home there than on the Continent. In Liverpool I could scarcely believe my eyes when I saw the blackness of the buildings, compared to which the downtown district of Pittsburgh looked as if it were covered with freshly fallen snow. On the first day I tried to scratch the soot off one wall with my fingernail, just to see how deep it was, when a policeman came sauntering along and smilingly discouraged me. The dirt coating had been there for centuries and would probably be there for centuries to come.

Of oils, paints and varnishes our European confrères knew much less than we did in America. Even the famous Dutch linseed oil, known the world over as *Standoel*, would not have impressed American buyers, except perhaps to evoke a smile.

A few weeks after my return to Chicago, I was engaged to Bertha. No fuss was made over our engagement. We spent the next few months buying our furniture at sales and then were married as quietly as possible. Our wedding trip took us south as far as Sixty-third Street, where we had furnished an apartment.

We agreed that a honeymoon in our new home was enough romance for the time being.

In the meantime, the management of the American Linseed Company had changed, and a few weeks after our wedding day I was suddenly discharged. There had been no previous warning; there never came a subsequent explanation. Perhaps my salary, which had climbed to four hundred dollars a month, was considered excessive, or else the new president disapproved of my outside activities. The blow had fallen at an inopportune time, I confess, and no doubt my vanity also suffered. Then I recalled that I had always advocated throwing people into the water to make them swim. Well, someone had pushed me in, and now I would have to strike out for myself or sink. I took a deep breath and stretched my arms. I vowed that I had lived my last day as an employee. Never again would I depend on the whims of higher-ups. I had lost a job, but hoped to have found freedom instead.

The next morning I took charge of the Scientific Oil Company. My only regret was that I could not take Gertie into my new venture on full time. She volunteered, however, to come to our house evenings and help with the office work. We were both looking forward to the time when conditions would permit a permanent reunion. As it happened, we did not have to wait long.

CHAPTER 11

ONE PROBLEM AFTER ANOTHER

$\mathcal{T}$HE SUDDEN READJUSTMENT of my career was not accomplished without some inner strain. I had stepped from the comparative luxury of a well-paid position into the primitive surroundings of a homemade plant, and exchanged a regular income for the vagaries of a small business, still in its infancy. My new daily routine was no bed of roses. I began work in overalls at six o'clock in the morning and labored with my men until twelve. Then I washed up in the rest room of the public park across from us and walked out in street dress. At six o'clock I came home for supper, and the rest of the evening was given to letter writing and other office work. The Scientific Oil Company was to be a chemical consulting office with a manufacturing annex, conducted along the lines of professional ethics. There would be no salesmen, and I never would advertise. If I proved to be good, people would eventually discover me, just as they discovered good surgeons and lawyers, and if I proved bad, I had no right to succeed. Orthodox business stood aghast at such heresy and was quite justified in its skepticism. I still guard among my treasures the first commercial reports on my new venture. They intimated plainly that credit men had better keep a wary eye on me.

Billy, my new superintendent, was a small man, but much stronger than he appeared. His skill in handling barrels and drums, empty or full, was remarkable. He had a way of spinning them around with two fingers that would have done honor to a vaude-ville artist. It usually took two or three men to load a full oil barrel on a truck, but Billy always did it alone and seemingly without effort. It was a pleasure to watch him work. I soon hired another man named Tom, who had once been employed in the White Sox ball park, and whose conversation, such as it was, centered solely around the great players he knew and to whom he always referred as Fred or Jim or Joe. At noon he used to sneak into the restaurant where they assembled prior to an afternoon's game, and if they bestowed as much as a glance on him he was the happiest man in the world.

In the course of time I got to know many of the White Sox players. One of them had once strolled into our office by mistake and found it a convenient hangout for a clandestine cigarette or two. Soon others followed, and at times we had quite a crowd. The older players often regaled the rookies with wild yarns, to which I listened with amusement. Some of them still cling to my mind.

"We were playing in a little town one afternoon," an old-timer said, "and the game dragged out into extra innings, until it was getting dark. I hit a double and was taking a big lead off second base, when what does the fool of a catcher do? He tries to catch me off second, but throws wild, way over the shortstop's head, into the outfield. I leg it for the plate, of course, and when I slide into it, there stands the catcher with the ball in his hand and touches me for an out. Naturally, there was a big hullabaloo. The out-fielders were still looking for the ball out there in the dark, and here this fellow had it in his hand all the time. When he sees me take that big lead he pulls a potato out of his pocket—I guess he had figured that play beforehand—and throws it over second, and when I come in I am just a plain sucker.

"We almost killed that catcher, but he calls the umpire for a decision. The umpire pulls out his book of rules and sure enough, there's nothing said in there that a fellow can't throw a potato if he wants to. I was out for good, and we lost the ball game."

"That reminds me," drawled another veteran, "of an overtime game I was in once out in one of the western bush leagues, when I was a young fellow. They had a pitcher in there I could not hit at all, and when I came up to bat in the eleventh inning, with the score nothing to nothing, I decided to bat lefthanded. I couldn't do worse than I had done before. So when the pitcher starts to throw the ball in, I close my eyes and swing. Bang, goes the ball

218

over the fence for a home-run. I got so excited, I forgot I was standing the wrong way, and started to run to third instead of first. The crowd yelled like crazy, but I thought they were just cheering me on, and I went all the way around, third, second, first and home, and when I crossed the plate, the umpire said the score was now nothing to minus one and that I had lost the game by hitting a home run."

I liked the White Sox players, but I could never warm up to them as a team. In my heart I was still pulling for Pittsburgh, for Fred Clarke, the "Flying Dutchman" Honus Wagner, for little Tommy Leach on third, and the big pinch-hitter Hyatt, who made a three-bagger every time they let him bat. In Chicago my team was the Cubs, who were going at top speed. Those were the days of the stonewall infield—of Chance, Tinker, Evers and Steinfeld, of Kling and Three-Fingered Brown and many other baseball immortals. Frank Chance had a saying which I have never forgotten. When he was asked how he won championship after championship, he answered that he did it by keeping the best utility players in the league on his payroll.

"A team is as good as its substitute players," was the way he put it. "Whenever a star player of another team gets hurt, the whole team goes to pieces. My substitutes are as good as the first-stringers, and that's the whole secret of my success."

I have watched many businesses for thirty years, and I think Frank Chance was right. A business is as good as its pinch-hitters, no better, whether it is out to produce merchandise or baseball victories.

The All-proof Cloth Corporation, now about a year old, was beginning to attract nation-wide attention. Orders were coming in from all over the country, and we had to enlarge our quarters time and again. From the manufacture of sanitary bed sheets, the company had progressed to baby clothes and waterproof raincoats which could be folded up to fit into a pocket or handbag. They were a great novelty in those days. We had a very able young lady named Marie in charge of the enterprise, and her energy, together with the unflagging enthusiasm of Doc Marshall, was putting the invention over. Unfortunately, none of us knew enough about finance to avoid the obvious pitfall ahead of us. Our very prosperity, with insufficient capital to back it up, proved our undoing. We were handling so much business that we could not meet our bills, and finally had to sell out to the Ladies Garment Corporation, an internationally known house specializing in women's accessories. The new owners built a large plant for All-proof Cloth in the little town of Montmartre, about one hundred miles from Chicago, with Doc in charge of the manufacturing. I was retained as consultant and still held the exclusive right to furnish the waterproofing fluid. We had exchanged a large slice of a small pie for a small slice of a large one which, as a rule, is not a bad swap.

The Montmartre plant had an interesting crew. Our superintendent, Gilchrist, had been a conductor on the Trans-Pacific in his earlier days and entertained us by the hour with his stories. He had been freight conductor between Gibson City and Dunkirk, and one day, as he took over a fast freight train at the western terminal of his section, his incoming colleague cautioned him about a car containing silk valued at some thirty thousand dollars. Gilchrist laughed.

"Do you want me to sit on the car all the way to Dunkirk?" he asked. The silk car was in the middle of the train. If the train got to Dunkirk the silk car would get there too. But it didn't. When the train reached Gilchrist's eastern terminus, every car was there but the one with the silk. There had been no stop, no accident. Gilchrist was suspended from service, as were all other men on that train. The railroad detectives got busy on the case and scoured the country. A freight car could not vanish into thin air, and the silk would have to show up in some trade channel sooner or later. But month after month passed, and all hope of getting to the core of the puzzle remained unfulfilled.

Then, after a lapse of two years, a great drought hit the entire western country from Gibson City to Dunkirk. A cowboy in search of cattle came near a trestle of the railroad and under it, half buried in some mud that once had been a river, was the missing freight car. The silk was ruined, of course, but from the evidence found it was easy to figure out what had happened. The trestle made a sharp curve there, and as the train had passed over it, the silk car must have broken loose from the two cars which held it and gone over the side. The engineer most likely had then slowed down, and the rear end of the train had caught up and automatically coupled itself on again.

It was a good story; we had our doubts about it, but no one expressed them audibly.

A few weeks later I met by chance one of the railroad detectives who had worked on this case, and he confirmed the story in every detail. The next time I saw Mr. Gilchrist I held out my hand to him. It is not always safe to call a man a liar, not even in your own mind.

Our master mechanic at Montmartre was a Bible student. Everything that had been, was or would be, he believed, could be found in the Scriptures, although few people were able to interpret them correctly. I challenged him to foretell something that would happen within our lifetimes. He predicted a World War which would last from 1914 to 1918. We thought that this was carrying a joke too far and did not even laugh at it.

The Ladies Garment Corporation soon added to our old line sanitary aprons, dress shields and other ladies' accessories, the uses of which I could not guess until they were explained to me. Once a week I met saleswomen who brought me articles about which complaints had been received. The freedom with which the most intimate functions of female bodies were discussed was something to which I had to get acclimated. Each saleslady had customers whose excretions were abnormal in one way or another, and each wanted individual service. Sometimes I met their customers in person, and my sessions with them, no matter how often repeated, always remained a source of embarrassment to me.

I had my shingle out as a consulting chemist, but most of my early clients were either crackpots or too poor to pay for chemical services. Most of them acted greatly surprised, not to say offended, when I asked for a retainer. I could not blame them a great deal for that. Legislatures all over the country were creating state laboratories, where everything from soils to apple jellies was analyzed free of charge. State socialism to protect all people may be justified, but I did not see it extend into fields where other professions were affected. If a man wanted to know if something was against the law he could not ask the state's attorney's opinion; he had to hire a lawyer and pay for the information. That most legislators were lawyers may have had something to do with this one-sidedness. Regardless of all social theories, however, the fact remained that state and federal laboratories made it difficult to ply an analyst's trade and make it pay.

Most problems submitted to me were not real chemical problems anyway, but pipe dreams. No self-respecting chemist would have wasted an hour of his time on them. I remember a small, secretive-looking man who assured himself that all doors were shut, before he disclosed his secret to me. Could I make iron into a metal that would not rust, or dissolve in various acids, in short, iron that would have all the characteristics of platinum? If so, he could sell more than I could ever produce. I told him that what he needed was not a chemist, but an alchemist. I had people come in with suggestions for using water instead of gasoline in motors. One man wanted to make candies out of glue; another was looking for a kerosene that would not burn, Heaven knows why. None of these people had even a speaking acquaintance with the chemical aspects of their problems. I found that the best method to rid myself of their presence was to ask for a five-hundred-dollar retainer. After that they quickly remembered that they had business elsewhere.

Once in a while I landed an interesting consulting job. In the summer of 1913 I was asked by some moneyed men to investigate a number of abandoned western gold mines. They intended reopening them, should this appear profitable. I protested against an assignment so far out of my line, but I protested in vain. Soon Bertha and I were on our trip, which began in the Black Hills of South Dakota and ended in Denver. The mountain states had few good roads then, and while it was possible to use automobiles now and then in the back country, we had to do most of our traveling there on horseback.

The Black Hills were as yet unknown to tourists, the Rocky Mountains almost inaccessible. I spent weeks among old mines, walking through abandoned shafts hundreds of feet under the surface, climbing up and down rickety ladders that had not been used for years, and listening to many strange tales from old-timers. They were hanging around formerly prosperous mining districts, dreaming of the days when the glorious past would be revived; they saw in me an angel of hope and showered me with information and misinformation. To be on the safe side, I hammered out and assayed my own samples, a difficult and wearisome task. On the whole, our trip was interesting, but for my clients without profit. With one exception, I considered all the abandoned claims worthless. The exception was a mine in Colorado near Idaho Springs about which I was doubtful. Some of my employers took a trip out there, concluded that the chances were good, and decided to reopen the mine. They invited me to come in on the deal with my fee of six hundred dollars, which is why my work as a mining expert has left me with nothing but a pleasant memory.

While traveling from the Black Hills to Colorado, we passed the Crow Indian Reservation, and on the spur of the moment got off the train to visit Custer's battlefield. Evening was setting in, and the Indian settlement presented a dismal appearance. The only light in town came from a kerosene lamp in the little station house, and that was extinguished at nine o'clock, after the last train had passed. There was no hotel. Luckily, an Indian trader, the only white man around, offered us two beds in his garret. They had not been made up for weeks, he said; the last persons who had slept in them were Mr. Josephus Daniels, then Secretary of the Navy, and his wife, which was evidently sufficient reason for our host to leave things undisturbed. I am sure Bertha would have gladly deserted me, had there been a place for her to go. As we took a walk through the shacks and tents which made up the village, shadowy forms passed us or seemed to lurk in the corners. Bertha clung to me for dear life, but when an old squaw suddenly lit her pipe right in front of our faces, it was the last straw. Bertha fled to our room, pulled the blanket over her head, and was not herself again until the sun shone on us next morning.

Custer's battlefield is situated on a knob, a short distance from Crow Indian station, and at that time was guarded by an old veteran, who was delighted to have us break in on his loneliness. He had been a soldier in General Gibbon's army, which was the first to arrive after the massacre. I asked him why the victorious Indians had not been pursued. He took me aside and described to me how Gibbon's army of youngsters, most of them not over eighteen years old, had come upon the naked and horribly mutilated

223

bodies of their comrades, and why no threats or orders would have induced them to risk a like fate.

The battlefield was overgrown with grass as high as a man's head, and abounded with rattlesnakes. We dared not get off our horses while we followed the trails over which Custer had traveled. The four-mile ride to Reno's battlefield was surpassingly beautiful. On our left a rolling desert stretched for many miles to the banks of the Yellowstone, far beyond the horizon. On our right, at the foot of a sharp precipice, the Little Big Horn wound its way through a landscape which looked alluring even in its desolation. On the opposite bank dense groves of cottonwood trees hid the spot where Major Reno, following Custer's orders, had tried to pit his handful of men against thousands of infuriated Indian warriors. He had been forced to retreat across the river to seek refuge on a little hill and had slaughtered his horses to form breastworks. Piles of bleached animal bones still encircled his old campsite. The place was cut off from drinking water, and during the night volunteers had stolen down to the river bank to fill their canteens. Little white stones showed where they had been slaughtered.

In 1913, one could still pick up cooking utensils and shells on Reno's battlefield, and I even found a loaded army revolver, on which were engraved the initials of its owner.

My visit to the site of Custer's last fight moved me more deeply than anything had ever done before. For many years, a picture of the massacre hung in my office, until I had it removed because it distracted me too much. I resolved to see every battlefield in America, and I was fortunate in seeing many of the more famous ones before paved roads and peanut stands turned their hallowed soil into picnic grounds.

One of my few early consulting jobs originated with an express company. The wheels of their little baggage trucks were made of hickory wood which warped to such an extent that they became useless. Covering the rims with steel hoops would have meant cutting up the cement platforms on which they traveled. Was there any way in which the warping could be avoided? I thought there was. All we had to do was impregnate the wooden wheels with oil so that the moisture which was causing the warping could not enter.

My work on transparent envelopes had acquainted me with penetration problems. Of course, a thick slab of hickory wood was different from a thin layer of paper; but the principle was the same. When I had worked out a formula for an oil which dried satisfactorily inside a wheel, I found that I could not coax it into the dense structure of hickory wood. It just lay on the outside as on a plate of steel. I tried a vacuum tank, but that proved too expensive. I then inserted the wheels in a vat filled with hot oil. The moisture and air left the cells of the wood, and the oil moved in. The scheme was as simple as it was effective. I charged nothing for my service, but instead added another account to our list of customers. Perhaps I could show the financial reporters that chemistry and business sense were not incompatible.

Another problem, submitted to me by a local glove manufacturer, has remained in my mind, not because of its chemical difficulties, but because of its unusual background.

Many years ago, I was told, one of the big league baseball teams had a pitcher whom I shall call Jones. He was a good pitcher, but in the course of time his prowess waned, and he went down the ladder until he was even too old for the bush leagues. He drifted back to the place of his former triumphs and asked the manager to let him do some work, any work at all. I suppose baseball managers have sentimental streaks in them like other human beings, and Jones was allowed to catch for rookie pitchers during morning practice. It was also part of his work to break in new gloves, and Jones had to do a lot of spitting, for spitting was the only method then in vogue for softening them. One evening as he rummaged through the cupboard of his washroom, he had a happy thought. He would try out oil, rather than wear out his saliva glands. What he used, I do not know. It may have been castor oil or vaseline, or any of the oily substances in ordinary household use. At any rate, the results were astoundingly good. A sporting-goods house adopted the idea and the Jones gloves soon became popular.

It was my job to do for my client what Jones had done for his— and for baseball in general. I figured that leather, being a product of animal origin, should absorb animal oils with greater ease than vegetable oils like castor oil, or petroleum products like vaseline.

225

Hence, I tried lard oil, fish oils and wool grease, and brought my work quickly to a satisfactory conclusion.

That oiled baseball glove gave me much food for thought. I did not feel very proud of my success. It was the old pitcher who deserved the glory, not I. Thousands of chemists must have used mitts in their younger days, but it had taken a baseball player to recognize this nugget when he saw it. Why had no chemist picked it up before him?

I am not sure that I ever found a satisfactory answer to my question, but I made what was perhaps the most important discovery of my chemical career. I recognized for the first time that each chemical task consists of three entirely separate parts: the first is to find a good problem; the second is to solve it; the third is to sell the solution. Colleges only taught their students to solve problems. They did not point out that problems do not present themselves of their own accord, and no one ever lectured on how to sell the solution after it was found. Probably the teachers themselves did not know. To find worthwhile problems one did not have to be a chemist. The glove problem had been discovered by a baseball player; the waterproof cloth idea had come to me through a hospital orderly. Like so many other chemists, I had been sitting in my office waiting for people to bring problems to me rather than seek them myself.

I had also taken it for granted that after problems were solved they sold themselves. They don't. If you handed the solution of a problem to two different chemists, one would make a fortune and the other cigarette money. I once heard a consulting chemist discuss one of his recent cases. A candy manufacturer had complained to him that he could not control the quality of his lemon drops. At times they turned out as clear as a crystal, at other times they became cloudy and unsalable. My friend had diagnosed the case quickly and correctly. The trouble lay in the citric acid used, which sometimes contained an excess of water. He had charged his client fifty dollars and considered it fair pay. Another chemist might have done differently. He might have supplied his client with a citric acid guaranteed to produce clear lemon drops, thereby protecting his customer permanently and securing for himself a steady income through commissions or profits on the sale of merchandise.

226

That would have been good salesmanship. But the average chemist, I found, had about as much acumen in money matters as a prize fighter; the difference was that prize fighters had sense enough to put themselves under the guidance of hard-boiled business managers.

One chemist who knew how to sell his services at high prices was Freddie. He owned a doctor's degree from an obscure German university where rumor had it that money talked, and he never let anyone forget his title or that he had studied in Germany. He was a member of several high-class clubs and played billiards with the best prospects in town. Freddie was that smart he could have made money sitting on a rock in the middle of the Sahara.

I happened to run into him once at a fashionable resort, and we went to a prize-fight together. While we were mingling with the crowd, someone stole his billfold. The poor pickpocket could not have made a greater mistake. Stealing money from Freddie was a sure bid for trouble. He went back to the hotel, asked the clerk for a telegram blank, and concocted a message which was addressed to his secretary. It read something like this:

> CALL COLONEL J. IN WASHINGTON AND TELL HIM I
> HAVE BEEN ROBBED IN THIS TOWN. HE WILL DO THE
> NECESSARY.

Then he bought himself an evening paper and sat down to enjoy it.

Half an hour later, a man approached us and said he was a private detective. Would Freddie split the contents of the pocketbook if it could be recovered? Freddie would not. The chief of police was the next to put in an appearance. Would Freddie give the police twenty-four hours to catch the thief? Freddie would not. Finally the manager of the hotel walked up to us and offered to make good the entire damage if Freddie would withhold his wire. After much persuasion Freddie accepted four hundred dollars in settlement. The pocketbook had contained seventy-five dollars, he told me later.

"Who is this Colonel J. in Washington," I asked him, "with whom you are so chummy?"

"Colonel J.?" he asked me, raising his brows in surprise. "I don't know any Colonel J. in Washington. Have a smoke?"

The selling of solved problems, in its broader sense, does not necessarily involve money. Some chemists work out important improvements and see them rejected by the management; others earn promotions or bonuses. The clever ones know how to get the workingmen on their side, the less clever ones antagonize them. One chemist will take care to have his achievements recognized by the man on top, while another sees his credit stolen from him by a dishonest foreman.

Lack of salesmanship in chemists showed even in little things. Applicants for jobs came in at nine o'clock on a Monday morning before I had read my mail. Not one in a hundred had informed himself beforehand as to whether we were manufacturing oil compounds or fire bricks. Any lead pencil salesman knew better. Perhaps if the study of chemistry included courses on what to do with chemical knowledge after you possessed it, the lot of chemists might improve.

On one of our educational institutions I used to read the sign, "Knowledge is Power." That simply is not so; at best it is only a dangerous half-truth. Knowledge is no more power than a stone on the roof of a building is power; before it becomes power it must be released, and then the extent of its power depends on the speed of the drop. The old formula $M \times V^2$ describes it: mass times the square of velocity. Until released, the stone is a dead mass; until knowledge is sold, again in the broader sense of the word—cleverly used would be a better expression—it is worthless.

At that, I thought, it would be a good thing if colleges dispensed more knowledge and fewer credits. A young woman who worked in the office of a leading university once told me that students and teachers came in from morning till evening, asking if certain credits were valid if they changed to another school, or how many credits this or that study was good for.

"Doesn't anyone ever ask you," I inquired, "how he can really learn something in your college?"

"Nobody has asked me that yet," she declared, "and if he did, I for one would not know what to answer."

Unforgettable among my clients is Mr. Ainsworth, president of a jobbing house. He was a stately man, with a long white beard that gave him the appearance of an Old Testament patriarch. People who met him for the first time and listened to his honeyed prattle about himself and his charity toward the world usually opened their hearts and purses to him. Those who knew him longer noticed a cunning gleam shoot from his closely-set eyes when he thought himself unobserved. Mr. Ainsworth was a man who always took much and gave little. At our first meeting he pushed a check for twenty-five dollars on me as a retainer, before he had even stated the purpose for which he had called me in. He then leaned back in his chair, and with his most benevolent smile unfolded a program which five chemists could not have accomplished in as many years. For this work I was to receive a constant stream of checks, which he said I could safely leave to his discretion.

Mr. Ainsworth belonged to the type of client who tries to impress chemists by his technical knowledge. He used words such as "oxidation," "saponification," or "polymerization" with great frequency and always in the wrong context. My old doctor in Morningport used to tell me that patients with a half-baked knowledge of medicine were the hardest to treat. Mr. Ainsworth was like that. He had absorbed just enough encyclopedic chemical terms to drive a professional chemist to distraction.

Somehow we two did business with each other for quite some time, and he never lost an opportunity to express his regret that he had been too poor to go to college; with the advantages of a higher education, he felt sure, he would have become the greatest power in America. I had heard similar outpourings before and was heartily sick of them; so one day, in sheer self-defense, I told him a fable which I made up on the spur of the moment.

Once upon a time, I yarned, there were two wolf cubs who had lost their mother. A hunter found them and, leaving one in the lair, took the other home with him. There the pup became civilized; but one day the house burned down, and he wandered back to the woods. He grew hungrier and hungrier. Rabbits abounded, but he did not know how to catch them; when he sat up on his hind legs and barked his prettiest, they only ran the faster. Thoroughly discouraged, he sat down on a log. There he was presently joined by another wolf, who looked strong and well fed. The two wolves sniffed at each other and realized that they were brothers. The tame wolf then

229

related how he had learned to jump through hoops, dance to music and eat at the table.

The wild wolf stared in amazement. All he had learned was to catch mice and rabbits.

"Great heavens," he exclaimed, "just think how much fatter I would be today if I had had the advantages of your education."

Mr. Ainsworth listened to this fancy tale but professed not to see the point. I therefore explained to him one of the principal axioms in physics—that two things cannot occupy the same space at the same time. As knowledge is pumped into a man's head in college, a proportionate amount of natural shrewdness and incentive goes out of him. If Mr. Ainsworth had gone to college, he probably would be getting fifty dollars a week as chief clerk in someone else's office rather than making a hundred thousand dollars a year as president of his own company.

Others besides prospective clients dropped into our office from time to time. The one I liked best was Father O'Leary, the priest of a neighboring Catholic church. Father O'Leary was a heavy-set man, with a skin affliction which gave his face and hands a mottled appearance. To do good was his religion, and people clung to him with genuine affection. Wherever he walked, groups of children crowded around him. In the evening, I often saw him sitting on a doorstep, while some woman sobbed out her sorrows to him. In his quiet, unobtrusive way he managed to persuade stern-faced business-men to accompany him on his evening trips through the poor neighborhoods of his parish, and I know that some of them gave him large donations. Sometimes he became confidential and told me of the friction he had with his immediate superiors, who did not approve his methods. Mediocrity, he mused, has always abhorred originality, much as nature is said to abhor a vacuum. Father O'Leary liked nothing better than to sit in a quiet corner of the office and be left to himself. These were the only times, he said, when he was really at peace with the world.

Another of our frequent visitors was a big, red-haired Irish police-man named Hogan. He had come in once during a blizzard, be-numbed by the cold, and we had revived him with a bottle of cognac which we kept in our medicine closet. By and by, Father O'Leary and Hogan became fast friends, although they never agreed in their views on the one subject they discussed most frequently. Hogan boasted that if he were allowed to pull all people into his station house, he could beat a confession of some crime or other out of every one of them. Father O'Leary, on the other hand, contended that he could take all prisoners then behind bars and make useful citizens of them.

Father O'Leary and Hogan have now both passed out of my ken, but memories of them linger with me.

In the course of time many queer characters became steady visitors at our office. Everyone was welcome, and high-hatting was unknown. There was a Negro undertaker who was always working on new methods of embalming; there was an oil salesman named Chamberlain, whose great-uncle, the chemist Guthrie, had been a co-discoverer of chloroform back in 1832. A boulder at the western entrance of Washington Park in Chicago was to have borne a memorial plaque for him, but the plaque was never put on. Every time I drive through the park I see the boulder lying there, by the world forgot, much like Guthrie himself. After all, Guthrie was only a chemist and had done nothing but usher in the era of anesthesia. Chamberlain was blessed with a nice voice and would often sing for us. He was one of the most loyal, decent and modest men I have known, and when he died, every member of our little group went into that kind of mourning which is no less sincere because it scorns outward display.

Our office door was never locked, not even during the days of the race riots in 1919. We were located only two blocks from the so-called Black Belt, and policemen who had drawn a cordon across 35th Street advised us to stay away. Negroes were running amuck, they said, drunk with liquor and lust. This bothered us not at all. Gertie and I remained in the office every day while the rioting lasted, listening to panicky people who came rushing in with tales of brutality and bloodshed. Half a block away from us a poor Negro teamster had been pulled off his truck and a mob had jumped on him until his head was pulp. Drink-crazed Negroes in automobiles were racing along the streets, firing on white pedestrians. Dog-tired policemen reeled in, their clubs full of blood and kinky black hair.

During all this excitement, our office was an open haven for all

231

comers, black and white alike. No one fought on our premises, no one molested us. Negroes hid in our yard or called openly for mail, food and papers which friends of theirs had deposited with us. White men with places of business in the Black Belt engaged Negro caretakers in our presence. Police and militia men rested up in our chairs and took a drink or two on the fly. It was very strange and exciting, but we all felt much relieved when racial peace was re-established in Chicago.

One day news reached us that the plant of the American Linseed Company in South Chicago had blown up. There had been just one flash in the percolator room, followed by an explosion and an upheaval which obliterated everything. Only a deep crater indicated where nineteen buildings had stood. The office and the laboratory, located somewhat apart, were all that was left. By a miracle the explosion had occurred during the lunch hour, while most of the men were outside, and therefore only few lives were lost, although many workers were injured. The cause of the explosion never was definitely learned.

Gertie and I had been intimately acquainted with the dead and the injured. Naturally, we were greatly depressed. Moreover, Gertie's father and most of the other survivors were left jobless. I was certain that the plant would never be rebuilt, and it never was. Mr. Stock did not survive the catastrophe long. He stood for hours at the rim of the crater which once had been his linseed oil plant, tears rolling down his cheeks. At home he talked only of the dead men, of improvements he had contemplated, of past triumphs. One morning he was found dead in his bed. The grief and strain had been too much for his heart.

The destruction of the South Chicago plant had a disturbing effect on my own fortunes. The city of Mulberry, a community of about 250,000 souls, needed a new garbage plant and had engaged me to draw plans for it. Here would have been a rare opportunity to utilize the experiences for which I had paid such a handsome price in worries and annoyances. The plant was to have used the naphtha-extraction process, but the explosion at South Chicago changed the minds of the Mulberry city officials. Instead of trying to extract the garbage, they decided to incinerate it. Not only did I lose this contract, but with it went all my hopes for the erection of garbage-extraction plants as part of my future career.

During my activities as a consulting chemist I had some rather narrow escapes. In a Milwaukee plant where I was installing a laboratory, I had ordered the construction of a hollow steel plate, about the size of a small desk, which was to serve for the evaporation of water and other volatile substances. It was really nothing more than a flat radiator designed to withstand a steam pressure of five pounds. The boilers of the plant were geared to a hundred twenty-five pounds of pressure, but it was easy to throttle it down. When the steel plate went into action for the first time, the engineer forgot to regulate the valves. I was just demonstrating the use of the hot plate to several men when it exploded. Pieces of steel flew through the room like so much shrapnel. The men next to me had to be taken to the hospital; I was thrown to the floor but suffered no harm.

I had another miraculous escape while engaged in my preliminary work on the garbage plant at Mulberry. Bertha accompanied me on this trip and we were seated on the rear platform of the observation car when she suddenly left her chair and went inside. She cannot tell to this day what prompted her to do so. For a while I paid no attention to her absence, but finally I got up to look for her. She was calmly sitting in her parlor car chair looking at the landscape. I was about to make a jocular remark on what happens to deserting wives, but the words were never spoken. Just as I sat down, the air was rent by several short, sharp whistles, following each other in rapid succession. From my days in the Pittsburgh switchyards I knew what that meant. The engineer saw a calamity ahead against which he was helpless and was signalling the passengers to look out for themselves as best they could. A few seconds later we ran head-on into a passenger train coming the other way. Two men who occupied the chairs Bertha and I had so recently vacated were thrown through a partition and had their backs broken. Our own injuries were hardly worth mentioning. Bertha suffered a slight wrench of the right shoulder and I had my head thrown violently against the pillowed back of my chair. I felt no pain, but must have been slightly dazed, for I found myself distributing towels without being able to recall where I had picked them up or why I had left Bertha.

I was not quite so lucky on another occasion. Red Wing, Minnesota, had an oil plant where I was introducing a new refining process. The vat containing the oil stood on a platform about twenty feet above the floor of the building. Some narrow boards had been laid alongside it so that the operator could see what was going on, and a stepladder led up to these boards. For the purpose I had in mind, the oil had to be heated by steam, and as linseed oil below 560° is not inflammable or otherwise dangerous, I had no idea of impending danger as I stood on that narrow ledge watching the oil beneath me.

Then one of those little things happened which, coming from a source so inconspicuous that it is overlooked, have so often upset well-laid plans of mice, chemists or statesmen. The plant was equipped with a sprinkler system, and the heated air rising from the vat caused the popping of a safety valve directly above it. Water spurted into the vat where it at once became superheated steam; the hot oil rose toward me with incredible speed. I had only a split second in which to think. If I tried to reach the stepladder I would be scalded to death; if I jumped I would probably kill myself. I jumped, but not quite quickly enough. Some of the oil had already reached my hands, and splashes of it reached me in mid-air. I landed safely enough, probably due to my handball training, but already the skin was hanging from raw flesh on my hands and forearms, and there were ugly wounds on my body and legs.

I still think with gratitude and respect of that little Red Wing hospital, so small and yet so efficient and friendly. I knew, of course, that if a third of my skin was destroyed I would die, and between the chief surgeon and myself we decided, after taking the proper measurements, that it was a tossup. After five days of such excruciating pain as only victims of burns can appreciate, I was fit to return to Chicago. It was many weeks, however, before I could use my hands again, and in the interval I had to be accompanied by a personal attendant who had to do everything for me that an armless man cannot do for himself.

In my professional work I now began to meet small businessmen for the first time and found that I had to study a new style of approach. In the large concerns I had become used to suave presidents, steely-eyed purchasing agents, rough-mannered superintendents, skeptical chemists. Smaller establishments had no superintendents, no purchasing agents, no chemists. I had to deal with one man only; he filled all these positions himself, but usually made up by shrewdness and experience what he lacked in book learning. While this simplicity in the organization made for quick dealings, it also had its disadvantages. For the first time in my life I stepped into doubtful credits. I never was a good credit man and probably never will be, but the errors I made in the beginning were elementary. I trusted everyone. If a man wrote out an order for me on a printed form it looked to me like a government bond. I had to learn to temper trustfulness with suspicion and to press collections without giving offense. Taking it all in all, it seemed to me that doing business with smaller houses was more interesting. There was more of a human tie between buyer and seller. The employer-employee relationship also was better. Where men felt themselves directly under the eyes of their boss they worked harder, and their efforts were more likely to be rewarded. In the early years of the 1900's much fear prevailed that the trusts would crowd small business from the face of the earth. From what I saw I doubted that such a thing would ever come to pass. It was the old difference between mercenary soldiers and men defending their own homes.

There were many things about business which I could not understand. Wherever I called, I heard that sales were so many per cent more or so many per cent less than last year. When I questioned the importance of constant growth, people looked at me with amazement. Everybody was striving for growth, were they not? To stand still meant stagnation, and stagnation meant death. There was truth in that, of course, but did things have to keep on growing forever? When a tree reached a certain size, it stopped growing; why not a business? When a business furnished everyone employed a good living with fair provisions against a rainy day, it looked to me as if it might stop. Not a single man to whom I talked agreed with me, so I was probably wrong.

Even before Bertha and I were married we had decided to pool all our resources once and for all. A marriage was a partnership, we reasoned, in which the man did the earning, and the woman reared the children. The man was no more entitled to his earnings than the wife was to the offspring. I had always thought it a medieval custom to have husbands dole out money to their wives. We decided to study our financial condition each month; then either of us could spend as much money as we thought the treasury could stand. In this fashion it became my habit to make up a monthly statement for my wife and hand it to her with minute explanations. It usually showed that we were making progress and accumulating a surplus at a fair rate. In reality, these monthly inventories did more than picture our financial condition. They forced us to keep all our affairs shipshape, to discuss investments, insurance and the like. These inventories were like a monthly inspection tour of our lives, with a spotlight thrown into dark corners so that no dirt could accumulate and breed trouble. We have never abandoned the custom. To let your wife in on your business deals is not only a sign of respect and trust, but on occasions pays big dividends. Women usually can see through false friends more accurately than a lie detector.

One of my early clients was the Florsheim Shoe Company, a large house, well known for the high quality of its merchandise. Mr. Milton Florsheim, the president, invited me to go through his plant to suggest chemical improvements. At first thought, a shoe factory seemed to me the last place for the application of chemistry. I was greatly astonished, therefore, to find that modern developments had laid many chemical problems at the old shoemaker's doorstep. Inks had to be made for improving the appearance of the footwear, inks for heels, inks for soles, inks for shanks. The elimination of nails, a goal ardently sought, could be accomplished by a chemical binder, such as rubber cement. Threads had to be waxed and leather scraps disposed of. One invention, then only a few years old, excited my particular admiration. It had been the custom to equip shoes with strips of felt to fill the hollow space between the inner and outer soles so as to provide a cushion for the feet. These felt strips had many shortcomings. They were neither water- nor sweat-proof, and once wetted would curl up, stiffen and make walking uncomfortable, if not downright painful. Felt also was expensive, being practically pure wool. Then there was the difficulty of holding the strips in place and preventing their piling up in the front of the shoe. To overcome all these drawbacks, some inventor had replaced the felt with a mixture of ground cork and rubber cement, the latter a solution of rubber in naphtha. The mixture was stirred up into a dough and spread over the inner sole, where it was left to dry. This innovation, ingenious as it was, still had one principal fault. The naphtha was slow in evaporating, which tied up a lot of expensive floor space. Moreover, its inflammability played havoc with insurance rates. At this point a new inventor entered the arena and cut the knot in a simple and brilliant manner. He mixed the ground cork with a hot, pitchy substance and spread the mixture on the soles with a hot knife. As soon as the pitch cooled, which was only a matter of seconds, it made a plastic covering for the sole. The pitch-cork mixture was cheap, light in weight, waterproof, and stuck to its appointed place with commendable tenacity. The invention was a perfect little gem in its own realm.

From Mr. Florsheim's point of view, only one thing was wrong with it. The idea had been patented, and he thought the royalties too high. I was asked to invent something just as good, but minus the overhead. As I needed additional products for the factory annex to my consulting office, this problem appealed to me, and I set out to solve it.

The patents covering the shoe filler, as it was called, were well drawn and had no apparent weak spots. Secretly I was glad of it. Whoever had been clever enough to conceive this invention was entitled to his reward. On closer study, I found I could change the product in one respect. I stumbled on a proper material, one which had been overlooked by the patent holder, and applied for a patent of my own, which was granted. Thus fortified, I immediately began the manufacture of shoe filler. After the installation of the necessary machinery and just when deliveries began hitting their stride, we struck a nasty little obstacle. One morning I received a frantic call from the Florsheim Shoe Company. The plastic mixture which had been left over from the previous day's operation had burned up. I had grave misgivings, for I perceived in the fire earmarks of a spontaneous combustion. But what could have caused it? Cork comes from the bark of a tree and does not burn easily. The binder was an asphalt material and as innocuous as cobblestones. I could not explain the fire on any known grounds.

Before long my fear that the combustion had been spontaneous was confirmed. In going over our own stock, ready and packed for shipment, I found several burned packages, mere ashes which crumbled to dust when I touched them.

There was no doubt that ground cork and our binder reacted in some way to create heat, although this was against all chemical precedent and looked to me like a vicious exception created for my especial benefit. My college training must have reasserted itself at this stage, for I consulted with many experts in spontaneous combustion for a possible explanation. Someone suggested that the trouble might lie in fine particles of dust in the cork. I immediately installed a sieve and made shoe filler with both the screened and unscreened cork. The expert had hit the bull's-eye. The more dust the cork contained the more it inclined toward spontaneous combustion. We installed a big revolving screen and sifted out as much dust as we could. But how could we determine when all the dust had been removed?

Again I conferred with the experts, but this time they could not help me. Apparently no method was known by which the presence of small amounts of dust could be determined, much less measured. One manufacturer of scientific apparatus devised a complicated testing machine for me which would have cost hundreds of dollars. I decided to forget experts and go native. Abstractedly fingering some ground cork one day, I discovered that the clean product would glide off my hands, leaving no traces; but if even an infinitesimal percentage of dust was present, it clung to the ridges of my fingers where it was plainly visible. That moment our files on the subject of cork dust were closed, and until this day cork has been tested in our plant by the finger-ridge method, a fact which, now that I have made it known, may lead to my expulsion from every scientific society in the country.

In February, 1914, Bertha and I decided to take a belated honeymoon trip to Europe. It was a wise decision for, as it happened, it was our last chance to see Europe in its pre-war days. We held a family gathering at Abbazzia on the Adriatic Sea. Incidentally, Bertha and I had another miraculous escape. At Venice we were scheduled to take a boat to the Lido, but changed our minds at the last minute. The *vaporetto* we almost took collided with an Italian torpedo boat, was cut in two, and sank with all aboard. As Abbazzia had no newspapers, we did not know of our close call until the Vienna papers arrived the next day.

The number of my nephews had now increased to three, and my mother, finding an outlet for her energies, had taken a new lease on life. The sunny days we spent together remained in our memories a long time, for it was many years before we were to see each other again.

During our stay in Vienna, my older sister's former employer, who had once tried to find me a rich dowry attached to a wife, invited me to speak before the Austrian Chamber of Commerce. I called my address "The Austrian Cinderella." Austria had everything a tourist's heart could wish for; beautiful scenery, quaint customs, a territory not overridden by visitors, the best food in the world. Yet Austria was almost unknown outside her own borders. Many people in America thought I hailed from Australia, and even the name *Habsburg* was consistently spelled *Hapsburg*. It is the only historical name I have ever seen spelled wrong, although I have never discovered the reason therefor. The syllable *Habs* is an abbreviation of *Habicht* (hawk), and its meaning in English does not become plainer by the hardening of one consonant.

The audience listened to my talk with that mixture of courtesy and indifference which was so characteristic of pre-war Vienna. Tourists only increased the cost of living for the natives, they thought, and if anyone wanted to believe that Vienna was the capital of Australia, that was all right, too.

The Austrians of that era were engrossed in the real values of life. They were happy; could anyone, they asked, be more than happy? I had mentioned the inflow of foreign moneys; what was the good of it? The tourists would want everything changed to suit themselves, and the easy, languid, peaceful past would be gone forever. One had only to look at Paris, which had sold its soul to become the Mecca of Americans. No, the Viennese wanted none of that; they had their coffee-houses, their wine gardens, their theaters. That was all they wanted, and they were content to leave well enough alone.

Europe was then already rushing toward the abyss. During the war years the world was to hear almost nothing of Austria. The country was little known and therefore not news. When the Big Four drew up the peace treaty they also were in ignorance of its history, geography and economy.

Among other things, they did not know what to do with the town of Teschen, an important mining center, greatly desired by both the Poles and the Czechs.

"How many members have heard of Teschen?" Lloyd George asked the House of Commons on April 16th, 1919. "I do not mind saying that I have never heard of it . . ."

And so to the Poles it went. A year or so later, when the Poles were fighting Russia, the Czechs took it away from them; and when Hitler threatened Czechoslovakia and the Czechs were helpless, the Poles took it back. For the sake of this town, of which Lloyd George had never heard, these two Slavic nations had remained at daggers' points during all the intervening years. Divided and hostile as they were, it was easy for Hitler to swallow them both. Had they stood together, they might have resisted him.

People knew the names of little villages in France, in Italy, in Switzerland, but even the heads of important governments did not know Teschen. If they had, Hitler could possibly have been stopped. Old Austria had loved her privacy too much, and the whole world paid dearly for her shyness and her earnest wish to be left unvisited, unsung and unknown.

Forerunners of the approaching war were already discernible, although few people recognized them. A Pan-Slavic Congress was in session at Belgrade; the Serbians took pot shots across the border at frequent intervals, forcing Austria into expensive mobilizations; Russian troops were maneuvering close to the German frontier. I spent a great deal of my time in Vienna with a young couple whom I had known a long time. The girl always had been a favorite cousin of mine, and I still feel grateful to her, for it was she who introduced me to the beauty of Wagnerian music. She had married a young banker, known to all his friends as Lutsch, a man of great intelligence who possessed a lot of inside information on political and financial matters. I took to him because, like myself, he used to ponder and worry about many things which led to nothing in particular. He wondered, for instance, why, if wheels were a better mode of locomotion than legs, Nature in her wisdom had not equipped animals with wheels. Or why no attempt was being made to measure people's intestines; it was a factor which seemed to be so important in determining their dietary needs and preferences. This banker told me that in the spring of 1909 King Edward VII of England had visited the Austrian Emperor at his summer home in Ischl and urged him to sever his alliance with Kaiser Wilhelm II. Instead he was to help form an iron ring around Germany which, with its world-wide ambitions, was beginning to disturb English complacency. The King argued that of the fifty-five million Austro-Hungarians only ten million were Germans, and that it would be easy to swing the remainder into an English-French-Russian combine. But King Edward pleaded in vain. Francis Joseph had given his word of honor, and nothing could induce him to break it.

Kaiser Wilhelm was advised of this intrigue and made a warlike speech. England countered by withdrawing credits from the Austrian money-market, and Austria struck back by annexing Bosnia and Herzegovina, two Turkish provinces over which she had held only a protectorate heretofore. Military men thought a European war inevitable; for the Central Powers it seemed a favorable moment to strike. Russia had not recovered yet from her defeat by the Japanese, and the English-French Entente was still in the making. But Francis Joseph, who so far had followed his German ally, could not be moved further. There would be no more war during his reign if he could help it.

Thus ran the backstairs gossip of European politics. The intellectual classes of Central Europe sensed the danger and desperately tried to stave off the approaching conflict. A congress of peace-loving German and French parliamentarians met in Switzerland to compare ideas, especially about Alsace-Lorraine, which was the main source of the mutual distrust and irritation. German and French parents interchanged thousands of children during vacations, giving them an opportunity to learn the language of their supposedly implacable enemies and discover that common people everywhere had the same daily worries and problems, and only wanted peace. But the statesmen willed it otherwise. A few days after our return to America the heir to the Austrian throne was shot and the war was on.

CHAPTER 12

SERVANTS OF MANKIND

PON MY ARRIVAL IN CHICAGO I
received the surprising news that during my absence I had been
elected chairman of the Chicago section of the American Chemical
Society. I had been vice-president of that group before, but had
never taken an active interest in its affairs. The friends who had
sponsored me expressed the hope that I would get the Society out
of its rut and "start something," whatever that meant. After the
unexpected outbreak of hostilities in Europe, I had to start things
indeed, and start them fast.

The sudden interruption of commercial relations with Germany
was immediately felt by business in the United States. Industrialists who had to do without German products were seized by a panic,
and a hectic search for substitutes was the order of the day.
Chemists, the forgotten children of a society which was in the habit
of catering to the non-creative occupations, were suddenly hailed as
saviors. A prominent Chicago daily carried a full-page appeal,
which sounded almost like an indictment of the profession..

"Where are our chemists?" the paper thundered in effect. "Why
don't they do something? Are there no chemists in America?"

The country was stranded; the admirable Crichton was asked
to take charge. Overnight the servants of mankind were pushed
into the driver's seat. Being well-trained servants they went to
work without a murmur.

The first thing we did was to form an Emergency Chemical
Council to advise businessmen regarding substitute materials. Every
chemist in the territory was willing to donate his services, and those
who hesitated were drafted ruthlessly. We could not help every-

242

body, but we helped many and did valiant work for very little thanks.

Among those who offered their services with genuine enthusiasm was A. V. H. Mory, chief chemist for one of the big mail-order houses. By his scientific control of general merchandise, he had helped bring the meaning of chemistry to the consciousness of the farmers and housewives of America. It was his pride to draw around himself the best young chemical talent of the country; where other chemists displayed to visitors their laboratories, Mory displayed his assistants. Most of them, like Leon Logan, landed near the top before they were out of their forties. One of Mory's most promising chemists was a tall, powerful-looking young man, who had graduated from the University of Missouri and against whom none of us could prevail at tennis. His name was Donald M. Nelson.

With such men as these, and many others of big caliber putting their shoulders to the wheel, the affected industries were kept on the move, even if at times the obstacles seemed overwhelming.

A problem which I handled myself comes back to my mind, for it led to the one time in my life when I was literally thrown out of an office. There was a manufacturer in town who specialized in toe boxes. A toe box is a stiff, round half shell which is put into the fore part of a shoe to make it hold its shape; without it the shoe would cave in and show the outline of the toes. These toe boxes were made of felt which heretofore had been impregnated and hardened with Montan wax, a German specialty. I was called into consultation and substituted for Montan wax an asphalt of American origin. The work required a great deal of study and experimentation, but eventually one of my samples proved satisfactory, and I let a felt manufacturer take over from that point on. All arrangements had been made, when the felt concern received such a large and profitable contract from the British government that it withdrew from the bargain. I knew nothing about this upset, and when I called at the toe-box plant to see how things were progressing, the owner took me by the collar and pushed me down the stairs. I was too astounded to resist. I had done all this work without either compensation or hope of profit.

A few days later the toe-box manufacturer found out that I was innocent of the untoward developments and called me up to renew our connection. I merely hung up on him. He then wrote me a plaintive letter, and when that brought no results he called on me in person. I let him state his plea and then threw him out. I think it is the only time I laid violent hands on anybody.

By the beginning of fall, things had quieted down a bit and I began to pay attention to my duties as chairman of the American Chemical Society. The Society was devoted entirely to science and disregarded the human problems of its members. This neglect had led to dissatisfaction on the part of the younger element. Originally all members had been pure scientists, most of them college professors who needed a common meeting-ground for the exchange of scientific ideas. But lately the profession had been edging its way into industry and a new class had grown up, calling itself chemical engineers. Problems that were outside the realm of pure science were coming to the fore, and the human side of the profession was pressing for an outlet. We had about five hundred members in our Chicago section, but they were not personally acquainted with each other, nor was there any forum for the exchange of opinions on many economic questions which agitated their minds. I saw a big task ahead of me, and having been elected to tackle it, I determined to do so, regardless of precedent.

There were several points in my program. The first was the creation of a chemical newspaper. In this publication there was to be no mention of scientific matters. It was to serve merely as a bond between the chemists of Chicago, registering their joys and woes, their weddings and deaths, or such commonplace items as changes of position. New members were to be introduced by special articles, and a discussion of all our common interests was to be invited.

The next point covered the promotion of our financial welfare. One committee was to act as an employment agency, another was to advise younger members on their personal problems, such as the utilization of an invention or the proper recognition of their department. A publicity committee was to connect us with the outside world. Even little things were being revolutionized, such as the seating of our members at the suppers preceding the meetings. Up to then we always had been placed at long tables, which made serving easy but intelligent conversations impossible. You talked either to your neighbor on the right or your neighbor on the left, turning your back to one or the other, and you had to shout if you wanted to converse across the table. Arrangements were made for small tables seating no more than six persons, and so from a mere feeding of our bodies the suppers were lifted into a meeting of minds and a means of bringing about closer personal relationship among those who attended.

All these innovations had been thoroughly discussed and approved by the officers of the Society, and finally were submitted to a full meeting. A howl of dismay went up from the old guard. For two evenings the deliberations continued. The critics had the floor, and their oratory filled the hall. My friends were remarkably quiet and subdued; many friends are while the outcome of a fight is in doubt. In the end, we went ahead with the plans as contemplated. In this way the first chemical newspaper in America was born. We called it the *Chicago Chemical Bulletin,* and its first issue consisted of only eight pages. By "we" I mean Dudley French and myself. French was the secretary of the section and as loyal as he was industrious. For two years we two wrote practically the entire publication and did all but print it ourselves. It was a constant struggle for existence. We could have had many scientific contributions from people who did not understand our purpose, but we stood firm on our platform that we would print news only, and our test for every item was whether or not the readers would be prompted to ask their brother chemists, "Did you see in the *Bulletin* that . . ."

Within a few months the Philadelphia and Pittsburgh sections followed our lead and started local papers. Our own *Bulletin* spread to Milwaukee, Champaign, Louisville and other chemical centers west of the Alleghenies. As we grew in circulation and paid advertisements, additional sections came in. Before long we were an established institution.

Twenty-odd years have gone by since I left the editorial staff of the paper I founded. Now it is a magazine containing some thirty pages, with enough advertising matter to yield a substantial profit to the Society. The *Bulletin* and its sister papers are today read more religiously, I am told, than most other publications which circulate among the chemical profession. Even the parent Society eventually adopted our idea and began the publication of a news organ. What was radical in 1914 has become conventional today.

Shortly after the outbreak of the war, Chicago was stirred by a poison case which is still remembered. One morning two students in a northern Chicago suburb, a young man about twenty and a girl a little younger, were seen getting off at a lonely way-station of the electric railroad which parallels the shore of Lake Michigan. A day or so later the girl's body was found in a thicket nearby. The autopsy showed that she had died from cyanide poisoning. Traces of the dried liquid were discovered on her coat and on her face, indicating that she had taken the poison in liquid form and that some of it had spilled as she drank it.

The young student was arrested and put on trial for murder. What aggravated the suspicion against him was that detectives had dug up a can of cyanide in the back yard of his father's house. The father, who was a gardener for a large estate, explained that he had used this poison experimentally but, finding it useless, had buried it to make it innocuous. This explanation, although later found true, was taken with a grain of salt. Letters the girl had written indicated that she thought herself jilted. Things looked black for the accused, and most likely he would have been hanged, had it not been for the powerful defense which his father's employer made possible. He had known the boy from childhood and was convinced of his innocence. Fortunately for all concerned, the defense counsel had secured the services of Carl Miner, a chemist engaged in consulting and laboratory work who was rapidly forging ahead toward the top of the profession. At the suggestion of the boy's father, Miner compared the analysis of the cyanide found in the stomach of the girl student with that of the poison found in the can, and made the startling discovery that they were two different compounds. The poison which had killed the girl was shown to be cyanide of potassium, while that used by the gardener was cyanide of sodium. This dénouement exploded the case of the prosecution. Subsequently it was established that the girl herself had had access to potassium cyanide in her high school laboratory, and a verdict of acquittal logically followed.

What made this case so noteworthy was that, for the first time, chemistry had saved an innocent man's life. It was also memorable for the fact that Dr. William McNally, chemist for the coroner's office, who had found that three spots on the girl's coat had been made by a cyanide paste, rather than a liquid, refused to interpret his evidence in any but a strictly scientific manner. When reminded by the prosecuting attorney that he was a witness for the state, he gave the classic reply that as a chemical expert he was a witness for truth, and for truth only.

"I have some information that is of the utmost importance to the defense," he stated, "and I am going to take the stand to testify to it. You may say that it is not because I am conscience stricken. I have told the truth. I am simply going to tell some more truth, and this time it happens to favor the other side."

This little speech should have been given world-wide prominence; it could well serve as the motto of expert witnesses for all time to come.

Miner was ably assisted by Drs. John Long and L. I. Shaw; Judge Wilkerson was a defense counsel. After the war, Dr. Shaw became assistant chief chemist of the Bureau of Mines, and then turned his attention to development work in the telephone industry, where he now occupies a leading position. The one man in the case who suffered severely was the expert chemist for the prosecution, an able professor of toxicology. He had made the small but fateful error of taking the presence of potassium in the gardener's cyanide for granted, a mistake easy to understand, yet hard to excuse. All our hearts went out to this elderly colleague who had almost sworn away a man's life. He died a short time afterward.

The European war redounded in a way to my advantage. A small exporter whose office and warehouse were located on the premises we jointly occupied had to close up shop, and I took over his lease. It was a great day when Gertie and I moved into our new office, even though it was a dark and dismal place which, with its barred oval windows, looked more like a medieval prison than an office. Nevertheless, to us it looked like the throne room in a king's castle.

The office opened on the stub end of an ordinarily quiet street which, however, could be mighty noisy when the White Sox played to a full house. With thirty thousand people yelling in unison it is difficult to keep one's mind on oils and chemicals. In time, Gertie and I became quite efficient in interpreting the noises of a howling baseball crowd. We could distinguish yells of triumph from those of disappointment, and we could tell when a Sox player had made a hit and how far around the bases it had carried him. There were no radios in those days, but when we ventured to guess the score we seldom missed it by much.

Gertie was married just as we moved into our new office, and her husband Bill, a healthy and likable young man of Irish descent, joined our organization. Gertie's match was an ideal one in every respect, and she was always proud that I had taken no hand in arranging it. Ever since I had met her, she used to say, I had shaped her life in all its details, but her husband she had chosen for herself. Bill had no chemical training, but his native wit more than made up for that. He and his brother Frank took charge of our manufacturing department, and soon were as much part of our official family as was Gertie herself.

One of the war problems which came my way, and which I worked out with my former assistant Copthorne, concerned the coating of barbed wire used in trench warfare. In the damp climate of Belgium and Northern France, wire entanglements rusted away rapidly. This spelled danger, and the danger was the greater as the weakening of these defenses was often not discovered until a successful enemy attack disclosed it. The Allied Governments therefore urgently demanded that all barbed wire sent to them be covered with a rustproof coating. This coating had to be flexible and weather-resistant, but it also had to be cheap, for the quantity of wire used during the first World War, even in its early stages, amounted to figures that almost surpassed comprehension.

Like every war problem, this one had to be solved quickly. Without much time for experiments, Copthorne and I had to do some bold guessing, but we were lucky, and the formula we recommended was not changed throughout the war.

The coating of wire barricades was only one of the vexatious technical questions which modern warfare brings with it. Being involved in them gave one an opportunity to understand the importance of what each nation, in the course of the conflict, learned to designate as its home front.

The war brought me another oil problem which, however, did not have such a successful ending. In fact, it turned out to be one of the outstanding failures of my career. It was a problem which today, with the much larger variety of domestic oils at our disposal, would not be nearly so difficult as it was a quarter of a century ago. The Catholic church prescribes for its services certain sacred lights, known as eight-day lights, because they should burn eight days without adjustments. Originally the rites of the church prescribed the use of olive oil, but when the Christian religion spread to regions where this product was not obtainable, the use of other vegetable oils was permitted. Previous to the war, French rapeseed oil had been used in American churches, but now its importation had ceased, and a substitute became an urgent necessity. The problem was put up to me and I began to study it. The universal practice, I found, was to burn a cotton wick in a red urn-shaped glass. The flame was expected to be smokeless; the wick was not supposed to char, but to burn steadily until, at the end of a week and a day, the oil had been consumed.

All this sounded fairly easy, and I had no doubt that I would soon find a solution. I had not yet learned that apparently simple questions often are the most difficult to answer.

As usual, the literature on the subject was worthless. Some oils were described as burning and others as non-burning, but evidently no one had ever determined the basic difference between the two. I tried cottonseed oil, soybean oil and a flock of others, alone and in combinations, but not one of them answered the purpose. Some lit up with a beautiful clear flame, but went out after minutes or hours, or whenever the wick had burned down to the surface of the oil. Others started to smoke, and would char the wick into a black knob which choked the flame to extinction. The reason for these different behaviors was a mystery to me.

In order to eliminate all errors, I used only genuine church urns for my experiments; they were beautifully shaped and made of purple-red glass. The office, the laboratory, the storerooms and the basement of our house presented the weirdest kind of spectacle at night, illuminated as they were with innumerable flames and their colored reflections. Eight days was a long time to wait for the conclusion of a test, but patience became a virtue by necessity. At times a flame would actually last eight days, but on repetition the results would differ. At other times a light would start off beautifully, but die without apparent cause. Father O'Leary, the Catholic priest of our neighborhood, was much interested in the outcome of my work and visited us regularly. He looked over the collection of flames much as a gardener might look over rows of flowers, and kept mumbling to himself all the time during his inspection.

These tests went on for months and months, until I felt that human endurance could stand no more. Then, slowly and painfully, a theory began to form in my mind. Oil, as everyone knows, is drawn into the protruding portion of a wick by capillary action; I inferred that if the wick clogged up, the light went out because the oil could no longer penetrate; if the wick did not clog up, it was often consumed by the flame before the oil could saturate it. The right kind of oil evidently had to preserve the wick just long enough to support the flame, but no longer. The idea naturally suggested itself of providing these properties synthetically by strengthening the fibers of the wick with something which would form a skeleton to hold it up for a time, but not strengthen it so much that the pores would close. This led to the deduction that the burning qualities of an oil depended on the proper amount of mineral substance which it contained. Obviously, this was the right hypothesis, for it accounted for all the vagaries I had encountered. Still better, it made the proper regulation of the burning process a comparatively simple matter. As always when the goal was in sight, my activities became feverish. I removed all minerals from one of the oils and, as I had expected, the flame went out a few minutes after it had been lit. I then introduced certain quantities of soluble mineral salts into the oil, and the light lasted in proportion to the percentage of skeleton-furnishing substance. Theoretically, the problem was solved. I wiped my brow and began to speculate on an evening of celebration.

Unfortunately, my exaltation did not last. I could make oils perform in the laboratory, but I never got beyond that stage. The oils, I found to my dismay, had to be used at once. Whenever they were allowed to stand, the mineral salts settled out, leaving the oil lifeless. I never succeeded in overcoming this fault and finally gave up. Like many inventions, this one flagged on the last lap. In chemistry a ninety-nine per cent success is a one hundred per cent failure.

As chairman of the Chicago section of the American Chemical Society, I came in contact with many of my colleagues, most of whom were employed in laboratories or chemical plants. As my acquaintance with them grew, I was amazed at their low financial status.

There was a young chap from Cleveland who functioned as one of our minor officials in the Chemical Society; his business life consisted of running gas tests in a coke plant, and his salary for a seventy-two-hour week was sixty-five dollars a month. There was a pretty girl chemist who ate her heart out within the four laboratory walls of the Good Hope Hospital, running Wassermann's and urine analyses for seventy-five dollars a month. The chief chemist of a large metallurgical plant, who had left analytical work behind him long ago, looked prosperous to me; but his wife confided to me that if it had not been for her private income they would have gone without winter coats.

Then there was a blond Norse who was holding down a position in one of the smaller packing houses. To put it correctly, it was the other way around; the position was holding down the man. He was allowed no funds for laboratory supplies or replacements. A chemist was outlay enough, he was told.

Perhaps the most forlorn figure in this medley of Chicago chemists was Hilda. She had been an honor student at a prominent state college with the mirage of a glorious future ahead of her. But that had been long ago. For a while she had stayed on as an assistant instructor, until she found that she was merely standing still, because one dominant—or domineering—figure on the campus implanted his ideas on the next generation by selecting his assistants from his own graduates. Mental inbreeding, she called it. So she quit and was now working for a chewing-gum firm testing chicle, day in and day out. Hilda made no secret of her innermost thought; she said she could feel herself turning into an idiot.

251

The stormy petrels of the profession were a young married couple, both chemical graduates, one more rebellious than the other, although the other was rebellious enough. John worked in a stockyard laboratory, Joan in a pharmaceutical house. Neither of them made any money to speak of, but both made a lot of noise. They were constantly threatening to organize chemists. I think they did finally form a union of chemists, but it never became important. The last time I heard of the couple, John was writing for a radical paper and his wife was painting picture postcards.

Small wonder that many a chemist, like Doc Skinner, who once had conducted a commercial laboratory, had long since gone into other lines. Skinner was now doing well in the chinaware business. Two colleagues of my earliest days, William Schmidt and Ervin Wilson, decided that the brokerage business held out greater promises than chemistry, and so the community gained the services of two expert brokers, while the world lost two more fine chemists in the process. Three others of our group, who had been chief chemists of large enterprises, went out selling life insurance. Bernard Schaar, who had been working for the Health Department of the City of Chicago, started to deal in scientific apparatus and chemicals together with his brother Adolph, which business later was to assume substantial proportions.

One chemist who had attracted general and favorable attention in his early days by the intelligent way in which he used to participate in the discussions at our chemists' meetings was Paul Van Cleef. Before he left school he had been offered the princely sum of twelve dollars a week to enter the laboratory of a prominent rubber firm. Instead, he wisely took a position as packer in the shipping room of another rubber concern; for it was characteristic of those times when chemists were little understood that this seemed the only way in which one could earn a living wage while utilizing his chemical knowledge. To introduce chemical control overtly was not considered advisable, but as a man in overalls Van Cleef succeeded in gaining the confidence of his fellow-workers and so exerted a beneficial influence. He soon struck out for himself and started to make rubber cement for his own account, thereby laying the foundation for a large enterprise.

Another able chemist who left the profession was Forest Sweet

After working in the stock yards and in a breakfast food plant for a few years, he found chemistry an unprofitable investment and decided that taking a quick loss would prove cheapest in the long run. So he wrote off his chemical training; but he never succeeded in writing off his chemical thinking. Sweet chose dealing in autographs as his career, which was lucky for me, for he was of great help to me later during my historical studies. All I ever had to do was to tell him the problem which was worrying me, and he would immediately set out to solve it, just as one brother-chemist helping another. I recall one case in particular which proved that "once a chemist, always a chemist." I happened to be tracing the fortunes of a Washington detective named Lafayette C. Baker, prominent in Civil War days, but whose trail had been pretty well obliterated in the course of time. By merest accident, I found that he had left some papers with his Washington attorney, one Albert G. Riddle, but what Riddle had done with them, I could not imagine. When Sweet heard of my dilemma, he went to work, without even telling me about it. First, he discovered that Riddle had at one time been a congressman from Ohio; then he went with a fine comb through all the libraries in that state and, after drawing quite a few blanks, located the missing papers in the archives of an historical society in Cleveland. There, in wooden boxes stored away in a basement, lay what I had been looking for. When I offered to compensate Mr. Sweet for his service, he only laughed. Was it not compensation enough to have the fun of stumbling on a problem and solving it? I did not say much, but I wondered how many professional men, except chemists, would accept intellectual satisfaction as the only, or even as the best part of their reward.

Most of the chemists who had stuck to analytical work were being paid about as much as stenographers but were treated with less respect. Non-analysts did not fare a great deal better. I doubt if a single chemist in Chicago prior to the war earned—or perhaps I should say was paid—as much as five thousand dollars a year. Of course, a great many were doing analytical drudgery, working in day-and-night shifts, performing tasks which any normally developed high school graduate could have done as well, and for which college-trained chemists were being hired merely by force of habit.

The State of Illinois, under a law enacted in 1907, had set up a peculiar standard of compensation for chemists. "Expert food chemists of known reputation," so the statute read, when hired by the State to draw up standards of quality, purity and strength for food products, were to be allowed a compensation of fifteen dollars per day. Think of trying to hire a lawyer, a surgeon, or an architect of known reputation for fifteen dollars a day. Real estate experts engaged to guess at the value of vacant property were paid one hundred dollars a day. The State of Illinois also had a chief chemist; his salary was twenty-five hundred dollars per annum. It was his duty to supervise milk, butter, canned goods, drinks and cosmetics, thus helping to carry the responsibility for the health of the entire state. All this for forty-eight dollars and eight cents a week. Judges of the Circuit Court in Cook County (in which Chicago is located) had an income of ten thousand dollars a year, certainly not an excessive amount. Was the standing of the state's chief chemist or of "food experts of known reputation" so much inferior to that of jurists on the bench? Did they not both belong to highly honorable professions which had to be above reproach and suspicion?

It took a crusader like David Klein to take the position as state chemist of Illinois and feel satisfied, at least for a time. Later he found—as Donald Nelson aptly expressed it when he started to spread his wings—that some jobs have a low ceiling; eventually Dr. Klein put his knowledge and energy to wider use and attained the presidency of a large concern manufacturing pharmaceutical products.

For forty-eight dollars and eight cents a week, the third most populous state in the Union undertook to buy expert chemical knowledge, knowledge that was expected to be infallible. Twenty-five hundred dollars a year for a chief chemist, ten thousand a year for a judge. The relative esteem in which the community held these two professions could not have been expressed more plainly—or more brutally.

Once we tried to take a census of what remuneration chemists in Chicago were receiving, but although every precaution was taken to facilitate the filing of anonymous and truthful reports, only a small percentage of replies came in, too small to allow a correct estimate. The salaries of those who filled in their blanks ran between twenty and thirty-five dollars a week. Even if these low-salaried chemists

254

represented only a minority—we could not tell—it was a pitiful return for the investment in time, money and effort which had gone into their making.

There lived in Chicago at that time an ex-chemist whom we all knew as Mac. He and his wife used to come to our house to play a friendly game of five hundred, and in between rounds Mac talked about the chemists he met on his daily calls. He was salesman for a house dealing in chemicals and probably knew more members of the profession than anyone else in town. His remarks usually were jocular, but only his lips smiled, not his eyes. The youngsters, those who had just left college, were his particular worry, and he could talk about them by the hour. Every mother and aunt, Mac would say, every minister and high school principal out in the country seemed to have read in the papers what a tremendous field chemistry was offering. Here at last was an answer to the perennial question of what to do with the new generation. Let them all become chemists. The career question was settled.

Mac's comments were caustic. Sure there was a big field in chemistry; so there was in telephony; but telephone operators were not getting rich, nor were linemen. Parents were bundling off their youngsters to far-away schools for the "advantages" of a college education; but need knowledge necessarily be gained in a classroom? When universities were first founded, there existed few books, no libraries; there was no other way to gather knowledge than by personal contact with the scientists of the times. Today anyone thirsty for education could get it at home, except where laboratories or clinics were necessary adjuncts. Our colleges, so far as they were not devoted to sports, had become places for gathering credits, not knowledge, and even their credit departments were none too good. Credits went to those who knew the most answers in quizzes; but any simpleton with a factual memory could answer quizzes. A genius with a poor memory stood no chance at all against some mediocrity who could learn the pages of a textbook by heart.

According to Mac, young chemists had no friends. Colleges, eager to make a showing, were luring them on. Let there be two students where before there had been only one; that would enhance the reputation of the school. What happened to the students after graduation was something that concerned only the graduates. Chemical journals wanted more readers (and want ads), supply houses more customers, chemical industries a big pond of chemists to fish in. You really could not blame any of them; it was just that their interests were on the other side of the fence. Mac knew a young chap who had played on the Iowa University baseball team, a strong, straight-thinking farmer boy who had been turned into a chemist. He had found a job in a small Illinois town, twelve hours a day, Sunday and Fourth of July included, all for sixty-five dollars a month. One day he looked out of his laboratory, saw the sun shining and walked out; never even collected his back wages. Eventually he ran into a semi-pro baseball manager, showed him what he could do, and now was pitching every Sunday for fifteen dollars a game. This, he declared with a laugh, was what he had been getting for a full week of chemistry. Good old baseball!

Mac estimated that in his midwestern territory no more than five per cent of all chemists made a good living out of their profession; ten per cent, he thought, drew comfortable or at least decent salaries; the rest were either underpaid or unemployed. I asked him if the graduates of the highly touted and expensive colleges were better off than those who had studied in smaller schools. He shook his head emphatically. There was no difference; why should there be? It was the student who counted, not the university; a big money investment was no guarantee for big financial returns. Many dubs bought golf sticks for twenty-five dollars apiece with the name of a celebrated professional engraved on the handle, and then made scores of a hundred and thirty; other players took nothing but an old mashie around and shot the course in par. One of the best chemists both Mac and I knew had graduated from an obscure pharmaceutical college. No, short-cuts through life could not be bought for money.

Once I asked Mac if he had any plan in mind that might remedy the situation. Would he establish laws calling for minimum salaries, or for restricting the output of chemists? Mac laughed. In his opinion, what chemists needed were not more laws, but the antiseptic effect of publicity. Not only newspaper or magazine articles, but publicity brought right to the door of the students and would-be students of chemistry. Mac wanted to see each college run a course on the business side of chemistry, where only practicing chemists or those who once had practiced would do the lecturing.

Let the speakers be chosen so as to represent a cross-cut of the profession; old ones and young ones, successful ones and others who were not. By listening to their varied experiences, future chemists could form their own opinions. Further than that no one had a right to go. Would the colleges be willing to cooperate? Mac doubted it. Would a storekeeper pay a man to walk up and down in front of his store with a sign reading, "Look before you enter"? No, the pressure would have to come from below, from the students themselves. If colleges were antagonistic, there were halls that could be rented. But students did not have enough gumption for such a scheme; what did their future matter when they could discuss credits and football scores?

When Mac seemed carried away by his own rhetoric, I used to interpose some objections. What he said about the miserable salaries paid to chemists was undoubtedly true; but not all the victims were complaining. I knew quite a few who appeared satisfied with their lot. This remark would invariably raise my guest's wrath to the boiling point. Satisfied! They were not satisfied, they were merely contented, like cows in the meadows. No pep, no ambition. And how about the wives? Were they satisfied? Look at them, talk to them and see. Mac sounded just like my old friend, the book agent.

But there was something Mac did not mention which I thought was holding many chemists back, and that was their inability to become well-fitting cogs in the machinery of which they were a part. They and the front office did not speak the same language. Laboratory reports were written out in technical and high-sounding words which meant nothing to laymen; but chemistry was too young yet to have its exponents indulge in professional snobbishness. Fact was that the front office did not know enough about chemistry to ask the right questions, while chemists, instead of trying to be helpful, failed to grasp the problems which worried the management. What was wanting was a liaison officer to connect two branches of business which lacked mutual understanding. I knew of one case where a chemist had supplied this missing bond and had not fared badly by doing so.

A young girl chemist in Chicago had become dissatisfied with her lot. She took up shorthand and, after acquiring proficiency, found work in an eastern city where no one knew her. One day the president of her firm received a letter containing some puzzling chemical terms. No one but the new stenographer could interpret them, and so it came to light that she possessed a chemical education. Her desk was immediately transferred to the president's private office, and in a short time the young woman was making thousands per year as a chemically trained secretary where she had made hundreds as a full-fledged chemist. Perhaps it was a case of the one-eyed shining forth among the blind; but why not shut one eye, if the remaining one led to success?

In many places, such as purchasing or claim departments of railroads and large industrial concerns, chemists might find promising liaison careers, provided they were willing to use their chemistry as avocations only, if and when needed. But chemists were like most other human beings. They preferred to travel with the crowd, never thinking that berries do not grow on cement highways, and that one has to tramp along the byways to pick them.

Nor did I think that lack of ambition alone made these poorly paid chemists contented. The real reason lay deeper than that. There was something satisfying about being close to Nature and her eternal laws. Like Antaeus of old, who replenished his strength from the earth, chemists constantly drew strength from their science. Elements and reactions were refractory at times, but they did not lie or cheat; the fight was fair, and even small victories were worth striving for. Few chemists I knew, no matter how successful in their subsequent careers, were without a secret nostalgia for the quiet peace of their early laboratory days.

At times Mac was unusually glum, and on one of these occasions I asked him why he looked so unhappy.

"I look unhappy because I am unhappy," he said. "And I am unhappy because I think that since I stopped being a chemist I am not doing anything worth while. I walk from one laboratory to the other selling chemicals and glassware, but nobody needs me for that. If I should die tomorrow, they would get their supplies just the same."

"You are making a good living, aren't you?" I remarked.

"Too damned good a living for what I am doing," he burst out.

"I look at these chemists to whom I am selling and see them do real work that benefits the whole world. What do they get for it? Next to nothing. My work only benefits myself and my firm, yet I make five times as much as they do. It simply isn't right. We read so much of new developments and improvements, all due to modern science. To science, mind you, never to the scientists.

"Chemistry is doing great things for the world," Mac suddenly piped in a high voice, as if mimicking an orator on Commencement Day. Then his voice became natural again. "Chemistry, indeed! It is the chemists, not chemistry, who are doing things for the world. Is literature writing books? Of course not. Authors write them, not literature. The difference is that people know authors, but no one knows chemists. I bet you that not one layman you ask can name you three chemists, or engineers for that matter; ask them about authors, or actors or doctors, and they can rattle off names by the dozen. Publishers brag about their authors, producers about stage stars, hospitals about staff physicians, even restaurants about their chefs; but did you ever hear any firm brag about its chemists or engineers? Do the papers ever print their pictures? I have never seen any, and I read a lot of papers."

I had to interrupt him here. The papers, I told him, printed news, and news was something that interested people. If Mac could show the editors that minor technical inventions were news, the papers would print them fast enough.

"News is not born, it is made," Mac retorted with some heat. "If a magazine editor with imagination would pick out some new automobile gadget, let us say, and print the story of its development together with the picture of the inventor, the idea might take like wildfire. Then the imitators would fall all over themselves to get on the bandwagon. Why, they could run a string of articles a mile long with those stories and not even scratch the surface."

He stared gloomily through the window.

"I'll tell you something," he started again after a pause, without turning around. "The day will come when society will judge people not by how much they take out of the common pot, but by how much they put in. Did you read all the fine things they said about that real estate man who died the other day? They could not praise him enough for his business acumen and whatnots. What did

259

he ever do? He bought houses at foreclosures and resold them at a profit; didn't even build any himself. All he left behind was higher rents. Why, I know a little chemist up in Milwaukee who has already produced enough inventions to equip a museum. These inventions will do you and me and everybody no end of good. He sure has put plenty back into the pot. I wonder what they'll say at his funeral. Perhaps it won't matter much; no one will know that he's dead, because no one knows he's alive now.

"You and I won't live long enough to see it," he continued after a while, "but when we become really civilized, each community will keep a ledger for everybody and make an entry for everything he does. If a fellow writes a beautiful poem or makes up a new tune or invents new gland preparations like that fellow in Milwaukee, we'll say he's done enough for the pot and put him on a pension. That goes for everyone who invents a new gadget or improves an old one. And that's not Communism, either. Nobody begrudges Henry Ford his millions, because he has brought autos to the doors of the little men who could not afford to own them before. He is putting a lot back into the pot, I should say, and has earned his share. But speculators, usurers and a lot of others I could name, how much are they giving back for what they take out? Mark my words, there will be a reshuffling of cards some day such as no one can now visualize. And after it's all over, people will wonder why it wasn't done long ago."

With that he picked up his hat and walked out without giving me so much as a nod.

Ordinarily, though, Mac ended his observations with a shrug of his shoulders. Why should he worry about the fate and fortune of chemists? He was a salesman, not a reformer. Had we not better play another hand of five hundred?

Many young chemists visited me in my capacity as chairman of our chemists' group and asked my advice. Most of the time I could offer scant help, but now and then I was more fortunate. I recall a youngster, no more than twenty-four, who came to see me and talked of suicide. He had been out of school three years and had never made a living out of this "damned chemist's profession." Now he was through. He only wanted to blow up his college and his professors before he quit for good. They were grinding out chemists like sausages, he said, hundreds of them annually, thousands, tens of thousands. Evidently they knew nothing of the law of supply and demand. There never could be enough jobs to go around, even at starvation wages.

I pointed a way out to him. If he would buy himself a dollar's worth of shoe-strings and sell them for two dollars, I would obligate myself to get him a job. At first he thought I was joking; but I assured him that I had never been more serious in my life. He left me, a trifle dazed. I did not see him again for weeks.

At last he came back, a foolish grin on his face. He had succeeded in selling a dollar's worth of shoe-strings for two dollars. Now what would I do for him?

"If a man can do what you did," I told him, "he can sell anything; and if a man can sell things, he would be silly to remain a chemist."

The light dawned on him. At my suggestion he took a newspaper and put his finger on the column "Salesmen Wanted." A few days later he was out selling liquid soap and sanitary appliances to hotel washrooms. It was a tough job, but not for a man hardened by selling shoe-strings to people who did not want them.

One day he stormed in looking as Napoleon might have looked after the battle of Austerlitz. His firm had been buying its liquid soap at an exorbitant price. He offered to produce it for half as much, and was now making more money brewing soap in his basement than he had ever made selling it. A few years later he owned a big soap factory in one of the southern states, and for all I know may now be a millionaire. People usually stop writing to me when things go well with them.

So long as chemists changed their occupations and continued to do things in which chemistry played a part, I felt that they followed the line of natural evolution. But it hurt when they went into selling life insurance or chinaware. What a waste of potential creative power that was, and what damage to our national wealth! Was it really a matter of indifference to the community if men who had advanced the science of food, metals and any number of other items, went into the free-for-all fight known as competitive salesmanship? Just as in my old days as a student in Vienna, when I had rebelled against an opera singer retiring from the stage for private reasons,

I felt that some wrong was being done. Again I discussed this matter with many people, but found no more understanding now than I had then. Of course, it was all right for a chemist to become a salesman. Was not selling a perfectly honest way of earning money?

This temptation to give up constructive work for the sake of an increased income did not only concern others, it concerned me too, and vitally so. I had now lived a jobless life of freedom for five years and found that chemists in business for themselves had to struggle just as hard as those working for others. Analytical work was being paid for at scandalously low rates, and not only because of competition from public laboratories, which were free, or from college teachers and chemists employed in industry who were willing to do the work for very little. There was another drawback; analytical work brought few repeat orders, and therefore the overhead expense was burdensome. Every businessman knows that first sales are generally made at a loss; the profit comes from repeat orders. People who brought in samples for analysis were mostly one-time customers whom one never saw again. To be sure, some firms did arrange for continuous analytical supervision, but such contracts were difficult to get, and I had never been able to land one.

Consulting work suffered from the same drawback. As a consultant I was practically without competition in my line, but although I put my fees pretty high, I never came out with a real profit. Once I designed a linseed oil refinery in a neighboring city and charged fifteen hundred dollars for my work, but it took so much of my time getting things started that the fee represented only a small wage when spread over weeks and months. Another time I made a somewhat bizarre contract to teach a man to run a linseed oil plant in Alberta by remote control, as it were. He paid me fifteen dollars a day for the privilege of hanging around me a couple of weeks and hearing me talk oil. I am glad that he thought he got his money's worth.

No, the chemistry part of my business was not doing well. Driven by necessity, I cast about for other fields without knowing which way to turn. Then Fate stepped in and made the decision for me.

CHAPTER 13

ON THE WITNESS STAND

ONE HOT AFTERNOON in midsummer a man dropped into my office and asked my permission to tell me a story. Nothing could have suited me better. I shoved a box of cigars toward him, lit one myself, and listened.

A few weeks before, so my visitor related, an implement store in a small Arkansas town had run out of gasoline. The manager of a local station, appealed to for quick service, had one of his men roll a drum of high grade gasoline down two blocks to the store. While the gasoline was being drained into an underground storage tank it suddenly caught fire. The conflagration destroyed the entire store, causing a damage of some fifty thousand dollars. The owners claimed that rolling the gasoline over the hot pavement of the streets had caused it to catch fire spontaneously while it was being discharged; hence they had started suit for damages against the oil company.

What did I think of the case, my caller asked me, and would I care to take part in it as a chemical expert? With this he handed me a visiting card on which I read the name of a legal firm in an Arkansas city.

My answer was prompt and decisive. If the lawyer represented the oil company, I would gladly help; if, on the other hand, he represented the store, I wanted nothing to do with the case. There was no such thing as spontaneous combustion of gasoline at ordinary temperatures, and I was not going to prostitute myself by arguing a chemical impossibility.

"I represent the oil company," said my visitor, "and you may consider yourself engaged. What will be your charge?"

I was cautious enough not to give a direct answer. I only intimated that I usually charged seventy-five dollars a day during court attendance, and half that amount during the preparation of the case. The lawyer smiled and left, promising to familiarize me with all the details I needed to know.

In due time the case was called. Seldom have I approached a trial with more confidence, and never have I been more thoroughly upset. The opposing lawyer was a small, wiry Irishman by the name of Shaughnessy, the wittiest and most dangerous adversary I have ever encountered in a courtroom. He seemed to enjoy taking witnesses to pieces and putting them together again. While they squirmed and suffered, the jury and the audience roared with laughter at his witticisms, and more often than not I had to join in these outbursts of hilarity. Even our lawyers and the judge were not immune. Thus our case went from bad to worse, and when one of our chief witnesses became so bewildered under Shaughnessy's crossfire that he contradicted himself several times, the little Irishman created a sensation by swearing out a warrant for perjury against him. This just about finished us. When we assembled in our room after supper that night, we were ready to give up. I was looked upon as our last hope, but I knew that I was no match for Shaughnessy. One thing only might save us. I had figured out an unusual plan and proposed that we try it. The next day would be the last, and if we could not then sway the jury, we were lost.

I shall never forget my duel on the witness stand that day. Shaughnessy was a champion boxer. I never knew from which side his blows would hit me, and when he let loose they came like a whirlwind. He started out by doubting my right to call myself a chemical expert and examined me at length from a handbook of chemistry which he evidently had obtained at the local high school. To be quizzed a score of years after graduation is a mean ordeal at best, but in that little Irishman's clever brain each question turned into a barbed arrow dipped in poison. My own lawyers could have protected me more than once, but they left me to my own devices. Finally an idea struck me. I let Shaughnessy think that he had me going; then all at once I disagreed with him and told him he was dead wrong. He waved the book, proclaimed that it was in use in the Arkansas schools and therefore the last word in chemical science.

"Will you let me see the book for a minute?" I asked.

Everything now depended on the correctness of my hunch. If the volume was not as antiquated as it looked, I was sunk. But my hunch had not been wrong.

"Nineteen hundred and five?" I asked with a fine show of scorn. "You are using a chemistry book twelve years old on me, Mr. Shaughnessy?"

Shaughnessy dropped the book like a hot brick, but came back from another angle, slyly, insinuatingly.

"How much do you get for testifying here?" he asked me.

It was a good question. In the minds of the country lads on the jury anyone would perjure himself for seventy-five dollars a day.

"I don't know," I answered blandly.

"You mean to tell me you don't know?" Shaughnessy bellowed at me. "You aren't working for nothing, I assume."

"No, sir," I said, "are you?"

My opponent cried out that he was doing the questioning, not I; but the shot had told. Anyway, my precaution of not arranging a fee beforehand had not been wasted.

Shaughnessy drove me from corner to corner with his barrage of questions and had the laughs on his side most of the time. Only once did I succeed in turning the tables on him. He was curious to find out how I had obtained my knowledge on gasoline explosions, and I was answering to the best of my ability. Then my adversary pulled a pamphlet from his pocket.

"You have not said anything about this pamphlet here," he said. "It's a government publication called *Hazards of Gasoline Explosions*. Written by a Mr. Pollard. Have you any opinion of him?"

"Yes," I said, "he's a good man."

"Oh," he mimicked me, "a good man. Goes to church on Sundays and never beats his wife. That what you mean?"

Laughter. I had to explain that I meant something different, and was given a lecture on how to express myself properly.

"Now look here," Shaughnessy continued, "you haven't mentioned this pamphlet at all. But you've read it, haven't you?" And before I could answer, he hissed audibly: "In fact, haven't I seen you reading it right in this courtroom?"

The way he said this must have made the jury think that Shaughnessy had caught me in an unspeakable crime. I almost felt guilty myself; but this time my little friend had left an opening for me, and I was hoping that he would not suspect the trap I was setting for him.

"I am not going to answer this question," I said with grim determination.

"What?" cried Shaughnessy excitedly, "you refuse to answer?"

"I do."

The courtroom became as still as a tomb. The judge woke up, as do people on a boat when the engines stop unexpectedly, and looked at me sternly. He did not know exactly what was up, but he probably felt the tension. He was informed of what had transpired and ordered me to answer under penalty of contempt of court. Still I refused. The judge then asked me why I was so stubborn. This was what I had been praying for.

"Because I am incompetent to answer," I said. "If Mr. Shaughnessy wants the court to know what he saw me do, he will have to take the witness stand and testify himself."

This time I had scored. Even Shaughnessy joined in the general storm of laughter.

My little triumph was short-lived; Shaughnessy quickly turned the tables on me. How dangerous was it to roll a drum of high grade gasoline over a mile of pavement on a hot day? I did not think it was dangerous at all. Was that so? How much pressure would form in the drum through heat and agitation? I did not know. No? What did I know, anyway? What kind of expert was I, not to acknowledge that pressure inside a gasoline drum was dangerous? Any child in Arkansas knew that much. If the temperature in the shade was 84° F., how hot was the pavement and how much would fifty gallons of gasoline heat up during a mile-long roll? Carelessly I declared that no one could answer these questions. No one? I meant I could not answer them. Who was I, to sit in judgment over other experts, real experts and not imported chemists who had gotten their education outside the great United States?

When the forenoon was over, I felt as if Shaughnessy had wiped the floor with me.

We adjourned for noon recess, and there and then decided to spring the coup I had thought out. When the afternoon session opened, we startled everyone by putting on our own lawyer as first witness. By asking about my fee, the opponents had opened the way for our daring play. Innocently enough the lawyer-witness was asked to report our conversation regarding my rate of compensation and then, as an apparently harmless afterthought, came the question of what else had been said on that occasion.

"The chemical expert said," the witness stated, "that he would not undertake the case if I represented the plaintiff, for gasoline never ignites spontaneously."

The judge suddenly became interested. His Honor possessed a Ford car, and the testimony introduced had made him feel uneasy. He asked me to take the witness stand again so that he could examine me himself. Was it really dangerous to fill a gas tank on a hot day? Was there any hazard in driving a car in which the sun had heated the gasoline supply? The jurymen also leaned forward in their seats, and the entire audience listened with rapt attention. Twenty-five years ago automobiles were still something of a novelty, especially in the more sparsely settled regions, and from what Shaughnessy and his witnesses had indicated, a man took his life in his hands every time he filled his gasoline tank in summer weather. Up in the witness chair I enjoyed the situation to the utmost. No one dared interrupt me, and I made it plain that the fire in question must have been caused by an accidental spark. When I had finished, the judge instructed the jury to find a verdict for the defendant. After ten long days the trial was at an end.

Outstanding in my mind are two little incidents of this case that gave me a great deal of satisfaction at the time. One was the confession of a man shortly afterward that he had thrown a lighted cigarette into the basement of the implement store just as the gasoline was being unloaded. The other was that Mr. Shaughnessy looked me up as I was packing my grip.

"Next time," he said, "I hope we'll be on the same side of the case. Then I'd like to see anyone lick us."

That Arkansas victory certainly had not been due to my knowledge of chemistry, such as it was; it had been achieved by one pointed question asked at the right time. Nevertheless, my reputation as a court chemist was made and grew rapidly. I was asked to take case after case, and was lucky enough to be on the winning side each time; the fact that I accepted no case which looked doubtful to me may have helped some. Soon I was charging one hundred dollars a day, then one hundred and twenty-five, and later I raised my price to a hundred and fifty dollars a day. The more I charged, the more I was in demand. I believe that for a few years there was no important gasoline explosion case in the Middle West in which I was not asked to appear for one side or the other. Once I lost a golden opportunity because both sides tried to engage me on the same day. A former judge of a state supreme court put a blank check on my desk as the acme of seduction. I refused him because I thought his side was wrong, and then I had to refuse his opponents because I had already listened to his confidential communication.

I remember one case with particular distinctness. The trial took place in the spring of 1917 in a small Pennsylvania town of about two thousand people. The courthouse stood opposite the hotel which was headquarters for all—judge, attorneys, reporters, jury and witnesses. The trial dragged on, and all those engaged in it became well acquainted with each other. As the town had no newspaper, and radios were then still unknown, we depended for news on one of the reporters who used to call his wife in a nearby city every night before supper. He had her read part of the paper to him and then reported the latest events to the rest of us. One evening a heavy snowstorm disrupted the telephone service in the midst of his conversation, and the last sentence he had understood was that a revolution had broken out in Russia or Prussia, he was not sure which. For three days we discussed which country had revolted, while the continually falling snow kept us busy shovelling our way to and from the courthouse. We lived by candlelight and ate out of tin cans, but it was all done with a smile. Only one thing mars the memory I have of those days in the little mountain city. The mail carrier started on horseback to the nearest railway station, about twenty-five miles away, to fetch a newspaper, and he never returned. Next spring, when the snow melted, his body and that of his horse were found in a ravine into which he had stumbled and from which there had been no way out.

The most intriguing case in which I appeared as an expert centered around an explosion in a small Missouri village. I first heard about it at a conference in a Chicago hotel to which I had been called in haste. It appeared that a local oil company had a station in the town of Frederick and distributed kerosene and gasoline from there to the smaller settlements in the vicinity. One day urgent orders came from the town of Jonesville; the village had run completely out of kerosene, which was used there almost exclusively as fuel in kitchen stoves and heaters. The man in charge of the Frederick station had rushed out to Jonesville and supplied kerosene to several stores and households. Upon his return he found to his horror that by mistake he had delivered gasoline instead. In spite of night and rain he had retraced his steps, collected all his earlier deliveries, and replaced them with kerosene. Every gallon placed during the day, so he claimed, was properly exchanged and accounted for. Nonetheless, small explosions occurred in the village from then on. They did not amount to much, being largely puffs of smoke which scattered soot through living-rooms and kitchens, but a general feeling of nervousness spread through the little settlement. Finally one of these explosions ended in real tragedy. A girl of fifteen was preparing lunch for her family over a wood fire. Being pressed for time, she did what was common usage in her community; she poured a little kerosene over the flame. A terrific explosion shattered the can she was holding, and the burning fluid not only set fire to the kitchen but also to her clothing. Screaming in agony, the poor child ran through the main street of the village until she collapsed. She died in unspeakable pain before she could be removed to a hospital.

When I heard this gruesome story I refused to become involved, for I could not see how the oil company could possibly win before a local jury; nor did I think that it should be absolved from blame. I doubted that all the gasoline had been gathered in, but in any event I believed that, both factually and sentimentally, the other side held all the trump cards. Hence I argued seriously that my would-be clients should not burden themselves with the expenses of a trial. The officials of the company acknowledged the force of my arguments, but insisted on going through with the fight. Evidently more than this suit was at stake. I listened to their story with amazement and, although I still believed that we had little chance to win the case, I determined to go into it with all I had. My only reservation was that the child's parents were to be compensated regardless of the outcome, and that I should have a free hand in preparing my end of the case. Upon receiving assurances to that effect, I went to work.

The first thing I did was to hire the professor of chemistry in the Frederick high school as one of our witnesses. Not that he was an expert on explosions, but he looked dignified, and his testimony would carry weight. I then engaged a young professor of chemistry at the state college, whose duty it would be to study the explosiveness of kerosene. He was to demonstrate that kerosene, once brought to the point of explosion, was more dangerous than gasoline, a fact which could be proven. To myself I assigned the task of taking the bulk of the cross-examination which I knew would be loosed with full fury on me, the outsider. That the explosion really had been one of kerosene and not of gasoline I now considered a fair probability, for a minute inspection of the books had convinced me that the station agent at Frederick really had collected every gallon of gasoline he had erroneously delivered. The problem was how to convince the jury, and in that respect I could not help remaining pessimistic. Our battery of lawyers, gathered from the state capital, from St. Louis and from Frederick, confided to me that they, too, felt rather hopeless. We all would have been much happier on the other side of the counsel's table.

I happened to be out of Chicago when I was summoned by wire to Frederick. The suit was to open on the following Monday. All trains were delayed by heavy snowstorms, and as Frederick was not on a main line, I had to cover the last ten miles on horseback, with two suitcases dangling from my saddle. When I reached the courtroom it was Tuesday noon; the jury had long been chosen, and the father of the girl who had been burned to death was on the witness stand. He was describing the condition of the kitchen after the fire. The ceiling was charred, he testified, the windows broken, the cupboard gone, and there were holes in the linoleum. I pricked up my ears on hearing this last statement. Edging my way to our chief counsel, I asked him to suggest a noon adjournment before cross-examining the witness. He looked at me in surprise, for I was mud-bespattered and must have looked like a tramp, but he did as I asked. Over the lunch table I gave him my reason.

"I wouldn't have bet a nickel on our chances when I started out from Chicago," I told him; "but now I'll lay you even money on our case, provided you can get rid of these holes in the linoleum before the day is over." He wanted me to give him details, but I preferred to keep them to myself. He promised to do his best, and the case continued.

All afternoon witnesses came and went, and our lawyers dutifully doubted the existence of the holes in the linoleum. The result was curious. Where there had been only ten holes the size of a dime in the forenoon, there were about fifty by the time all the antagonistic testimony was finished, and their size had increased to the dimensions of dishpans. When we met after the close of the afternoon session, our legal advisors were quite downcast. They felt that they had let me down. I only smiled. What had happened, I told them, was just what I had expected. I would now lay them still better odds on our case. In the meantime, could I be excused for a day or two? I would be back in time for my testimony.

After my return the case dragged on for another week. The entire population of Jonesville must have trooped to the witness stand, and every time an inhabitant testified, our lawyers would tear into him and disclose shady chapters of his past life, discrediting most of these poor people to the point of ridicule and robbing their testimony of all its value. What was not said openly was insinuated. The social life of that little Missouri town was stripped of all privacy. Jonesville must have been a queer place to live in after this trial was over.

At last our turn came, and at the tail end of it we experts went on. The two professors did well, although I doubt that the jury understood them. The young college professor in particular ignored my suggestion to talk in one-syllable words. It was on a Saturday noon that he finished his testimony; I was to follow in the afternoon.

It was a great day for Frederick. Everyone in town seemed to feel that the climax was at hand, and when court opened every seat was taken, with people occupying windowsills and all other available space. My name was called, and I took the stand. After the usual preliminary questions our chief counsel pulled out a paper and read to me a long hypothetical question. It was one we had prepared with great care. In short, it amounted to this. If a person had used a liquid to revive a wood fire on a certain forenoon, and

271

if the ensuing explosion had left many holes in the linoleum of the room, what was it, in my opinion, that the container of the liquid had held—gasoline or kerosene?

"The liquid," I answered deliberately, "was kerosene."

Would I or could I prove this to the court? I could, I said, provided I could do so in my own way; and over the violent objections of our opponents the court ruled that I was at liberty to do all the demonstrating I wanted to.

I now pulled up my suitcase and from it I took a piece of linoleum. It had been bought in a local store and was accompanied by a bill and a price tag. The jury inspected it solemnly and decided that it was linoleum. It was our Exhibit A.

Next, I brought forth a small sealed bottle labeled "64° gasoline, Standard Oil Company of Missouri." A certificate of the state university showed that the sample had been bought and sealed by the head of one of its departments. It was introduced as Exhibit B. Another bottle, similarly attested, contained kerosene and was our Exhibit C. This much accomplished, I asked the judge to clear a space in front of his dais and to invite the jury closer to the arena. The show was about to begin.

By this time the excitement in the courtroom had almost reached the point of hysteria; one could hear only occasional nervous giggles and suppressed whispers, as everyone crowded toward the front of the room to see what I would do. I fed the tension by giving the jurymen a short resumé of what the exhibits were, while I spread the little piece of linoleum on the floor. I then produced a thimble, also bought in a local store, and filled it with gasoline from the bottle. Getting on my feet, I held the thimble at arm's length by means of a pair of prongs.

"I am a person holding a container with gasoline in my hand," I explained. "I shall now set it on fire." I applied a match to the fluid, and the resulting flame terrified those who stood nearby.

"Watch out!" I cried. "Here goes the fire!" With that I dropped the thimble on the linoleum. There was a flash through the air; the thimble struck the floor, but the fire was out. The draft in midair had consumed the gasoline.

"Look at the linoleum," I said. The little square of fabric was picked up and passed around. It did not show even a speck.

By this time the audience was wild with curiosity and emotion. The judge, who was none too calm himself, and who stood by my side as in a trance, left it to the bailiff to pound for order. In spite of his efforts, I could hardly make myself heard.

I next took the kerosene and repeated the experiment. When the burning liquid hit the floor this time, it kept on burning until I quenched the fire, and wherever splashes of it had fallen, the linoleum showed large round holes, like those on the floor covering in the dead girl's kitchen.

There was no need for further explanation. The jury went back to their benches, talking, gesticulating, shaking their heads. The break had come. Our opponents, taken off their feet, did not even cross-examine me; if they had, I might have had an unpleasant time. As it was, the battle was over. I boarded the next train home, and at the station Bertha waited for me with a telegram. It read, "You have won our case," and was signed by all our lawyers. I heaved a long sigh of relief and slept for a day and a night. A couple of weeks spent in court work are not exactly a vacation.

My record as an expert would have been perfect had it not been for one defeat. It was a funny case. A Chicago firm of oil dealers, Potthauser and Mettendorf, were being sued for adulterating linseed oil and asked me to help defend them. I had known both men a long time and had often been amused by their antics. They were easy-going, generous, not over-scrupulous; in this instance they had tried to enlarge their profits by putting ten per cent of naphtha into their boiled linseed oil. Both deserved whatever punishment awaited them, and at first I was disinclined to listen to their plea. What changed my mind was the form of the complaint drawn up against them, which seemed quite out of proportion to the offense committed. A ten per cent admixture of a volatile substance like naphtha weakens the dried oil film in the paint proportionally; but the paint is still serviceable and would not, as the plaintiff's attorney claimed, ruin thousands of dollars' worth of property. I took the case under the condition that my clients should plead guilty. It would be my job to mitigate the verdict.

Everything might have gone well had not Mr. Mettendorf had a hunch. The war against Germany was on and he was disturbed.

"Look here," he said, "my name is Mettendorf, my partner's name is Potthauser, and your name does not sound like that of a Yankee either. I have a hunch that if we can get a lawyer by the name of Wettlesborough, we'll win the case." We all jumped to the telephone directory and, curiously enough, there was a lawyer by that name in Chicago. We made a date with him to acquaint him with his task.

When we got to his office, we found that Mr. Wettlesborough was a young man of twenty-three who had never handled a case in his life and who had never even been alone in court. Mr. Potthauser and I wanted to call the thing off, but Mr. Mettendorf would not hear of it.

"My hunches have never failed me," he insisted, "and they will not fail me now." That settled it. Mr. Wettlesborough remained our attorney.

When the case came to trial, the young lawyer was in a funk. He begged me to sit next to him and guide him, but instead of picking up courage as the opposing attorney unfolded his rather weak attack, he became more and more panicky and finally, with a short, "I quit," literally walked out on us.

That ended it. My clients pleaded guilty and got off with slight damages, but I debited myself with the loss. Perhaps there was a silver lining to this cloud. These court cases were taking too much of my time anyway, time which I thought I might devote more profitably to the development of my oil business. At any rate, I rejected many flattering offers from then on, and gradually withdrew altogether from court work.

My courtroom experiences did not imbue me with much reverence for our judicial system in technical cases. I found faults in everything—laws, judges, juries, experts. I heard laws cited dating back to 1818, and wondered why one generation should take it upon itself to legislate for another, as yet unborn. Conditions change, but laws do not. Why should not all laws be allowed to expire automatically, say thirty-three years after their enactment? They could then be re-examined, to be renewed or discarded, as experience and the progress of events indicate. This would eliminate the unwieldy accumulation of statutes which, in the light of newly created conditions, may have become obsolete or downright silly. A law in a western state, said to be still in force when I was doing court work, stipulated that when two railroad trains met at a crossing, neither should proceed until the other had passed. When you ran into similar statutes in chemical cases it was not funny. The judges I found universally well-meaning and honest, but incapable of understanding technical testimony. Their instructions or decisions often flew not only into the face of the evidence, but also into that of plain common sense. This was not due to the judges' lack of intelligence, but to their lack of technical knowledge. A logical remedy that suggests itself would be to have certain judges undergo special training to fit them for cases involving chemistry or engineering. If patent lawyers handle patent cases, why not have technical judges handle technical cases? And the poor juries! They usually did not know what it was all about and were locked up until they arrived at a unanimous verdict. If the justices of our Supreme Court are frequently divided in their opinions, why expect twelve laymen to agree? We do not lock up the Supreme Court to force unanimity, therefore the majority opinion of a jury should be equally acceptable. Such a majority opinion would, at any rate, mirror the honest convictions of the panel and be of help to any higher court called upon to review the case.

As to experts, I hope the time will come when they will undergo state examinations like certified public accountants and be called by the court, not by either of the contending parties. It is the only way, as I see it, by which judges and juries can be reasonably sure of the facts on which to base their verdict.

C H A P T E R   1 4

*

A JOY RIDE IN COMMODITIES

THE WAR YEARS from 1914 to
1917 were not happy ones for those who were acquainted with European politics and knew how to interpret current events. They could read between the lines and see propaganda being infused into the United States with subtle skill.

I saw how one of the foreign propaganda machines worked. I employed at that time a German stenographer who happened to be engaged to the owner of an advertising firm in Chicago. One day I found her in tears. She had broken off her engagement, because she had discovered that her fiancé was a German spy and his advertising agency a blind. The young man begged for a chance to explain his position to me.

The German was no spy, he explained, but a propagandist, working under orders from his embassy. He had entered the United States from Canada under a forged passport and was given money to establish an advertising agency in Chicago. He let it be known that he was holding two million dollars for distribution in advertising matter; the slogan was "Travel in Germany After the War." Of course, if certain papers chose to adopt a hostile attitude toward Germany, it would be inadvisable to use their columns. From his files this German propagandist pulled letter after letter from well-known publications, in which he was assured that their political attitude was not inflexible. One daily in a midwestern city even printed for him a pro-German trial editorial in order to snatch some of his gold. The unbelievable part of the contemptible story was that a whole string of American papers had been held in line by this bait for two years, although the two-million-dollar fund was a will-o'-the-wisp and not a single dollar was ever paid out.

276

When America entered the war in 1917, I, as a chemist of Austrian birth, naturally became an immediate target for every professional and amateur sleuth in Chicago. For weeks I knew that I was under secret observation. My friends were accosted in street-cars and other public places by persons unknown to them, who wanted to find out my views on the war; I suspected that my mail was skillfully opened and resealed, and certain signs pointed to the tapping of my telephones, both at home and in the office. I was not surprised when two high officers from the Department of Justice, one a general, the other a colonel, entered my place of business one morning and, after a short introduction, began asking me a bewildering array of meaningless questions. When had I been in Gary last? Who did I think would win the war? Did I know a girl by the name of Wolkenbruch?

"Gentlemen," I said, after I had endured this hurricane for several minutes, "you are wasting your time. Your tactics amuse, but don't confuse me. May I suggest that you ask me one question which you perhaps should have asked first?"

What question had I in mind? Just this, I told them: Was I born an American citizen? The two officers looked at each other in amazement.

"You weren't, were you?" one of them asked at last.

For reply I went to the safe and brought out my father's citizenship papers and my own passport. The result was electrical. From being a suspect treated with icy politeness, I became the object of profuse apologies. Before they left, the two Intelligence officers gave me their secret telephone number with instructions to call them should I be pestered by any minor sleuth. In truth, they went further than that. They tried to help me get food to my mother in Vienna as the widow of an American army officer.

The visit of these two officials proved a good thing for me, for it protected me from further annoyances. One runt once walked into our office with his hat on, cast impudent glances in all corners, and even went to our desks to look at letters. During all that time he had not introduced himself nor stated the nature of his errand. I told Gertie to call the police. This forced his hand and, with a contemptuous gesture, he showed us his government star. Calmly I went to the telephone and called Hartford 7777. It was comical how quickly the man's hat came off when he heard this number. He wanted to leave at once, but I bade him stay. When I got my connection, the general asked to speak with my visitor. I could only surmise what he said, but I was greatly pleased to see the runt leave in a hurry, bowing himself out backward in the manner of a courtier. I was never bothered by bona fide sleuths again.

Nevertheless, attempts to win laurels at my expense never ceased while the war lasted. A young Irish girl who was selling magazines dropped in from time to time. She evidently hated the English, for her remarks invariably turned in that direction. Gertie and I became suspicious and asked her to cease talking politics in our presence. After this admonition she disappeared.

One terribly hot day an old man came in. He was carrying a tray containing buttons, suspenders and the like and looked completely exhausted. I asked him to sit down and gave him a glass of water which he drank thirstily. Speaking with a broad German accent he then complained that in most places he was told with a sneer to go back to Germany and fight for the Kaiser; often he was the subject of personal insults, and once he had been beaten up by some super-patriotic hoodlums.

I bought his entire stock of goods and offered him a job as night watchman. It meant no more than sleeping on our premises; I would pay for his board. He was so grateful he cried. We closed the bargain and I sent him home in my car. He lived, so he told Gertie's husband who drove him, in one of the flophouses on Madison Street.

Two or three nights went by without a trace of my new watchman. I became slightly alarmed. Perhaps the poor fellow had fallen sick. I went to his hotel to look after him. To my astonishment he did not live there any more. I became curious and decided to investigate. With the aid of a few drinks, judiciously distributed, I found that he had left the flophouse on the day he had called at my office. I then visited several small hotels in the district, but failed to find my old peddler.

A few weeks later, as I was driving along a West Side street, I noticed a well-dressed man walking toward me. Something about him looked familiar. I stopped the car for better observation; yes, it was my German friend, only much younger looking, dressed like a dude and jauntily swinging a cane. I got out of the car and confronted him.

"What about that watchman's job?" I asked him.

He turned pale, but did not say a word. Then he suddenly swung around and started to run away, but was not quite quick enough. I just had time to plant a juicy kick where I thought it would do most good, and then watched him disappear down the street. What the man's mission was, or in whose employ he worked, has always remained a mystery to me.

Not long afterward I had another experience with a peddler, but this time the ending was happier. My visitor was selling soaps and perfumes; his object in coming to my office, however, was not to sell me anything, but to buy samples of oil. At his home he was working on a new soap which was to clean and bleach cloth at the same time without damaging the fabric. Could I spare him a small bottle of this oil and that, and hold the price down to his means? I questioned him thoroughly and found that he really was a student. A few bottles, I told him, would hardly carry him very far in his experiments, and therefore I handed him with my compliments several gallons of various products, waving aside his profuse thanks and wishing him the best of luck.

A year or two passed and I had forgotten the incident. Others must either have worked out the same idea or stolen my peddler's secret, for I noticed that a bleach-cleansing soap was being advertised by a Chicago concern. I paid no particular attention to the matter until one day I received an invitation to call there. I was surprised at the size of the plant in which this soap was being turned out. When I presented my card to the switchboard operator, she told me that the president was expecting me. A few seconds later I was ushered into a sumptuously decorated private office, and there at the desk, dressed in a natty business suit, sat my erstwhile soap peddler. He grinned all over his face when he saw my astonishment, asked me to sit down, and told me the story of his climb. His ambition, he said, had been to buy a carload of oil from me and he had waited all this time to have his dream come true. Now the moment had arrived and the order was mine. I could have all his business, if I cared to handle it, and I did handle it for many years.

Another example of bread thrown on the waters comes back to

me. It concerns an insurance agent who had written some small policies for me and who owned a piece of property out West on which a mica deposit had been discovered. He did not know much about its value and had no one to turn to but me. I ran some tests for him and gave him my professional opinion, which was favorable. He told me that he could not pay me anything, and I assured him that I would cheerfully put it on the cuff. We both laughed and I gave it no further thought.

Then the war broke out, and the price of mica went skyrocketing. One morning's mail brought me a check for fifteen hundred dollars. The mine had proved a success. I banked the money and returned a cuff marked "paid in full." For a long time insurance salesmen must have wondered why they received so pleasant a reception at my hands.

Not all people with whom I came in contact during the war were considerate. There was one man, especially, against whom I had sworn revenge at the first opportunity. He was the purchasing agent of a large firm for which we prepared some special oils. He had always been disagreeable, but when the United States entered the European war, he became downright vicious toward me. He showered me with impudent remarks and wanted to fasten on me the sins of all Germans, dead or alive. I vowed to myself that some day I would get even with him.

One afternoon I called at the office of his company and found a new man at his desk. The purchasing agent had been demoted to the shipping department. I could not get downstairs quickly enough. There, in a far-away corner, I espied my old enemy. Even before I approached within speaking distance, the words which I had so often rehearsed rose to my lips. But when I stepped close to him he looked up and I saw tears come to his eyes. Jumping from his chair he almost embraced me.

"My friend!" he exclaimed, "my only friend! They have all forgotten me since I have been transferred and you, of all people, you whom I have so often abused, come to see me." He pulled out a box of cigars, and then told me how a once powerful man feels after he has been made impotent.

What was I to do? Before we parted I, too, had tears in my eyes, and the best rehearsed speech of my life was never delivered.

When the war was on in all seriousness, and the first outbursts of oratory were over, a remarkable separation took place between the essential and the nonessential functions of the national body. The country divided its citizens into those who could do things and those who could not. Among the latter were most of the former pillars of society. What good were lawyers, brokers, advertising agents and psychoanalysts now? A fighting nation could get along very well without them. On the other hand, chemists, engineers, mechanics and inventors were suddenly lifted from the social gutter to the pinnacle of public esteem. No chemist was allowed to go to the front, not even as a volunteer. America expected every chemist to do his duty as a chemist. It was, at least by implication, a great compliment to the profession.

One of the queer war problems that came my way had its origin in a fire which destroyed a large chocolate factory in the East. Although the plant had been gutted, much of the chocolate was saved; but it was mixed with ashes, broken glass and other debris, and therefore useless for edible purposes. The problem was to save its most valuable constituent, the cocoa butter. A chemical process for its recovery was worked out by the Miner Laboratories of Chicago almost before the last fireman had left the scene. The plant work was then turned over to me.

All we needed to start work was a large tank, for which we received a priority order from the War Department. Nevertheless, it took a week or two to build it, and in the meantime carload after carload of chocolate began piling up in our yard. Our plant became the most popular rendezvous of all South Side children, and our night watchman had to ask for police reinforcements to cope with the crowds.

But no army of watchmen could keep away the flies and bugs. I never saw them in such numbers or in so many varieties. They seemed to breed in the chocolate, and the specimens were of a glittering beauty that reminded me of the plumage of tropical birds. Their vitality was far above that of ordinary insects, and even the buzzing of the flies was different and testified to the joy of living amid such luxury. We barricaded our office with triple screen doors and still went swinging swatters all day long to keep peace and order in the place.

Much of the chocolate had come through the fire unscathed, and we found whole barrels which were fit to be taken home to eat. All our men helped themselves liberally and got sick, one after the other. I did not dare inquire about their children or their children's friends. We were at the same time handling a tank car of castor oil, and generous samples of it may have relieved the situation somewhat.

It took months to clean up all the wreckage of that chocolate plant, but we turned over to the government almost every pound of the cocoa butter contents. The flies stayed with us hopefully for a while, probably living on scraps which had lodged in invisible crevices. The kettle we salvaged for future use, and the older men in our plant still call it the "chocolate kettle."

The Ladies Garment Corporation also received a war order. When I first heard about it I could not suppress a smile, for I had difficulty connecting baby diapers, sanitary aprons and dress shields with the needs of soldiers. Nonetheless, the report was true; the government needed waterproof coats for the aviation corps. Our oiled silk lent itself splendidly to this purpose, at least theoretically, being light in weight and waterproof, and promising protection against changes in temperature. We went to work on this order with much enthusiasm, but without much success. Where the chemist had succeeded, the tailors failed; they could not sew buttons on our material or find other means of fastening the garments. We tried all kinds of adhesives, and at times I had a dozen tailors around, each of them asking my advice. I felt as so many of our newly commissioned officers must have felt when giving orders to recruits. It was a good thing that our flying aces did not depend on my dressmaking ability, for I did little to aid them. I made up for it in a way by furnishing the government an oil preparation for gasproofing army balloons.

Every chemist in the country was busy in his line. Hoskins, our dean, headed a committee which examined suggestions for new inventions and, although confronted with many serious decisions, he also got some amusement out of his work. When secrecy was no longer necessary, he entertained us for hours by telling about plans he had passed on or passed up, and the correspondence he had carried on with real inventors as well as crackpots in every state of the Union.

One chemist who achieved national fame during the war was Lee Lewis, then professor of chemistry at Northwestern University. He developed and perfected Lewisite, the deadliest of all poison gases known. It was never used in actual combat, but it is believed that the Germans knew of its existence, and that this hastened the Armistice. Lewis' friends could not decide which of these two facts gave him greater satisfaction. In later years, when Dr. Lewis recalled those days, he never mentioned Lewisite. He preferred to dwell on his fundamental contributions in the fields of organic arsenicals and sugars, on his efforts as a teacher and counsellor of young people, or on his promotion of higher sanitation and more precise chemical methods in the packing house industry.

Lee Lewis would have made an equally enviable name for himself as a writer or public speaker. His choice of words was something at which I always marvelled, and his humor brought to mind the fable of the man who wanted to award a prize for the most heroic deed. There were three contestants. The first told of a child he had rescued from a fire. The second had kept a boat from foundering. The third, who received the prize, had suppressed a good joke at a dinner table because it might have hurt one of the guests.

Lewis' humor was and still is like that. It has that rare quality which makes friends instead of estranging them.

Ward Evans of Northwestern University, a confrère of Lewis, also did valiant work during the war. When hostilities ceased, he probably knew more about the proper filling of hand grenades and shells than anyone else in the United States. Evans was destined to be one of the great teachers of chemistry; it would be said of him that he instilled more fear and affection in the hearts of students than whole faculties at other schools. The secret of his success has never been made known to outsiders.

An important invention of the war years, one made under somewhat peculiar circumstances, was that of a chemical called furfural. A shortage of molasses had developed, and in order to offset this shortage, the Miner Laboratories endeavored to produce a sugary substitute from the hulls of oats. They did not attain that goal, but found instead that oat hulls could be made to yield furfural in commercial quantities. Today, millions of pounds of it are used in the petroleum, the rosin and many other industries.

One of the romances that brighten a chemist's life is the hope that although he may fail to find the product he is seeking, he may hit on another, perhaps more valuable than the first. The discovery of Hoskins' epoch-making heat-resisting wire had come about that way. Hoskins had originally tried to manufacture synthetic rubies and diamonds, and was forced to study reactions under very high temperatures. In the course of time, this led to the discovery of heat-resisting metals. His idea of producing gems had not worked out, and Hoskins was secretly glad of it. In his whimsical way he would point out that an electric toaster on a woman's table was many times more useful than a string of rubies around her neck, and that even if the woman might not agree, her husband would.

The Armistice struck American industry like a bullet hitting a bird in full flight. There were a few flutterings, then the silence of death. A million wheels stopped all at once. War orders, some half filled, were cancelled overnight. Raw materials of all kinds were dumped on a prostrate market. Stagnation was the order of the day. We had never made any money on war orders, but all our customers had. We were hurt as much as the rest, but without the cushion of their profits.

Vegetable oils, our primary interest, suffered a violent decline, together with all other commodities. This did not concern me directly, but it did involve me in a deal that was to cause me many a headache. Among the concerns which had mushroomed up during the war was that of Clark, Roberts and Company. By 1918 this firm had offices all over the world, including Chicago. I was well acquainted with the local manager, a shrewd Scotsman named MacDowell, who often consulted me on technical matters. One day, during the dreary winter of 1918, I called on him to swap tales of woe. Among his troubles was one which attracted my attention. Clark, Roberts and Company had imported great quantities of China wood oil during the war, and amid the hustle and bustle of those days some off-grade oil had found its way into their cargos. These bad lots had been culled out in Seattle, but no one would take the time to bother with them just then. Now that quiet reigned again and everyone was taking inventory, it was discovered that about ten thousand barrels had accumulated, all adulterated, and all considered useless. China wood oil was then, as it is now, used as a base for varnishes and had to be pure to be marketable. Adulterating it was like putting kerosene into wine; it made the wine unfit to drink and the kerosene unfit to burn.

We talked on the subject for a few minutes; MacDowell showed me an analysis and asked me what I thought the oil was worth. The market value of pure China wood oil was then about twenty-one cents per pound. I hazarded an estimate that eight and one-half cents would be a fair valuation, and that I myself might take on a few hundred barrels at that price.

"Sold," MacDowell said. "You have just bought yourself three hundred barrels of adulterated wood oil."

I must have turned a sickly green, for my host laughed and offered to let me out of the bargain. This I would not accept. In trading, a man's word must be good, and a sale once made is a sale. With a heavy heart I turned my steps homeward. I, who was not a merchant but a chemist, had just bought ten thousand dollars' worth of merchandise, and merchandise which I knew to be practically valueless.

Two or three weeks elapsed before the unwelcome shipment reached us. In the meantime I had spent many sleepless nights; but my tossings had not been in vain. I concluded that ten thousand barrels of any kind of oil would not be dumped into the ocean, and that anyone who found a way to utilize them would reap a handsome profit. Had the problem been presented to me as a chemist, I would have tried to solve it for a fee. Why not solve it for myself and make whatever profit there would be in it? Eagerly I sampled each of the three hundred barrels. No two of them were of the same grade, and I had to analyze each individually. It takes about twenty minutes to test a wood oil sample, hence I did not relish the prospect. Under the pressure of war, however, chemists had learned to think and act quickly. If a sample of wood oil had to be analyzed in five minutes, it would be done. I developed a fairly good method, and the testing of the three hundred barrels was completed a few hours after their unloading. To my surprise, I found that much of the oil was pure, and what delighted me still more was that some of it was of a lighter color than I had ever seen. The whole lot was immediately assorted. I sold the pale oil to a specialty manufacturer at twenty-eight cents a pound and disposed of the other pure oil at twenty cents. This left me some two hundred barrels, with which I did not know what to do.

Then an idea struck me. I had heard that a St. Louis manufacturer used wood oil in a waterproof cement paint. In his case purity might not be of paramount importance. To a varnish plant an adulterated oil would be anathema; in cement paint, it might be usable. At any rate, it was worth taking a chance. A few hours later saw me in St. Louis, and soon after, I held in my hand an order for one thousand barrels at fourteen cents a pound. A thousand barrels was more than I owned, and tremblingly I called up Mac-Dowell in Chicago. Before I hung up I had bought an additional lot of two thousand barrels at the old price of eight and one-half cents. My head swam when I computed my profit. I had made about twenty thousand dollars on this deal. It certainly beat anything that consulting work could offer in the way of money-making.

MacDowell saw a lot of me during the next week. Each time I visited him I dared him to sell me more of his refuse, as I called it, and each time I talked him out of another few hundred barrels. In this way I gradually amassed five thousand barrels. Then someone else tumbled to my private gold mine and bought what was left of it. I borrowed all the money I could, paid for my goods, and waited. Luck was with me. News of this new off-grade oil spread through trade circles, and now that no more of it was available, everybody wanted it, human nature being no different among oil buyers than anywhere else. I sold out my holdings at steadily advancing prices. The last five hundred barrels went, for some reason which has always remained a puzzle to me, to the government of a British Colony at the fancy price of seventeen and three-quarters cents a pound. When I closed my books on the entire transaction, I found that it had yielded me over fifty thousand dollars. Applied chemistry, when applied properly, evidently could be quite profitable.

While the sale of this adulterated wood oil had been going on, a peculiar question came up which caused me some uneasiness. Was adulterated wood oil subject to an import duty as a compounded oil? It was a neat legal question, and I called on Jeremiah Hynes, the Chicago Custom House chemist, for a decision. I had never met a custom house chemist before and was secretly in fear of having to face a lot of official dignity; but my fear proved groundless. Hynes was a jovial and informal man and only too glad to help. He had been born in the pine country of Michigan, and some of the healthy fragrance of his native earth seemed to cling to him. He constantly encountered strange problems, but he met them all with a clear mind and a sense of humor. No one could make a bureaucrat of Jerry Hynes.

In the course of time he had to give answers to many quaint questions. Once he had to analyze a Christmas tree made of wire frame and fancy green pine needles. Did it take duty as a toy? Jerry did not think so. The imitation pine needles were made of dyed goose quills. So far as the Custom House was concerned, the Christmas tree was bird feathers. Are animal glands crude drugs or fresh meat? Is an elephant's foot, made into an umbrella rack, a piece of furniture or a stuffed animal? If a man imports Salvarsan and it proves to be ninety-five per cent ordinary kitchen salt and five per cent color, does the swindling importer escape the high tax on pharmaceuticals, even though he sold the preparation as Salvarsan? The Custom House laboratory took such problems in its stride.

Only once did I see Hynes slightly perturbed. A law had been passed prohibiting the importation of artificially colored tea, and the presence or absence of coloring, so the statutes said, was to be determined by chemical analysis. A sample of imported tea was put before Jerry, and he immediately recognized it as artificially colored. Moreover, he proved his point conclusively. After the dust had been shaken out in a sieve, the coating was easily identified under the microscope as Prussian blue. Jerry considered the case closed, but it was not. The importer fought back and showed in court that the presence of coloring had been determined by a physical and not a chemical test. The tea came in, color and all. Jerry's unofficial comments, made in the privacy of a chemists' gathering, were something to be remembered.

Only once again did I have an opportunity to make big money by handling off-grade wood oil. Many years later I was invited to New York to consult with a large importer. Over the lunch table he told me a curious story.

A few months prior to our conference a boat which he had chartered was lying in the harbor of Hong Kong. It was a bulk cargo boat, a vessel containing two parallel egg-shaped shells, arranged lengthwise and designed to transport oil in large quantities. This particular boat was waiting for a twelve-hundred-ton cargo of China wood oil. Half the load had been received and was stored on the port side, when news was received that disturbances had broken out in the interior and that the arrival of the remainder would be delayed. The captain cabled for instructions and, receiving orders to proceed with half the cargo, pumped Hong Kong drinking water —so he said—into the starboard tank to equalize the load. Then he weighed anchor. A few days out at sea the boat ran into a typhoon and nearly foundered. It then pulled into Singapore for repairs. When the hold was inspected, the captain found to his dismay that instead of having oil on one side and water on the other, both tanks were filled with a white substance. Evidently a leak had sprung between the two compartments, and the contents had been churned into a cheesy emulsion.

When the boat reached New York the cargo looked worthless. The importer refused to accept the load, and a three-cornered fight started between the importer, the steamship line and the insurance company, the latter claiming that the captain had used salt water instead of drinking water and thereby had damaged the oil beyond repair. Chemist after chemist tried to break the emulsion, and I was called in to offer suggestions, if I had any.

I had an idea, but I took my time before disclosing it. I no longer considered myself a mere consulting chemist, and was not inclined to give away chemical advice free or for small change; long before this, my intercourse with lawyers had taught me to adjust fees to the sums involved in a case rather than to the difficulty of handling it. I would take a leaf from their book of experience. This cargo was worth two hundred and fifty thousand dollars, and whatever advice I gave would cost proportionately. In fact, it had to, if I expected my opinion to be respected. I remembered something that had happened in the war days while Clark, Roberts and Company were in their prime. They had called me from New York to ask for my opinion on a sample of linseed oil which they proposed sending me. I pointed out to them that there were chemists in New York quite competent to analyze linseed oil, and I did not see how I could benefit them. They stuttered and stammered for a while, before they told me that they had had the oil analyzed; the chemist, well known and capable, had pronounced it pure. But he had charged them only fifteen dollars for his work; how could they buy a cargo worth a king's ransom on the strength of a fifteen-dollar analysis? Would I just look at the oil and tell them whether I would buy it in their place?

I received the sample, smelled it, made a few elementary tests and phoned to New York that if the shipment were offered me, I would accept it as good merchandise. A few days later I received a check for five hundred dollars. The antics of what Bert Leston Taylor often referred to as the so-called human race certainly were peculiar.

This Oriental cargo of emulsified wood oil offered a tough problem, but I was confident I would find the solution. I had broken stubborn emulsions before, and I thought I knew how to do it. At least I thought so until I tackled this one and found that all my past experience availed me naught. Try as I might, the oil and the water would not separate; if the issue was forced, the oil was irretrievably ruined in the process.

When I had worried myself into a state of idiocy, and no further ideas came to me day or night, I decided to go back to my boyhood remedy of taking a few days off to give my brain an airing. My best thoughts had always come to me on long walks; perhaps the old method would still work. So I literally walked away from my work. I walked all the way from Chicago to Madison, Wisconsin, a distance of about a hundred and fifty miles. On the way I found the solution of my problem. Again it was Poe's "Purloined Letter" in a different setting. No ordinary emulsion was likely to withstand all the known methods of breaking it up. But what if the emulsion had been formed by sea water? True, the captain's story was that he had used drinking water, and I had no reason to doubt it; but even so, the storm-tossed boat might have sprung a leak. How could I have overlooked such an obvious possibility? Sea water contained ingredients that could very well react with wood oil. As in a medical case, to diagnose a case correctly is to win more than half the battle. If my diagnosis proved correct—it did eventually—the treatment would be more or less a routine matter.

The case looked really too big for a consulting fee. If my advice was good, it was worth keeping for myself. I went back to New York and bought the entire cargo at a low price, with an arrangement to reprocess the oil and share the profits, if any, with all other parties concerned. For a while it looked as if a large reward was in the offing. But this time luck was against me. The market on wood oil broke wide open before I had proceeded very far. The initial profits soon turned into losses, and at the finish, like the colored preacher who had passed his hat around and received it back empty, I thanked Heaven that at least I had got my money back.

Peace came with exasperating slowness. In the meantime many thinking people wondered if the real lessons of the war had been rightly learned. It was said that in 1915, Professor Nernst of Hannover had submitted to the German high command the idea of gas warfare. When it was reluctantly adopted—rumor said by imperial decree—it was put to use in a crude, unbusinesslike manner. Instead of waiting for the invisible phosgene to be developed, chlorine was loosed. Five thousand Allied soldiers died, but the next day one hundred thousand primitive gas masks were on the field of battle. It was the one great chance Germany had to win the war. No army could have stood up to an attack against which there was no defense. When the English sprang their tanks on the enemy two years later, they showed that they had not profited by their enemies' mistake. With a few of these novel monsters they crushed a mite of the German front; it would have been just as easy to crush it decisively with a larger tank corps. In future wars such basic errors would be impossible, of course. Shrewd businessmen would sit on all army staffs to tell the military men how to utilize good ideas to their best advantage. If one army, for instance, left some specially made cardboard tanks stranded on roads in a campaign, and news of it was allowed to pass the censor, the businessmen on the other side would see through the trick and refuse to let their governments be trapped into premature declarations of war. Inventors and experts, known in industry as research men, would work hand in hand with both army officers and businessmen. It would be all the brains of one country against those of the other. Potsdam and West Point were going to be no more than advisers to national boards of directors in far-off cities, for military schools could only turn out military experts, but could no more instill ingenuity into their students than civilian colleges could instill it into graduate chemists or engineers. Like chemical problems, military questions of the future would have to be answered by three different kinds of minds—the visionary which foresees new possibilities, the inventive which provides practical tools to develop them, and the military which knows how to use them. The nation which first recognized this truth and coordinated dreamers, inventors, strategists and businessmen, would hold an immeasurable advantage in the next conflict.

After the silent demise of Wilson's famous Fourteen Points, the peoples of all countries cherished one more hope. The statesmen had failed, but the returned soldiers would surely succeed in bringing about real peace. The veterans' associations which blossomed forth everywhere would raise such an outcry of "No more war," that the politicians would bow to it. Here was a made-to-order world slogan leading to mutual understanding and general disarmament. It was a great rallying cry and needed only a few far-seeing leaders to make the world thereafter safe against bloodshed. The returned soldiers of all nations were holding the future of the world in the palms of their hands. There never could be any more wars.

The slump in business and commodity prices which had followed in the wake of the Armistice did not last long. Before the sap began to rise in the trees, a lot of quiet buying began to take place. Reports were flying about that, as soon as the peace treaty was signed, the Central Powers would have to replenish their empty larders. In particular, the shortage of fats and oils would have to be made up. For years the Germans and Austrians had gone practically without butter and cream, even without soap. All this was to be bought now. I recall sitting in MacDowell's office one morning, when he suggested that I buy myself five tank cars of Manchurian soybean oil. What on earth was I to do with them, I inquired.

"Sit on them, you fool," he said crisply. "Can't you feel the market is on the go?"

I replied that I felt nothing but cold air. MacDowell was one of those fresh-air fiends who glories in freezing everyone out of his office. I had never before bought a drop of any oil on speculation;

nevertheless, I asked him to give me an option on those five tanks for a couple of hours. I would know by then if I could use them. He agreed somewhat reluctantly. A few minutes later a wire was handed him and he turned to me.

"I'll pay you three hundred and seventy-five dollars for your option," he announced in a matter-of-fact tone. "Here's a bid for your five tanks at nine and one-quarter cents. Our firm will take one-eighth and you take the other."

This was great. Perhaps if I remained sitting on my chair doing nothing I would make more money. I certainly was not missing anything at my own office, which was as quiet as a cemetery at midnight.

"I'll wait," I declared.

"Wise boy," was MacDowell's curt comment.

I remained in the office of Clark, Roberts and Company for two hours and left with a profit check for two thousand and seven hundred dollars. Thus was I ushered into the most exciting period of commodity speculation this generation has witnessed. Before long everybody was buying commodities. The number of brokers increased week by week, and all did a land-office business. Most of them were tempted to speculate on their own account; at times, they were practically driven to it. There was a broker named Parker, for instance, who once called me up in evident distress. He had an order to sell a few cars of cottonseed oil at ten and one-half cents and at the same time someone else had wired in to buy an even quantity at eleven cents. Brokers were accustomed, of course, to see a spread between bid and asked prices, but never before had anyone seen the bid price the higher of the two. Here was a man willing to pay more than the seller demanded. What was a poor broker to do? Let three hundred dollars per car go into the sewer? Rather than do that, he acted as both buyer and seller, and besides his commission pocketed the tidy extra sum which had been thrown into his lap.

Whatever one bought was higher the next day. People actually became dizzy on these steadily rising markets and acted as if they were intoxicated. My old friends Mettendorf and Potthauser were in the vanguard of the procession. They took fliers on anything the brokers offered them, and did not care if what they were buying was used in peach pies or roof paints. I was in their office when they took a certified check for forty thousand dollars out of an envelope. They had bought a contract for ten carloads of Kauri gum, and the seller had bought back his own contract for that amount. They quarreled about what to do with the money. I suggested that they split it and put their respective shares into savings accounts in their wives' names. Some day there would be an end to this orgy, and the money might then come in handy. Strange to say, they took my advice and thanked me sincerely. For a long time I felt that I had done a good deed. Later, when the crash was on and I dropped into their office, their faces bore woe-begone expressions. Everything was going wrong. But that forty thousand dollars, I reminded them, that surely was a nice nest egg? Oh, that forty thousand dollars? Yes, they remembered. They had taken the money out of the bank the next day and bought more Kauri gum with it.

Many people did not want it known that they were speculating and therefore did their trading through my firm. Our books became a secret receptacle for private gambling accounts. Presidents of concerns, capitalists little and big, even bankers bought and sold through us. We became a regular clearing house for commodities and made more money in brokerage than in manufacturing and chemistry combined. The work was intensely exciting. I met people from every walk of life, all actuated by the passion for easy money. A group of speculators instructed me to buy them a thousand barrels of linseed oil. They wanted it for immediate delivery, so as to have it under their own control; I pleaded with them to buy the oil in the form of contracts and not as physical property, but I probably was too forceful. They placed their order elsewhere, to our mutual sorrow, as we were to find out later. One man high in ecclesiastical ranks had heard of money to be made in China wood oil and bought it by the train load. An attorney I knew called me up and wanted to know where peanut oil came from and what it was used for; he had just bought a thousand barrels on a tip. A few days later he sold out with a substantial profit, and his sudden scientific interest died a-borning.

By the end of the year, the speculative rage had gotten out of hand and I decided to quit. When mailmen and stenographers were beginning to discuss markets, it was time for old hands to get out.

Everyone was now convinced that Europe's needs for replenishment were infinite; but I had my doubts. I knew German and Austrian habits. There was no such thing as a given consumptive amount for Europeans; their requirements were what they could pay for, and their ability to reduce them to a minimum was unbelievable. When I was still a boy and not permitted to read newspapers, my mother had told me of a strike in New York, where workers had only bread and butter for their meals. Bread and butter! We thought it a misprint. Butter was a luxury, and as long as people had bread, what could they complain about? But those were things the average American knew little about.

All this made me thoughtful. I was convinced that Europeans would not pay exorbitant prices to satisfy American speculators, and that there would be the devil to pay when this fact became known. In spite of protests from many quarters, I therefore closed shop, so to speak, and decided to go abroad.

CHAPTER 15

AUSTRIA IS DYING

J HAD NOT SEEN EUROPE since the beginning of the World War. I did not anticipate a pleasurable trip, and hence was not disappointed. Paris was still a bedlam of confusion. Tourists had to report to police headquarters for permits of many sorts. Foreign embassies and consulates were scattered all over the city; no one knew if, where and when they functioned. Waiting lines blocks long in front of them testified to their lack of efficiency.

I had in tow an American who wanted a passport for Riga. To determine what country Riga was in, now that Europe's map had been redrawn, was our first problem; after we found that it was in Latvia, we could not find the Latvian consulate. Taxi drivers were reaping a harvest carrying helpless victims from pillar to post, and porters of hotels were amassing fortunes by giving questionable information and procuring or promising tickets for the few trains and planes that were leaving Paris at irregular intervals.

It was lucky that I had learned a trick about besting crowds. When I got to Paris, I was well supplied with American cigarettes. Warnings were posted everywhere against importing more than a handful per person, which bothered me not. If I were caught, the Custom House officials would be glad to take the cigarettes as a peace offering. I was not caught, and each package was a sesame which opened locked doors and sweetened the most sour-looking official faces. At the Austrian consulate, where I had to get a visa for entry, I was given a number which, I was informed, would be called in about three days at the rate they were progressing. I did not have three days to waste. I sat in the waiting room until the consul opened the door to let someone out and then jumped at him with a joyful cry.

"Hello, Fred," I exclaimed, "think of finding you here!"

The consul looked at me in surprise; he could not place me, of course, but invited me in, probably to avoid a scene. Was he not Fred Kassler, I asked, who had gone to school with me many years ago? Decidedly not, he declared, his name was neither Fred nor Kassler. I apologized profusely and gave him a handful of cigarettes; a minute or so later I left with my visa. In a like manner my Riga companion and I got our papers stamped at all other consulates, procured tickets on a fast train to Vienna and left.

The German trains were unpainted, but clean, and ran on time. At the Austrian border, however, conditions changed abruptly. The carriages had no windows, the plush seats had been taken out and replaced by planks; customs officials, police and train crews were clad in dilapidated uniforms which might have looked funny had they not been pathetic. During the war, so the saying went, Germany had been optimistic and serious, Austria pessimistic and gay. Now Germany seemed poor but proud, Austria starving and devoid of hope. Beggars and invalided soldiers crowded the streets. Restaurants served poor food on bald tables. Vienna had become a dying city.

I had more friends in Austria than I knew. Following the Armistice I had sent food packages to my European relatives and friends by registered parcel post, but only a small percentage had ever reached their destination; the remainder was stolen on the way, sometimes by starving post office employees, more often by bands of discharged soldiers who boarded the trains and helped themselves to anything eatable. One spot in particular where the railroad was plundered with great regularity was on a steep grade about thirty miles west of Vienna. As the trains slowly worked their way upward, the robbers found it easy to board them. Curiously, many of these marauders sent me letters of thanks acknowledging their thefts. Whether they were prompted by gratitude or a sense of humor I do not know.

By the summer of 1919 conditions had become more stabilized, and the so-called Hoover packages were ready for distribution. These were made from food originally intended for American soldiers. One paid to American banks for any number of packages wanted, and the delivery was handled by Americans from European warehouses. I cleaned out my bank account and sent packages to Vienna more or less at random. I felt my chance had come to repay Vienna for her hospitality to a foreign boy who once had been given all the privileges of a citizen.

One day I received an invitation to visit the office of a factory whose owner I did not know. My visit was soon over, but my host begged me to remain until closing time and was so insistent that I hardly had any choice in the matter. At last the whistle blew, and in trooped a long row of men and women, the entire working force of the establishment. As they passed me, each one stopped and made a little speech; how my Hoover packages had saved his child, his wife, himself; how they had come in the nick of time to prevent suicide or death by starvation. The owner of the plant was the last of the speakers. It had been New Year's Day, he told me, and there had not been a bite in the house, when one of my packages was delivered. In it he had found bacon, flour, chocolate, beans. It had been a great event in his life.

My own family had not fared too badly. A considerable percentage of my shipments had reached them and, as I had made them the dispensers of many Hoover packages, they had been able to barter for them a comfortable amount of coal, wood and other materials of which they stood in need. My brother-in-law was on the board of the Vienna stamp exchange, which was taking on increasing importance in view of the impending inflation.

The population of Austria, although impoverished and emaciated, showed little bitterness toward Americans; nor, did it seem bitter toward any of the victorious Allies. The clothing one saw on people, regardless of class distinction, was worn out, patched, shabby. Whenever I invited friends to eat with me, they did away with amazing quantities of food. I felt ashamed every time I ate alone, and when I did, I ordered only what I saw others eating, which was next to nothing—a cup of coffee with dry bread, or the like.

Tales of misery abounded, although here and there a ray of humor would break through the clouds. One story, which was told me by a milliner who owned a fine downtown store, amused me because it was so typical of easy-going Vienna. The Viennese milliners, she told me, had resolved during the war never again to buy French *chapeaux;* "Austrian styles for Austrian women" was to be the future slogan. When the Armistice was declared, the high resolve was reaffirmed in open meeting; but when the first train left for Paris my milliner friend had a ticket, and when she took a look around, she saw that the entire millinery guild of Vienna was going along.

A Chicago committee for Austrian relief had entrusted to me for distribution a fund of fifteen hundred dollars. In the face of the calamities confronting me, it was ridiculously inadequate; moreover, I could not make up my mind which institution to support. To stretch the money as far as possible, I decided to turn it into a revolving fund and use it for individuals only. Thus I became treasurer for four Viennese groups which had been doing good work in their respective districts during the war, but had now completely run out of funds. I invited them to submit to me their worthiest cases, but only those where we had a sporting chance to get repayment. The money would have to be used over and over again.

At first this idea was not well understood. The social workers who, like all Austrians, had a childlike faith in everything and everybody coming from America, brought me their pitiable charges, each one so poor that I felt like giving him or her all the money I had. But my mind was made up; I hoped to accomplish more than mere stop-gap help. To people on a desolate island a three-day supply of food is not charity but cruelty; it would have to be no supply at all, or else a milch cow or some other permanent source of nourishment. I would build our work on this principle and steel my heart against everything else.

The first case I accepted was a former army officer who was lying in a suburban hospital. He had been shot in the back and was a hopeless paralytic. Nevertheless, he wanted to continue his study of law, convinced that his physical handicap would not prevent him from practicing; what he needed were books, and these I was requested to supply, with the understanding that their equivalent would be paid back when and if his earnings made it possible.

It was late in the evening when I arrived at the hospital, and I was immediately shown to the room where the young man was lying. A kerosene lamp spread only a small circle of light; all I could see was the thin, bearded face of a very sick patient and, close by, the head of a young girl who was reading aloud to him. Both looked up in surprise when I entered, and for a moment there was an embarrassed silence. I explained my mission as delicately as I could, but both occupants of the sick-chamber remained motionless, and neither of them uttered a sound. I felt uncomfortable. Finally I beckoned the young girl to the corridor. Rising slowly from her chair, she followed me as in a dream, and it was not until we stood in a corner of a hall smelling of disinfectants and the exhalation of human bodies that she spoke to me.

The officer was the son of a Vienna carpenter, she told me, and the doctors did not expect him to recover. To make matters worse, the hospital which had taken him in was one for transient patients only, and he had already occupied his room for eighteen months. There was no other place to send him, and the hospital officials, so the young girl hinted, were covertly hoping for his early death. Her own connection with the case was odd. Her father, a Polish count, had fallen in the war and she had resolved to do her bit by nursing another officer. She was alone in the world, made a scant living by knitting and darning, and spent all her spare time at that suburban hospital. Her protégé could be saved, she believed; he was dying, not of his injuries, but for lack of food and lack of hope. The hospital, she thought, was letting him die by inches.

I talked to some of the doctors, but they were unanimous in their opinion that only a miracle could save the young man. So far as food was concerned, the doctors themselves had not eaten a square meal in years.

I gave the volunteer nurse enough money to buy the officer nightshirts and plenty of food; then I made arrangements to send her regular contributions sufficient to take care of all reasonable wants. She thanked me and promised to send me monthly reports. Then we parted. When I stood outside the hospital again, I took a deep breath of the pure night air. I had absorbed a lot of misery in the past few hours.

For several months after my return to America, the promised

reports arrived regularly; they contained only routine matters, although as time went on I sensed something unusual between the lines. Then suddenly the news came out. From the moment I had entered that hospital room, a subtle change had come over the young officer. He became more cheerful, studied harder, took on weight. One morning there had been a wild cry from his cot. When the nurse rushed in, she found that he could move one leg. The entire hospital staff assembled and gazed at the miracle which had come to pass. Renewed efforts were made to help the healing process along, and soon muscular activity returned to the whole body. He could sit up and even move around without the help of others. Jubilant letters kept me informed of the latest developments; a few weeks of salt-water baths at an ocean resort would complete the cure. I sent the girl enough money to pay for this trip, but I sent too much, it seemed. Her next letter was the outpouring of a broken heart. When the young man heard of the sum at his disposal, he declared he would not take the salt baths, but instead give the money to his father, who was badly in need of it. The girl remonstrated, but to no avail. He had her thrown out of his room and even accused her of having mismanaged previous funds entrusted to her by me. The curse of gold had descended upon what once had been an idyll.

I never again heard from the patient, nor do I know what happened to him. His good angel wrote me a few melancholy epistles; they came at longer and longer intervals and then ceased altogether. Of the money advanced, none was returned.

We had better luck in other cases. Living in a poor quarter of the city was a former opera singer who had been shot through both lungs and had thereby lost his ability to provide for his wife and three girls, aged twenty-one, seventeen and thirteen. I walked into their apartment at noon one day to see what they were eating. They had four potatoes, all told, boiled in water, and a little salt. There was not another eatable thing in the house. The girl of seventeen, a stenographer, represented the earning power of the family. After deducting carfare, about five dollars was left of her month's salary. The older daughter had contracted tuberculosis and was dying in a local hospital.

I invited the family out to a café, which was a polite way of helping them to a real meal. They accepted avidly, but the results were piteous. None of them could hold their food down, and they had to live on soup and eggs for several weeks before their digestive organs returned to anything like normal.

I had rented an automobile for my exclusive use—at one dollar a day—and we visited the oldest daughter at her sickbed. She was a beautiful girl. Her dark eyes were the more lustrous as they glittered in constant fever. When I asked her what I could do for her, she smiled enigmatically.

"Don't be offended," she begged, "if I don't ask for eggs, wine and other delicacies usually given the sick. They would never reach me in the first place, and I would not care for them if they did. I am dying and I know it. All the doctors here are tubercular and need the nourishment more than I do. My doctor and I have a bet who is going to outlast the other. But if you really want to do something for me, buy me a volume of Shakespeare. I would like to read *Romeo and Juliet* and *Hamlet* before I die."

I bought her a set of Shakespeare. She wrote me a beautiful poem of thanks which I still have. A few months later she was dead.

The family needed clothing badly, especially the stenographer, who was wearing the only pair of shoes in the house. It was not difficult to take care of their wants, for an American dollar went a long way in those days. We visited the sick daughter at intervals, but once the stenographer asked me to take her to the famous Vienna Woods instead. Although born in the city, she had never seen them. When the rest of the family left us at the hospital, the mother took me aside and asked me to treat her daughter with consideration.

"We don't expect you to do all these things for us without payment of some sort," she said, "but my daughter is so young yet and so pure. She also has a touch of tuberculosis. Just listen to her little coughs. Treat her kindly—please!"

I assured the mother that her daughter was quite safe with me, but I don't think she believed me until I brought her back unharmed. That was Vienna after the war.

Eventually I had the young stenographer taken in as a patient in an exclusive Alpine tubercular asylum. It was there that this story found a fairy-tale ending. A rich banker from Budapest who was also a patient there promptly fell in love with my beautiful ward and almost as promptly married her. Both recovered from their affliction; they not only took care of the girl's family but paid back to our revolving fund many times what they had taken out. I hope they all lived happily ever after.

Our committees handled a great variety of cases, and by and by I was able to separate quickly the wheat from the chaff. Many of our applicants were repulsive to me, and on the whole I suppose I earned as many curses as blessings. Yet it gave one a lot of satisfaction to build new lives on the ruins of the old. There was a photographer, who had pawned parts of his apparatus to buy a few meals; we redeemed his articles and he re-established himself in business. We bought models for a hatmaker and rented a store for her. I particularly remember one aged couple whom we fitted out with trays and a little merchandise which they could sell from door to door. They provided their own livelihood after that, and whenever they could spare a few pennies, dutifully paid them back into the fund. I visited most of these people in their homes and must have climbed thousands of steps. The poor of Vienna all lived next to the roof, and the climbs to their doors were no pleasure trips.

As the weeks rolled by, the inflation grew, gathering speed on the way. Prices jumped almost hourly. Public institutions which depended on endowments folded up, as their income shrank in purchasing power. Tourists from countries with good money swarmed in like locusts and bought everything in sight. Priceless heirlooms of aristocratic families, kept hidden from the world for hundreds of years, found their way to stores and private brokers. The natives of Vienna disappeared from the streets and their beloved coffee houses, and their places were taken by loud-mouthed, ill-bred upstarts from the backwoods. Those whom the Viennese detested most were the people from the eastern countries, only recently ruthless enemies on the battlefield and now on a rampage against which there was no defense. The foreigners not only bought the Viennese treasures, they also bought the Viennese women, and this the natives could not forgive. In the night clubs one could hear more eastern tongues spoken than German, and cultured Austrians would turn away in fury rather than see some "Roumanian swineherd" put his arm around a starving Viennese beauty.

It was said that every second woman in the Austrian capital was for sale that year. This may or may not have been literally true; from my own observation I am inclined to admit reluctantly that feminine virtue seldom, if ever, has been put up for auction at such low prices.

Underneath all this superficial corruption, however, the old sterling Austrian character still lived on.

A friend of our family named Leo, and his wife had joined us in Vienna, and we determined to move away from the city into the Alps. We rented rooms in a modest but comfortable small hotel, and our vacation would have been enjoyable, had Leo not shown signs of mental distress. A hard-pressed government had put him, at the age of fifty-four, into military uniform and trained him as a soldier. Our friend was small of stature and not very strong, and the camp experience had affected his mind. I first noticed it during a game of chess; he made some foolish moves, although I knew him to be a good player. I then began to watch him more closely; there was no doubt that he was becoming insane. A council was called, and we decided to lodge him in a private Viennese asylum. Leo's brother was a physician and concurred in our decision. So as not to arouse the patient's suspicion, we all were to take an afternoon train home.

Our plan did not quite work out that way. With the cunning of the mentally afflicted, Leo saw through our scheme and could not be induced to board the train; hence his wife and I stayed behind and took him in charge. We were not to let him out of our sight for a minute; but we had underestimated Leo's powers of dissimulation. During supper, which we took at a restaurant, he was gay and apparently quite normal. He then excused himself for a moment to go to the washroom. I planted myself in front of the door and waited. Minute after minute passed, but Leo did not reappear. Finally I had the door opened by force. The washroom was empty. The deranged man had jumped through a second-story window to the street below, a distance of at least fifteen feet.

While his disheartened wife roamed the few streets of the town on the off-chance of picking him up, I hurried to the depot. No train had left for several hours. I gave an exact description of our patient to all the railroad officials, from the *Stations-Chef* to the ticket agents and platform guards, waited until the last train to Vienna had pulled out at midnight, and then went back to the hotel.

Early morning saw me at the headquarters of the local *gendarmerie*, which had to police a large tract of this mountainous district. The captain received me with the greatest consideration, but held out little hope. It was his guess that Leo had climbed into the mountains, become panicky and jumped or fallen into some abyss. Insane people, according to his experience, often acted that way, and his records were full of similar cases. Half his police force was ordered out on a search, and the captain spent an hour telephoning to neighboring towns for volunteer rescue squads. The response was wonderful. One of the local constabulary, although off duty, offered his services and also his privately owned and specially trained dogs, and walked eight miles to bring them into play. Mountaineers all over the territory were notified by telegraph, telephone, heliograph and messengers to be on the lookout. All I could do for the moment to spur the search was to offer a reward of about one hundred dollars which, in the diluted currency of the country, looked fantastically large on the posters we had ordered printed.

As I was no mountain climber and therefore of no use in the field, I decided to do a little detective work. Perhaps Leo had boarded a freight train during the night after all and had been seen by some of the trainmen. I would soon find out.

The night crew was now probably asleep. Nevertheless, I took their addresses, got myself a guide, and started on my mission. The men lived in widely scattered little huts, far away from passable roads, so that it took us many hours to cover the ground. I had to awaken each railroader in turn and question him. Never have I been treated with greater courtesy, never did men try so hard to aid a stranger who had broken their much needed rest. I offered them compensation for the trouble I was causing, but at the slightest hint they stiffened and proudly refused; they were only doing their duty. I protested that they were not in service during their free hours, but they insisted that they were; my questioning made them so. All the huts I visited gave mute testimony to the extreme

304

poverty of the owners, but only in one case did I succeed in leaving a little money behind. After one of the men had retired again, his old mother, who had listened to our conversation, snuggled up to me and, with tears in her eyes, said she would accept something for her son, but he must never know. They were so terribly poor.

My calls drew blanks everywhere. Upon my return to the *gendarmerie* I found that their search had been equally unsuccessful. The telegraph instrument was still clicking incessantly, as one after another of the rescue parties signed off for the day. At home Leo's wife was close to losing her own mind.

The next forenoon brought us to the end of our trail. Leo called us long distance from Vienna, telling us gleefully how he had eluded all our traps. He was then on his way to the asylum, which he himself thought was the best place for him. I may add here that his mental disorders were cured in time, although he never became quite well again.

I notified the *gendarmerie* of the latest developments and suggested that the captain distribute my reward among all the men in his force. He declined so sternly that I substituted the volunteer searchers instead. The captain's refusal was just as prompt and emphatic. I came down to a box of cigars, only to be met with the smiling threat that even this would be considered attempted bribery. In desperation I donated the reward money to the poor of the district, which was the only way in which I could get rid of it without conflicting either with the law or with the ethics of these stalwart mountain folk.

My visits to Austria continued at intervals almost to the day of Hitler's invasion. My favorite spot was the town of Baden, the place where as a student I had met with such a kindly reception. Perhaps it was a case of returning to one's first love, for Baden certainly was a city with which one could easily fall in love. Prettily strung along the Alpine foothills in the valley of the Schwechat river, it is surrounded by vineyards that cover every available mountainside on which the sun shines. Little dells reach out like so many fingers into the mountain vastnesses. The roads are spaced by ancient Roman milestones; between them are scattered homemade tablets which record the tragedies of long-forgotten people who met with misadventure on the public highways. On one you may read in faded letters that Johann Nuttelhauser lost his life here in 1642 by falling under the hooves of his horses. The story ends with a sermon: "Wanderer, whoever you may be, pray for his soul, and may the Lord forgive him."

I saw nothing about forgiving the horses. Around the bend of the road, under a crude crucifix, Franz Huber had been stabbed to death a hundred years ago in a drunken brawl; at least this was indicated by the primitive painting of the rural artist. Tablets, chapels and taverns alternate. Signs that have stood for ages advise the traveler to eat *Krautstrudel* at the inn of the Jammer-Pepi (the whining Josephine) or taste delicious trout at the house of Schiel-Hansl (Cockeyed John).

On top of steep hills the ruins of old castles stand like sentinels. They have long since been off duty. Along their crumbling walls lizards glide gracefully, enjoying the sunlight. As you sit there, friendly ghosts play around you. When the Turks came through here centuries ago, these fortresses gave shelter to the local populace, who lived here in security while the Ottomans devastated the countryside.

In one of the woods I was shown a cave where an Archduke of Austria had once taken refuge from his pursuing enemies. Tradition has it that he was saved by a spider that wove its net across the entrance. It was a cozy cave in which to sit and chat. The little light that entered shone on some hanging rocks which formed a precarious roof over this old refuge. A game warden in uniform marched by and was hailed in to keep us company. When I expressed some anxiety about the unstableness of our den, I only aroused amusement. The roof had hung in its perilous balance for many generations and would probably hang so for many more to come.

Next morning I was awakened early. It was the game warden who had called to see me. He was dignified and deferential, but I noticed that he was pale. During the night the cave had collapsed, and the stone bench on which we had sat had been buried under tons of debris. Perhaps it was our laughter that had disturbed a finely adjusted equilibrium.

Baden and history are inextricably interwoven, and of the two, Baden is undoubtedly the older. Prehistoric animals of eras long gone by used to come here, attracted by the thermal springs and the luxurious vegetation which surrounded them. Prehistoric men followed, and their primitive earthworks are still plainly discernible in less frequented spots. Eons later the Celts came, but their traces were obliterated by the Romans who conquered them. The Romans quickly recognized the curative powers of the hot springs and called them *Aquae* (baths) of which *Baden* is a literal translation. The bathhouses, erected before the days of Christianity, still stand in their ancient beauty. It is odd to read that "the officers of the Eleventh Legion thank the gods and these springs for relief from their rheumatism." I had never associated officers of Roman legions with rheumatic knees.

The road from Rome to Vindobona, the Vienna of today, led through Baden and is still being used. I was told that it requires fewer repairs than the modern road which roughly parallels it.

Where Caesar's legionnaires once marched, a local historian had dug for relics and been rewarded by an unexpected find of Roman silver coins. Inspired by his discovery, hordes of youngsters were constantly digging along the highway; they found no more silver, but they did unearth a large stone table which had been left there by an army outpost of Charlemagne.

Baden's local historian was a man named Calliano, who had sprung from old Italian nobility. In his private life he was the theatrical critic of a newspaper and a poor man even according to Austrian standards; but his home was full of historical treasures worth a fortune. He had started to write a six-volume history of Baden, which was not an easy task, and was made more difficult by his lack of means and the indifference of a population which preferred to discuss race-horses, homemade wines and the town's theater.

When I became acquainted with the mayor of Baden, he asked on one occasion if he could grant me a favor. I told him that what I wanted most was financial assistance for Calliano. The mayor was as good as his word, and not only undertook to finance Calliano's historical work, but also made him an honorary citizen of Baden. It was an event not easily forgotten. The festival chamber of the City Hall, which had remained closed for no one knew how long, was dusted for the occasion. The pictures of town-fathers, dead for hundreds of years, were draped with flags and flowers, and the floor was covered with carpets which probably had been captured from the Turks. Every seat was occupied by an awe-filled crowd. Then bugles blew, and six heralds marched in, clad in medieval uniforms and rendering the national anthem with precision and enthusiasm. They were followed by soldiers in armor, with spears in their hands. They looked hot but proud and appeared scared by the noise they made every time they moved. Finally forty aldermen, led by the mayor, marched in, all in full dress and with flowers in their buttonholes. They occupied chairs on a platform on which one seat remained vacant.

When the music had finished, the mayor gave a signal, and Mr. Calliano was ushered in by two pages. The poor man looked decidedly uncomfortable and sat down gingerly on the chair reserved for him. The mayor then rose and delivered a little speech, after which he pinned a medal on Calliano, making him an honorary citizen of Baden for the rest of his life.

According to an old custom the meeting then adjourned to a nearby *Weinstube,* where the mayor and the aldermen tried to drink me under the table. After a few hours of steady drinking I still held my own. No one had ever drunk down the mayor, but every one else gradually passed into oblivion. The respect shown to me in Baden after this display of prowess could not have been greater if I had saved the town from an invasion.

The mayor's name was Joseph Kollmann, and I think of him with a good deal of admiration. He was a short, stout man of about fifty, with a large mustache, a deep voice and urbane manners. He could call nearly every one of his twenty-two thousand co-citizens by name and was re-elected time and again. Even those who fought him politically were personally fond of him. After the military collapse of 1918 he had led expeditions to nearby Hungary to barter for food, and in the absence of all federal authority had organized a troop of vigilantes to protect life and property against threatening communistic uprisings. The grateful *Badeners* never forgot his services and worshipped at his feet. In turn, he did everything possible to put Baden on the map as a leading international resort. He financed a *Strandbad,* a sort of synthetic seashore, in competition with the Adriatic coast resorts which had passed into Italian hands; he gave

Baden a *casino* à la Monte Carlo; and he kept the theater going in spite of its perennial deficit.

My main interest was with the local theater, of course, with which I had an old account to settle. I had the manager distribute a few dozen tickets every day to deserving people, and at times I bought out whole performances for poor children. Even giving things away can be difficult at times, as we discovered. The superintendent of an orphan home, to whom some fifty tickets had been allotted for a certain night, returned them with the intimation that he preferred the money instead. His wards, he said, needed caps and shoes more than they did stage shows or the candies we used to distribute to the children in the audience. I argued that the little orphans would probably remember the performance long after they had forgotten caps and shoes, but he remained adamant. Somehow the boys must have heard of what was in the wind, because when I left, they crowded around me with tears on their wan little faces, begging me not to give in. I stood pat, and when the curtain rose, the entire orphanage was there and roared with delight. Even the stern-faced superintendent enjoyed the evening; probably he himself needed the relaxation more than he had realized.

The personnel of the theater—actors, singers, musicians and stagehands—were simple folk, much underpaid and living for what little applause came their way. Sometimes I took them to supper after the play, and it did one good to watch their appetites. The leftovers were carefully wrapped up in paper, to be eaten on following days in cheerless homes. Unfortunately, the intimacy brought about by these nightly gatherings had one drawback. The actors became more and more enthusiastic, and finally declared that they were playing for me only. Whenever a particularly good line was in the offing, they would look at me, and if I did not laugh heartily enough, tears were shed behind the scenes. Many sentences were improvised as flattering references to Americans in general or to me in particular. This was not at all to my liking, but I could not stop it. Moreover, it put me under a moral obligation to be present at every performance; when I was absent, so the director complained, the show went dead. In addition I was urged to watch the morning rehearsals, and as a consequence I almost lived in the theater and was considered part and parcel of it. I was even initiated into the secret song by which members of Austrian choruses know each other and which is kept as sacred as a Mason's password. It is a mournful song, full of obscenities, but I thought it quite beautiful, nonetheless.

The management of the theater tried to abide by my wishes in the choice of plays, and I took advantage of this opportunity by requesting old and half-forgotten operettas. Thus I heard Offenbach's *La Belle Hélène, Orpheus,* and *The Grand Duchess of Geroldstein;* Suppé's *Fatinitza;* Milloecker's *Obersteiger* and Strauss' *Waldmeister*—all gems of tunefulness, untarnished by time. The only trouble I ran into was when I suggested an operetta of German origin, called *Das Schwarzwaldmaedel (The Black Forest Girl),* a production which I had seen performed at the German theater in Chicago, then playing at the Busch Temple. Austrians did not look with favor upon German compositions, which they considered intrusions into their special field. It so happened that I was not satisfied with the rehearsals, and on a dare staged the performance myself. It meant several hectic days and sleepless nights, and after everything had gone off well I found myself filled with new respect for the work of a stage manager.

Amidst all their poverty the Austrians never forgot their politics. Each party was opposed to all others with undying hatred. The Socialists controlled Vienna and the industrial centers. The Clericals exerted their influence among the farmers. The Pan-Germans wanted *Anschluss* to Germany above everything else. Besides there was a Peasant party and a party of Monarchists, both of whom wanted the Habsburgs to return and bring the good old days with them. Baden was a staunch Monarchist stronghold. The town had been headquarters for the Austrian high command during the war and still stood by the old order of things. In Vienna they had even changed the names of streets; those perpetuating the memory of former emperors had given way to Twelfth of November Avenue and the like; but Baden still boasted of a Prinz Karl Square and a Kaiser Promenade. Baden was too historical-minded to be swayed by temporary changes, which was as it should have been in a town where every second building bore an historical inscription. In this old house Grillparzer had dreamt his *King Ottokar,* and there Brahms had composed his *Fourth Symphony.* In the hotel where

I lived, and which in medieval days had been a fort surrounded by wall and moat, Beethoven once had occupied some rooms, and tradition had it that he was so dirty, the maids had frequently refused to make up his apartment.

Mayor Kollmann and I often discussed the political situation. He belonged to what was known as the Christian-Socialist party, a name which had lost all its original meaning. He deplored with me the energy wasted in the constant fights between opposing groups of one little nation, all half-starved. There was nothing to be done, he thought. Children were born with party labels on them and became fanatics before they entered the grade schools. Even on peaceful occasions one could pick out Pan-Germans by the cornflowers, or Socialists by the red carnations in their coat lapels. None of the parties had a majority, and each delighted in killing projects proposed by its opponents, no matter how vital to the country at large. Kollmann wielded considerable personal influence, and I suggested to him that he propose a political armistice for five years to pull Austria out of the mire. He smiled indulgently and rather sadly.

"You have lived in America too long," he remarked. "Opponents over here do not congratulate each other after the election, as they do over there; they are more likely to shoot each other. I heard of an American saying that people will not cut off their noses to spite their faces. But here they do and probably always will."

The time was to come when I had to abandon Baden as my headquarters. I was becoming too notorious. Weeks before my arrival the newspapers would announce my coming. Mayor Kollmann made an official welcome call at our hotel, drawing up in an ancient carriage de luxe, with the city's coat-of-arms painted on both sides. He was followed by several city officials in full dress who left cards and flowers. Hundreds of letters were written to me, and the hotel had to throw a cordon of bellboys around me for protection. The theater greeted me with a gala performance, on which occasion our usual seats were draped with a carpet of roses. It was notoriety both unwonted and unwanted.

Most of the people who wrote me wanted a donation; others wished me to become a partner in their business or expected me to

311

buy anything they had, villas, stamp collections, anything. Actors asked me to give them jobs, singers wanted their voices trained, sick people begged for hospitalization. Six mothers offered me their daughters as mistresses.

In defense I threatened to publish this correspondence in the local papers, but that did not help. One woman tried the old badger game on me, and another threatened to shoot herself if I would not elope with her. Only those can understand the embarrassment of undesired publicity who have had to brave its glaring limelight. Baden had been a nice place for an unknown student to live in; now that I had returned with money to spend, the city had become unbearable. On my later visits to Austria I stayed in an obscure Vienna hotel, but never again did I find complete privacy.

The old Austria was breaking up; on each successive visit the signs of impending dissolution became more apparent. A new army had been created, but the singing, love-making soldiers of the old monarchy were no more. These new soldiers were grim, tight-lipped young men who worked hard at their profession and did not mingle with the civil population. On the boundary lines the Austrian, Czecho-Slovakian and Hungarian custom houses had been moved half a mile apart, perhaps to prevent a revival of the old camaraderie. The Vienna police were hand-picked country boys, supposedly loyal to the government and anti-Nazi; but they did not fit their positions. They knew nothing about the city, and it was difficult to understand their mountain dialects. I ran afoul of the police one time by taking some people for a ride in my car. They had begged for it, and when I unloaded them after a few minutes, a hundred more people had accumulated who wanted to ride in an automobile with an American license. When I disposed of my load the second time, the crowd must have grown to a thousand—men, women, and children. It was then that the police arrested me. I was taken to headquarters, and the only question put to me was: In whose service was I making propaganda?

The carefree, happy Vienna of the Habsburgs was gone, even before the tramp of Hitler's soldiers echoed through her ancient streets.

posing of the oils, but it was a heart-rending task. Clark, Roberts and Company had, for instance, paid an average price of twenty-four and one-half cents for their peanut oil. The first bid we succeeded in eliciting was fifteen and one-half cents; the next was nine. We took everything that looked like ready cash, but the losses were tremendous. We wound up with two tank cars of sardine oil in a storage tank at Seattle; they had cost one dollar and five cents a gallon out there and we could not sell them at any price. In the end, the bank offered them to me as a present for my assistance. I refused politely. The oil was not worth its freight to Chicago. Eventually I accepted it at minus five cents a gallon, so that its net cost in Chicago was two cents. At that, it was a year before anyone even asked me what I would take for it.

Other outgrowths of the commodity cataclysm kept coming to light. That group of speculators who had bought a thousand barrels of linseed oil and had stored it for safekeeping found themselves in an embarrassing position. Storage and insurance charges were beginning to be a serious factor, now that the speculative fever had worn off. Finally I received their appeal for help. I was not very sanguine but consented to examine the stock. A painful sight met me at the warehouse. Most of the barrels had sprung leaks, and some were total wrecks. The floor of the basement where the goods had been piled up was covered with several inches of oil, mixed with sawdust, dead rats and various debris. To merchandise this conglomeration was impossible, and I so reported to the owners. They were hard losers. Every broker in town was asked in turn to take a hand in disposing of what once had been a thousand barrels of linseed oil, but without success. In their extremity the unfortunate speculators came back to me. I sent a tank wagon, a pump and a portable filter press to the warehouse and, from a wooden platform I had ordered built, took command of the situation. The sawdust clogged up our filter press and the rats plugged up the pump; the remainder of the flotsam impeded our work impishly. Nevertheless, by sheer perseverance and stubbornness we succeeded in getting out most of the oil. It is not a task I should care to have thrown into my path again.

The only speculator I knew who came out of the great debacle with a whole skin was the broker Parker. He had accumulated seventy-five thousand dollars in a year's time, and this had gone to his head. He had to be taken to a sanatorium and was still there when the bubble burst. Shortly afterward he was released as cured and took possession of his fortune. He was forever after pointed out as the one smart gambler who had known when to quit.

The great commodity crash ushered in the end of my career as a chemist. I had been merchandising small amounts of oils before, but only in special cases. The fall of Clark, Roberts and Company brought about a change in the retail oil distribution in the Chicago area. They had handled most of this business and had gradually replaced older firms such as Hoffner & Meighs, who had been the only ones in the field prior to the war. Now Hoffner & Meighs were tottering, too. Others who had striven for a share of this business were bankrupt. Chicago was without a retail market for oils required by the paint and varnish trade. Every lot needed had to be ordered from New York, Boston, or San Francisco, which meant delays and annoyances. Rush orders could not be filled at all. It was an intolerable situation.

One day three Chicago paint manufacturers walked into my office. If I would care to retail vegetable oils, they said, they would give me enough orders to keep me going. Someone had to fill the gap which had been left by the failure of the old firms. I was well known as a chemist and had visited practically all paint and varnish plants in the Chicago district at one time or another. It would be nice to buy oils from a man who knew what was inside the barrels; it should be easier to turn a chemist into a merchant than vice versa. That was the way they argued. To make their speeches more effective, each of them drew from his pocket a signed order for a sizable quantity of an oil he needed; the order was made out to my firm and the price column was blank.

I asked for a day or two for meditation, but my mind was already made up. There was nothing in chemistry to induce me to continue with it. With the conclusion of the war, our old-time pillars of society, the non-creative professions, had again pushed chemists into the back seats; chemists once more were the servants of mankind.

I had now been given a taste of business life. From my earliest days people had dinned into my ears that no chemist could be a good

316

businessman. When I asked "Why not?" this platitude withered away, as most platitudes do when put into a crucible. Business, I had discovered, was nothing but applied common sense, no more difficult than the art of salesmanship, which had not proved so terrifying when attacked without fear or prejudice.

I had found the short chapter of my life as a businessman exciting and amusing. Reporters had interviewed me, the speculator, the parasite. No one had ever interviewed me, the chemist. I had met men in high positions and exchanged ideas with them. I had made more money than ever before. For the first time in my career I had been treated as an equal. The former servant had been acclaimed a gentleman.

What had I done? Bought and sold commodities for myself and others for the sole purpose of profit. I had returned nothing of value to the pot, as Mac would have said. My economic importance was on a par with that of a crapshooter; but evidently a crapshooter could become a man of prominence if his dice were large enough to attract attention. When, as a chemist, I had given to science a new method of analysis, to technology new processes either cheaper or better than those in practice heretofore, I had, voluntarily or otherwise, contributed a few grains of sand to that ever-growing structure called human progress. The reward had been comparative poverty and obscurity.

Yet, much as I had learned to appreciate money and its power, it was not the lure of a larger income alone that was swaying me. I wanted to get out of a profession whose members were considered second-class citizens; few people looked at chemists as anything else. Apparently the world had nothing but mild contempt for anyone who created for it things of beauty, usefulness, health. Creators were people to be looked down upon. Farmers who grew wheat were hayseeds; the brokers who sold the wheat, snatching at little profits without producing anything, were considered men of importance. Inventors were long-haired nitwits; but those who promoted their inventions were moving in the best circles. People raved about movie actors, yet not one in a thousand remembered the author of the play. It did not pay to be on the creative side of things, financially, socially or otherwise. Salesmen, bridge-players, jockeys, dancing masters, fine citizens all, no doubt, but contributing nothing constructive to the community at large, were feted in public; but no one knew or cared who had discovered aspirin, synthetic plastics or concrete. In a few years a man would make a daring flight across the Atlantic and become world-famous; no one would ever talk of the men who had built his plane. For two decades I had watched the procession go by. Nothing had changed; nothing was likely to change. The world still asked, like that insurance man in Pittsburgh, what a chemist ever did that entitled him to more than twenty-five dollars a week. Tens of thousands of chemists produced better lights, better medicines, better perfumes, better crops, better everything, but they remained the "who-on-earth-are-they?" men with the small pay checks. Yes, chemistry was a good profession to get out of.

Nevertheless, my heart was heavy. I had been active in chemistry for twenty years. Never had I met nicer, cleaner, more generous-minded people than among chemists. Like the Rhinedaughters in Wagner's operas, they lived in the depths, far removed from the world's meanness, and had retained much of the decency and love for truth with which most men are born. I would become a businessman from necessity; my choice might have been different, had chemists been regarded with more respect, and had the financial returns been anywhere near adequate.

A few days later I announced my decision. From now on chemistry would be an avocation to me; by vocation I would be a distributor of raw materials. I said goodbye to several of my old clients and to my laboratory. My days as a chemist were over.

CHAPTER 17

PROFITS—WHAT TO DO WITH THEM

$\mathcal{T}$HERE WE WERE, Gertie and I, launched on a real business enterprise, and as helpless as babes in the woods. To conduct a business as an adjunct to a consulting laboratory was one thing; to go out and compete with the business world was something else again. Between the two of us we literally did not know the difference between a sight draft and a credit memorandum; for years to come we would have our bills of lading printed blue and our invoices pink so that we could tell them apart. It was a decade before we learned to send out monthly statements. When we received notes in payment, we discounted them, whether or not we needed a cash balance, because one of our customers had told us to do so. We did not stop this practice until a kind-hearted bank cashier laughed us out of it.

Neither Gertie nor I cared a great deal for money; we used to draw whatever the traffic could bear or our judgment dictated. Gertie had my full power of attorney and I had hers. We shared one safety deposit box, and only changed this loose system when the Income Tax Department went after us once, because some of the coupons from our bonds had become mixed up in our tax returns.

One of Gertie's great worries came when we had to hire additional office help. Again and again she put off the sad moment by working overtime and Sundays. In the end she had to give up; but I felt that with each new girl who joined us Gertie saw another part of her beloved past crumble away. She lived to see the office force grow to a dozen workers or so, but it seemed she was never again as happy as when she had been alone. She became a very well-to-do woman, with a beautiful home of her own, a country estate and two cars. She could come and go as she pleased, and everyone revered her; but I was willing to lay odds that she would gladly have exchanged her stocks, bonds and real estate for that peaceful little underground office near the White Sox ball park, with its rough floor and coal stove, where she had not only been queen but also cook, dishwasher, stenographer and private secretary all in one.

My worries were of a different kind, and I was seldom free from them. I was now over forty years old and had made for myself a new bed into which I fitted about as well as one of Procrustes' guests. The businessmen I met talked a language I did not understand— turnover of capital, labor troubles, sales resistance, golf scores. What capital turnover meant I did not know; I never had experienced labor troubles, always had had plenty of customers and had never held a golfstick in my hand. I thought clubs existed for men of leisure, card players, sport enthusiasts. They certainly did not exist for me. As to sales promotion, I wanted none of it. I believed that advertising, unless it served to acquaint the public with a new product, was a sign of weakness. Nor would I ever have salesmen on our payroll. The chemical laboratory with its manufacturing annex had done well on the principle that professional people neither advertise nor solicit business; would it fail me now? I was going to wait and see.

I do not know how much faith to put in the common superstition about beginner's luck, but we undoubtedly had a liberal quota. The sudden demise of the oil dealers who had heretofore served the middle-western market had left some unfinished business dangling in midair, and the brokers for these defunct concerns asked me to wind up their half-finished contracts. I trembled when I saw the sums involved in these transactions which I only partly understood, but it was now sink or swim, and I could not afford to sink. The profits were in proportion to the size of the sales and the risks that had to be taken; but the brokers knew their ground, and my guardian angel was on the job. Our business received quite an impetus, and people actually believed that I was what they called a shrewd operator.

The distributing business which I had inherited seemed an easy way to make a living. I was to learn later that it was not so easy when competitors were in the field. For the time being, though, it was all sunshine. Then Lady Luck once more played my cards for me.

Around Christmas time our two children were taken sick, and after they had recovered somewhat, our family physician, Dr. Oppen, advised us to take them to California for the remainder of the winter. Dr. Oppen was a Hungarian from a town near the Serbian-Roumanian border where the populace spoke four languages. As a boy he picked them all up, of course; Latin, French and Greek he learned in school; his German he acquired in a clinic in Vienna, and his English in Chicago. Dr. Oppen was an excellent physician, but he seldom charged for his services and when he did, almost never collected. As a consequence he was always low in funds, but this did not detract from his ever-present good humor. He had come to America with cheeks like apples, and he looked the picture of health and happiness to his last day.

Dr. Oppen's wife did not and could not take money matters so lightly and, in the belief that as a consulting chemist I knew everything, begged me to imbue her husband with the necessity of turning his services into less humanity and more dollars. So it came about that one afternoon I sat in his study, clad in white, watching patients come and go and listening to the proceedings. The very first visitor gave me an idea why Dr. Oppen's practice was so barren of monetary results. An elderly woman was ushered in; she looked haggard and ill at ease.

"Doctor," she said in a language I could follow, although not identify, "I have pains in my head and I cannot sleep."

"Well, well," said Dr. Oppen, "let's see what is the matter with you."

He gave her a thorough examination in a little side-room, and emerged from it laughing.

"There's nothing wrong with you," he told the patient. "Go home and take a bromide, and don't bother me any more. No charge."

The old lady walked out, shaking her head. It was plain that what she had wanted more than anything else was sympathy and fuss, with a fairly expensive prescription to top off what she had probably envisioned as an adventure in her drab life. I have no doubt that she went straight to another physician to get what Dr. Oppen had withheld from her.

The result of the afternoon was twenty-two callers and fifteen dollars. Dr. Oppen thought it a successful day.

My consulting service in the medical field soon came to an end. Dr. Oppen had asked me to accompany him on one of his rounds, and after a few uninteresting calls we found ourselves in the bedroom of a young woman who complained of sharp pains in her abdomen. Dr. Oppen could find no symptoms of appendicitis and, in his usual gay manner, shrugged off her pains as unimportant and asked if there were any cookies or candies around. He always asked that, wherever he called, sometimes even before examining his patient. Just then the telephone rang; Dr. Oppen was urgently wanted in a nearby hospital. He told me to stay in the sickroom, hold the woman's hand and, if she seemed restless, give her water with a little sugar in it. Then he departed, leaving me in an uneasy frame of mind; but he would be back in no more than twenty minutes, and not much was likely to happen in so short a time. That is what we thought, but we were wrong. My patient suddenly let out a pain-filled scream, threw herself around, and yelled for help. I stood at her bedside, frozen into immobility. The woman was inarticulate, and I could only guess at what was happening. I threw back the covers and saw that my worst forebodings were true. A fountain of blood was streaming over the bed. I had come just in time to witness a miscarriage.

I unfroze myself by sheer force of will power. Rushing into the bathroom, I scooped up all the towels I could find and, remembering what I could of first aid, tried to stop the flow of blood, much as I once had stopped the flow of naphtha from a broken pipe line in my South Chicago days. When the towels were exhausted, I raised the woman's legs, put ice on her abdomen, covered her up and waited. I could think of nothing else to do.

Never had twenty minutes seemed so long as those spent in that little bedroom on the North Side. If I had erred in my treatment, both Dr. Oppen and I would be sharing a police cell before nightfall. At last I heard the welcome sound of screeching brakes, and Dr. Oppen reappeared. He took the situation in at a glance.

"Clumsy lummox," he mumbled to me, and then his happy laughter sounded as unperturbed as ever. Humming a song and telling stories in between, he did a workmanlike job of rebandaging our patient. Then we left.

"Pretty good work for a chemist," he said to me, when we were seated in his car. "Terribly amateurish, but just the same you saved the woman and most likely our two necks in the bargain."

In spite of his apparent nonchalance, I would have followed Dr. Oppen's advice blindly in all medical matters. Hence, when he told Bertha and me to take the children to California, we did so. Sunny California, sunny Dr. Oppen. The children would get well.

I felt that I needed a real vacation, and left orders with Gertie not to disturb me with business news. Every contingency we could foresee had been anticipated. Spring would bring increased orders, and we had provided for them. Among other things, we had purchased about one thousand barrels of China wood oil, which was one of our staple articles, but I had found no time to sell any part of it. We had bought it in advance, because experience had taught us that prices were usually lowest at the end of the year. The average price we had paid was around eleven cents a pound, which was normal. Nothing on the horizon foreshadowed any important market movement either way.

We had never been in California, and enjoyed our holiday to the utmost. Week after week passed, and I hardly remembered that I had a business back home. Then my complacency was rudely shaken. A business friend of mine, also sojourning in Los Angeles, met me and we exchanged greetings.

"What do you think of these crazy wood oil prices?" he asked me.

I felt my knees turn watery. What could have happened? We were sitting on a thousand barrels of wood oil, and each cent decline meant a loss of four thousand dollars. Had the bottom dropped out of the market?

"What's the latest you have heard?" I managed to stammer with a show of unconcern.

"The last I knew when I left Chicago, wood oil was selling at twenty-four cents," he replied.

Twenty-four cents! Was I hearing aright? Could it be that, unbeknown to me, our family tree traced its roots back to Midas?

My first impulse was to rush to the telephone and sell all we had; but Gertie was in charge and on the field, while I was out of touch with conditions. I suppressed the impulse to call, deciding that a good auto trip next morning was of more importance to me than all the markets in the world.

A few more weeks passed, and then I started on the home trek. Gertie and her husband Bill were at the station to meet me, and naturally my first question turned on wood oil.

"I bought fifty barrels this morning at thirty-eight cents," Gertie told me.

"You *bought* wood oil at thirty-eight cents?" I blurted out.

"Yes," she smiled, "and resold it two hours later at forty-two."

I could only gasp.

"How about the thousand barrels we bought at eleven cents?" I shot at her.

"Oh, they are still intact," was her cheerful reply. "You told me not to touch them until you came back. Remember?"

It was almost too good to be true. While I was imbibing California sunshine, trouble had broken out on the Yangtze river, and all shipments of wood oil had been held up. Stocks in the United States were low because, according to a time-honored rule of American business, January first statements must show large cash assets and low merchandise inventories.

My desk was covered with a foot-deep layer of telegrams. Wood oil, wood oil, wood oil—everyone wanted wood oil. Price was no object. It looked as if we had the only unsold stocks of wood oil in the whole country.

Wood oil is not a commodity quoted in daily papers, and I naturally was curious to know what prices prevailed in other centers of distribution. I called up one of our eastern importers and asked him what the wood oil market was in New York. He put his answer into one sentence.

"*You* are the wood oil market," he growled, almost vindictively.

So we were the wood oil market. Our little office in Chicago had assumed a new role in the whirligig of commerce. We held in our hands the power to dictate to an entire section of American business. Our word was law. It was an intoxicating feeling.

Gertie and I decided to peg the price at forty-two cents. People

324

were willing to pay forty-five, even fifty cents, for more than we were willing to let them have, but we stood firm. Forty-two cents was enough for us; that was the price to all comers, and no hoarding.

For a few weeks the dizzy spin of the wheel went on. The constant stream of messenger boys bringing wires and the incessant ringing of the telephone gave us the appearance of a miniature stock exchange. The strain was sometimes relieved by little adventures in human emotions. Once an out-of-town customer walked in, a picture of dejection. He was practically ruined, he moaned, by these high prices in wood oil. One of his competitors was lucky enough to have a stock of wood oil that had cost him fourteen cents, and with this cheap raw material was running our friend out of business. I asked him how much wood oil he needed.

"Ten barrels," he said lugubriously.

"You have just bought ten barrels at twelve cents," I told him. He stared at me.

"I thought you said the market was forty-two cents," he said.

"So it is," I assured him. "It just happened to drop back to twelve cents for a few minutes."

After he had left, Gertie shook her head.

"You know," she confided to me, "if we had a board of directors in our company, they would fire you about once a week. But," she added happily, "I am glad we have no board of directors."

After a while Gertie and I both tired of our little game; even making money can grow tiresome, strange as that may sound. We therefore made up our minds to get rid of our dictatorship by the simple expedient of breaking the market. The next buyer got his oil at thirty-eight cents, the one after him at thirty-six. Before the week was over we had the price down to twenty-four cents, and the last lot went at fourteen. A few days later the Yangtze river valley was opened up for traffic again, and the market steadied at the old price level of eleven cents. People in the trade said that I was one of the keenest speculators of the age. Gertie and I just grinned at each other. We were the only ones who knew.

The money we had made was put into a reserve fund. We figured that markets which could go up could also go down, and we would not always be lucky. Not long afterward, the wood oil market took another spurt, but this time one of our importers defaulted on his contracts and folded up. As a result we lost thirty-five thousand dollars in as much time as it took us to read a telegram. Thanks to our precautions, we took this blow with a shrug. Naturally, we kept this misfortune to ourselves; let the trade keep on believing that I was a shrewd operator.

No business can live on speculative ventures. Windfalls may now and then provide a bit of cream to sweeten the skimmed milk that is earned by hard work; but of the two, skimmed milk is the more wholesome and can be procured with a reasonable degree of regularity. Windfalls are likely to be interspersed with tornadoes. We found it good policy to sidestep both of them.

Our honeymoon of doing business without competitors did not last long. When people stopped buying merchandise of their own accord, I was confronted with the problem of selling it to them. Against firms who used advertising, salesmen and all the usual paraphernalia of commercial warfare, I could pit only myself. I had no idea how to proceed, but a new card game known as bridge was just becoming popular, and our teacher, a schoolgirl who lived next door, preached the doctrine of always playing one's strongest suit. It seemed a reasonable rule; perhaps it was also applicable to business.

My strongest suit, so I fancied, was my knowledge of the oils we were handling. I knew what was inside the barrels that went to the trade; my competitors did not, or did not know it so well. They were salesmen; I was a chemist. They sat in downtown offices, miles away from their warehouses, while I saw the cars switched into our plant from where I sat. I knew what various oils could do and how they had to be handled to get the most out of them; I doubted if many of my competitors were able to do more than quote prices. I held a pretty good hand, I thought; but I realized that even good hands must be played well in order to win. How to play mine well would take some planning.

As a consultant I had sold goods to the Florsheim Shoe Company, the Window Envelope Company and to other clients, after I had worked out the formulae that fitted their respective cases. But raw materials required no formulae. Or did they? If they did, I was out in front and could go where others would not find it easy to follow.

A long period of trial and error began, while we endeavored to put this idea into practice. Our competitors were men with large capital and long business experience; we had nothing but a theory; but I had faith in this theory, because I could not break it down, no matter how earnestly I slashed at it during sleepless hours. I reasoned this way. If I were a buyer of a certain staple oil, I would not care much from whom I bought it, other things being equal; but if one of the sellers were a chemist who was rated an expert and gave me his services free of charge, I would receive a sort of guarantee policy with his merchandise. Ordinary salesmanship could not prevail against such an inducement. True, the idea had never been tried before, but that was no hindrance. My very ignorance of ordinary business methods might prove an advantage. Had I not once checkmated an expert fencer by a highly unorthodox method?

There was something else I had learned in my consulting days from business dealings with client-customers. More than once competitors tried to break in, anxious to match the material we had worked out; but they were handicapped by conventions. They disposed of their goods through salesmen whose commissions added from ten to twenty per cent to the cost price. Then they made shipments in fine-looking containers, which meant an additional, and I believed unnecessary, expense. Our direct method eliminated sales commissions, and by mutual agreement with our customers we used the same containers over and over again. The conventional way of selling merchandise seemed to have its vulnerable points.

Having decided on the principle of our campaign, Gertie and I set out to make it work. It was a long and uphill fight. Predictions of failure were plentiful. Many of them came true, others did not, and some of them turned out to be quite amusing. One of our competitors was an Italian whom I had once helped over a bad spot when a carload of his oil had arrived in damaged condition and no public warehouse would take it in. He invited me to lunch and, being a much older man, talked to me in fatherly fashion.

"You'll never make it, my boy," he told me. "The least you must do is go out golfing with the fellows you expect to do business with and get drunk with them. Everybody is doing it."

When I expressed doubt, he offered to prove his point. One of the large varnish houses in town was just then in the market for a substantial quantity of oil. The deal would be closed in a few days, and my Italian friend felt sure of getting the order.

"It's as good as in the bag," he told me confidentially. "I'm paired for golf with the purchasing agent, and I'll sell him before we leave the clubhouse."

I had known about the pending purchase, but I did not go golfing. The morning following the tournament our telephone rang bright and early. The purchasing agent of the varnish house was at the other end. He asked me the price of various oils, my views on the market, some statistical information. Then he placed his order with me. My surprise must have been apparent, even to one who could not see the expression on my face.

"I know what you're thinking," he said. "That Italian is a darned nice fellow, and I enjoy playing golf with him; but when it comes to business, I prefer to do it with a fellow who has no hangover from the night before."

The Scientific Oil Company was forging ahead. The profits on individual transactions were small, but we made money, more money than I thought Gertie and I were entitled to. It was time to take care of our co-workers. They would have to share in our profits somehow.

Our working force was a congenial crew. It was not easy to become one of us, but once on the inside, an employee (I don't like that word, never did and never will) almost had to commit murder to lose his or her position. To insure harmony in the office we adopted a peculiar rule, which has never been changed. No new girl was considered hired until she met with the full approval of all the older employees. Gertie and I did the provisional hiring on the strength of certain tests which had proved their value; never did we ask for references, and if they were given to us, we did not follow them up. About family life, religion and other private affairs of our employees we knew as much as they chose to tell us, no more. If, however, after a short period of probation the new girl was not considered desirable, if only one thumb was turned down on her, out she went. But if the newcomer was welcome, she was almost bound to succeed, for everyone helped her along. Once people have put their money on a horse they usually pull for it to win.

Each new member of the office staff was immediately made the head of a specific department and held responsible for it. At the start it might only be the routing of delivery trucks, the filing of letters, or the purchase of office supplies. No one supervised her, no one ordered her around. The older girls headed departments with greater responsibilities; otherwise, there was no difference between them. If they felt like switching their activities, they did so with Gertie's blessing. In this way everybody acquired a variety of experience, and each girl eventually found the job for which she was best fitted. Out in the plant Bill followed the same system, and he was as successful there as we were in the office.

Gertie and I never had had any secrets from each other, and as soon as new employees proved themselves worthy of being taken into our confidence, they were not only allowed to read all incoming and outgoing mail, they were actually requested to do so in order to get an insight into the workings of our business. Everything was open to everybody; the petty cash drawer had no key, and stamps could be had for the taking. No desk, including my own, was ever locked. Gertie and I had private offices, but we never used them, except when Gertie had newly-born babies. Then the young arrivals were lodged there during working hours. More than once callers were startled when a baby's cries suddenly interrupted a business discussion, and it was comical to see their faces when Gertie rushed away to attend to her motherly duties.

Gertie died several years ago, a victim of cancer, and her kindly influence is no longer felt in the office over which she presided so superbly for thirty-four years. She knew better than anyone how to handle our workers, especially the more difficult ones, of whom we had a few in the course of time. She loved Josie, the elderly accountant, who spoke with such a lisp that no one could rightly understand her; she was the confidante of a French girl who had quaint love affairs in out-of-the-way quarters; she sympathized with Marjorie of the baby-blue eyes, whose husband beat her; and she was the only one who never stopped listening to old Henry, the worn-out bookkeeper whose only adventure in life had been a trip around the world. Gertie was gentle, placid and just, an ideal office manager whom everyone liked and trusted, a balance wheel in an organization which housed a goodly variety of odd characters and quick tempers.

Of all the strange people who ever worked in our office, the strangest was Ruthie Marie.

Ruthie called in reply to an ad we had inserted in a daily paper; the only qualification we had specified was that the applicant should be not less than twenty-three years old. Out of hundreds of letters we picked thirty, and when we finished interviewing the writers, Ruthie remained as the only one who had passed all tests. Nevertheless, I could not warm up to her. She was a freckle-faced youngster with straight hair, strong teeth and an impertinent stub nose which she held at a disdainful angle. I looked for an excuse to get rid of her, but could find none that sounded convincing. Then it occurred to me to ask her how old she was. Ruthie admitted readily that she was only nineteen. That settled it. I told her that we were not running a kindergarten, and if we specified girls aged twenty-three, that is what we would get.

"Pardon me," Ruthie said, "but did you ever hear the story of the man and the pork chops?"

I was dumfounded. No, I did not know that story. What on earth did it have to do with what we were discussing?

"Well," Ruthie said with that toss of her head we all came to know so well, "a man once went into a restaurant and ordered pork chops. When the plate was put in front of him, he looked at it with suspicion.

" 'Are those pork chops or veal chops?' he asked.

" 'If you don't know the difference,' the waiter replied, 'what is the difference?' "

I had no comeback to that.

"You win," I said resignedly. And that is how Ruthie came into our office.

At first I did not like her and never spoke to her if I could avoid it. She constantly did little things that went against my grain. She was invariably late in the morning, although she knew that I was a stickler for promptness. When I dictated a letter to her and hesitated a moment for a proper expression, she would impatiently tap a tattoo on the desk with her pencil, throwing me entirely out of gear. But she did her work exceedingly well, and the other girls adored her.

There was something about Ruthie that puzzled us all. At times she looked pretty, at other times almost commonplace. Most of the time she was sprightly, witty and full of life; then came other days when she was morose and almost rude. I would then call her by her middle name Marie, which infuriated her. Her moods had a singular influence on the whole office force, and I was no exception. When she was ebullient, our spirits soared; when she was depressed, we all became gloomy. Although Ruthie never could have been called beautiful, visitors who happened into the office seemed unaccountably attracted to her. I used to tell her, half jocularly, half in earnest, that she possessed the ancient gift of casting spells over people.

Ruthie died in the prime of young womanhood, and died as strangely as she had lived. The attending physicians were as much mystified as anyone, and Dr. Oppen who, at my urgent solicitation, visited her several times a day, shook his head in utter perplexity. She was devoured by a burning fever, her digestive organs stopped functioning, yet she fought on bravely and with outward unconcern, long after the doctors had given her up. Six hours before she died she sat up in bed smoking a cigarette, and the intern called me up in the middle of the night to tell me that he thought a miracle had happened and that she would live. It looked as if she had cast her powerful spell over her new entourage and almost over Death itself.

Under Ruthie's pillow was found a note for me. It said only that she had made all arrangements with a certain railroad to reimburse us for an overcharge, and that I need not worry about it. A few days later the check came in. It was as if Ruthie's capable little hand had stretched out from the Great Beyond in one last loyal gesture toward a business that she had served so devotedly for eight happy years.

To share our profits with those who helped create them was not so easy as it seemed. I had been on the receiving end of a profit-sharing system in my days with the United States Steel Corporation and had noticed its damaging effects. To have employees buy shares in the enterprise for which they worked had serious drawbacks. After considerable thought, I had come to the conclusion that any system which required money contributions from the workers was looked upon by them with suspicion. In some cases, at least, this suspicion was not groundless. When I had been manager of the linseed oil plant, the superintendent of a neighboring mill had invited me to join in a movement to have all our workers buy their own homes. The employers would acquire the properties outright and let their employees pay for the little houses out of their wages. I objected to this idea as unfair, for a workingman who owed a balance to his employer had a chain around his neck and would not be able to quit or fight a reduction in wages.

My neighbor gave me a sidelong glance.

"That's the idea, of course," he said.

I handed him his hat.

Yet there was more to these housing plans than met the eye. I had been through some large factories in Germany and Austria where benevolent managements had provided homes for their workers, free from all encumbrances; but even these outright gifts had not been received graciously. Evidently men did not like to be compelled to do anything; they wanted to live their lives and spend their money according to their own recipes for happiness. They did not care to move into homes built for them by someone else, even if the houses were free gifts. A gift with a string attached to it only bred discontent, even if the string meant no more than that the gift was to be put to its proper use. We would have to hit on a profit-sharing plan devoid of this evil. Apparently, the easiest way would be to add a certain percentage to the workers' annual wages and give it to them as a Christmas present. But I had become afraid of easy ways; they were usually full of pitfalls. That this particular method was faulty was soon demonstrated. The employees of a firm I knew were receiving regularly ten per cent of their wages as a New Year's bonus. They quickly came to accept these bonuses as something they had coming to them, cast their budgets accordingly, and almost rioted when business reverses forced the management to omit this extra remuneration.

Could it be that employees did not want any kind of profit-sharing system?

Workers, like everyone else, wanted to make as much money as possible, and if the enterprise which employed them was exceptionally successful, they were entitled to a share in the prosperity. That much could be accepted as axiomatic. Perhaps the best way to give it to them was to apportion certain specified portions of the profits to capital and others to labor. But against such an arrangement the arguments were again obvious and irrefutable. For one, the workers would never believe that they had received their full share. Their inborn mistrust of finance, which they did not understand, was something that would not be easily overcome. Of course, the employees might be allowed to appoint their own auditor to look over the manager's shoulder and see that the rules were lived up to. But here another obstacle was sure to arise. The workers would insist on distributing all the money that had been earned in one year, leaving nothing for plant improvements, repairs or emergencies. Nor was there any reason why they should do otherwise. They were not permanent stockholders, and to leave part of their earnings as surplus for others who followed was too much to expect of them. Arguments for the proverbial insurance against a rainy day would fall on deaf ears, if the ears belonged to people who did not know where they would be when the rains came.

Other doubts assailed us. Suppose we made so much money in one particular year that the workers' share would be more than they could wisely spend. What would happen? I remembered a little girl of about fourteen whom Bertha and I had employed in our home during the first few months of our married life. Her father, a carpenter, had made high wages the year before and had given our girl twenty-five cents each night. With this she had, day after day, bought herself a new hair ribbon and thrown it away at night. The following year business was slack, and the whole family had to go to work; not a cent was left of last year's prosperity. The silk-shirt era of 1919-20 also was still fresh in our minds. Workers and farmers then had been buying not only silk shirts they could not wear, but a piano or gramophone for each of their children. No, too much money was not a good thing for anyone and was positively dangerous for those who were not used to it.

Altogether, the sharing of profits seemed quite a complex problem.

One innovation there was, though, that we could inaugurate at once without doing any harm, although it had nothing to do with either profits or wages. Whenever there was a new opening for a position in our office, the faces of the applicants haunted me. They had that desperate look one sees in those who have lost all hope and faith, both in themselves and in human kindness. I recalled my own job-hunting days and the unfriendliness with which I had been met. People searching for positions were apparently looked upon as outcasts, to be kept waiting and to be asked impudent questions. Everyone kicked them around, although they were unquestionably the most desirable of the jobless and deserving of real sympathy. Once while I had been making the endless rounds of a job-hunter, I had been given a cigar and a few kind words. I had never smoked the cigar, but together with the kind words it had been a tonic which buoyed me up for weeks. I would see to it that all who came to us for an interview would be treated with consideration. In place of a cigar we would give them a dollar for their time and carfare. And why not? When a man invited another man to a meeting, it was he who set up the drinks. I was ashamed that I had not thought of this before.

The profit-sharing problem held Gertie, her husband Will and me in many serious conferences. Gertie's husband had been superintendent of our plant for many years, had a kind heart and a lot of common sense, and was of great help to us in our deliberations. He knew workingmen as only one who mingles with them every day can know them. What was it that would make a workingman happy? Well, what was it that made anybody happy? It was manifestly wrong to speak of men in overalls as a class, distinct and separate from white-collar workers, be they clerks, managers or capitalists. What workingmen wanted was what everyone else wanted, and that, we agreed, was first of all, security. We all wanted security in one form or other, but above everything we wanted to be sure of our livelihood. Most capitalists wanted security of income, security more than size. They invested their capital in mortgages or bonds in the hope of preserving their capital and having a safe income, though a safe investment would necessarily pay only a moderate rate of interest. Very few speculated in gold stocks. A workingman was not much different. His capital was his body and his health, and these had to be protected at all hazards. Next in importance were his wages; if they were secure, they need not be excessively high. So far we felt ourselves on safe ground. The thing to do was to provide security of employment at fair wages to all our co-workers. We thought this could best be accomplished by putting the bonuses which a profit-sharing system would have yielded into a special security fund, earmarked "payroll reserve." Whenever business became dull we would tap this fund, just as a water reservoir is tapped when the streams run dry. There was nothing new in the idea; it was as old as the Bible, Gertie commented, as old as the story of the seven fat and the seven lean years in ancient Egypt.

I talked to several businessmen about our newly founded payroll reserve, but they disapproved this innovation. Between capital and labor, they contended, peace was unthinkable. Lions and lambs did not lie down together. Force was ranged against force; it would ever be so. I argued that every good businessman put aside a certain credit reserve each year against losses that might accrue in the future, and that he figured this percentage as part of his cost. Why not apply the same rule to wages? My friends only shook their heads. It was not being done. Give the men a Christmas bonus, if you were generously inclined, but that was all. Why worry about the workingman's daily bread? Who guaranteed the employer his daily bread? America was a free country, and the relations between capital and labor were regulated by the law of supply and demand. When the supply of labor ran short, as it had during and after the war, the workingman was on top; when labor was plentiful, capital wielded the big stick. It was all very simple. What we were practicing was paternalism. Yes, paternalism, that was it. You could see the joyful relief in people's faces when they had found the right word with which to torpedo our ideas; for one word, spoken with the proper intonation, can save much thought and argument.

If the idea of keeping our co-workers' incomes intact was paternalism, that was all right with us. We still proposed to keep our men on the payroll during slack periods and give them as much security as we could afford.

In time, our payroll reserve began to pile up. When it reached thirty-five thousand dollars, we became impatient. We did not know then that the depression of the early thirties was in the offing, and that all we had accumulated would be needed to keep our crew on full time and without a cut in wages. Gertie and I felt that some sort of distribution was in order, but handouts were contradictory to our theory that workers were investors looking for a fixed income, and that extras would do more harm than good. Suppose a man holding a five per cent mortgage on an apartment building were suddenly to receive, in addition to his interest, a bonus from the mortgagor. What would be his reaction? Would he believe it, if he were told that the extra check was a token of brotherly love? More likely he would conclude that the profits on that building were so high that the owner did not know what to do with his money and was throwing it around. Instead of being happy he would be dissatisfied at having loaned out his capital at such low interest. Moreover, if an extra check were not forthcoming the next year and the next, he would feel that he had been robbed of what was due him. Bonus checks were dynamite, no question about it; we had to evolve a different method of transferring some extra money from our checkbook to the pockets of our workers.

We knew of no immediate answer to this riddle, and therefore Gertie and I decided to wait, rather than force the issue. A revelation would come to us sooner or later. It came sooner than we had thought, and from an unexpected source.

Our office force had grown to substantial proportions, and with its growth we had added a few refinements. Among other things we had built a dining room, where all of us assembled for breakfast and lunch. Gertie and I had always lunched together, since our earliest days, but our meals had then consisted of a glass of milk with crackers or something equally frugal. By and by Gertie's husband and other workers had joined us, until we found it best to pool our purchases and prepare a cooked repast, which one or the other girl usually volunteered to prepare. Sometimes I had a nearby club serve us a better lunch, and our tastes gradually moved into higher spheres. Before long we hired a regular cook; a real kitchen took the place of the laboratory stoves, and when the cost of the meals threatened to become a serious item for some of the employees, the company acted as host to all who ate with us. It worked out very satisfactorily. At breakfast it became customary for each department to air its troubles, and we discussed the pros and cons of whatever advice was being offered. Each worker was thus painlessly educated in our affairs, and the entire force developed into a board of strategy on which each member had a voice.

One morning at breakfast the gay mood which usually prevailed at our meals was absent. One of our bookkeepers, ordinarily a fluent conversationalist, sat crying into her handkerchief and got up from the table before the meal was over. I asked Gertie to find out what was wrong, and she did. The poor girl had been robbed of her handbag the night before and, as hard luck would have it, that day had been payday, and she had, together with her purse, lost a whole week's salary.

What to do? Gertie had a ready suggestion. We would buy the girl a new bag, fill it with whatever knicknacks it was likely to have contained, and put a week's salary into it. Two girls were quickly dispatched to a store and succeeded in matching the lost handbag. Then it was properly filled, and suddenly turned up on the desk of our weeping bookkeeper.

I looked at Gertie, and she looked at me, and I knew that to both of us had come the same thought. Here was at least a partial solution of our problem. We would start a fund through which to distribute profits by taking care of unusual situations. We could not very well penalize the other employees for not having lost their bags or other belongings, and so they all, men and women, were given the equivalent of the recovered bag and its contents. From that time on the new fund became known as the Happiness Fund.

Incidentally, we had discovered another principle of human reaction, just as applicable to employer-employee relationship as it is to any other group. It was the principle of the expectation of the unexpected, if it may be so called. It was the justified hope of our workers that at certain intervals the management would provide a treat for them. A story which my old boss, J. W. Hirst, had once told me flitted back into my mind. As he looked over his mail one morning he found a parcel with a book in it. It was one that a friend of his had liked and had sent to Mr. Hirst in the hope that he, too, would enjoy it. Mr. Hirst told me that tears came to his eyes. He was a rich man by that time, and could afford to buy all the books he wanted. That someone should send him a present, rather than ask for one, touched him to the quick. The monetary value of the gift was not over three dollars at the most. Had Mr. Hirst received three dollars as a present, he would have been highly indignant; the book caused him to cry with joy. Gertie and I thought this episode contained the germ of a serious lesson.

Our first opportunity to apply this lesson arose with the arrival of fall. It was one of those days when the whole world seemed steeped in gray, and when the rain poured down mercilessly on our yard workers. In the afternoon, when the men were ready to leave, we invited them to the office and Gertie poured a glass of brandy for each of them, handing him at the same time a check for an extra day's work. The men understood what was in our minds, and while they did not say much, they showed their appreciation in a way that we on our part understood equally well. How different their reaction would have been, had we omitted the personal touch. Our crew in overalls were men, and their feelings were the same as those of other men, no matter how rich or well educated.

One early spring we learned another interesting lesson in profit-sharing. Looking over the price list of the oils we were handling, we noticed that linseed oil was selling at what appeared to be a very low price. I had not studied under Mr. Hirst for years without learning something about markets. Gertie agreed that linseed oil was bound to rise in price before many months. When we discussed our theory at next morning's breakfast table, one of the stenographers suggested laughingly that if she were sure of a rise she would buy a few barrels of linseed oil for her own account. Again Gertie and I looked at each other and nodded. Within an hour we had bought a few cars of oil for speculation. One lot was entered on our books for the account of our office force, another for the men in the plant. Everyone was told of his or her allotment and why we had bought it. If our speculation turned out well, all the profit would go to the workers; if it turned out wrong, the company would take the loss.

This time we really had rung the bell. Never had our working force been so well posted on the oil market, and never before had they sweated with us during the day-to-day fluctuations which usually precede important market movements. Quotations rose slowly, then faster and faster. Soon I could not walk through the factory without being accosted by one man or another. Their paper profits were mounting, and they did not know whether to cash them in or wait. I let them tremble for a while. It would do them good to experience some of the worries of those who try to make money without working for it. At last I suggested that the market seemed pretty high, and quoted the old saying that no one ever went broke taking profits. When the checks were distributed, the universal joy rose almost out of bounds. It really seemed a little out of proportion to the profits realized. Perhaps we had hit on another important point we had so far overlooked.

We had. For a while we could not define it, but when we did, it appeared obvious enough. What we had done was to give our men an opportunity to see a dream come true. This time it had been an expected present, not an unexpected one, that had turned the trick. Perhaps it would be wise to mix up our presents in the future. There was fun in surprises, but there also was fun in giving people a vision, something around the corner that would be pleasant if it should materialize.

On one of my European trips I had asked the Mayor of Baden whether the Austrian lotteries had helped the government's finances while he had been Secretary of the Treasury.

"Financially they helped some," he told me, "but that was not so important. What these lotteries did was to keep the masses from suicide or rebellion. Any one of them might draw the big lot and become rich; he probably wouldn't, of course, but he might. Don't ever take people's hopes away, whatever else you do; when hope is gone, it is the end of everything."

The people's hopes. I thought Kollman had put his finger on the core of our problem. People's lives on the whole were so gray, so monotonous, so hopeless. Ordinary profit-sharing did little to make them more interesting. Money alone never would make workers contented. They had to have hopes, visions, perhaps also fears. Gertie and I decided to add one more item to our system. Whenever a particularly large or profitable order was in the offing, we let everybody know about it. If we landed it, there would be a celebration in the form of checks; if we did not, we all suffered. Thus we added fear to the list of our emotions. But this is where we stopped. Neither Gertie nor I, nor the two of us together, would be able to set this world right and eradicate all its shortcomings. We felt fairly satisfied with what we had accomplished, and the results were reassuring. We would leave it to wiser heads to work out a profit-sharing system that was perfect.

CHAPTER 18

*

THE LURE OF HISTORY

$\mathcal{A}$s TIME ROLLED BY and the pressure of business duties eased, I decided to fulfill the promise I had made to myself years before on that little knob in Montana where Custer had made his famous last stand. I began to read up on history, because I wanted to visit the battlefields of America with true understanding. It was a vast undertaking, and one that was to instill drama into many a future vacation. Bertha usually accompanied me on these trips, although without much enthusiasm, I fear. Each trip was preceded by intensive study of one battlefield. We would then stay on the ground for days, marching into the fight with regiments or brigades, pursuing with the victor, retreating with the vanquished. Only the most prominent historical sites had as yet been converted into national parks or monuments, and this added zest to the task. Maps did not help much in orienting ourselves; the real picture always was so different from what we had imagined. The absence of guides proved a blessing; in their stead we struck up acquaintances with old-time residents of the neighborhood, many of whom had personal recollections that lent color to our visits.

Our itinerary was without system. One jaunt might take us to Virginia, the next to New Mexico. Never did we take in more than one battle at a time. Each was a storybook in itself, and we were loath to ruin its impression by undue crowding.

Many spots stand out in my memory. That hillside at Fort Donelson, over which three raw Illinois regiments had once stormed and where hundreds of wounded died miserably when the underbrush caught fire; the little house in Boonsborough from which two old ladies with whom we talked had watched their brother march to the battle of South Mountain; the bushes and trenches at Chickamauga through which we crawled with a veteran of the 61st Ohio. He had been through that battle, and together we relived those September days when men fought each other on a field so obscured by natural obstacles that they scarcely knew whether they were killing friend or foe. An old man whom we met on the banks of the Big Black river had been a boy of ten when Pemberton's men were being pushed into Vicksburg by Grant's army. He had crossed and re-crossed the stream all night long on a homemade raft to exchange Confederate tobacco for matches and newspapers. After the armies had moved on, his father paid him ten cents a bucket for lead bullets, and the boy made a small fortune; bullets were so plentiful they had to be carried in wagonloads to a lead-hungry market. Nor shall I ever forget that half-buried trench near Corinth, where an Alabama regiment had shed its blood during Van Dorn's attempt to take that little Southern town. A wounded soldier had engraved his name on the bark of a tree. He had started to add, "I am dy—," when death overtook him. I was probably the first and last man who walked by his forgotten grave.

Of all the battlefields we visited I thought Shiloh the most intrigu-ing. No novelist could have packed into a space of two days more action, romance and surprises than history did on that occasion. If Grant had not been miles away when the firing began, would he have stemmed the gray tide in the morning? What if the Northern army had thrown up trenches, or if rain had not delayed Albert Sydney Johnston's advance, or if General Buell's relief army had arrived two hours later? Like an overtone to these questions one ever-recurring thought haunted my mind: where had my father fought on these blood-drenched miles of fields, woods, marshes and ravines? How close had he been to Death?

Some claimed that Grant was drunk while his men were fighting off the Southern onslaught; but people said many things, even that Grant had done his best to hold off Buell's relief troops, so as to gar-ner all the laurels for himself. A Federal colonel who had been in the fight made this accusation and was court-martialed for it.

My father had at times talked to me about Grant. The few conversations with him I could recall had usually dealt either with Grant or Lincoln. He had admired Grant without stint, both as a general and as President. I confess that I could not share his enthusiasm. Grant's conduct seemed to be constantly in need of explanations. Why had he not been with his troops at Pittsburgh Landing? Why had he been so sure that his army would not be attacked? Later, when he battled Lee in the Wilderness, he coined the phrase that he would fight it out along that line if it took all summer. His panegyrists immortalized the pledge, but soft-pedaled the fact that he had not lived up to it. Studying Grant's career with a critical eye, I stumbled on another queer event in his life that was destined to have a curious influence on my own. Grant, I read, had accepted an invitation to accompany Lincoln to Ford's Theater. And Grant did not go. An apparently unimportant incident this, and completely overshadowed by the tragedy of the assassination. Yet the more I pondered over it, the more extraordinary it looked to me. How could Grant have broken his promise without being rude, if not actually insubordinate? Furthermore, if Grant had been in the Presidential box, the entire course of history might have been changed. My curiosity increased when I discovered that Grant's own explanation, given in his autobiography, was trivial, evasive, highly improbable. I tried to shut my mind against the challenge of this riddle; but in my heart I knew I would not be able to rest until I had satisfied myself as to why Grant had left Washington an hour and a half before the curtain rose in Ford's Theater that fatal night.

In my Pittsburgh days I had become acquainted with the city editor of a paper to which I sent occasional contributions. This editor had a favorite anecdote with which he used to regale his young reporters. A young boy in a small Pennsylvania town, it appeared, one morning had met a railroad conductor.

"What time is it, mister?" he asked. The conductor pulled out his watch.

"It's seventeen minutes past eight," he replied. The boy looked at the stranger for a moment with a calculating eye.

"You ain't no railroad conductor," he declared. "A conductor would have said eight-seventeen."

The self-styled conductor started to run away, the boy after him, with half the little town joining in the chase. When they caught the man, he confessed that he had just murdered a railroad conductor and donned his uniform to make his escape.

The editor thought this story made to order for young men in the newspaper business.

"Boys," he used to say, "when you run into a story that doesn't click, there is a story behind that story. Get it. I want them both."

Long after I had left Pittsburgh and newspaper work, the editor's advice remained with me. What would he have done if one of his men had reported to him Grant's unusual behavior? I could almost hear him shout for the story behind that story. Well, I decided I would get it if it could be got, not for him, but for myself. Little did I know what I was letting myself in for.

Up to then I had handled some chemical problems, but I knew nothing about historical ones. After many dismal failures I began to wonder if I could not find my answer in the archives of the War Department in Washington. The archives would certainly make interesting reading, no matter what they contained. In my innocence I believe that all I had to do was to go to Washington and ask to be ushered into the archives. And so to Washington I went, adventure-bound.

No one in the War Department was overly glad to see me. The idea of going through its archives had evidently occurred to others before me, but almost without exception they had been turned away. The colonel in charge, a kindly, jovial officer, put the case to me succinctly.

"If you are a real historian," he said, "we will put no obstacles in your way. But if you are one of those cranks who come in here every day of the week to accuse us of withholding vital evidence that John Wilkes Booth escaped, the quicker you leave, the better we will like you."

I had only vague ideas on Lincoln's death and none on the fate of his assassin. I assured the colonel that I harbored no sinister intentions; but how would he go about finding out whether I was a crank or an historian?

The colonel was quick with his rejoinder.

"I come from an historical town myself," he declared, "and I intend to find out how much you know about it."

My heart fell. America boasted many historical towns I had never heard of. The colonel's clipped military enunciation had given no indication of his nativity.

"What is the name of your home town?" I asked with inward trepidation.

"I come from Perryville, Kentucky," he replied.

Perryville. What luck that the colonel had chosen to be born near a battlefield. I took a pencil and a piece of paper and drew a map of Perryville. These small circles on the outskirts of the town were the pools of water in Doctor's Creek where a few thirsty Federal troops had met the outposts of Bragg's army on October 7, 1862, and from where the conflict had spread until it involved both armies. General Rousseau was out in front of the Federal troops, along the crest of a hill which I marked with a line. At one o'clock in the afternoon, just as his brigades were reforming, the Confederates attacked him furiously and drove his men pellmell before them. He appealed to Sheridan, who stood on the ridges to his left, but . . .

Here the colonel interrupted me.

"Stop right where you are," he laughed; "if you go a step further I may have to admit that you know more about Perryville than I do."

From that day on the Government archives were open to me.

Only those who have gone through piles of dusty documents, written generations ago, can appreciate the emotions I felt when I unfolded these yellowed papers and with them the pasts of men long dead. Their troubles and hopes, their successes and their mishaps all lay before me in one heap, and no one cared now for either one or the other. The specters of dead men seemed to press around me, asking to be remembered. Had they not lived, fought, died? Should they be completely forgotten? Many times I was on the point of dropping my work on Grant and Lincoln's death to write up, instead, the lives of these unknown dead, whose fates were so vividly depicted in the files of that gloomy room in the old War Department.

Not all my work could be done in Washington. As question after question arose, and one solved problem only led to another equally puzzling, I needed help, and therefore surrounded myself with a corps of young assistants, to all of whom were allotted tasks that must have astounded them. One young student was asked to look up the time tables of trains between Washington and Burlington, N. J., in 1865, another to study the court records of California land condemnations in 1859. A young lady in Vermont helped me trace the alleged movements of a conspirator through that section of the country, a retired lawyer in Macon read old Georgia newspapers for me. Eventually I employed eleven assistants, with headquarters in my library under the direction of my niece Virginia. Sometimes it took years of work and much thought to clear up one little point, and we had our share of disappointments. Nevertheless, the excitement of the hunt never waned. Most of the time we were like explorers on uncharted ground, working our way through jungles and swamps to new discoveries, more often to frustration. Virginia and I visited many places, wherever the latest clues led us. In Anderson, Indiana, we followed Lloyd Lewis' footsteps in search of material on Louis Wiechmann, the star witness of the infamous trial of the so-called Lincoln conspirators. In Bowling Green, Virginia, we endeavored to find who it really was that had been shot at Garrett's barn, the assassin Booth or someone else. We interviewed people in Pittsburgh, Indianapolis, Beloit, Cadiz, Port Tobacco and innumerable places of whose existence we had been unaware heretofore. One elusive diary of which we had heard rumors lured us through six states before we located it. But after we had done yeoman's work, the question which had intrigued me so at the beginning still remained unanswered: why had General Grant failed to accompany President Lincoln to Ford's Theater? Somehow I sensed that if we found the right answer to this query we would hold the key to many others that still plagued us.

Of stories that did not click there was no dearth, and we followed each with eagerness and persistency. It was fascinating work and, after all, not unlike the solving of chemical problems. The only difference was this. In chemistry one dealt with elements and compounds that could be depended on; whether neutral or corrosive, harmless or poisonous, they always were honest. In history one dealt with human beings and their testimony. Neither was ever quite dependable or quite honest.

One of the in-between problems that came our way and had to be solved was similar to many more that beset us.

On the night of Lincoln's death, all commercial telegraph wires out of Washington went dead for two hours. Strangely, the wires used by the War Department remained intact; and as the War Department did not choose to send out its first dispatch until most papers had gone to press, the news of the assassination was not printed in the early morning editions of many American newspapers. After the deadline had passed, the telegraph system started functioning again. No one had ever taken enough interest in this event to investigate it.

What a story behind that story! Of course, the few historians who had mentioned it at all offered a ready explanation: the conspirators had cut the wires to impede pursuit. But this offhand explanation was palpably wrong. Aside from the fact that it would have taken more conspirators to perform this task than ever were under suspicion, something else pointed in a different direction. Wires that have been cut do not go back into service again of their own accord; and the conspirators would hardly have stopped to repair the damage they had wrought. Our suspicions were aroused; yet we dared not jump to conclusions. This matter would have to be examined without bias or prejudice.

If the wires had gone out of commission for two hours and then had returned to normalcy again, they had done so either through natural causes or else through intervention by human hands. There was no other alternative. But which was the right one?

Our next step was plainly outlined. We would have to study the workings of the telegraphic system in the nation's capital at the time of Lincoln's death. This was not difficult. Before long one fact emerged indisputably: a break in the service could not have remained unobserved in Washington, especially with a swarm of reporters trying frantically to file their dispatches. The break must have occurred away from Washington, out in the open; but how?

Questions that looked easy we often found the most baffling. Their very simplicity proved disconcerting. My own knowledge of electricity and telegraphy was limited; but the telegraph companies and various technical institutes, we confidently believed, would quickly provide us with the information we needed. In this we were mistaken. A country-wide correspondence had to be carried on before we could form a clear picture. The experts agreed with us that a leakage of the batteries in the power stations would have

caused a gradual weakening of the signals, not their outright extinction. Crude sabotage, such as the demolition of sending instruments would, of course, have been discovered instantly. Nothing
remained but a possible breakage of the lines out in the open. But
how could this have happened in such a way as to bring about an
automatic resumption of wire service after the lapse of a few hours?

According to the experts, such a natural interruption and subsequent resumption could have occurred, at least theoretically; but
it could only have been brought about through a freakish combination of circumstances. If, during the night of April 14, 1865, a
windstorm had snapped the topmost wire between two telegraph
poles and had thrown it across the remainder, the whole system
would have been short-circuited, provided the top wire had touched
wet earth. If, two hours later, the storm had hurled the severed
wire to the ground, thereby breaking its contact with the remainder,
the other wires would have been restored to their normal function.
All this sounded extremely unlikely, but it could have happened.
Therefore, the next question was: had there been a windstorm around
Washington during the night of April 14, 1865?

The answer to this question would be a matter of routine. All we
had to do was to make inquiries at the Weather Bureau. But now
an unexpected stumbling block appeared. The Weather Bureau in
Washington informed us that the wind velocimeter had not yet been
invented in 1865. Without a wind velocimeter, we knew that the
strength of air currents could not have been determined.

This was a body blow and it looked like final defeat. But
human nature rebels against accepting defeat. Somewhere, somehow, we might still reach the goal of our quest. The first thing we did
was to make a search through contemporary newspapers. In describing the events of such a fateful night as that of Lincoln's death, reporters would take note of everything to weave into their stories.
Unluckily, most of them had made undue use of their poetic license.
They dwelled on the fact that it had started to rain almost as soon
as Lincoln had breathed his last, as if even the elements had wept;
to some writers the air had seemed oppressive; others, less imag-
inative, had not noticed this. Some had seen the moon hiding behind clouds, others had seen it shine brightly; still others did not
refer to it at all. Two experts employed by the United States Naval

Observatory differed by more than an hour regarding the time the moon had risen. All in all, the contradictions we encountered only tended to obscure rather than clarify what we were trying to ascertain.

From this hopeless maze we fled into the records of court trials during which witnesses had made formal statements about the weather. The sworn testimony, we found, proved no better than that of the reporters. Firemen, soldiers, civilians and policemen who had roamed the streets of the capital after the tragedy often made casual mention of the weather, but their observations left much to be desired. No one mentioned any atmospheric disturbances, such as a heavy wind, which was negative evidence; but negative evidence is not conclusive. It took a long time to wade through these legal tomes, and the reading proved highly interesting; the results, however, were practically nil, so far as they concerned our object.

We could think of only one more possible source of enlightenment, although the odds were ten to one against success. We would ask for photostatic copies of the weather reports issued by the Weather Department for the month of April, 1865, to see if they contained any reference to air currents. We included the stations at Baltimore and Annapolis for the sake of a wider perspective. If the wires had been broken deliberately, they might not have been broken within the limits of the Washington Weather Bureau.

The arrival of these records was awaited with understandable impatience. At last they came. They consisted of the usual notations on temperature, humidity and barometric pressure, which is what we had expected. To our pleasant surprise, though, a column had been devoted to wind observations. A column marked "Wind" showed figures ranging from one to seven. Unintelligible as these figures were to us, we felt we were making headway.

Then came the break. Someone in the Washington Weather Bureau had become interested in our little problem and, by diligent search, had found an ex-employee who remembered the days before the invention of the wind velocimeter. Still better, he also remembered the meaning of the figures which had so puzzled us. Before the strength of the wind could be measured by an instrument, the Bureau had estimated its velocity and designated it by figures. One stood for perfect calmness, two for a slight breeze, and so on up the ladder. At last the answer was in our hands. There had been no wind around Washington strong enough to disrupt the telegraph service.

Someone, therefore, had interfered with the wire system connecting the capital with the rest of the nation during the night of Lincoln's death. This dénouement fitted well into a startling pattern which was slowly emerging from our investigations. As it grew in size and distinctness, we became almost frightened at the form it was taking. Could it be that Lincoln's murder had been an inside job?

Years of additional work went into the pattern before it was complete, or as complete as we could make it. We had enough stories behind stories to have satisfied even my old Pittsburgh editor. We also thought we knew why Grant had not gone to the theater with Lincoln. Now we would have to find someone to write our story in book form.

I had never written anything longer than a magazine article and shied at writing a book. Several authors whom I approached were too busy with work of their own. Then my good neighbor, Miss Clara Laughlin, came to the rescue. Many years before she had published her admirable *The Death of Lincoln,* and from the very beginning of my historical studies she had listened patiently to my ideas, plans, theories. Since her book on Lincoln, Miss Laughlin had wandered from historical to literary fields and was now writing travel books with equal ease and success. According to her, the way to learn book writing was to write a book. What I was afraid of were shadows, and even they existed only in my own imagination.

Miss Laughlin was right. After one had a story, the writing was not too difficult. To my surprise the manuscript almost wrote itself. The first publisher to whom it was offered accepted it. I had become an author.

I have since talked to many writers, and they all agree that the greatest moment in their lives was when their first book was accepted. It marked the summit of their literary happiness. After that contracts must be signed, changes made, proofs read. The triumphant joy of that first moment never comes back; I know it never came back to me. By the time the book was on the market, it had almost become a child of sorrow.

I had nearly forgotten that I was a chemist; but the readers quickly brought my profession home to me again. Worse, they apparently considered it my outstanding feature, if not my chief crime. Among the reviewers scarcely one in a hundred failed to mention the chemist in me; the vast majority did it with astonishment, some with anger, one or two with contempt. A chemist had come out from his kitchen and mingled with the crowd in the parlor. It was evidently all right for ministers, librarians and others to write history, but not for a chemist. I felt as welcome in my new surroundings as an unwashed tramp at a banquet table.

I did not blame my critics, professional or otherwise. The fault did not lie with them, but with the chemists. Why were they content to let the world think of them as bewhiskered old men holding test tubes against the light or carrying on distillations from medieval-looking retorts for no reason that anybody could see? Men like that did belong in the kitchen. Their dissertations on anything beyond their limited horizon could not be of value. Let them stick to their test tubes and retorts and gas burners.

I am glad that some of my readers found the situation humorous. Would they have to dust off their schoolbooks on chemistry in order to understand my language? Was H_2SO_4 still the symbol for sulphuric acid? One of them had even dug up my half-forgotten treatise on the detection of fish oils, which discovery gave him cause for great merriment. Fish oil and Lincoln—what a combination! It really was funny. An unsophisticated young chemist had spent a year of his spare time in an excursion into science. With what had he come back? With an analytical method. What utter rubbish! When people led expeditions to Africa they came back with the pelt of a lion. Even those who went vacationing came back with a sunburn. One could see those things, feel them, show them off. But a scientific discovery—pshaw! I could not blame anyone for laughing.

Perhaps my publishers would have done better not to proclaim my profession on the book jacket. If they had called me an oil merchant, things might have turned out differently. Everybody knew what an oil merchant was and either had a friend in the oil business, or a cousin who ran a gas station, or an uncle who owned stock in a Texas oil well. People understood the oil business, and I would have been one of them. An oil merchant could conceivably be also a Lincoln author; he stood almost as high as a librarian or a minister. But the publishers, unfortunately, had introduced me as a chemist; like Parsifal, I had been sent into the literary world clothed in an outlandish garb, and people had laughed at me.

The people were right, as they always are. *Vox populi, vox Dei.*

CHAPTER 19

*

ROAST BEEF AND GREEN PEAS

*T*HE FIRST THING the author of a controversial book should learn is to grow a protective skin. I learned it the hard way. It took me many weeks before I could scan reviews without loathing myself, and I was surprised that my friends still shook hands with me. I longed to be left alone in my shame, but even this privilege was denied me. People wanted to see what an iconoclast looked like, and ask him questions. These questions never varied: how had I first become interested in Lincoln, how long had it taken me to finish the book, how much money had I spent in collecting my material? I became so bored, I seldom gave the same answer twice, trusting my imagination would hold out. I had never in my life tabulated expenses, be it for living, traveling or collecting, but an enterprising reporter estimated my expenditures at twenty thousand dollars. I do not know how he arrived at this total, but I neither affirmed nor denied it. It wove quite a halo around me. Twenty thousand dollars to write a book! Some book, no doubt, by all common standards. Few people forgot to mention that sum when introducing me, and it always assured me a respectful reception.

For weeks after the publication date, invitations to speak simply rained in through the mail. I felt flattered—what fools these mortals be—and accepted them as fast as they came. My first engagement taught me one of the painful lessons that amateur speakers need to remind them of their proper status. The engagement called for a lecture at a church in one of Chicago's proudest suburbs. I had often addressed meetings of chemists, and anticipated a similar audience of serious listeners. Forty-five minutes of speaking, a few questions, then some handshaking and it would be over. But at this meeting, the last thing the audience apparently wanted was to hear me. I listened patiently to the reading of minutes, less so to a soloist at the piano, and—horror of horrors— to community singing. An elderly lady announced a picnic, a Boy Scout a prize contest. My pride shrank with every number on the program and collapsed when a group of dancing children earned a storm of applause. I never would get that much attention or approval. What did these folk want me for anyway? They were having a wonderful time without me, and I did not feel at all inclined to interrupt their vaudeville show. In fact, that is what I told the minister who sat next to me. But he met my remonstrance with raised eyebrows and genuine perturbation. Why, they always had these preliminaries, but I was the *pièce de résistance*, the speaker of the evening. Everybody was dying to hear me. I wondered.

A few days later I met a friend who was a speaker of renown and told him of my misadventure. He laughed immoderately.

"That's what you get for speaking free of charge," he chided me. "Charge them, my boy, charge them. What people get for nothing can't be much good. That's your answer."

My friend was right. These gratis performances were thankless jobs and disconcertingly alike, with few exceptions. They were not only tiresome, at times they were almost humiliating. One late afternoon, for instance, I received an emergency call from the secretary of a prominent charity organization. He was in an embarrassing predicament and asked for my help. A crowd in a hall was waiting for a speaker, but he had not appeared. Would I jump into my car and hurry over to entertain the audience? He would join me as soon as possible.

I did as told. The meeting was held in a public clubhouse, and when I entered I found myself part of a sweltering, milling mob, all trying to gain admittance. I elbowed my way to the platform and looked at my prospective audience. It consisted mostly of women of undeniably foreign extraction, and I counted at least two dozen babies who were feeding contentedly at their mothers' breasts.

"Lordy," I thought, "how these people will enjoy it when I talk history to them."

There was no one on the platform but myself, not even a chairman to introduce me. Only a janitor stuck his head out from the wings and admonished me to "get a-going." Obediently I got a-going. My listeners, to judge from their stupid looks, were totally oblivious of my message. I must have spoken for about three minutes, when a hatless, freely perspiring man stormed in and joined me.

"Enough of that," he whispered to me, "now do your stunts."

It was my turn to look stupid.

"What stunts?" I asked.

"The stunts, the stunts," he repeated. "Aren't you a magician?"

The heck, I told him, I was a Lincoln speaker, or at least posed as one.

"Good gravy!" he exclaimed, wiping his brow. "That's my secretary again. She always gets the index cards mixed up. What'll we do? Can't you think of something?" I thought I could.

"Hold the stage for a while and talk," I said. "I have an idea." Then I put my idea into execution. I left through the back door and drove away as fast as I could.

After this experience I turned a new leaf and began to charge in earnest for my speeches. The vaudeville stopped, and so did the community singing; the programs started on time; but another evil started to haunt me—suppers. They were as alike as the proverbial peas in a pod; worse, the peas were there. I detest green peas and I abhor roast beef, yet nine times in ten that is what was put before me. I believe I ate more roast beef and green peas in one year than most men, with the exception of speakers, eat in half a century. In the end I could not look at that dish without feeling sick, and under the pretense of eating I would roll the peas around the meat in a self-taught game resembling pool, in which the peas had to drop into the crevices between the meat and the fat.

The meals were not always bad; sometimes I even partook of veritable banquets. One night, in a city famous for its food, I sat at a table that would have done honor to a king, and we were entertained by an orchestra. I was sorry to see the chairman rise to say his piece.

"We have with us tonight," he announced, "a Viennese-born American author, who . . ."

I felt vaguely uneasy when he brought up the city of my birth, but I was grateful he had omitted the usual reference to my chemistry, which always led to many vexatious questions and explanations. I only half listened to the remainder of his words, and when he sat down, I assumed it was my cue to get up. To my surprise, however, the musicians started to play again, this time *The Blue Danube*. I was waiting for them to finish, when the chairman nudged me.

"Rise, you numbskull," he hissed, "don't you hear they are playing your national anthem?"

There was nothing for me to do but rise, whereupon the audience applauded enthusiastically. Had I been the butt of a joke? But at my next scheduled stop the orchestra in the dining room played the same tune again at my entry. After that it was played for me in all places where I appeared. Before the trip was over I almost began to believe that it really was the Austrian anthem. For months to follow, whenever the radio in my car rendered *The Blue Danube*, I felt like getting out and standing at attention until it was over.

My speaking schedules were sometimes difficult to fill and made me feel like a one-night-stand actor. Once I spoke at Lima, Ohio, at eight o'clock in the evening and had to appear at Oshkosh, Wisconsin, next noon. It took hard driving all night and morning to make my appointment. I arrived in time after a sleepless night, but with no more than five minutes to spare. On another trip I had to speak in South Bend at a supper meeting and deliver addresses in Cleveland next afternoon and Detroit in the evening. It may look like easy money to cash in checks with three figures, one after another, but the consumption of energy was considerable, especially as I had no prepared speeches and did not know in advance what I was going to say. I was probably more curious than the audience about what would come out of me next. The settings were not always ideal, either. In one large city, for example, I had to speak in a department store, where a section had been fenced off by means of wallboard. Behind the temporary stage on which I stood, I could hear the employees of the wholesale music department fight over pianos, harps and delivery tickets, and I became so interested in their squabbles that more than once I lost the thread of my thoughts and had to step over to the chairman to hook in again. Unfortunately, he himself then became intrigued by the backstage discussions, and when next time he could not help me out, I had to start a new chapter. To judge from the expression on the faces confronting me, it did not fit any too well into what I had been saying before.

Newspaper publicity hit me both favorably and otherwise. In a Michigan town an enterprising reporter offered me a large picture on the front page in exchange for an exclusive story. I gave him the story, but doubted that his editor would ever put a lecturer's picture any other place but next to the obituary column. When I left the auditorium after having finished my program, I passed a newsstand, and saw with amazement my likeness, almost life size, glare back at me. I debated with myself whether to feel elated or foolish, when a woman and a young girl walked up. The girl looked at my portrait with interest.

"Look, mother," she exclaimed, "they caught the murderer."

I fared worse in a western city, where I had been asked to address a noon meeting of businessmen. The chairman in his preamble had proceeded to the point where he was to announce the subject of my talk, when he suddenly bent over and whispered:

"What is the title of your speech, anyway?"

I whispered back, "The Drama of Lincoln's Assassination." Thereupon the chairman straightened up and announced that I was now going to discuss "The Glamour of Lincoln's Assassination."

The afternoon papers repeated this title in their headlines, with the result that for a month I received such a flood of abusing and vilifying letters that I envied Siegfried his bath in Fafner's blood; only I would not have dared let a leaf fall on my shoulder.

The audiences were strangely akin in all places. There always was an old man in the front row who fell asleep; in the back sat women who gossiped; in between, people were interested or genteel enough to appear so. I became used to hecklers and discovered a polite way of handling them. I asked them to come up to the platform and make my speech for me. The only ones who really bothered me were the old ladies who buttonholed me after the lecture with the solemn assurance that their father had once seen Lincoln. I never have been able to think of a more appropriate answer than, "So what?" and it hurt me to suppress it.

The size of my audience varied from twenty-five hundred to six.

Of course, the six people who braved a blizzard to hear me had paid their admission, and I had received my fee, so there was nothing left to do but go on with the program. But when two men walked out to see if their cars had frozen up and did not return, I proposed a game of bridge, and my suggestion was accepted with delight. Even the lecturer had a good time that night.

I remember one engagement on which I made no money in spite of a good-sized fee. It happened at a mid-western university which was located some fifty miles from the nearest large city. I took a taxi out there, as train connections did not fit into my schedule. The taxi fare would be about twenty dollars, which I could easily afford. The address came off on time, and ended at eleven o'clock in the morning. I was about to leave, when I was informed that a luncheon had been arranged in my honor; to decline the invitation would have been discourteous. The luncheon was eaten and enjoyed by all, with the exception of one diner who fancied he heard the ticking of a meter throughout the meal and the speeches that followed. When I finally made my escape, a very happy taxi driver and a less happy passenger started on a belated trip home.

Sometimes I have tried to estimate how many people I met in my years of lecturing. Twenty to thirty people were introduced to me at each meeting, and I had as many as nineteen engagements in one month. When I came home after a prolonged journey, I sometimes had trouble recalling the names of my own children.

I had often read how actors improve shows by extemporizing, and my lectures also went through several changes, as I watched the effect of certain remarks on my audiences. Some quips that had accidentally crept into my speech never failed to arouse laughter, although I could see nothing funny in them. Others, that I thought quite good, made no impression at all. Even certain mannerisms found their proper place in my repertoire. One time, on a hot summer evening, I had to appear in full dress at a college gathering. I felt mighty uncomfortable, but the wife of the president, who sat next to me, put me at my ease. When she saw me constantly pulling at my bow tie to set it straight, she assured me that she would fix it for me before I started speaking; she had often done it for her husband. The chairman started to introduce me and, probably because the heat annoyed him, broke off his preface with unexpected abruptness. I rose, and suddenly remembered that my tie had not yet been adjusted. I bent down to my kind neighbor, who half rose in her seat and pulled on both ends, taking an ungodly time before she was satisfied. The audience began to snicker and apparently enjoyed the spectacle, for when I was finally released I received a most generous applause. The stiffness went out of the atmosphere as if by magic, and I could feel the presence of that sympathetic chord for which every speaker so fondly wishes. After this experience I made a similar deal with the lady next to me, whenever I had to appear in full dress, and the little trick never missed fire. Perhaps a psychologist can find an explanation for it. I can't.

A radio appearance now and then provided a welcome break in the monotony of speech-making. My radio programs mostly took the form of interviews, and we tried to make them tolerably interesting, with what success, I am unable to say. I liked radio programs because they always came off on the second and ended with equal precision. You could not see the audience giggle, whisper, yawn or fall asleep, and it was therefore easy to imagine that you were a hit. Only once did I go through a disturbance of sorts. I was being interviewed by a somewhat nervous announcer, and just as we got into swing, he made an imprudent gesture which brushed his typewritten sheets into a scattered heap on the floor. He almost fell off his chair in his scramble to retrieve the script, and I faced the microphone alone, my sheaf a useless tool without my partner to shoot his questions at me. For fully three minutes I extemporized, only half conscious of what I was saying. Aside from a boxer I once saw getting pommelled around the ring by a stronger man, I think I am one of the few men who knows how long three minutes can really be. At last my vis-à-vis had straightened himself out, and the situation was once more under control. We started in where we guessed we might have normally been by that time and hit the end point within five seconds. Then we both went to a Turkish bath. So far as I know, no outsider noticed the mishap.

My career as a public speaker is not yet ended. What the future will bring forth I do not know but, like Mary MacLane, I pray that Satan may deliver me from—

Chairmen who cannot pronounce my name,
Microphones that whistle or shriek,

People who want to sell me antiques,
Girls in the audience who giggle,
Roast beef, green peas, community singing, dancing
   children,
And, above all, may Satan deliver me from
My urge to write another unorthodox book on Lincoln.

CHAPTER 20

*

AT THE CROSSROADS

*J*HE FIRST WORLD WAR had brought many revelations to American industry, none more startling than that research chemistry could be profitable. During the years of conflict chemical research had contributed to national safety; from now on it was destined to create national wealth. Thousands of chemists had enlisted behind the lines and given freely of their ideas; but with the exception of Lee Lewis—I do not recall anyone else—whose Lewisite was named after him, all had remained unknown soldiers. Their achievements, however, had not remained unknown to industrial leaders. If chemists could do constructively what they had done destructively and defensively, research was an attractive speculation. All one had to do was to put a group of chemists to work on a problem and, given time and working tools, they would probably yield a good profit over their salaries and expenses. Those who wanted to venture still further need not concentrate on specific problems; they could turn chemical knowledge and inventive genius into vaster fields and wait for results. The odds would be greater, but so were the possible gains. It was all a matter of dollars and cents. Industrialists were intellectually honest; they did not claim to be serving mankind. They tried to serve their stockholders and themselves, and let mankind take care of itself.

As it turned out, research chemists served both, as creative workers invariably do. It is the outstanding difference between them and the non-creative professions. If Smith sued Jones, no one except the litigants and their lawyers cared who won; if clever advertising made Black's apple cider outsell White's, it meant no more to others than if these two gentlemen had matched coins. But when chemists in their daily work, without altruistic illusions, invented, discovered, improved or reclaimed, they could not restrict the benefits to themselves and their employers, even had they so desired.

The effect of research work soon manifested itself in many lines. Radical progress became the order of the day. The paint and varnish industry, with which our own business was affiliated, was no exception; it jumped forward in several directions at once, dislocating established practices and endangering industries of long standing. Someone, for example, had found a new use for the nitro-cellulose films heretofore used only on cut fingers, and began selling in train-loads what had previously been sold in bottles. As a result, the entire automobile industry was revolutionized. Cars had always been daubed with twenty-odd coats of varnish, each of which had to dry before the next one could be applied; these new nitro-cellulose solutions, called lacquers, dried in a few minutes, and the job was finished in hours instead of weeks. Varnishes made from oils and gums seemed a matter of the past. I attended more than one conference of worried old-line varnish makers who thought they had come to the end of the road. Oriental importers, terrified by this industrial earthquake, wrote me, wired me, called me up, asking if I thought wood oil would still be used. I could not tell them. But when the year ended and the dust had settled, it was found that the consumption of wood oil had scarcely been affected at all; for the old varnish maker had struck back with an innovation of his own, a four-hour varnish, which caught the public fancy. It was but another demonstration of the truism that new inventions seldom are hurtful. The contrary is true; they fertilize the consumptive field and stimulate rather than retard the use of competitive products.

Another bombshell that fell in the varnish field was the advent of synthetic resins. Up to then fossil gums, which gave varnishes their gloss and hardness, had been considered indispensable and irreplaceable. In out-of-the-way places, on the shores of the Congo and in South Africa, in New Zealand and in the bushlands of Australia, natives had been wont to gather fossilized resins, once the sap of trees; their very names, Copal, Kauri, Damar and Pontianak, suggested the heat of the tropics and the mystery of the jungle. By and by these treasure mounts had become exhausted; the price of the

361

gums rose, their quality deteriorated. How to maintain the lustre of varnished surfaces loomed as a big problem. It would take Nature thousands of years to replenish the devastated supplies.

At this juncture two chemists stepped into the breach, Leo Hendrik Baekeland and Lawrence V. Redman. Working independently of each other, they produced resins from phenol and formaldehyde which did things no natural gum had ever done. For once chemists thought of embodying their names in their inventions. Each time the world used Bakelite and Redmanol, it would pay homage to their originators. Baekeland already had anonymously given to his fellowmen new photographic papers and an electric cell. Perhaps both men believed, audaciously no doubt, that even chemists had a small claim to immortality.

The one-time monopoly of fossil gums was broken; again the laboratory had triumphed over Nature. The century-old gum industry, stretching from distant lands to American varnish plants, thought itself threatened with extinction. But once more these fears proved groundless. The gum pickers in New Zealand and South Africa would never hear of synthetics; the world consumed all the resins Nature and laboratories could produce, and then asked for more.

Research chemistry gave birth to a new species of chemists, the research chemist. Just as miners and prospectors rush to new gold fields and farmers to new profitable crops, so chemists rushed to research when it became the vogue. Every chemist wanted to become a research chemist. Not one in ten knew what the term implied; but most of them, like myself, had become chemists in the first place without knowing why, and they followed the crowd. Superficial prospects looked alluring enough—interesting work, fair salaries to begin with, the dream of world-shaking discoveries. Of course, things did not, as a rule, turn out quite so roseate. There was not much room at the top. Youthful enthusiasm was stifled by detail work that had to be done. The cost of diplomas increased, because colleges insisted on their graduates studying two or three extra years for degrees with which to stamp them. Titles became fashionable and set one group of chemists apart from others. What one could do did not count so much as the kind of degree one had acquired. Creative ability and inventiveness, those rarest and most precious of all mental qualities, were being forced into a straitjacket. The *Meistersingers* had invaded chemistry and sat in judgment on the composers of chemical prize songs.

By and by some of the human debris created by this research wave was washed ashore. Good-memory students failed miserably when life asked them questions that were not in textbooks. Others could see nothing but the scientific angles of their problems and stumbled over the inevitable commercial hazards. Still others landed in *cul-de-sacs* through no fault of their own. A bright young man came to my office one day, head hanging low. At the age of twenty-six, after seven years in college, he had taken his Ph.D. degree; highly recommended by his school, he had found a position in the research laboratory of a nationally known establishment. Highly recommended graduates always found ready placements, for the colleges usually recommended only those who had all the degrees. Thereby they created an artificial market for graduates whose brains were crammed with book chemistry, but who had become *weltfremd* in their collegiate hothouses. This particular young man had been put to work on the recovery of a waste material and, together with a group of other chemists, spent years on the problem; then the employers gave up. The speculation had not turned out as expected. There was no complaint, but the research laboratory was closed, and our chemist, now thirty-two years old, went tramping the streets. He was too old to start again at the bottom. His college would not or could not do any more for him. No one wanted a specialist in something that had not worked out. He had become an expert navigator of a ship that could not float.

Most research chemists, even if they were doing well in their respective fields, became specialists by necessity. This did not matter so long as they remained with their original employers; on the contrary, it enhanced their usefulness. On the other hand, the longer they remained with one organization and one line of work, the more their horizon shrank and the more the market value of their services narrowed. Like a rare old book, they commanded either a big market price or else none at all.

All young chemists who applied for positions now wanted to do research work. They did not realize that chemical knowledge, to be applicable, must be fertilized by inventiveness, tempered by common sense and guided by experience. When I asked these boys if they had a problem in mind they wished to solve, they stared at me dumbly. When I asked them if they could make practical use of a problem after they had solved it, they stared some more. Time had not changed the old school methods. The best research chemists knew only how to find the answer to given questions. The art of finding their own questions and selling their answers, if and when they had them, was still being left to the few independent thinkers among them, or to outsiders. Most Doctors of Philosophy were fine chemists, nothing more. They had longer training, but like ordinary chemists, they were only trained to be servants. With a few exceptions the masters still hailed from a different world.

Chemistry was coming of age, and its youthful democratic ways were disappearing. A new aristocracy had sprung up, the aristocracy of academic degrees. Chemists looking for employment were required to fill out endless application blanks on which to bare their entire past, how many years of study, what degrees and all. The one point the blank did not cover was their native ability. Under the new system the Thomas Edisons or William Hoskinses would not even be granted an interview.

The professors of chemistry, leaders of the aristocratic group, were highly satisfied. Their pedigreed output was doing well, if drawing a fair but limited salary meant the height of a career. Those without degrees might go jobless or work for low wages; they had only themselves to blame.

Nevertheless, chemists without degrees still constituted the vast majority, and the new order had done nothing to improve their lot. The supply still overtopped the demand. Salaries remained low, so low in fact, that the American Chemical Society, heretofore devoted to scientific rather than human problems, felt impelled to recommend modest minimum remunerations for chemists and chemical engineers. The directors of the Society went still further; they invited those who were not worth their hire to leave the profession and seek their livelihood in other fields. No secret was made of why the leaders in chemistry did not sleep well. Labor unions were making progress in enrolling disgusted and despairing chemists into their ranks.

And so twenty years after I had stepped out of the profession the picture was much the same as it had been before. Chemists still served mankind by doing choice parts of the world's work. And mankind paid them no more in respect and wages than it ever had paid to any kind of servants.

All this time black clouds had gathered over the world, and now bolts of lightning struck in quick succession. Austria, Poland, France, Pearl Harbor. America was at war again. A country devoted to the establishment of permanent peace had to gird its loins for a life-or-death struggle. The decision would go to the one who outfought the enemy in battle and production. Anguished cries arose. More aluminum, more magnesium, rubber, oils. Bigger and faster planes. More ships. Production, more production, quicker production!

As in the first World War, chemists and engineers sprang into action. Factories doubled their output almost overnight. Substitutes for badly needed materials appeared as if from nowhere. Inventors were importuned for ideas. These orphan children of society, long laughed at as crackpots, friendless even while a paternal government had fed tap dancers and wandering minstrels, now crowded to the fore in obedience to urgent calls from their country. How quickly things changed when a nation in distress was reduced to fundamentals. Instinctively it turned for help to those who could originate ideas, possessed creative minds or hands, or knew how to make two blades of grass grow where only one had grown before. A bushel of wheat suddenly outweighed a bookshelf of Court decisions, a ton of synthetics a carload of advertising slogans. As on a warship getting ready for battle, the useless superstructure went overboard. What remained was all bones, sinews, vitality. Once more the chemists marched near the front of the procession. I thought with a wry smile of that cosmetics manufacturer who had resented the cream he had to put into the jars, because selling, label-printing and credit problems took so much of his time. In making a bomb, nothing mattered much except what went into it. Sales managers, credit men and label printers were superstructure. The men who counted were the chemists who calculated the charge, the engineers who provided the machinery and the workmen who produced; a countless army of obscure patriots, none of them ever singled out for distinction, yet each plodding along without pause, without complaint—and without fame.

In the midst of war, the far-seeing among the nation's thinkers are beginning to lay plans for future peace. Are they far-seeing enough, deep-seeing enough, to include the creators of things among their new leaders? Will the wheel be left in the hands of those who are holding it during the emergency, or will they again have to relinquish it to others?

Reconstruction, to be successful, calls for the pooling of the world's most potent brainpower. All of it will be needed to prevent the worst cataclysm in history, if it can be prevented. No one knows how long the Ship of State will sail in troubled waters; why not leave it in charge of those who can navigate it, run its engines, repair possible damage? Let all others compose themselves until a safe harbor is reached.

In whom shall the nation invest its biggest rewards, while it walks in the twilight zone that lies between war and peace? A difficult decision, and fraught with tremendous consequences. Precedent points one way, common sense and justice another. A lawyer once snatched two degenerate boys from the gallows and thereby earned more money than the discoverers of the life-saving sulfa-compounds will earn in a lifetime. That is precedent. The community, owing little enough thanks to the lawyer, glorified him; to the chemists it should erect a monument of gold, yet does not even ask their names. Is that sound judgment? What if all brilliant chemists should tire of making discoveries and defend criminals instead? The hottest flame of idealism consumes itself unless it is fed, and Cinderellas wait for Princes only in storybooks. In real life they run away and find themselves new homes. The country is already too full of big-caliber chemists who have exchanged altruism and poverty for a place in the sun and a more comfortable living. In the public interest it is vital, now more than ever, to hold them to constructive work and, if possible, rally more of the talented around their standard.

But, so runs the counter-argument, have not chemists and other doers always worked without individual recognition and large financial rewards? Leave well enough alone. All is right the way it is and has been.

All is not right, though. True, some chemist do perform miracles on insignificant wages and without public honors; but who can tell what greater miracles they might perform should they receive more gracious acknowledgement, and if their ranks were not constantly being thinned by those who are losing hope?

Real peace will not come with the dropping of the last bomb. Not after this war. Too much wealth has been destroyed for that. If the world is rebuilt again with outmoded tools, under a management discredited by previous failure, it might easily go down in chaos before the task is completed. A new formula is needed, and none is at hand. Yet, whole continents will have to be rebuilt physically before other plans for the future can take root. Who can restore them better than those who have accomplished the seemingly impossible during the struggle? A few inventors, a corps of skilled experts and an army of brawny workers will be worth many times their number of orators and parlor theorists. Shock troops of restoration these, out to re-erect the edifice of civilization with the same combination of genius and technical knowledge they used to bring it down during the conflict. Reconstruction is war in reverse and should be conducted on the same principles and by the same men. Everything else, everybody else, is superstructure until the ultimate goal is attained.

Eventually, bugles of war will change to hymns of peace; but the cry for more production, better production, faster production, will go on. From the moment destruction ceases, genius, still triumphant, must be made to travel through creative channels, and the most alluring inducements to do so should be held out to it. Fine minds should not be wasted on the defense of criminals or on purely selfish occupations. To insure the rebuilding of the world, creators should be voted the foremost positions of responsibility and honor. A Supreme Court of eminent technicians should sit, and sit permanently, to tell the nation what it can do with its resources, its manpower, its learning, and should continue to gather and coordinate, as it did during the war, the best thoughts of the nation. Courts of Law should bow to this Court of Progress, because to know what to do tomorrow will be of infinitely greater importance than to know what should not have been done yesterday. If real reconstruction is to be achieved, all of the country's efforts must be concentrated on the common go... ...s, need be, let competitive struggles be suspended for the time b...ng. What if Black's and White's apple ciders must temporarily sell on their respective merits, and the case of Smith vs. Jones be adjusted by arbitration? Millions of lawyers, salesmen and other non-productive members of society will thereby be released and their power added to the forces that create new wealth. Only by such drastic measures can the world escape from the darkness and despair which threaten to engulf it. It will take real patriotism to bring about and endure these changes, but surely patriotism can work for Peace as well as it has worked for War. If it can not, or will not, all our protestations that we are fighting for a better future are nothing but sham and humbug.

Those who look into the future see America at the crossroads. One path, well charted, has been trod in the past; its guides, competent in fair weather, faltered in the whirlwind. The other path, never traveled before, leads over lofty heights, clear of the swamps and the fog of the valleys. New leaders are ready who have on their side science, imagination and a record of steadfast performance in storm and stress.

America must make her choice of new leaders. On her decision will rest the fate of the post-war age and the happiness of generations yet unborn.